THE SPANISH CROWN
1808—1931

QUEEN MARIA LUISA
After the portrait by Goya in the Alte Pinakothek, Munich.

" Maria Luisa has her past and her character written on her face,"
wrote Napoleon ; " it surpasses anything you dare imagine."

THE SPANISH CROWN
1808—1931

An Intimate Chronicle of a Hundred Years

by

ROBERT SENCOURT pseud. for

George, R. E. Gordon

"On the throne of Spain sits the destiny of Spain."
Sir Henry Bulwer, Lord Dalling,
Record Office, F.O. Spain, Series 72, No. 698.

NEW YORK
CHARLES SCRIBNER'S SONS
1932
uGE

PRINTED IN GREAT BRITAIN

TO

WILLIAM FORCE STEAD

IN ADMIRATION OF HIS POETRY AND PROSE

" From all sedition, privy conspiracy, and
rebellion ; from all false doctrine, heresy,
and schism ; from hardness of heart, and
contempt of Thy Word and Commandment,
Good Lord, deliver us."—CRANMER's *Litany*.

PREFACE

THE story of King Alfonso is not simply his own. His triumphs and disasters can be understood only by a view of the forces which played around the throne, and a review of the family history which he inherited. It is those rather than his own deeds which account for the unexpected events of 1931.

As for the dramatic story I have to unfold, I looked for light on it in Paris and London, as well as in Madrid. Except the Marquis de Villa-Urrutia, the Spanish historians, admirable as they are, have not yet searched the archives of London and Paris ; nor have they yet realised how much they have to learn about the last hundred years of their history, from the account of it in *The Times*. It is, more than any other, *The Times* correspondent in Madrid to-day, M. Grimaud de Caux, who is giving the world a full account of what is now happening there, and it has been the most precious of my privileges to have enjoyed for many years his friendship and his guidance. I cannot conceive a greater advantage than to draw on the rich stores of his information, and weigh them with his serene though relentless judgment.

I could never have written this book but for the work of Spanish historians, and for the personal help distinguished Spaniards have so generously and so graciously given me. Anyone who knows how thorough and how scholarly is their work is bound to pay them a tribute of admiration, even though he grieves they have left so little new to glean among the various archives in which I studied in Madrid. And to their work, so fully documented and yet so vivid, I have many memories of personal kindness which threw open to me both public institutions and private means of information. The President of the Historical Academy, the Duke of Alba, again opened his archives to me ; the President of the Centre of Historical Studies, Señor Menéndez Pidal, arranged with the Director-General de Propiedades that I should again work in the Archives of the Royal Palace ; the Marquis de Villa-Urrutia, formerly Minister for Foreign Affairs and the leading authority on the earlier periods of my study, guided me from week to week in Madrid. I should like also to mention by name, as those who went out of their way to do me kindness : Count Romanones, Viscount Güell, Señor Calvo Sotelo, Señor Castillejo, Don Miguel Gómez del Campillo, Don Miguel Artígas, Don Antonio Sierra y Corella, Don Pedro Aguado Bleye, Don Eugenio d'Ors, Don Miguel Asín Palacios, Don Agustín Millares, Don Juan Cueto, Miss Catharine Moran, and the Republican Ministers, Don Alejandro Lerroux, Don Fernando de los Ríos, Don Marcelino Domingo, and Colonel Maciá ; as well as Sir George Grahame and his staff at the British Embassy in Madrid.

The Ministers I mention will not, I hope, think me cavalier if I cannot accept all their contentions. But, in writing history, a foreigner can do no greater service to a country than to tell as much of the facts about it as he is able, and to guide himself by those

Liberal historians who are the fountains of our knowledge of Spain through the period under my review.

I am especially grateful to M. de Caux and to Professor Don F. de Arteaga y Pereira, for each reading through chapters of my MS. and proofs ; as also to the courtesy which enables me to draw on articles I have, in the course of the last six years, published in *The Times Literary Supplement*, the *Edinburgh Review*, the *Nineteenth Century*, the *Contemporary Review*, the *Atlantic Monthly*, and *Current History*.

R. S.

HYÈRES, *February* 2, 1932.

CONTENTS

PAGE

PREFACE vii

GENEALOGICAL TREE xiv

PART I

I. THE CONSPIRACIES OF DON FERNANDO . . 1

II. THE USURPATIONS 30

III. THE GOOD INTRUDER'S REIGN 65

IV. THE KING THEY LONGED FOR 91

V. THE LEOPARD CHANGES HIS SPOTS . . . 129

PART II

VI. THE PASSIONATE REGENT 151

VII. THE GREAT MARRIAGE INTRIGUE . . . 182

VIII. QUEEN ISABEL AND REVOLUTION . . . 208

IX. CONFUSION 232

X. ALFONSO XII AND HIS WIVES 247

PART III

XI. ALFONSO XIII : ACCESSION AND MARRIAGE . 263

XII. KING ALFONSO : THE ROYAL DIPLOMATIST . 287

PAGE

XIII. KING ALFONSO : THE BREAKDOWN OF PARLIA-
MENTARY GOVERNMENT 313

XIV. THE DICTATORSHIP OF PRIMO 329

XV. KING ALFONSO : THE FINAL CRISIS . . . 351

CONCLUSION 372

CHRONOLOGY 386

SOURCES 388

INDEX OF PROPER NAMES 395

LIST OF ILLUSTRATIONS

QUEEN MARIA LUISA. After the portrait by Goya in the Alte Pinakothek, Munich . . . *Frontispiece*

FACING PAGE

QUEEN MARIA LUISA. After the portrait by Goya in the Museo de Arte Moderna, Madrid . . . 4

MANUEL GODOY, PRINCE OF THE PEACE. After the portrait by Goya in the Académia de San Fernando, Madrid 32

FERNANDO VII. After the portrait by Goya in the Prado . 44

KING CARLOS IV. After the portrait by Goya in the Prado 56

QUEEN MARIA CRISTINA DE BOURBON. After the portrait by López in the Prado, Madrid 130

ESPARTERO, DUKE OF THE VICTORY. From an old photograph 166

QUEEN ISABEL II ON ASSUMING POWER. After a portrait in the possession of the Facoltád de Medicina, Madrid . 180

NARVÁEZ, DUKE OF VALENCIA 216

QUEEN MARIA CRISTINA IN HER MATURITY . . 220

QUEEN ISABEL II WITH HER SON, DON ALFONSO. After the portrait by Winterhalter in the Royal Palace . 230

KING AMADEO 240

KING ALFONSO XII IN THE ROBES OF THE ORDER OF THE GOLDEN FLEECE. After the portrait by Padrò in the Royal Palace, Madrid 252

QUEEN MARIA CRISTINA DE HABSBURG. From a photograph 260

QUEEN VICTORIA EUGÉNIE OF SPAIN. After the portrait by M. de Laszlo in the Royal Palace, Madrid . . 288

KING ALFONSO. After the portrait by Casals . . 294

GENERAL PRIMO DE RIVERA, MARQUIS DE ESTELLA. After the portrait by M. de Laszlo. 338

xiii

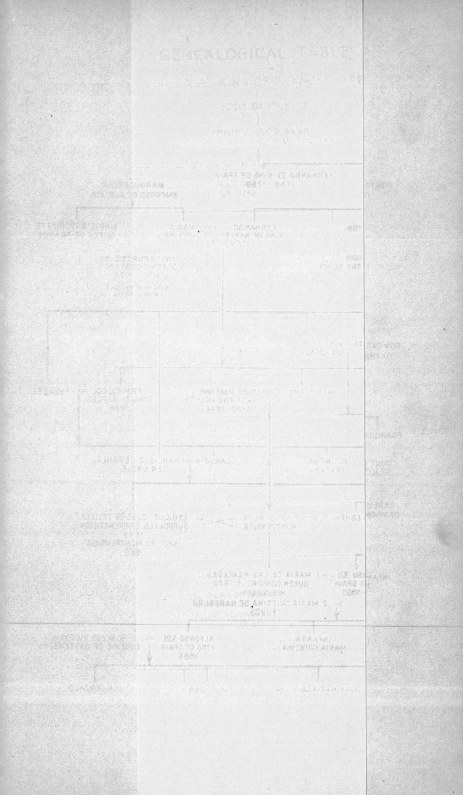

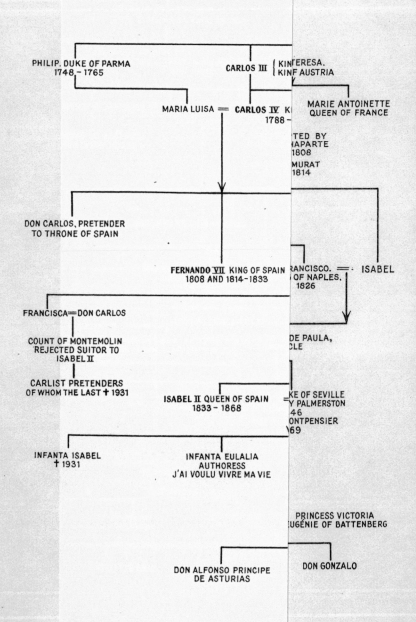

PHILIP. DUKE OF PARMA
1748 - 1765

CARLOS III | KIN|TERESA.
| KIN|F AUSTRIA

MARIA LUISA ══ CARLOS IV K|
1788 -

MARIE ANTOINETTE
QUEEN OF FRANCE

|TED BY
|NAPARTE
|1808

|MURAT
|1814

DON CARLOS, PRETENDER
TO THRONE OF SPAIN

FERNANDO VII KING OF SPAIN
1808 AND 1814-1833

|RANCISCO. ══ ISABEL
|S OF NAPLES,
1826

FRANCISCA══DON CARLOS

COUNT OF MONTEMOLIN
REJECTED SUITOR TO
ISABEL II

|DE PAULA,
|CLE

CARLIST PRETENDERS
OF WHICH THE LAST ✝ 1931

ISABEL II QUEEN OF SPAIN
1833 - 1868

|KE OF SEVILLE
|Y PALMERSTON
|46
|ONTPENSIER
|69

INFANTA ISABEL
✝ 1931

INFANTA EULALIA
AUTHORESS
J'AI VOULU VIVRE MA VIE

PRINCESS VICTORIA
|UGÉNIE OF BATTENBERG

DON ALFONSO PRINCIPE
DE ASTURIAS

DON GONZALO

PART I

I

THE CONSPIRACIES OF DON FERNANDO

Fecunda culpæ sæcula nuptias
Primum inquinavere et genus et domos
Hoc fonte derivata clades
In patriam populumque fluxit.

    ·   ·   ·   ·

Damnosa quid non imminuit dies?
Ætas parentum peior avis tulit
Nos nequiores, mox daturos
Progeniem vitiosiorem.

HORACE : *Odes*, iii. 6.

I

AT the beginning of the nineteenth century fierce uncertainties played havoc within the Court of Spain. England's rivalry with the ambition and glory of Napoleon, now that he had led France back from the Terror to order and victory, was to make a plaything of the crown of Catholic Majesty, while comedy, intrigue, dethronement, incest, and scandal hedged it so close around as to provide in themselves melodrama complete.

The Bourbons had come to reign in Madrid in 1700, when fear of French influence dominating the Peninsula had made the War of the Spanish Succession. In 1800 Carlos IV had been reigning for twelve years. A good, mild, kind, bland man, with the tastes, the perceptions, and the simple honour of a country gentleman,[1] he was hardly equal to the task.

[1] Comte de Ségur : *Mémoires.*

1

He was too careless of his sceptre, too fond of his gun. " Every day, winter and summer," as he himself said to Napoleon, " I went shooting till twelve, had dinner, and at once returned to shooting till the fall of the evening. Manuel told me how things were going ; and I went to bed to begin again the same life the next day unless any important ceremony prevented me." [1] So did he govern Spain for twenty years. And yet he had gifts with which he would have shone as king : he was quick at understanding things ; he had a great memory ; he loved justice ; and when at times he busied himself in the conduct of affairs was swift and skilful.[2] He was furthermore informed and prudent in his judgments ; he was virile, he had excellent health, and he was determined to have things done. After the French Revolution there was a certain change : his mind became a prey to the fear of tumult or disturbance : he had always been impatient of even the slightest delay in having his wishes performed ; but now the sense of impending anxiety made him fearful lest any accident should be attributed to his neglect.[3] Yet, in spite of his anxiety, he liked to leave things to other people, no matter what was at stake : like many physically active people, he had a sluggish will ; he meant well, but he was inadequate, and since the age of sixteen, when he married, he had been dominated by his remarkable wife.[4]

Queen Maria Luisa was also a Bourbon, with the Bourbon nose and the Bourbon lip. Of her youth there is less to learn than of her middle age. She bore her husband no less than twenty-two children,[5] of whom survived three daughters and three sons, Fernando, Carlos, and Francisco de Paula. She and

---

[1] Beausset : *Mémoires.*   [2] Toreno : *Historia,* i. 56.
[3] Godoy : *Cuenta Dada,* i. 11.   [4] Escoiquiz : *Memorias,* p. 49.
[5] Lady Holland : *Spanish Journal,* p. 75.

her husband had ascended the throne in 1788. While he went shooting, she occupied herself in other ways ; for she attended Councils of State, and even chose the Ministers.

Magnetic, resolute, acute at ruse, Maria Luisa was at once both queen and witch. She was firstly mistress of the art of dressing herself.[1] Her manners combined the highest dignity with perfect ease.[2] In the shape of every limb and in the suppleness of every movement, she displayed a voluptuous grace ; her eyes were aflame with the power not only of a queen but of a courtesan ; yet there was in the intensity of her expression an unmistakable ruthlessness ; and as her lips tightened to show her teeth in a smile, she looked at once both cruel and winning. Adder's poison was under those lips. And who could look at the underset mouth which shot out above the salient chin without feeling the tyranny of her will ? Dressed as for a royal portrait by Velazquez, with the crown by her side on a cushion of scarlet silk, and black feathers rising out of her hat, she struck her painter as hardly short of devilish. Riding astride over the slopes of the sierra, she was manifestly equal to all the demands made upon the woman of the world. For her face, though not beautiful, was alluring, and was stamped with queenly power.

Her temperament, we are told, was fiery and voluptuous. Free in her early youth from the constraints of Spanish etiquette, she showed no small power over the hearts of men. She added to charm passion, and to passion fury, and to fury wit, and to wit cunning, and to cunning enterprise. Although she was a girl of only fourteen when she married, she had at once entirely mastered the kindly, innocent,

---

[1] Marquise de la Tour du Pin : *Mémoires.*
[2] Jung : *Lucien Bonaparte et ses Mémoires.*

and well-intentioned boy of whom she was the bride. He had had no experience whatever of other women ; whether or not in his simplicity there was also inherent weakness, so straightforward a youth could hardly have been equal at any age, least of all at sixteen, to cope with a girl of such brilliant appearance and so sharp a brain. It was said that to this she added a heart which was naturally vicious, a heart capable not of true affection but of unmitigated selfishness, and this with a refined astuteness and an incredible power of hypocrisy and deceit,[1] that her remarkable personal abilities (for no one could deny those) were used for nothing else than to indulge her dominant passions as they arose, and that she regarded it as insufferable to apply them to any matter really serious—except of course when she arranged with obsequious priests the ritual and worship of her chapel.

The reason why such things were said of her was too plain. She retained the confidence of her husband so fully as to induce him to place her favourite in unprecedented power. Manuel Godoy arrived in Madrid in 1784 and came into the palace simply as a gentleman of the bodyguard. Born at Badajoz in 1764, his sovereigns singled him out for every power and privilege. The post of Generalissimo was created for him. He was at once made High Admiral and " Universal Minister of Spain and the Indies." He was also made a Knight of the Golden Fleece ; he was given the Dukedom of Alcudia, then the title of Prince, and his titles of honour filled a hundred parchments. Horsemen cleared the way for him as he drove.[2] He married a Bourbon princess, a descendant of the Grand Monarque ; he

[1] Escoiquiz : *Op cit.*, p. 50.
[2] Mesonero Romanos : *Memorias* ; Hans Roger Madol : *Godoy.*

QUEEN MARIA LUISA

After the portrait by Goya in the Museo de Arte Moderna, Madrid.

" She struck her painter as hardly short of devilish."

was called Your Highness, and he ruled absolute from Vigo to Valencia and from Texas to Tierra del Fuego. And what were his qualifications for such preferment? One and one only, says Toreno—that he had compromised the honour of the Queen.

Sensational tales were told. They said that once when the King was walking down a corridor, followed by the Queen and Godoy with their suite, Godoy had slapped her in the face, and that when the King had turned round to ask what the noise was, the Queen had said that she had dropped a book. They said (we shall hear more of it) that she had been surprised at night by her own guards entering the Escorial by a private door opening on a path from Godoy's house.[1] But such stories are hardly evidence. If, in a short time, all that mattered to the crown was in the hands of the Prince of the Peace must we needs infer, as ordinary Spaniards thought, that the explanation was a reason for the grossest scandal? During the long years—more than twenty-five years—that Godoy lived in daily intercourse with the sovereigns, he was not only by their arrangement married to the King's first cousin, but he also maintained a mistress to whom he was enabled to give the title of Countess of Castillo Fiel. Spanish women are not surprised to find the Eastern tradition of polygamy modify the constancy of men. It is true that the amours of middle age are more absorbing passions than those of youth, and Maria Luisa did not meet Godoy till she was forty. Yet it is a little difficult to suppose that Maria Luisa accepted Godoy's intimacies in the intervals of those he gave to two other women, one of whom was in low position, and one of whom the Queen herself had chosen as his wife. The explanation can only be that what immorality there was changed soon to

[1] Oman : *Peninsular War*, i. 24, 25.

another phase of passion, and that, in a love that could not reckon sacrifice, she sought out those who could gratify Godoy when her own cheek was wrinkled.[1] But whether her passion was, or had ceased to be, adulterous, it was entire and lifelong. During the twenty-five years of its duration, it seemed to become only more ungrudging. And during those twenty-five years, nothing interrupted either the King's confidence in his Queen, or the friendship of the King with her friend. If others thought her youngest son, Francisco de Paula, was the image of the Minister, Carlos was unconcerned.[2] If she had had other lovers before Godoy, and aroused the suspicions of her father-in-law,[3] her husband would not hear a word against her. He was no doubt an indolent and trustful man, but if through all these years he could not judge his wife's conduct, his simplicity could have been no other than idiocy.

There are other titles of attraction in personal relations, even between men and women, than the engagements proper to wedlock, and it is possible that from the beginning the admiration Maria Luisa felt for the man whom she had made Prince of the Peace was in the ultimate particular innocent, even though it was shockingly indiscreet. The Prince himself says that at the time of the French Revolution, which horrified the sovereigns of Europe, and not least such as had any kinship with the beheaded King and Queen, the Spanish sovereigns had in succession as Prime Ministers two men who were neither of them adequate to deal with troubles : first,

---

[1] *Westminster Review*, April 1836. The Marquis de Villa-Urrutia makes a brilliant psychological analysis in support of this explanation in his *María Luisa*.

[2] Villa-Urrutia : *María Luisa*.

[3] Escoiquiz : *Memorias*.

the timorous, wavering Floridablanca, and secondly, the imperturbable Aranda. Carlos and his Queen were shrewd enough to be content with neither. Godoy managed to capture their attention, he does not say how ; we know from other sources that his elder brother won the Queen by the way he played the guitar,[1] but Manuel himself was no musician : he did not need to be. To his fine manners, and dashing presence, he added magnetism. He had, however, other gifts, and as for the sovereigns, they wanted, he says, only a man whom they had found themselves, and on whom they could rely to carry out all their ideas.[2] And such was he. For fifteen years he held his own as ruler of Spain and Spanish America, and in a post of almost unlimited power. " Manuel," as the King summed it up, " told me how things were going." Those words tell the story of fifteen years of Spanish monarchy.

2

In those fifteen years Don Fernando, Prince of Asturias, grew from boy to man. He had been born in 1784. Education had not been forced on an Infante for several generations. King Carlos III used to relate that his tutor had complained to his father of his idleness.

" Doesn't the Infante want to learn ? " asked the King.

" No, Señor," answered the tutor.

" Then if he doesn't want to, he needn't," said the King, as he turned and left them. And the young prince cut two capers in the air, and never again

---

[1] *Westminster Review*, April 1836.
[2] Godoy : *Cuenta Dada*, i.

opened a book. So had Prince Ferdinand's education been.[1]

Then the Prince of the Peace had later appointed the priest, Escoiquiz, as his tutor. This man, according to Godoy, had the air both of a Christian and a philosopher ; he was at the same time both mild and serious, as he spoke a peculiar modesty seemed to grace the authority of his learning, and in the regard of his eye there seemed the power of every virtue. He seemed like a man who knew his duty and had no aim in life but to accomplish it. Such were his manners as a courtier : in his private life he spoke with an intolerable superiority, and had no patience with ideas other than his own.[2]

He was supposed to come and teach Don Fernando mathematics and classics. But these formal studies were laid aside, while the priest spoke to the young Prince of the art of governing men. To him the crown was sacred, and kings reigned by divine right. But they were to enforce this right in days of danger, as Machiavelli and France had already shown them, by a great astuteness in balancing man against man, and party against party. Both counsels found in the son of Maria Luisa a ready ear. The young man determined that to reign by the grace of God was to do as he thought best. He had no intention of compromising his absolute right by regard for the will of the nation. Even as a child, Fernando had been reserved and cold, he had never shown affection, even to his parents, and at times he would break out into acts of wanton cruelty. A smile was a stranger to his lips, truth still more so. Behind his silence, suspicion sharpened its apt weapon of slyness. As for his face, it had all his mother's bad features without her charm.

[1] Villa-Urrutia : *Fernando VII : Rey Constitucional.*
[2] Godoy : *Cuenta Dada.*

" My eldest son," said Maria Luisa to Lady Holland,
" you will find ugly ; he is the counterpart of myself." [1]

As early as 1801, Godoy, in consultation with his
royal lady, had sought a wife for this unsavoury
youth. The richest heiress available among the
Courts of Europe was Princess Augusta of Saxony, who
was supposed to be as beautiful as she was intelligent.
In Paris the First Consul, who had already begun as
a matchmaker, approved the choice, but in the meantime, another influence was brought to bear.

Maria Luisa intended that each of her three
daughters should be a queen. There had been one, it
is true, married to only a Prince of Parma, but she had
died shortly after. The eldest, Carlota, was married
when she was twelve years old to the King of Portugal ;
for the second, after a difficult negotiation, Maria
Luisa secured the hand of the King of Etruria, who
left her a widow at twenty-one, and she was then
offered to Lucien Bonaparte [2] who, being happily
married, refused her ; as for the third, the Queen
found that she could marry her as second wife to the
King of Naples, if in return she would reserve for one
of his daughters the heir to the throne. The bargain
appealed to her. So in 1801, at Barcelona, young
Fernando received the bride to whom by proxy he
had already been married in Naples. She was a type
of Princess beyond anything he could conceive—intelligent, curious, sensitive. " Her face conversed
with you," said the Duchess d'Abrantès,[3] but she was
pale, sickly, and not good-looking.[4]

In the picture she had seen of him he did not seem

[1] Lady Holland : *Spanish Journal*, p. 75. She says, " He was a
gawky lad like the Bentincks."
[2] Villa-Urrutia : *María Luisa*, p. 94.
[3] D'Auvergne : *Godoy, the Queen's Favourite*, pp. 178, 179.
[4] Lord Holland : *Journal*.

exactly elegant ; but the ugly portrait was handsome compared to the real Fernando. When she first saw him, she was shocked. " I believed," she wrote, " that I had lost my senses." The Duke of San Teodoro had described him as an amiable and kindly youth. " When one is well prepared," she wrote, " one feels the evil less. I, who believed what I did, was horrified to find that he was just the opposite." The poor girl fell to tears, cursing the moment she had ever agreed to such an espousal and the man who had led her into it.

It was not long before her young husband was bullying and humiliating her by refusing to treat his marriage as reality in that in which alone it is marriage. " My daughter is desperate," wrote the Queen of Naples on November 10. " Her husband is an absolute blockhead and not even her husband in the flesh, as well as being a hulking fellow who does nothing, and stays all the time in his room." Ten days later : " He is a fool who neither hunts nor fishes ; who hangs all day about the room of his unfortunate wife ; who busies himself with nothing, and is not even her husband from an animal point of view." [1] Such was the theme of the Queen of Naples, repeated with variations. But after a time, a change took place in the attitude of bride and bridegroom, and the Prince of Asturias was heart and soul with his bride. This did not please his mother. She feared perhaps that they would unite with the Neapolitans to work against the Prince of the Peace, to whom she poured out her mind on every subject, from affairs of State to the appointment of the servants, or the gossip about those who frequented the Court. She told him of her fears of the Neapolitan Embassy intriguing, for she had made up her mind by now that all Neapolitans

[1] Villa-Urrutia : *Fernando VII : Rey Constitucional*, pp. 21, 22.

were rascals. One can hardly think that she was courteous to her daughter-in-law : the poor young Princess had had two miscarriages, on which the Queen wrote with her accustomed sharpness—and accustomed frankness—to the Prince of the Peace ; for, after all, she told him everything. She did not approve of her daughter-in-law's reading. The King, she said, had seen the Princess reading a book called *Les Folies de ces temps : an neuvième de la République,* which had as frontispiece a plate of which the good old King did not approve,[1] and which she thought would be baneful to her son. But what reading was not baneful ? For her part, " I am a woman," she wrote to her confidential minister. " I abhor those women who claim to be intelligent and on a level with men, for I think it unbecoming to our sex—but as I am a Spaniard, by the grace of God, I am free from that fault." Her daughter-in-law, however, had it very badly ; and what was one not to say of the dreadful prints that came from Paris with these books ? For such a young creature no words could be too bad : from such expressions as " her mother's spittal " and " a bloodless little animal all venom and vinegar," " a half-dead frog " to " a poisonous viper," and " phlegm which crackles in the fire." [2] " What shall we do," she asked the Prince of the Peace on October 10, 1805, " with this diabolical serpent of a daughter-in-law, and this son who is a spiked vine of cowardice ? If we do not take them in hand, and cut their wings, I am afraid of a crash, for I shiver at the thought of foreigners, and specially the Italians ; and as they on small provocation use poison, it all horrifies me—not so much for myself, because I have no confidence in anyone—and so watchfulness with all, and

[1] Villa-Urrutia : *Mujeres de Fernando VII,* p. 36.
[2] Villa-Urrutia : *Ibid.,* p. 34.

most of all with this household." [1]   The Princess was spied upon by her confessor, her doctor, her servants, and those she thought her closest friends.   So that of everything that went on in their household, Maria Luisa had a more or less precise account.   All the Princess's letters, and even those of the Neapolitan Embassy—the Maccaronis, Luisa called them—were opened.[2]   The Ambassador had written to the Princess some letters which were very unpleasant to Maria Luisa—for she saw that he was influencing the Princess against the sovereigns and their ministers. "You will see the intrigues which these rascals have been and are carrying on," she wrote, referring to the young couple, in October 1805, a few days before the Battle of Trafalgar, " and which are due to those bandit Ambassadors as far back as in the spring."

The truth was that the Princess's mother, who was a Habsburg of Vienna, had brought her daughter up to detest Napoleon and everything to do with him, including his alliance with Godoy.[3]   And Godoy was at that time working day by day in secret treaty with Napoleon.   The Spanish Ambassador in Paris, Prince Masserano, was of Piedmontese origin : lest he should prove troublesome, Godoy employed another agent in Paris, who treated directly with two secret agents of Napoleon, Duroc and Lacépède.

Godoy's agent was named Izquierdo : he had had a post in the Court in connection with the Royal Gardens ; he was sent to Paris with letters saying that he was charged with several commissions concerning natural history ; that, on account not only of his character but of Their Majesties' trust in him, he was

[1] Villa-Urrutia : *Mujeres de Fernando VII*, p. 41.
[2] Villa-Urrutia : *Ibid.*, p. 34.
[3] Alcalá Galiano : *Recuerdos de un Anciano.   Mémoires du Duc de Rovigo*, iv. 18.

to be treated with distinguished consideration, and to
correspond freely with the Generalissimo. Two
things Godoy told him were required of him—truth-
fulness and circumspection. As for Napoleon, his
first preoccupation was to undermine any influence
that the Queen of Naples might obtain through her
daughter at Madrid ; and this was not difficult ; for
the Queen had already a suspicion of Godoy, and
thought him the father of her daughter-in-law.
" Napoleon," wrote Izquierdo, " knows and despises
the Queen of Naples, whom he thinks a woman
capable of anything," that she regretted the double
marriage of her children with the Spaniards ; and
Napoleon " would be much interested to see what
steps were taken to free Madrid from the intrigues of
this fiendish woman."

The Queen's agents in the Court of the Tuileries,
the Duke and Duchess of San Teodoro, also infuriated
him ; and he had taken steps markedly to avoid them.
But why he was so anxious to counter her " fiendish
intrigues " was that she was a friend of Nelson and of
England, as well as a daughter of Vienna. He would
have no confidence in the Spanish Government, said
Napoleon to Izquierdo, till their fleet had joined his
own to keep the English ships from their coasts.

Before long the Emperor sent another and a more
important representative than Lacépède to treat with
Izquierdo : this was no other than the Emperor's
own brother-in-law, Marshal Joachim Murat, who,
born as an innkeeper's son in Gascony, was now
the Grand Duke de Berg et de Cleves ; he was
characterised by Napoleon himself as a mixture of a
hero and a fool. And his diplomacy was distinguished
in turn by bluntness, venality, and ostentation. He
began his talks with Izquierdo at Neuilly like a plain
soldier, without equivocation, and without preamble ;

at the same time he showed such good will that Izquierdo recommended that it would be worth making him a bigger present—a present of a million pesos.

" In this way," wrote Izquierdo to Godoy, " we shall attain here whatever is for our advantage, and what has been done with Prince Murat can be done with Cambacérès, Berthier, Talleyrand. You must understand that my ship is already in harbour, and that nothing can hold it back from arriving at the wharf. Big affairs should be treated broadly. To succeed, cost what it may, is my motto.

" Only my zeal and loyalty to my country compel me to speak with this frankness to Your Excellency, impelled by the circumstances, and sure that all is so well guarded that no one but Your Excellency and I should know it." [1]

A fortnight before he had received an excited letter from Godoy. " The world is in movement," wrote the Prince of the Peace, on June 10, 1805. " The objects which may concern us are infinite, and yet none has been determined. We are converting the country. Great are our afflictions, extreme the need of what is not provided, but we have perseverance and energy, daring and hope. May God bring my work to an end, and you will see Europe surprised. But no one can hope for so much." [2]

No, it was too much to hope for. For Nelson was in command of the British fleet. And so, though the Queen of Naples might fall, as very soon she did,—so, though Queen Julie, the daughter of a merchant of Marseilles, might reign with Joseph Bonaparte in her place, all was not well for Godoy in Madrid : the

---

[1] July 3, 1805.

[2] These letters were taken from Godoy's house at his fall, and are now in the National Archives at Madrid, Legajo, 2881.

"bandit Ambassadors" of Naples had the powers of the sea on their side, and Maria Luisa therefore was more acid than ever with her daughter-in-law.

Small wonder that the Princess had wanted to escape and live in a separate house her own life with her husband. But this her mother-in-law would by no means allow. "The King does not want it," she said. "He knows that it would not do, and we have always lived together, always united and without fusses."

But gradually the poor young Princess, who had been compared to a half-dead frog, began to grow aweary of the sun. The rattle-snake Queen had bitten into her blood a slow but hideous poison. Cut off even from the undisturbed company of the husband whose figure had at first revolted her, she found a mysterious illness attacking her in the winter of 1805. On January 18, 1806, she received Extreme Unction, but she lingered on through the spring. Death did not release her from her sufferings till May 21.[1] She had supported almost five years of misery.

And Godoy was accused of having poisoned her.[2]

3

It is the peculiarity of royal dramas that, while their actors are exempt from neither the passions nor the pettiness of humble lives, in their eminence and power they can involve the issues of state which are at their disposal ; for they move central in a realm of principle and tradition, not always to be sundered from eternity itself.

This truth was forced upon the Spanish sovereigns in San Lorenzo del Escorial. Great powers and great

[1] Villa-Urrutia : *Mujeres*, p. 43.
[2] D'Auvergne : *Godoy, the Queen's Favourite.*

ideas, when they move the society of men, give out their life to stone. In the architecture, which is the monument of Spanish kingship, there is the mystery and press of a spiritual urgency which joins a suggestion of lightness to the austere yet mellow granite, so that the Gothic flight finds wings out of Roman solidity, and tinges the whole with an indefinable suggestion of the East.

Against the violet bloom of the Sierra, the royal creation hewn out of its rock raises the proportioned length and height of its immense façades ; the dormer windows, the angled roofs, the square towers at the square corners of the building or between its central courts rise to a pyramid, and on this their central spires are crowned with a ball of metal. Serene and central, over turret and campanile, over quadrangle and façade, over the angled roofs, the spires, the balls, the dome raises above another colonnade a smaller dome surmounted by a cross. On this, the central height, above a temple rises again a spire, and on the spire again a ball, and on the ball a cross. The whole is one with the rocks, the pines, the mountain. Thus, through clear and luminous air, fine because high and far from exhalations of sea or smoke, is the first vision of the Escorial. Such is the stone portrait of Catholic Majesty.

At the great entrance to this building, which is at once a tomb, a temple, a palace, and a cloister, six giant statues of the prophets of Israel—Solomon with his Book of Wisdom, and David with his harp, in the centre—stand crowned with glittering gold. Within, rising in immense piers, majestic arches show the scheme of architecture was that which Bramante and Michelangelo recreated from the models of imperial Rome to voice, at the consummation of the Middle Ages, the supreme majesty of the Church after its long conflict with the mediæval Cæsars. For the dran a of the Middle Ages in Europe was the struggle of the Church against the power to which she owed her safety. Yet,—though she contended so—to the Church there is and there has always been something sacred in civil authority; and among the things which are Cæsar's is a dignity to which it has been her privilege to give a hallowing and a crown.

The Escorial was built by Philip II, the son of one of the greatest monarchs of a power which called itself Holy and Roman and an Empire. Surrendering the ambition of dominance in Europe, it had received the compensation of mastery in new continents, over which it was to spread the order, the luminance, the warmth of Mediterranean Christianity, while it enriched the plains and hills and mountains of arid Spain with the wealth of those new Indies. All had been dedicated to the great convictions of a rule which was one with the freedom and the authority of the Church; and Philip's palace was so constructed that from his bed he had a glimpse of the High Altar of the temple, and could adore at the Elevation of the Host. And monks, day by day in sacrificial mysteries, raised the ideals of triumph and of life above the tombs of kings—for when the palace was built they had prepared resting-places for twenty-five sovereigns then unborn. Three of those resting-places for kings of Spain are waiting still.

In this serene and austere monument, and beneath the spiked insistence of its spires, the broom and lavender of early summer had faded from the hills, and the cistus had softened the pungent aroma which the sun spreads from its leaves, like living coal from grains of incense; the high air was sharpening at the approach of the autumn of 1807, when suddenly the personal intrigues of the Court were involved with the politics of Europe in a sensational conspiracy.

2

It was brought by a letter from the King to the ears of the new Emperor of the French, whom Habsburgs and Bourbons alike were compelled to acknowledge the Master of Europe.

"Monsieur Mon Frère (wrote Carlos to Napoleon),—

"At the moment at which I was concerned only with the destruction of our common enemy, when I thought that all the machinations of the ex-Queen of Naples had been buried with her daughter, I see, with a horror which makes me shudder, that the most horrible spirit of intrigue has entered into my very palace. Ah ! my heart bleeds as I refer to an attempt so frightful. My first-born son, the heir presumptive of my crown, had formed the cruel project of dethroning me : he had gone so far as to plot against the life of his mother. So horrible an attempt should be punished with the most exemplary rigour of the law. The law which called him to succeed should be revoked : one of his brothers would be more worthy to replace him on my throne and in my heart.

"At this moment I am toiling to discover his accomplices, to penetrate to the foundation this plan of blackest evil, and I do not wish to lose a single moment to give an account of it to Your Imperial and Royal Majesty, begging that you may aid me with your lights and counsels.

"And so I pray God, my good brother, that He may deign to hold Your Imperial and Royal Majesty worthily in His holy keeping.

"Carlos.

"In San Lorenzo del Escorial,
    Oct. 29, 1807." [1]

[1] Published in *Moniteur Universel*, Paris, Feb. 5, 1810.

It is not difficult to explain what had happened. Our judgments of others reflect our own character, and the King had had complete confidence in his son. "Fernando," he would say again and again, "is incapable of doing an unbecoming thing." But in reality the Prince was incapable of nothing. Even before his marriage he had lived much alone : he had passed the years of his youth, when spirits should be highest, in severe subjection to the will of his mother and the monotonous etiquette of the Court. His retirement was accentuated by the fears which his rise to manhood naturally inspired in those who were then directing the monarchy. Finding nothing to do, no way to exert either the influence or power of a Prince of Asturias, he began to intrigue. And his mother knew it. His conduct was observed, even his most innocent procedures were made the subject of inquisition. The Prince broke out into bitter complaints, and his expressions were often rather unrestrained. Guided by his example, the servants around him spoke with more freedom than was convenient ; those sayings and talks repeated, perhaps even altered as they passed from mouth to mouth, awoke the ever intenser hatred of those who naturally distrusted him.[1] And yet such trifling affairs were not sufficient to invite a judicial enquiry : they only gave occasion to new care and watchfulness. Both were redoubled, until it was noticed that the Prince received secret letters, that he stayed up late into the night writing, and that his bearing suggested that he was thinking out some important business. Any one of those suspicions gave sufficient ground to awaken the jealousy of the paid servants around him, and a lady-in-waiting gave information to the Queen

[1] Toreno : *Historia del levantamiento, guerra y revolución de España*, 7 vols., 1862.

of the mysterious life her widowed son was leading.[1]
Then an anonymous letter came to the King's hand,
saying : " Prince Fernando prepares a movement in
the palace : the Crown is in peril, and Queen Maria
Luisa runs great risk of death by poison. It is urgent
not to lose an instant to impede the plot. The faithful
subject who gives the advice can find no other way to
accomplish the duty." [2]

Some said that Godoy himself had that letter
written and placed among the prayer-books on the
King's faldstool. A curious story put it down to the
idea that the Queen had been accidentally arrested by
the palace sentries on her return from an evening visit
to Godoy. According to this she had been accustomed
to leave the Escorial by a secret door, and by an
accidental change the sentries were at hand when she
returned ; and she at this suspected Fernando, and
decided that no time must be lost in reducing him to
complete subjection.[3] But why the young man's
intrigues were discovered just at that moment no one
can really say. What is solid history is that on
October 29 they summoned the Prince to the King's
room, and cross-questioned him about the papers that
had meanwhile been seized. His servants were
arrested, and sentinels were placed to keep him in
custody, while the King and Queen went through the
papers. They discovered that their son had been
engaged in a far-reaching conspiracy.

4

Although the nobles of Spain had flocked to the
house of the Universal Minister, and he was offered,

[1] Toreno : *Historia*, i. 12.
[2] Vaya : *Fernando VII*, i. 41.
[3] Oman : *Peninsular War*, i. 24, 25.

by the very highest, the respect and flatteries with
which it was thought becoming for a *grand d'Espagne*
to address a member of the Royal Family, there were
not wanting those who were resolute to down him.
The chief of these were the Duke of the Infantado,
the Duke of San Carlos, and the Count of Montijo,
whose niece afterwards became the Empress of the
French.[1]   With this party the Prince of Asturias had
allied himself : he found an ally in the Count de
Beauharnais, the French Ambassador, a brother-in-law
of the Empress Josephine.   Beauharnais so hated and
despised Godoy that, even in official communications,
he refused to address the Universal Minister as Your
Highness, though King Carlos had given him the title.
Godoy complained ; Talleyrand intervened ; but
Beauharnais went on the way he had chosen.   The
Queen suggested, after the death of Maria Antonia,
that her son should marry a sister of Godoy's wife ;
and Godoy himself urged the suit on Don Fernando ;
but this was too much.   " I would rather remain a
widower all my life," the Infante shouted in the very
face of the Prince of the Peace, " or go into a monas-
tery, than be the brother-in-law of Manuel Godoy."
But if he was not to marry the sister-in-law of Manuel
Godoy, then whom ? Beauharnais whispered the
name of Joséphine's cousin, Rose-Françoise Tascher
de la Pagerie, and the Empress, in her foolishness, was
pleased.[2] Fernando himself was won over.   He was
induced by Beauharnais to address a letter to the
Emperor, appealing to him as " the greatest of heroes
whom the world had seen."   He applied both for aid
against his parents and for a bride from Napoleon's
circle.   " This is what my heart desires," he wrote,
" but it does not appeal to the perfidious egoists who

---

[1] *Moniteur Universel*, Paris, Feb. 5, 1810.
[2] Geoffroy de Grandmaison : *L'Espagne et Napoléon*, i. chap. iii.

surround my father, and who can for a moment get
the better of him ; I am full of fears on this point.
Only the prestige of Your Imperial Majesty can disconcert their plans, opening the eyes of my good and
beloved parents, and providing them with felicity at
the same time as the Spanish nation and myself." [1]

Fernando was phenomenally sly, but in all other
matters, as Godoy had complained before his marriage,
the Infante's education was deficient : he was clever
enough to remedy his own defects by relying on the
gifts of the tutor whom Godoy had given him. For
Escoiquiz was a master of diplomacy and a master
of the pen. He not only wrote the letter to Napoleon,
but made also separately to each of the parents a
denunciation of Godoy.

In this denunciation [2] the pretensions of Godoy
were compared by the priest to those of Haman
in relation to Ahasuerus. "The perverse man is he
who, abandoning all respect, is obviously aiming at
robbing us of the throne, and finishing with us," the
letter went on. "Godoy, in less than eighteen years,
has risen from a simple soldier of the bodyguard
and a poor private gentleman to Generalissimo and
Admiral, to not only a Grandee of the first class and
a Prince, but to a marriage with a close kinswoman,
and to being treated as a royalty, a thing up to this
time unknown in Spain, for there was no one with
whom the Royal Family could mix as equals.
What have been the artifices with which he surprised the kind heart and the candour of my beloved
Mother, and the goodness of Your Majesty, who,
measuring the generosity of others by his own, thinks
it impossible deceit and perfidy should find a shelter
in his heart ? A war badly led against France, a

---

[1] *Moniteur Universel*, Paris, Feb. 5, 1810.
[2] Escoiquiz : *Memorias*, pp. 281–331.

burdensome peace, the ruin and discredit of the inheritance, and a series of disgraceful calamities have been the fruits of government." And who could wonder if the sovereigns were unpopular?

" Ah, Señor ! the principal, or let me rather say the only, cause of the coldness of this poor and loyal people, and even of the whole nation, is no guilty disaffection for its monarchs, whom they have loved, love still, and always will love ;   it is, yes, the evil and tyrannic administration of this man ; it is the sorrow they feel at seeing a monster like him raised by the kindness of Your Majesty to a power which holds the whole kingdom oppressed and enslaved.

" He has used his authority, his power, and his compulsion to prostitute the flower of the women of Spain from the highest to the lowest." The King had been too trustful. Escoiquiz quoted a Spanish proverb, " Keep a good opinion of your neighbour and lock the door."   But this was too subtle for the young man transcribing the letter. " Keep a bad opinion of him," added Fernando, " and you will find it right."

And then the voice of jealousy, which was the voice of the many, burst out into a fresh account of the triumphant position of the Prince of the Peace.

" The nobles, the officers of highest rank, the judges, the ecclesiastics of highest place dispute with their inferiors the shameful honour of occupying for long hours, not only his ante-chambers, but his staircases, even his stables, to gain a glance, a word, a gracious gesture, thinking him fortunate who attains it, and wretched any person they see who does not pander to these vilenesses, or who disdains to give to him a reverence due only to their sovereigns."

Such was the letter to the King. And there was another like it to the Queen. When the sovereigns had finished reading them, the King turned to Caballero, the Minister of Grace and Justice. " What punishment," he asked, " does the law visit on a son who acts in such a way ? "

" Señor," answered the Minister, " he is guilty on seven accounts of the punishment of death."

" What ! " cried the Queen, " have you forgotten that he is my son ? With the right I have as his mother, I shall destroy the proofs of his guilt. They have deceived him : they have ruined him." And sinking into a chair, with tears in her eyes, she tore up the letter and hid the pieces in her bosom.[1]

What were the sovereigns to do ? It could not be obscured that Godoy was becoming unpopular. And yet they could scarcely dismiss him, for he was engaged in negotiations with Napoleon ; and if one thing was obvious it was that they must all unite in keeping Napoleon appeased. He had already placed his brother Joseph on the throne of Naples ; he had won the battle of Jena ; the peace of Tilsit left him free. He was a menace alike to Carlos and his son. So the first thing to do was to write to Napoleon. And meanwhile Maria Luisa used her influence with her son.

Godoy, who had been ill with fever in Madrid when the plot had been discovered, was apprised of the drama, and hastened up to the Escorial. He wanted quarrels neither with father nor with son. After the affair of Naples, he had published a proclamation speaking of an enemy of Spain ; and he knew that Napoleon knew what enemy he meant. That was the danger to Spain : he had been working to avert it, and on the very day that Carlos was writing to Napoleon, Napoleon had signed in Paris a treaty with Godoy agreeing to the partition of Portugal.

[1] Ceballos : *Hechos.*

So as one of Maria Luisa's daughters had lost the Two
Sicilies, and a second Etruria, a third was to lose
Lusitania. But Godoy was to be given an inde-
pendent territory : he was to be Prince of the
Algarve. Meanwhile, the troops of Napoleon who
were to assist in the negotiation had entered Castile.

The Universal Minister was still waiting for news
of his negotiation with Napoleon when he came out
to the Escorial. The King, he said, had sent him a
draft of Caballero's indictment of the Prince of
Asturias. And doubtless the Queen had also sent a
message that her son must be saved. Godoy knew
that, ill as he was, he must face a crisis. " It was the
depth of night," he himself said. " I could hardly
see : my head was like the boiling of a flood, and in
spite of all this I had to answer with the least possible
delay, without a moment's consultation, without anyone to help me even to hold my pen. But the great
excitement of my mind gave me power, as happens
from time to time in the access of delirium. Reading,
and re-reading, I began to correct what I could :
here I erased, there I altered. I cancelled this. I
wrote over that. Blots fell on the paper, and after a
time I could not myself understand what I had
written, and certainly no one else could have
deciphered it. I made up my mind to write out a
rough draft." [1]

When simple people are disillusioned, their distrust
makes no compromise. The King was not at first
disposed to accept the draft. " Neither as king, nor
father," he said, " could I forgive him without failing
in my duties and exposing myself to contempt. And
I was so good to him ! And such a kind father !
To have deceived me like that ! To have put me in
such a painful position ! To have trampled on my

[1] Godoy : *Cuenta Dada*, i. 200.

respect, and to have compromised the fortune of my kingdoms secretly seeking for a bride from the enemy of my house ! To have given him a free hand to place us in subjection ! And if I pardon him, what will my subjects say ? "

Godoy argued that to pardon him was the only way to outwit Bonaparte, the only way to close the door by which he could enter as a friend finally to destroy them. But someone must reconcile the Prince ; and to whom could the King entrust such an office without compromising his dignity but Godoy ? The Minister entered the room of Prince Fernando and folded the youth in his arms. " Manuel mio," Fernando cried, weeping. " I wanted to send for you, and I went to send for you. Those rascals have deceived me, and ruined me. I believe nothing against you. I want to be your friend. You can save me from this afflic-tion in which I have fallen." " That is the only reason I came, ill and feverish as I am, as you see." " Yes. You are burning hot." " And I am burning with love of Your Highness, the son of my sovereigns, him whom I took so often in my arms, for whom, if I had them, I would give a thousand lives." And he wept even more than the Prince—tears, he said, which poured forth from his soul.

Later Carlos told Fernando that Godoy wished to give up all his positions of power. " I only want a proof that you trust your father, and to ask you these two things : first, if you think that this faction which made efforts to have you at its head is submerged and silenced, the faction which, as you told me, has long been working at dividing and obtaining my govern-ment ? and second, if in your way of thinking it would be a good idea, so as finally to disarm it, to let Manuel resign ? "

" *Padre mio !   Padre mio !* " said Fernando,

throwing a glance at Godoy, the most gracious and kindly the favourite thought that he had ever seen there ; " he who led me back into your favour, when he found me so far from deserving it, should never leave us."

Such is the account which Godoy gave the world of this scene after Fernando had died.   It may be true, it may not ; for the Memoirs of Godoy are by no means always in accord with other documents.   But there is no reason to doubt it here.   That Carlos trusted in Godoy there can be no question ; and certainly Maria Luisa still felt a mother's feeling towards her son.   She could rate at him ; she could calumniate him ; but she did not want anyone else to harm him, and at the thought of it her mother's instinct was *chevaux de frise*.   And as for Fernando, he had many reasons to be ashamed of himself : the Prince of the Peace had been by no means a bad governor in Spain,[1] and was in almost every particular far superior to the Prince of Asturias, who by now perhaps had begun to realise that it was a dangerous plan to invoke the aid of Napoleon to settle his affairs.   So, after five days to think it over, Fernando found it most prudent very humbly to apologise.   He wrote two letters.   The first was this :

" Sir, and my dear Papa,—
     " I have done wrong.   I have sinned against Your Majesty as King and father ; but I repent and offer to Your Majesty the most humble obedience.   Nothing should be done without knowledge of Your Majesty ; but I was taken by surprise.   I have denounced the culprits, and beg

[1] See the important article by W.—probably Lord Wellesley— in the *Westminster Review*, April 1836, and Hans Roger Madol's new biography, *Godoy.*

Your Majesty to pardon me, permitting your royal feet to be kissed by your grateful son

"FERNANDO.

"SAN LORENZO,
"*Nov.* 5, 1807."

This letter was sent with one to the Queen :

"MADAM, AND MY DEAR MAMA,—

"I am very sorry for the great crime I have committed against my parents and sovereigns, and so with the greatest humility I beg Your Majesty to pardon me, as also in my stubbornness in lying to you the other night, and so from the depths of my heart I beg Your Majesty to intercede with Papa that he may allow his feet to be kissed by your grateful son

"FERNANDO."

And with these strange letters—which Ceballos accuses Godoy of having forged—the poor old King, who had so kindly trusted his son, was content. The son's letters of repentance were published to the nation, and the King declared himself to his vassals an example of Christian forgiveness. "The voice of nature," he said, "disarms the hand of vengeance, and when inadvertency claims mercy, a loving father cannot refuse it. My son has now disclosed the authors of the horrible plan which some villains led him to conceive : he has made all formally known, and all is scrupulously in accord with what in such cases the law demands." In other words, the Prince of the Peace continued in his place, the Duke of San Carlos (whom the Queen called the most treacherous of her son's friends) was exiled, the Duke of the Infantado was imprisoned, and the Court turned its full attention to the Emperor of the French.

5

Indeed, the very day before—November 4—the King had written to complain of the Count de Beauharnais, that brother of the first husband of the Empress Josephine, whom Napoleon had sent to Madrid as his Ambassador. The declarations of Fernando and Escoiquiz had made it clear how much he was involved in the conspiracy. Napoleon refused to admit any cognisance of the intrigue, and promised that his Ambassador should not interfere in the private affairs of the Spanish sovereigns. But meanwhile his troops were pouring into Spain, and at the head of them was his brother-in-law, the Grand Duke and Marshal, Murat.[1] He now overshadowed Beauharnais as the Emperor's Ambassador in Madrid. This was soon to menace both Carlos and Fernando with the loss of the crown of Spain ; and Frere, the British Ambassador, summing up his feelings to Lady Holland, said that were he an emigrant, he would have " no more scruple in sticking a dagger into B.'s heart than a knife into a leg of mutton." [2]

[1] Vaya : *Fernando VII*, i. 51, 52.
[2] Lady Holland : *Spanish Journal*, p. 174.

II

THE USURPATIONS

How carols now the lusty muleteer ?
Of love, romance, devotion is his lay,
As whilome he was wont the leagues to cheer,
His quick bells wildly jingling on the way ?
No ! as he speeds, he chants, " Viva el Rey ! "
And checks his song to execrate Godoy,
The royal wittol Charles, and curse the day
When first Spain's queen beheld the black-eyed boy,
And gore-faced Treason sprang from her adulterate joy.

BYRON : *Childe Harold's Pilgrimage.*

I

THERE can be little doubt that at Tilsit Napoleon
had discussed the Iberian Peninsula with the Emperor
Alexander of Russia. He knew of the old alliance of
Portugal with England : it went back a hundred
years before Vasco da Gama had sailed around the
Cape of Good Hope ; it also gave England a foothold
against the power of Spain on both sides of the
Atlantic ; and after the battle of Trafalgar it was to
Napoleon a great annoyance. Therefore it would be
of extreme advantage to combine with Spain in
cutting Portugal into pieces, and Napoleon's plans
fitted very well with those of the Prince of the Peace,
who had already been allied with him against
England, and who for personal reasons had supported
Napoleon in dethroning the Queen of Naples. The
intrigues and vendettas therefore in the heart of the
Spanish Court were of no small importance, both to
Napoleon and to the English. For the dead Princess

30

of Asturias had been working almost as an agent of
England : her mother, the Queen of Naples, as
Napoleon had suggested to Izquierdo, was, as we saw,
a particular friend of Nelson ; as an Austrian she was
heart and soul with the English against Napoleon,
and the English interests were at stake in every move
of the Spanish intrigue.

Napoleon's interests were undoubtedly still more
so ; but the Conqueror had not yet made up his mind
whether to unite with Spain against Portugal or
England, or to bring the whole Peninsula under his
sway. "There is," he said to the Spanish Ambassador in Paris, " no way to free Portugal but to
subdue it utterly, to divide it up, and to make it into
two or three princedoms of Spain." He had just
dethroned Maria Luisa's daughter, the Queen of
Etruria. Here was a chance to recompense her : she
could have the North ; the House of Braganza could
keep the middle, and as for the South, why not give
it to Godoy ?

Godoy, behind " the heavy, sleepy, voluptuous
eye, not unlike Lord Amherst," which struck Lady
Holland's attention,[1] was an accomplished man of
affairs [2] ; ever since the French Revolution he had
kept Spain, and even the Indies, secure and peaceful.
Such a task required a remarkable man, and so the
British Ambassador felt him to be. " Godoy's
manner," wrote Lord Holland, " though somewhat
indolent, or as the French term it nonchalant, was
graceful and engaging. In spite of his education,
which I presume was provincial and not of the best,
his language appeared to me elegant, and equally
exempt from vulgarity and affectation. Indeed, his

[1] Lady Holland : *Spanish Journal*, p. 74.
[2] Junot credits him with " statesmanlike faculties." Duchess
d'Abrantès : *Memoirs*, Eng. ed., ii. 390.

whole demeanour announced, more than that of any untravelled Spaniard I ever met with, a mixture of dignity and politeness, of propriety and ease. He seemed born for a high station. Without effort he would have passed in any mixed society, for the first man in it." [1] Don Fernando might talk of " the black and cancered conscience of this tiger." A traveller like Ford might call him a thing of avarice, and compare him to " a foul beast of prey always craving and swallowing." [2] Lady Holland, looking at the ruddy complexion which set off the sleepy eye, might describe him as large and coarse. Napoleon himself was to compare him to a bull, as the Duchess d'Abrantès compared him to a coachman.[3] But the Prince of the Peace was a man of most remarkable capacities ; " the foul beast of prey " made such a woman as Maria Luisa write : " Your fame and memory will end only when the world is burnt to ashes, and then they will after that be rewarded in glory." [4] It is proof enough of greatness to occasion such differences of judgment. Napoleon himself had at first felt only scorn for the man who next to himself had had the most phenomenal rise of any in Europe, and enjoyed the most extended power. But at St. Helena he changed his mind, saying finally, " That man was a genius." [5]

When he heard of the plot against Portugal, the Prince of Masserano, the Spanish Ambassador in Paris, demurred, if we may trust Godoy, to lending himself to a plan that would be held dishonourable. But since the whole affair was in the hands of Izquierdo,

---

[1] *Westminster Review*, April 1836.   [2] Ford : *Travels in Spain.*
[3] Duchess d'Abrantès : *Souvenirs d'une Ambassade*, i. 79. " Sa tournure était des plus communes."
[4] Villa-Urrutia : *María Luisa*, p. 33.
[5] D'Auvergne : *Godoy.*

MANUEL GODOY, PRINCE OF THE PEACE
After the portrait by Goya in the Académia de San Fernando, Madrid.

" That man," said Napoleon, " was a genius."

it is doubtful whether he knew anything about it. Napoleon, according to Godoy, lost his patience when they spoke of honour. " Would it be believed in Spain that, to make war in Portugal, I had to buy your Minister ? " he asked. " All that is necessary is to let my troops pass through the territories. Your Prince of the Peace is already worn out : he has done great service, he has kept Spain at peace from the revolution of Europe ; but apart from being worn out, he has very powerful enemies in his country : the nobility and the clergy are against him, and above all the Prince of Asturias. The great intrigue which the English are working up is affecting Spain." And then Napoleon developed his plans : it was above all necessary, he said, to keep the English out, and to prevent their political institutions undermining the Catholic monarchy. " Hardly a week passes," he said, " without my getting some anonymous letter which casts a doubt upon the loyalty of Carlos IV ; and, if I believed them, our friendship would have been broken long since. And in any case Carlos may die. The interests of the Empire require us to take a wide view, and to foresee any contingencies, among them that the Crown Prince may not be the instrument or toy of an imprudent faction." [1] By an imprudent faction he meant, no doubt, the friends of England. So, in the meantime, on the very day that Carlos was writing from the Escorial to tell Napoleon of the treachery of Fernando, Napoleon was signing a treaty for the partition of Portugal, which allowed the French troops to enter Spain. Between the dream of outwitting England in Portugal, of becoming Emperor of South America, and of seizing the throne of Spain, Napoleon had not yet made up his mind.

[1] Godoy : *Cuenta Dada.*

3

What of the Spanish sovereigns and Godoy ?   They
were beginning to see plainly that their interests were
in siding with the great Emperor.   He who had
dominated all Europe could hardly be kept back by
the Iberian Peninsula.   So the Prince of the Peace
spent the winter in making amicable arrangements
with Napoleon and Murat.   The English, ably represented by Frere, Holland, and Lord Wellesley, saw
plainly what was happening, and were naturally
furious.   Their one hope was with Fernando.   He
was obviously the head of the faction which could displace Godoy.

They suggested every possible suspicion of the
French, and indeed there is little reason to think,
however, that the Emperor's intentions, both towards
the Spanish sovereigns and their minister, through
the autumn and winter of 1807, were anything but
sinister.   " *Ce gredin*," said Napoleon, " *nous ouvrira
les portes d'Espagne.*"

French troops were coming through the Pyrenees in
ever greater numbers, and Fernando's faction grew
more and more uneasy.   Ceballos has left us a record
of their view :

" Napoleon," he writes, " had hardly concluded the
Treaty of Tilsit, in which he appeared to have decided
in his favour the destiny of the Universe, when he
turned his eyes to the West and resolved the ruin of
Portugal and Spain, or what comes to the same thing,
to take possession of this vast peninsula, to make its
inhabitants as happy as those of Italy, Switzerland,
Holland, or the Confederation of the Rhine.

" The plan was not so easy as he had imagined ;
for such a gigantic and daring project as to subject a
friendly and allied nation, which had already made
great sacrifices for France, and which the Emperor
himself had praised for its fidelity and nobleness

of character, it was above all necessary to seek a pretext.

"Yet, accustomed to work with that lack of delicacy in the means, which is proper to anyone who imagines that the conquest of the whole world, the devastation of the human race, and armed violence lead to true glory, he proposed to foment discord in the Spanish Royal Family by means of his ambassador in its Court."[1]

2

The Prince of Asturias had a supreme quality which, in that curious circle, was like a prick of poison in already disordered blood. This quality was his cunning. His father now confided everything in him, even to a plan for dismissing Godoy. But Fernando apparently would not hear of it : he said that the King should never part with the man who had brought peace back into the family. The young man gave his hand to Godoy : he took Godoy in his arms ; he spoke to him in the tone of warm affection, begging him to sacrifice his repose to the country's good—and the heart of the old king was full of content. He did not know that the plot of the Escorial, and his own pronouncements, had been a rock of offence to the Spanish people, who were weary of ordered government and jealous of the power which had preserved it ; that they had formed a new faction around the Prince of Asturias, and were plotting the death of the Prince of the Peace ; and that Fernando was using the confidence of his father to give to a seditious party the news of all the King's secret counsels.[2] It was enough for the French to have come at the invitation

[1] Ceballos : *Exposición de Hechos y Maquinaciónes.* Madrid, 1818.
[2] Vaya : *Fernando VII,* i. 61, 62.

of the sovereign for every French soldier to be regarded as a menace to the independence of Spain. And the English naturally had every interest in fomenting that suspicion.

While Godoy and the sovereigns were careful to remain in amity with the Emperor, Fernando thought of nothing but his intrigue against his mother's friend. The Duke of San Carlos and the Duke of the Infantado had been removed, but by a peculiar oversight a more dangerous and unscrupulous nobleman, the Count of Montijo, still remained at liberty. Fernando now summoned him from Cadiz to Madrid.

In the meantime, feeling that there was unrest in the capital, the Court had gone to Aranjuez. This palace is almost as far from Madrid as the Escorial, but in the direction of Toledo : it is set where the river Jarama flows into the Tagus. There the sovereigns had a palace as luxurious and charming as the Escorial was noble and austere. To it Carlos and Maria Luisa had themselves added a model of the Grand Trianon, which they called the Workman's Cottage, the *Casa del Labrador*. Profuse elms had been brought from England, and the gardens were beautifully arranged with the rivers into pleasaunces of spring flowers and summer fruit. Life in Aranjuez was a delightful relaxation in harmony with those luxuriant parts of Spain like the Huerta de Valencia, where the air is rich with the scent of orange blossom, and where the warm weather insinuates voluptuousness. And here, in the spring of 1808, Maria Luisa received the latest things in robes and toques from Paris.[1]

It was in this spot that at the same time the Prince of Asturias plotted with the Count of Montijo

[1] Madame Lunette was her dressmaker in Paris. See Villa-Urrutia : *Relaciónes*, i. 41.

Montijo was by nature turbulent and troublesome :
he had a strong grievance, because his mother, who
shared ideas with the French encyclopædists, and some
said with the masons, had been exiled. Her son's
mind was aflame with a patriot's ambition. Restless
and intense, his temperament made him a perennial
conspirator. Godoy he regarded as a monster who
was ruining the country by his avarice, and he
delighted to head an insurrection against him.[1] As
" Uncle Peter," he had been scattering money at
Aranjuez, and had a formidable faction at his command. His brother, the Count de Teba, had taken
the side of the French.

On March 16 the King prepared to go to
Andalusia, with the idea of possibly abandoning the
throne of Spain for that of Mexico, as the kings of
Portugal had transformed themselves into emperors
of Brazil.[2] But before he started, the feeling of rest-
lessness against the French was so strong that he
thought it wise to issue a proclamation.

" My beloved Vassals (it ran),—

" Your noble agitation in these circumstances
is a new testimony to assure me of the feeling of
your heart, and I who love you as a tender father
hasten to console you in the anxiety which
oppresses you. Breathe tranquilly ; be assured
that the army of my dear ally, the Emperor of the
French, crosses my kingdom with ideas of peace
and friendship. Its object is to reach the point
menaced by the risk of the enemy disembarking,
and that the mobilisation of a bodyguard is
neither to defend my person nor to accompany

[1] Villa-Urrutia : *Eugenia, Imperatriz de los Franceses.*
[2] Ceballos : *Hechos.*

me on a journey which malice has made you
think necessary. Surrounded by the concentrated
loyalty of my beloved vassals, of which I hold
unarguable proofs, what can I fear? And when
urgent necessity demands it, could I doubt the
forces which your generous hearts offer me? No,
my people will not see this urgent necessity. People
of Spain, calm your minds ; behave as up to now
you have done with the ally of your King, and in
a few days you will see peace established in your
hearts, and me enjoying what Heaven grants me
in the intimacy of my family and your love."

But next evening the beloved vassals of Carlos prepared for him, at his son's instigation, a most disturbing surprise. Fernando, whom his father had again
supposed to be incapable of an unbecoming thing, had
carried out a new plan to dethrone his parents, after
the capture, perhaps the murder, of their trusted
minister.

The evening of March 17 was cloudy and star-
less, and the murmur of the river at Aranjuez was
drowned by the noisy crowd which " Uncle Peter "
Montijo had gathered round the house of the Prince
of the Peace. Between eleven and twelve, a carriage
with curtains drawn across the windows issued from
the house. The carriage, although escorted by a
guard, was attacked by the crowd, and its curtains, in
spite of resistance, were drawn aside. Its occupant
was discovered to be the Countess of Castillo Fiel.
Meanwhile, a shot had been fired, and a light had
appeared in the Prince's room in the palace.

Immediately a trumpet sounded and a troop rushed
to the charge. They forced their way with a great
body of peasants into Godoy's house, and sacked it,
while they searched for its master. The rooms, which

were the most splendid of any courtier's, were invaded by a dirty mob, and the sumptuous treasures of the palace thrown on to a bonfire.

The Universal Minister of Spain and the Indies, meanwhile, snatching a piece of bread from the table, had tried to escape through the Duchess of Osma's house next door, but, finding it closed, he had run up to an attic and hidden himself in a rolled-up mat. There he had undergone two whole days of torment, until at last thirst forced him to move. A Walloon recognised him, and at once gave the alarm.[1] A crowd gathered, struck him, and gave him a nasty cut on the right eyebrow. But by an effort the guard saved him, to drag him off to Don Fernando. They met in a stable. Godoy was so weak that he could hardly stand. He looked so pitiable that even his worst enemies might have been touched. He fell at Fernando's feet.

" I beg Your Majesty's mercy," he said.

" Manuel, you seem to forget that my father is still alive."

" Well, will Your Highness pardon my offences ? "

" Manuel," said Fernando again, " the injuries you have done to me are pardoned, but you owe to Spain an account of the evil you have done her. The Council of Castile will judge you." And Godoy was flung into a dungeon.[2]

So came to an end in violence and flame the triumphant ministry of the Prince of the Peace ; a ministry of tranquillity and order, which had encouraged science and the liberal arts, and done great good for Spain. It was ended by the crowd crying, " Death to the sausage man ! " (For Godoy came from Estremadura, where Spain makes her sausages.)

---

[1] Toreno : *Op. cit.*, i. 82.
[2] Geoffroy de Grandmaison : *L'Espagne et Napoléon*, pp. 145, 146.

" What, do they want to kill the sausage-man ? "
asked a little boy, who liked his sausages and their
merchant. " They are not talking of the sausage-
man," answered his mother ; " they are talking of the
poor Prince of . . ."

" The Prince of Darkness," his father interrupted.
And the little boy, who went to a Pestalozzi school
which Godoy had founded, was much mystified that
his parents and the crowd should be shouting for the
death of the august benefactor, whose praises he had
learnt to sing.[1]

Meanwhile the King, his confidence in his degener-
ate heir again badly shaken, his limbs heavy with
rheumatism, and his heart cowed by the insulting tone
of his beloved vassals, who before had never been anything but humble, sought from the ministers and
nobles round him the counsel and support which had
never been withheld by Godoy.[2]

But he had been forced to dismiss his minister,
and with sorrow and misgiving in their hearts, the
sovereigns had to receive an ovation for having done
so. Next day the King announced to Napoleon that
he himself had assumed in his minister's place the
supreme command of his armies. But Godoy was
scarcely out of his hiding-place before Carlos was
forced to abdicate.

That was March 19. The pressure was strong.
Fernando had the crowd with him. But Maria
Luisa contrived to outwit them. In two days more
Carlos had made a formal protest, and sent off a
strong letter of complaint to the Emperor of the
French. Napoleon, who knew everything that had
happened, had already said that he would take no
notice of the abdication. It complicated and mud-

[1] Mesonero Romanos : *Memorias.*
[2] Villa-Urrutia : *Fernando VII.*

dled all the plans he had been working out with
Godoy. An abdication, he said, therefore should be
a solemn formal act ; and had not Carlos already
warned him that Fernando had been plotting to take
the crown by force of stratagem ? The dissensions in
the Spanish Court now involved the politics of
Europe, and history was immediately to be crowded
with events.

3

Fernando meanwhile made good use of his triumphant cunning. All who had been proscribed for their
complicity in the Escorial conspiracy were recalled
and raised to posts of honour ; all who had served
King Carlos with Godoy were disgraced and banished.
The Duke of the Infantado was made President of the
Supreme Council of Castile, the Duke of San Carlos
Majordomo of the Palace. Don Juan Escoiquiz was
named a Councillor of State, and given the Grand
Cross of Carlos III, while Don Pedro Ceballos, who
had, in spite of marrying a cousin of Godoy, worked
hard to dethrone the old King, was made the Minister
for Foreign Affairs.[1]

Fernando meanwhile prepared for a triumphal
entry into Madrid on March 24. During the night a
great crowd on foot, on horseback, and in all sorts of
carriages had gone out to meet him on the road from
Aranjuez, and on a spirited horse he rode into Madrid
on a brilliant spring morning. His escort was small ;
but what gave glory to his procession was the enthusiasm which greeted him. Had any Spanish
monarch received from his people such a spontaneous
and warm ovation ? Tears of joy streamed down the
cheeks of old and young ; the women strewed flowers

[1] Vaya : *Fernando VII*, pp. 90, 91.

in his way, or waved frenzied handkerchiefs from the windows and balconies, while the men would at times actually kneel to touch the horse he rode. Mingling with the salute of cannon and the pealing of countless bells, there were such enthusiasm and love in the shouts of welcome given him by the crowd that one would have thought they were inaugurating the age of gold.

But they were nastily deceived ; it was an age of disaster that was being inaugurated : the young man they were welcoming had a heart which was treacherous and chill, and the trumpets which sang out his arrival were

> Clamorous messengers of blood and death.

The horror of the position is described by the Marquis de Villa-Urrutia, in a telling passage that points to the tragedies of a century :

" The young King, who up to then had done no particular good, nor given any pledges of a tolerable character ; who in the Escorial plot had shown himself rebellious and unscrupulous as prince and son, who had been cowardly and treacherous to his companions, criminal to his country, approaching the French to overcome the favourite, and calling on the Emperor to decide family quarrels ; who in Aranjuez had been raised on the breastplates of soldiers who had got out of hand, and a suborned populace, led by some few discontented and rebellious noblemen, would say that he held in his hands to pour down upon his people all the prosperity, fortune, and glory with which a benevolent fairy had endowed his cradle, and which had been prophesied at his birth by a flattering nurse, more Jesuit than courtly.

" And yet the cunning youth, who was to be the most sinister of all the Bourbons, carried in his hand only Pandora's box. From it was to issue the war against the French, as great in feats of daring as it was sterile in its effects, for it encouraged the indiscipline of the people, and awoke a habit of fighting which was to work itself out through half a century in civil war. From this box came also the Cortes of Cadiz and the ill-fated constitution of 1812, the cause of so many *pronunciamientos* and mutinies, of a new French invasion, and of the impossibility of making a Parliamentary Monarchy into a national Spanish institution ; from it also came the loss of Spain's vast promising Empire in America, a loss to which he seemed amazingly indifferent ; for all he cared for was to destroy constitutions by the armed intervention of foreign powers which he secretly approached as postulant and beggar. From it came forth that bloody persecution of the Liberals which so well suits the Monarch's cruel instincts. From it issued the Camarilla and the ministry of favourites, and the double diplomacy against Ambassadors and Ministers who were won over or deceived. From it, in fact, issued the most lamentable decay of Spanish Monarchy, so that the King left at his death for heritage a civil war which continued for many years and had lasting consequences." [1]

Such is the sinister story of the reign of Fernando VII : he had been only a fortnight on the throne when his mother wrote of him to the Grand Duke de Berg : " My son has a very bad heart ; his character is cruel, he has never loved his father nor me ; his counsellors are violent ; their only happiness is to work evil, even on a father and a mother." And these thoughts were elaborated in other letters : " Of Fernando we can never hope anything but miseries and persecutions : he worked out this conspiracy to dethrone his father, the King ; he has no character

[1] Villa-Urrutia : *Fernando VII.*

of any kind, least of all of sincerity ; he is false and
cruel ; his ambition is unlimited, and he regards his
parents as though they did not exist. Nothing affects
him : he is without feeling and without mercy ; he
promises, but he does not always fulfil his promises ;
his love is neither for the Grand Duke, nor for the
Emperor, but for despotism." [1] And what is most
shocking of all is that these warnings from a mother
were not mere spiteful calumnies, but the literal truth.
This was the person whom the people of Madrid were
acclaiming, in exchange for a beneficent ruler, against
whom they had no charge but a suspicion of adultery
in a position where it was thought almost impossible
for a young man to live a chaste life. But the people
of Madrid are liable to errors of judgment ; and not
alone in this case were they to pay dear for the
delusions of their own indiscipline.

4

Foreign Ambassadors soon followed the crowd in
acknowledging the succession of Fernando, not the
least eager being the English. Nelson's country was
very glad to see on the throne of Spain the husband,
even though he was now the widower, of the Queen of
Naples' daughter. But amongst the congratulating
plenipotentiaries, there was one eminent exception.
It was the Grand Duke de Berg et de Cleves. He
commanded an army at the gates of Madrid under
orders of the Emperor of the French, of whom it might
be said, as of Mark Antony, that

> Crowns and crownets dropped from his bosom.

It was to him therefore that Maria Luisa, writing
now herself on her husband's behalf, and now in the

[1] *Moniteur Universel*, Feb. 5, 1810.

FERNANDO VII
After the portrait by Goya in the Prado.

" This is the person whom the people of Madrid were acclaiming "

hand of her daughter the dethroned Queen of Etruria, addressed her exposures of her son and her pleas for Godoy. For the two ideas were inseparable. The Prince of the Peace, she said, would be safer among devouring lions and tigers than in the hands of her son's friends, and " among all those bloody creatures " the priest Escoiquiz stood the very first of all—though at other times she thought San Carlos the most malign. Godoy, she insisted, was in prison simply because he was the friend of France : he was not only in prison, but she feared that at any moment they would kill him or poison him, and say that he had died of his wounds. On the 3rd she was told that Godoy was to be liberated in three days, and with Carlos she moved over to the Escorial. From there, after a new disappointment and a reassurance, she wrote again to Murat on April 8 :

" My Lord and Brother,—
    " The letter which your Imperial and Royal Highness has written us, and which we received early this morning, allays our fears. We are in the hands of the Emperor and Your Highness, we need fear nothing. My husband the King, our common friend and I place all hope in the Emperor who will soon decide our fate. It gives us the greatest pleasure and satisfaction to keep the time appointed to-morrow to meet and talk with Your Highness ; it will also be to see the Emperor. And in the meantime, we beg Your Highness anew to free the Prince of the Peace from the horrible hands in which he lies, so that he may be safe and that they may not kill him, or do anything to him ; for those false and accursed ministers who surround him will do all they can to forestall the arrival of the Emperor. My son will have started. I shall go and show the

Emperor just the contrary of that, which is truth [*sic*]. They will have so many inventions and lies to which they will give the show of truth that he may doubt unless Your Highness keeps him informed. My son has handed over all his own powers of command, and of deciding affairs, to Don Antonio, his uncle, who has a very limited talent and spirit, but who is bloody and inclined to do all possible harm to us three and my daughter Luisa. Really, he ought to consult with the Council ; but this Council is composed of all the factions, so detestable, which have been the cause of this revolution, and which have no love of the French ; nor has my son Fernando either, in spite of all he put in the *Gazette* yesterday ; because it is his fear of the Emperor which makes him speak so. I make bold to say to Your Imperial and Royal Highness that the Ambassador [1] is quite on my son's side, with that cursed clerical hypocrite Escoiquiz, who have done and will do more than can be imagined to deceive Your Highness, and above all the Emperor. Your Highness should give His Majesty warning before my son sees him. As he is leaving to-day, and his hand is so crippled, he has not written the letter my son asked, and to-day for the same reason the King cannot write to Your Highness with his own hand. And he feels it very much because we have no other friends except Your Highness, and the Emperor, of whom we hope all.

" Luisa." [2]

Since all she hoped was a life in peace with Godoy, Napoleon found no inconvenience in obliging her.

---

[1] Beauharnais, she meant.   [2] *Moniteur Universel*, Feb. 5, 1810.

5

But meanwhile there was the question of Fernando
to settle. The young man had hardly taken possession in Madrid when he was told he was to receive a
visit from the Emperor, or at least that Napoleon
would come to the frontier. So Fernando immediately sent off his brother Carlos to receive him there.
That was on April 5, just before his parents had moved
from Aranjuez to the Escorial. Two days later,
another agent of Napoleon arrived in Madrid in
addition to Murat and Beauharnais. This was
General Savary, afterwards the Duke of Rovigo, who
was supposed to be the forerunner of his master,
though the trunks which contained ostensibly the
clothes of the Emperor were really full of smuggled
goods on which the General hoped to make a turn.
The fact is that Savary was meant to lure Fernando
to the French frontier. He denies it in his biography,
which, like Godoy's, is very often at variance with
other documents. In this case, both Fernando
writing to his father, and Murat writing to Napoleon,
state that Savary had persuaded the Prince to start.

Fernando set out on April 10 with Escoiquiz and
Ceballos as his advisers, and a suite of nobles, leaving,
as we have seen from his mother's letter, his uncle
Don Antonio with full power as regent in Madrid.
Don Antonio, who had a curious resemblance to
Benjamin Franklin, was a simple old man whose
hobby was to cobble old boots, and whom the Queen
did not malign in calling his intelligence limited.[1]
They travelled quickly, and on the 12th they had
reached Burgos, where Fernando had hoped to meet
Napoleon. Two days later they had got as far as
Vitoria, but Napoleon came not. Then, indeed, a

[1] De Pradt : *Mémoires*.

message arrived from Don Carlos to say that he also
had not yet encountered the Emperor.   Fernando
consulted with Ceballos and Escoiquiz : it was all
very doubtful.   But Savary urged them to go on,
and how could they reject the advice of Napoleon's
own envoy ?   Besides, there was one very reassuring
thing : unlike Murat and Beauharnais, Savary always
addressed Fernando as Your Majesty.

At this point he received a letter from Napoleon,
so firm in tone that, whether he liked it or not, his
weak mind was mastered.   Ruthless in its reasoning,
inexorable in its judgments, it told Fernando without
any compromise exactly how he had behaved and
what his position was.   It began with a sentence full
of meaning to sovereigns, and not least to sovereigns
of Spain : " *The people are glad to avenge on us the respect
they pay us.*"   This guided him in an elucidation of
Fernando's intrigues against his parents, and his
accusation of their minister.

" How can you bring a case against the Prince
of the Peace," he asked, " without bringing it also
against the King and Queen, your parents ?
Such a case would foment hatred and rebellious
passions : the result would be fatal to your
crown.   Your Royal Highness has no other
rights to it than the Queen has transmitted to
you, and if the case would be fatal to her honour,
Your Highness destroys your rights.   Your Royal
Highness should not lend ears to weak and
treacherous counsellors.   Your Highness has no
right to judge the Prince of the Peace : his crimes,
if he is found guilty of them, fade into the rights
of the throne.   Many times I have manifested my
desire that the Prince of the Peace should retire
from the negotiations : if I have not been more

instant, it has been on account of my friendship
for King Carlos turning my gaze from the weakness of his affections. Oh, miserable race !
Weakness and error, such is our motto. But all
this can be arranged : the Prince of the Peace
should be banished from Spain, and I offer him
an asylum in France." [1]

As for the abdication of Carlos, the fact that it had
coincided with the entry of Napoleon's troops into
Spain seemed to suggest that the Emperor intended
to seize his throne. But, said Napoleon, it was not so.
If, on the other hand, Charles had abdicated freely
and not merely on account of the mutiny of Aranjuez,
then, Napoleon said, " I should have no difficulty in
recognising Your Royal Highness as King of Spain.
I desire to confer with Your Royal Highness on this
matter."

" Your Royal Highness," continued the letter, " has
not been exempt from faults. There is sufficient proof
of that in the letter you wrote me, and which I have
always wished to forget. When you are a king, you
will recognise that the rights of the throne are sacred,
and any step taken by an hereditary prince to approach
a foreign sovereign is fatal. The marriage of a
French Princess with Your Royal Highness I judge
harmonious to the interests of my peoples, and above
all as a means of uniting us with new bonds to a house
which I have had reason to praise since I ascended
the throne."

Fernando felt not unnaturally some misgiving when
he read this letter ; but Savary again reassured him.
" If within a quarter of an hour of Your Majesty's
arrival in Bayonne," said the French General, " the
Emperor has not recognised you for King of Spain and

---

[1] Ceballos : *Hechos*.

the Indies, you can cut my head off." Overcome by
this picturesque figure, Fernando gave in, in spite of the
warnings of his counsellors and his own misgivings.[1]

When he crossed the frontier his doubts increased :
no one took any official notice till he arrived at St.
Jean de Luz. Though the Mayor greeted him there
as a reigning sovereign, and addressed to him a
flowery harangue, it was obvious to all when he
reached Bayonne that he was being treated with little
ceremony ; the lodging prepared for him was mean.
The Emperor, who was reviewing troops when he
arrived, rode up to him, and allowed Fernando to
embrace him, offering first one cheek and then the
other. Then he rode back to his review.[2] Fernando
felt a little reassured. When he went to dine with
Napoleon in the great château at Marracq, the
Emperor came down to the carriage to meet him.
But conversation halted, for neither could speak the
other's language, and Napoleon did not admire his
guest. " *Il n'a pas encore dit un mot*," wrote Napoleon
to Talleyrand. " *Il est indifférent à tout, très matériel,
mange quatre fois par jour et n'a idée de rien.*" [3]

The Spanish Prince had hardly come back to his
quarters when Savary, with no word now about his
alluring promises at Burgos and Vitoria, appeared
with shocking news. He did not refer to the possibility of Fernando cutting off his head. He simply
said that the Emperor had irrevocably made up his
mind that the dynasty of Bourbon should abandon
for ever the throne of Spain and the Indies to that
of Bonaparte, and that Fernando would not be
allowed to return to Spain.[4]

[1] Ceballos : *Hechos*, p. 20.
[2] Ducéré : *Napoléon à Bayonne*, p. 68.
[3] Napoleon : *Correspondance*, 13778.
[4] Ceballos : *Hechos*, p. 22.

Fernando shouted, " We are betrayed ! " and tried
to escape at once. But he found that his host had
already made escape impossible.

6

What was he to say ?   It was felt that he owed both
to his subjects and to his reputation not to renounce
the crown ; that he could not hand over the rights of
other members of his family ; and that the claim to
the throne depended not on the order of a foreigner,
but the choice of the Spanish people.

As for the affairs of Aranjuez, Ceballos had himself,
three weeks before those, heard Carlos say, " Maria
Luisa, we shall retire to our province and live quietly,
while Fernando, who is young, will take up the
burden of the government." No violence, it was
claimed, had been shown to the old King, either by
the Prince or by the people. All the foreign representatives had congratulated the new sovereign,
except the French Ambassador, though none had
received definite instructions from their Courts.

Napoleon's agent, Champagni, replied to these
arguments that the Emperor could not be sure of
Spain in the case of a war in the north, as long as
those who reigned over it were members of a family
whose elder branch had been despoiled of the throne
of France. In vain, therefore, it was argued that
such considerations did not weigh with the sovereigns
of Spain, whose every interest invited them to friendship and alliance with their only powerful neighbour ;
that France had every reason to remain on good
terms with her Spanish ally ; that Spain had for her
sovereigns a generous energy of love that had passed
into a proverb ; that she had been loyal to them even
when they were arbitrary despots, so when they saw

their adored sovereign dependent and insecure, would
their well-known valour be awakened by such a
motive ? that if, by mischance, the French should
offer so atrocious an insult, they would lose an ally
whose army, whose navy, and whose finances had in
no small way assisted French triumph ; that England
who had so far worked in vain to seduce the Spanish
from the side of France, would naturally combine in
such a case in defence of the Spanish crown ; and
that England would have in commerce with Spain the
advantages formerly held by the French.

Ceballos was still talking in this way when the
Emperor himself summoned him into his office.
Napoleon's tone was brusque ; his words were uncompromising ; the name he gave to Ceballos was
traitor. Ceballos held his ground. But Napoleon cut
short his arguments. " *J'ai ma politique à moi*," he
said. " *Vous devez adopter des idées plus libérales, être
moins sensible sur le point d'honneur et ne sacrifier la pros-
périté de l'Espagne à l'intérêt de la famille de Bourbon*." [1]
The Emperor then sent a message to Fernando, saying
that he must treat with a more flexible politician, and
Don Juan de Escoiquiz took Ceballos' place.

7

Escoiquiz has left us a portrait of Napoleon which
might have been painted by Goya. It has Goya's
vividness and Goya's intensity, and gives us the
impression which the Great Emperor made on a
Spanish patriot who talked with him for hours.
Escoiquiz depicts Napoleon as a man of extremely
lively imagination, with a wide clear view, but not a
deep one, a judgment rapid but inexact. The base
of his character was boundless ambition, says Escoi-

[1] Ceballos : *Hechos*.

quiz, and a boldness that enabled him to conquer
very obstacle to his darling passion. Although he
never did harm for the pleasure of doing it, he would
stop short at no atrocity, if he deemed it necessary to
realise his projects ; and, if he felt it prudent to hide
his designs, would go to any length of hypocrisy.
Interests that others felt sacred and inviolable were to
him simply the instruments of his designs. Uniting
in his nature the lion with the fox, he struck Escoiquiz
as having a tiger's mingling of ferocity with treachery.
From this extraordinary mingling of qualities,
cultivated by a scientific education, he was enabled to
form vast and daring plans, and to execute them with
the quickness of lightning. But the fury of his ambition gave him an impatience which stifled the warnings of prudence, and enabled the man who could
paralyse his impetuous and sweeping attacks by astute
withdrawals to gain upon him in the end. And this
weakness, so Escoiquiz thought, made him a poor
diplomatist ; for politics demand a deeper wisdom
and a farther view than could be obtained by a man
whose genius was that of the military commander for
swift decisions.[1]
On two successive days Escoiquiz argued clearly,
gravely and at length with the Emperor, urging him
that alike for the interests of equity, and in the long
run of policy itself, it was better to remain on good
terms with Fernando and the Spanish people. Napoleon pulled his ears, and remained in an affable mood,
but complained that Escoiquiz would not look at
things, as he, Napoleon, did.[2] No Spaniard in
Bayonne, in fact, would cede to his arguments ; and
so, to give his projects a colour of honour, he was
forced to look farther for his instruments.

[1] Escoiquiz : *Memorias*, p. 40.
[2] Escoiquiz : *Ibid.*, pp. 401–455.

8

The Emperor wrote therefore to Murat that he mus[t] by some means tempt Carlos and Maria Luisa t[o] Bayonne. They made their condition that Godo[y] should go with them ; so, in spite of Fernando's stric[t] orders, the Prince of the Peace was released by Murat[.] Carlos was anything but well : his rheumatism ha[d] become a torture. Maria Luisa had been warned b[y] a courtier that Napoleon intended to drive them a[ll] out of Spain. " But I can't believe in such scandalou[s] perfidy," she said. " What I can assure Your Im[-] perial Majesty," she wrote to Napoleon from Arand[a] on April 25, " is that we are flying into your arms.[']

Meanwhile, Fernando and Ceballos were guarde[d] by an *alguacil*,[1] who refused to let them out of thei[r] lodgings ; while the spies within were doubled.

Fernando was plotting with Ceballos to receive hi[s] parents with filial affection. But if the most prepos[-] terous audacities of hypocrisy had helped the Princ[e] in the Escorial, they could not do so now. Carlos, a[s] we have seen, was not a man to admit of qualification[s] in a character : he was like his English counterpar[t] in life, to whom everyone is either a thorough goo[d] fellow or a damned scoundrel. Having found tha[t] Fernando was not, as he had thought, the first[,] Carlos was convinced that he must be the second[:] once he believed his son incapable of doing an un[-] becoming thing ; he was now convinced that the yout[h] was a scheming blackguard. And Fernando was t[o] be made well aware of it.

It was on April 27 that the Empress Josephin[e] arrived from Paris. Two days later, Carlos an[d] Maria Luisa arrived at the frontier to drive in nex[t] morning to Bayonne. The Prince of the Peace ha[d]

[1] *Huissier*, or police-sergeant.

arrived a little time before them, and their youngest
son, Francisco, followed them with the Queen of
Etruria. Fernando and Ceballos approached to
greet them on their arrival, Godoy tactfully keeping
away to risk no collisions. Escoiquiz said that the
King and Queen received Fernando and his suite
coldly and contemptuously, and that their faces had
an expression of hate and fury.[1] But, as at the
Escorial, it was Maria Luisa who was the milder of
the two. As he descended from his coach Carlos had
spoken graciously to all, even to those he did not
know.[2] But when he recognised his sons, he turned
his eyes away. He so far relented as to say " Good
morning " to Carlos, while Maria Luisa pressed him
to her heart. Fernando, who had not known what
to do, plucked up his courage, and now moved forward. Maria Luisa embraced him also, but Carlos,
with a gesture of disgust, moved away. " Infante,
you have done outrage enough to my white hairs,"
he said.[3] A moment later the old King and Queen
were exchanging expressions of devotion with the
Prince of the Peace. The eyes of all three ran with
tears.[4]

They had been received at the French frontier with
more than the marks of honour given to reigning
sovereigns. Napoleon now made them the visit of
ceremony, with every sign of considerate respect.
But while the Emperor paid them the compliments
of a sovereign to sovereigns, he wrote about them to
Talleyrand with extreme terseness. Maria Luisa,
wearing on her grey hair a wreath of red and yellow
roses, and on her body a garment of yellow crêpe
which she had borrowed from Josephine,[5] had struck

[1] Escoiquiz : *Memorias*, p. 268.   [2] Vaya : *Fernando VII*, p. 133.
[3] *Moniteur Universel*, No. 127.   [4] B. Constant : *Mémoires*.
[5] Marquise de la Tour du Pin : *Journal*, ii. 220, 221.

him as appalling. " Carlos is a good old man," he
wrote. " Maria Luisa has her past and her character
written on her face, which is all I need say. It surpasses anything one dare imagine. The Prince of the
Peace looks like a bull with a touch of Daru about
him." [1]   But of this judgment the Spanish party could
discern nothing. Napoleon had suggested that after
their long journey they should have a day's rest. He
wanted to be considerate to Carlos, and had been
told how the old man ached after his journey. Even
when he did arrive for dinner with the Emperor at
Marracq, he could hardly walk up the stairs. The
Emperor offered Carlos his arm. " I have no
strength," said the King as he took it; " they have
taken it from me." " We shall see about that,"
answered Napoleon. " But lean on me, I am strong
enough to hold us both up." " So I believe," said
Carlos; " and on that I found my hopes." [2]   A few
minutes later he was taking his seat at the table; but
as he looked round for the friend on whom he had so
long been dependent, he noted with concern that the
Prince of the Peace was not there. How could that
be? " Manuel? " he asked naïvely. " Where is
Manuel? " The Emperor at once repaired the
mistake, for Godoy had been waiting outside, and
Carlos ate his meal in peace of mind. And
Napoleon had prepared them an excellent dinner.
As one dish came after another, Carlos would
turn to his wife and say, " Eat that; it's good." [3]
Maria Luisa had not only to borrow clothes from
Josephine; she was disquieted that Godoy's mistress
had not arrived. She knew, she said, that her sons
were prisoners, and she was very glad of it; that no

[1] *Correspondance de Napoléon*, 1393.   See Frontispiece.
[2] Savary : *Mémoires*, iv. 342.
[3] Ducéré : *Napoléon à Bayonne*, p. 87.

KING CARLOS IV

After the portrait by Goya in the Prado.

" Carlos is a good old man," wrote Napoleon.

matter what happened to them it would be less than their deserts ; that they were both monsters, and all her troubles came from them.[1]

M. de Beausset, as he led the procession in to dinner, had heard the Emperor say, " Your Majesty thinks perhaps that I am going a little too fast ? " And the Queen, leaning on his arm, had answered, " Sire, you have rather a way of doing that." But whether she spoke in irony or adulation, her voice did not disclose, and no one but Napoleon saw her eyes.[2]

9

Next morning there was a fierce scene between father and son in the presence of the Emperor. Carlos began by demanding that Fernando should restore, at once and unconditionally, the crown that he had torn from his father's brows. The Emperor took up the argument. But Fernando, still obstinate, spoke of the enthusiastic unanimity which had raised him to the throne. Carlos rose from his chair—up to that time Fernando alone had been standing—and in a solemn speech denounced his son as having plotted the murder of his parents so as to seize their crown for himself. Maria Luisa at this point lost control of herself, and pumped insults on her sons from the Cloaca Maxima of her abuse. At the Escorial she had pleaded for Fernando ; now she begged the French to punish him on the scaffold for his crime. At this point Carlos struck at the youth with his whip, and Napoleon, who himself was hardly prepared for such a scene, hurried Fernando out of the room.[3]

[1] Marquise de la Tour du Pin : *Journal*, ii. 222.
[2] Beausset : *Mémoires*, 3rd ed., i. 222, 223.
[3] Oman : *Peninsular War*, i. 53. Cf. Napoleon's despatch of May 1 to Murat, and De Pradt : *Mémoires*.

Fernando was no sooner alone than with the help of Ceballos he indited his parents a very curious letter, not devoid of skill. He had, he said, been asked by Carlos to resign in their favour, and since they did not want themselves either to reign or to return to Madrid, he would give up the crown only on condition that he governed the country as their regent. And then in a confused sentence, as though the words had stuck in his throat, he wrote of himself as " a son who had always been distinguished by his love, respect, and obedience to his parents," and said that any indication which could qualify those sentiments did violence to his filial piety.[1]

After sending this letter, Fernando arranged an interview with his father, and again argued out his case.

" Papa," he began, " if Your Majesty did not voluntarily abdicate at Aranjuez, why did you not tell me then, knowing that in such a case I would never have accepted it ? "

" I did do it voluntarily," said Carlos.

" Then," asked the son, " why did Your Majesty protest against it ? "

" Because I did not mean it to be permanent, but for the time that I thought fit."

" Then why did Your Majesty not insert this clause, or at least mention it privately to me ? "

" Because I didn't feel inclined, and was in no way obliged to tell you of it."

" Then did I ever suggest to Your Majesty to do it ?"
" No."

" And was there anyone else who forced Your Majesty to abdicate ? "

" No. I did it because I wanted to, and no one forced me to it."

[1] Ceballos : *Hechos*, p. 71.

" And now Your Majesty wants to go back and reign again ? "

" No, far from it."

" Then why," asked Fernando, " does Your Majesty command me to give you back the crown ? "

" Because," said the old man with finality, " it takes my fancy, and I have no need to tell you why. I don't want you to say a word more about it, but obey." [1]

Carlos at this evidently went back to the Emperor and asked him how to put the case, for next day he answered in a letter as obviously influenced by Napoleon as his son's was by Ceballos. He began by saying that the treacherous counsels of those around his son had brought Spain to such a pass that only the Emperor could save it.

" You have been," he continued, " seduced too easily by your first wife's hatred of France, and you have shared thoughtlessly in her unjust rancours against my ministers, against your mother, and against myself.

" I felt obliged to assert my rights as father and as King. I had you arrested, and found among your papers the proofs of your infamy ; but at the end of my career, reduced to the sorrow of seeing my son perish on a scaffold, I allowed myself to cede to my sensibility at the sight of your mother's tears, and I pardoned you. Nevertheless, my subjects were agitated by the false prejudices of the faction you had joined. And from that moment I lost my peace in life, and I was obliged to suffer both ill-treatment from my vassals and afflictions due to the dissensions of my family. You have introduced disorder into my palace and incited my body-

[1] Escoiquiz : *Memorias*, pp. 270, 271.

guard to mutiny against me. Your father has been your prisoner : my Prime Minister, whom I had adopted in my family as my own child, was led from one dungeon to another, covered with blood. You have stript the gold from my sceptre, and have despoiled us of a crown which my fathers wore with glory and kept free from stain. You have seated yourself upon my throne, and you placed yourself at the disposition of the people of Madrid, and of the foreign troops entered there.

And you cast your glances on the plot of the Escorial ; the acts of my administration were the object of public disapproval. Anxious and overborne by sickness, I have not been able to support this new misfortune. I have had recourse to the Emperor of the French, not as a King at the head of his troops, in the midst of the pomp of the throne, but like a King, unfortunate and abandoned, I have found protection and refuge in his realms. I owe him my own life, that of the Queen, that of my Prime Minister. I have come at last to Bayonne ; and you have conducted this business in such a way that all depends on the mediation and protection of this great Prince.

The thought of returning to popular tumults is to ruin Spain : it would lead to catastrophes still more horrible for you, for my kingdom, for my subjects, and for my family. I have opened all my heart to the Emperor : he knows all the outrages I have received, and the violences which have been done to me ; he has declared to me that never again will he recognise you as King, and that the enemy of his father can never inspire the trust of strangers. He has furthermore

shown me letters in your hand which clearly show
your hatred of France.

" In this position my rights are clear, and much
more my duties : not to shed the blood of my
vassals, to do nothing at the end of my career
which could lead to Spain being isolated and
ravaged, and reduced to the most horrible misery.

.   .   .   .   .

" Your conduct with myself, your intercepted
letters have placed a barrier of bronze between
you and the throne of Spain ; and it is neither
to your own interest nor to that of the country
that you should claim it. Beware of lighting a
fire which will cause inevitably your complete
ruin, and the misfortune of Spain.

" I am King by the right of my fathers : my
abdication is the result of force and violence ; I
shall have nothing further to receive from you,
and I cannot consent to any meeting together,
or any new and sinister suggestion from the in-
experienced men who accompany you.

" I have reigned for the felicity of my vassals ;
and I do not want to leave them civil wars,
mutinies, popular meetings (*juntas*), and revolution. All should be done for the people and
nothing by them : to forget this maxim is to
make oneself an accomplice in all the crimes that
follow. My people have made me sacrifice my
whole life for them ; and in the age which I have
reached I shall do nothing which is in opposition
with their religion, their tranquillity, and their
fortune. I have reigned for them ; I shall ever
occupy myself with them ; I shall forget all my
sacrifices ; and when in fact I am assured that
the religion of Spain, the integrity of its provinces,
its independence, and its privileges will be secure,

I shall go down to the grave, forgiving you the
bitterness of my last years."

This extraordinary letter bore the historic date of
May 2, 1808. No day in their history is fixed
more irrevocably in the minds and hearts of Spaniards.
On that day, the people of Madrid, indignant at the
absence of their sovereign, annoyed with the ostentation of Murat, suspicious at the presence of a foreign
army, had expressed their patriotic feelings in a
demonstration against the French. Murat answered
it with shooting on the mob, and followed that by
ruthless executions. The two most powerful pictures
that Goya painted express with all the eloquence of his
art the fierceness of the revolt, the ghastliness of the
reprisal. He painted those pictures to argue with the
world that men were meant to be something better
than barbarians.

10

Four days later, May 6, 1808, Fernando replied to his
father at considerable length, and with some vigour.
He denied that he hated France, or that he was guilty
in the Escorial plot ; that his object in treating with
Napoleon was to free his father from Godoy. He
insisted that Carlos had abdicated freely, without
pressure, or even suggestion from outside ; he claimed
that he himself had been consistent in his friendly
attitude towards France, and that Napoleon, once
assured that his attitude towards France was the same
as his father's, had promised to recognise him as King
of Spain.

"Full of trust in these promises," he continued, " and believing that I would meet His
Imperial Majesty on the way, I came to this city.

And on the very day I arrived, verbal propositions were made to some members of my party, so alien to those which so far had been mentioned, that neither my honour, nor my conscience, nor the duties imposed upon me when I took my oath to the Cortes as their Prince and Lord, nor those which were imposed upon me anew when I accepted the Crown which Your Majesty abdicated in my favour, have allowed me to accede to them."

And if the abdication of Aranjuez had not been free, why was nothing said at the time ? In any case, Fernando would be prepared to give back the Crown, and act simply as his father's representative.

"I repeat once more to Your Majesty," he wrote, "that in such circumstances, and such conditions, I shall be ready to accompany Your Majesty to Spain, there to make my abdication in the form referred to. And inasmuch as Your Majesty has said that you do not wish to return to Spain, I beg you, with tears in my eyes, by all that is most sacred in heaven or on earth, that if you do not really wish to reign, you will not leave a country that you know, in which you may choose the climate that best suits your failing health, and in which, I assure you, you may enjoy more comforts and more peace of mind than any other.

"And lastly, I passionately beg Your Majesty to realise your present situation, and that what is at stake is the exclusion of our dynasty for ever from the throne of Spain, substituting for it that of the Imperial dynasty of France ; that this cannot be done without the express consent of the Spanish nation, united in Cortes in a safe place ; that in addition we are in a foreign country, and do not act freely, and this consideration would alone annul what we do, and produce fatal consequences."

But Fernando's struggle was in vain. The next day he was summoned to the presence of his parents as he had been on May 1. Once again the Emperor Napoleon was with them. On the former occasion, it will be recalled, when Fernando had quivered before the onslaught of his parents, Napoleon had hurried the frightened youth out of the room. But this time the Emperor showed no mercy. The interview lasted an hour, in which Fernando was again kept standing while all the others sat. The words that were said to him were insulting and humiliating. " Unless you sign an absolute renunciation," said Carlos, " you will be treated as a usurper conspiring against your parents' life."

" *Prince*," said the Emperor in his sternest tone, " *il faut opter entre la cession et la mort.*"

Next morning, the desired letter, protesting that he had no choice between signing and being declared guilty of contumacy, was put into his father's hand.

On May 19 a junta, called a National Assembly, was summoned to Bayonne to treat of the *felicity* of Spain, and the great plans that were to be made for the improvement of the country. The Spanish had now at their disposal, if they chose to accept it, the ordered liberty of the Napoleonic system. They determined, or rather, Fernando's supporters determined, to fight it to the death. And Spain went steadily backward into something like the Dark Ages.

III

THE GOOD INTRUDER'S REIGN

" Still alive and still bold," shouted Earth,
  " I grow bolder and still more bold.
  The dead fill me ten thousandfold
Fuller of speed and splendour and mirth.
  I was cloudy, and sullen, and cold
  Like a frozen chaos uprolled
Till by the spirit of the mighty dead
My heart grew warm.   I feed on whom I fed.

" Ay alive and still bold," muttered Earth,
  " Napoleon's fierce spirit rolled
  In terror and blood and gold,
A torrent of ruin to death from his birth.
  Leave the millions who follow to mould
  The metal before it be cold.
And weave into his shame, which like the dead
Shrouds me, the hope that from his glory fled."
SHELLEY.

I

MEANWHILE, the Bourbons of Spain found a home
in France.   To Fernando, with his brother Carlos and
his uncle Antonio, Napoleon asked Talleyrand to hand
over the Château of Valençay, near Bourges, while
Carlos, Luisa, and Godoy, with the Queen of Etruria,
made their way to Compiègne by way of Fontainebleau.   These were never to see Spain again, and
they were content to say good-bye to a country where
they knew they could no longer reign or rule.   Napoleon had saved the royal trio from ignominy, and
their favourite from perilous imprisonment :   this

party had good reason to be grateful to him. But Fernando had been given internment in exchange for a throne, and while he was feigning the most absolute submission both to his parents and the Emperor, his cunning, as was to be expected, was slyly at work in summoning the Cortes in Spain and inciting the country to war. No sooner had he done so than he wrote to congratulate his successor.[1]

Napoleon was not sure at first to whom he had best offer the captured throne. Murat had had some hopes of it, but Napoleon thought such a prize more suitable for a brother than a brother-in-law. He had at first offered it to his brother Louis, then reigning in Holland. But Louis, who had been happy with neither his throne nor his Queen, was not enthusiastic for the new enterprise. Napoleon then chose his elder brother Joseph, whom he had enthroned at Naples a year or two before ; and Joseph accepted.

Carlos had appointed Murat regent when he came to Bayonne. And no doubt the Grand Duke thought he might be the King. But Napoleon decided that his task in Spain was over, and at this juncture he had two crowns at his disposal for his brother-in-law. One was the Neapolitan, the other the Portuguese. Murat, when offered his choice, did not hesitate. Perhaps he had had enough of rebellion in Iberia, perhaps he foresaw the Peninsular War, perhaps he simply realised that Naples would make a pleasant home, especially now that Joseph Bonaparte had left things in good order. So Murat and his wife became the King and Queen of Naples, while Joseph was proclaimed at Bayonne King of Spain.[2]

As early as May 12, the Council of Regency at Madrid had asked for him. At first they had said they regarded the Bourbons as having no power to

[1] Vaya : *Fernando VII.*   [2] Oman : *Peninsular War*, i.

sign away their rights.   Murat then summoned them
to the palace.   He told them it was not a matter of
knowing their opinion about the validity of what their
princes had done : it had been already agreed that a
member of the Imperial family of France should be
their King : it was for them merely to choose which.
At this point the Council and the Municipality gave
in ; they said that, without prejudice to the claim and
rights of their princes, they would choose the King of
Naples.[1]

The choice could not have fallen upon a worthier
figure than that of Joseph Bonaparte.   He was as
admirable as Fernando was contemptible.   " Full of
distinction and elegance," a Spaniard describes him.[2]
A tall, handsome man of forty, with a splendid bearing,
and a high-bred courtesy of manner, he was like a
milder Napoleon : his features were as regular, but
his eyes lacked the extraordinary power which made
Napoleon's regular features so commanding.   Although vain, and rather indolent, he was an indes-
cribably better man than Spain had long seen, or was
to see, upon her throne, and Napoleon prepared for
him a Constitution that was at once both conservative
in its loyalty to the ancient traditions of Spain and
liberal in the preparation of a few necessary reforms.
The Catholic religion, according to a promise made
to Carlos, was alone to be secured and recognised, but
the tyrannies of the Inquisition were to be abolished,
the Government was to be organised in eight ministries, and there were to be two Houses of Parliament.
When the Spaniards had discussed this Constitution
and accepted it, Joseph Bonaparte accompanied the
promulgation of it with wise and courteous proclamations.   " We decree the present constitution," he
wrote, " that it may be kept as the fundamental law

[1] Vaya : *Fernando VII*, i. 172.   [2] Vaya : *Ibid.*, i. 189.

of our states, and as basis of the pact which unites our peoples to us, and us to our peoples." [1] So in accepting the crown, he had declared : " Our first duties will be to keep the holy religion of our ancestors in the prosperous state in which we find it, and to maintain the integrity and independence of the monarchy. We have a right to count on the assistance of the clergy, of the nobility, and of the people, so as to restore the time when the whole world was full of the glory of the Spanish name ; and above all, we desire to establish tranquillity and to assure felicity in the midst of every family by means of a good social organisation.

" To work for the public good with the least possible prejudice to private interest will be the spirit of our conduct ; as far as it is in our power to make our people happy, all our glory is inscribed in their felicity. For this no sacrifice will be too costly. For the good of Spain, and not our own, we intend to rule."

His words were lost like a cry against the wind of storm. Although Joseph Bonaparte offered Spain to safeguard her Catholic and monarchical traditions, and at the same time to join them with freedom to grow into the spirit of the age, a great instinct of patriotism made it seem heroic, seem even Christian, to identify the country's good with the " vulgar blackguard," as George Ticknor called him, who was now writing from Valençay in the most fulsome terms to congratulate Joseph on his succession and Napoleon on his victory.

2

The first motive of the patriots was no doubt pride in the nation's choice. The Spaniards did not want

[1] Mesonero Romanos : *Memorias*, p. 79.

to be outwitted by the partisans of Maria Luisa or the protector of her paramour.

But that pride mixed with subtle and august principles. The Spaniards as a people were more profoundly and uncompromisingly Catholic than any nation on earth. They believed with firm and simple faith that the voice of the Church was the voice of sacred truth, and that in obedience to her counsels, and by acceptation of her mysteries, they would rise from out of the world of nature to a celestial realm of divine powers and presences, the realm of grace, which was a direct participation in the life which was the light of men. Nothing compromised their faith that in the Host which they saw the priest consecrate at the Altar, the Lord of Heaven was with them till the end of the world to assume the nature of mankind into His own illimitable perfectness, like a flood of crystal water absorbing the trickle of a brackish pool. For though the Spaniards were the children of nature, with a health hardened by biting winter and a torrid summer till their blood ran strong with the instincts of life, they shared with the peoples of Africa and Asia, in a way no other people in Western Europe shared, the sense of the immediacy and the almightiness of God.

To them religion was both a pageant and a passion. With uncompromising fervour, at times even with fierce savagery, they believed in the Church they loved, like a passionate husband believes in his bride. And they would not even tolerate the slightest expression of any other view.

Although the greater part of Western Europe was still nominally Catholic, two kindred agencies had been at work to present an easier and more human view of Christianity. Spain would have nothing to do with either. One of these had come with the

Protestant Reformation : it began as a protest more against Paganism than against what was then really, and has since remained, the Catholic Faith : as time went on, however, its earnest spirituality had been more and more leavened with a reasonable view of human effort in which the doctrine of grace and salvation grew obscure and far. It tended to converge into a view that what men believed, or what their spiritual exercises were, did not matter ; that they must simply be kind and good : the power to be so was apparently in themselves ; at least, they did not need a distinctive spiritual discipline to supply them with it ; they were, in fact, better without that sort of thing. Somehow in the background there was (so most still believed) the good which was referred to as the Almighty.

Now, their ideal took also the form of a society ; it added to itself the thrilling attraction of being a secret society. The Church was a mystery of which all could study the system, but only a spiritual gift could reveal the holiness. The new society, if it was new, of Freemasons had from the very beginning a system of cabbalistic signs leading up by degrees of initiation to a hidden personal influence. The Spanish Catholic was apt to believe that influence Satanic, as he had believed the schisms of the Reformation to be also.

It was a perfectly natural principle of the Catholic authorities to forbid their people to enter secret societies. One could have expected that the Church would condemn a rival system, elaborately organised into an apparent competition with itself. There was, however, a greater reason for antipathy between the two societies ; for men wage the fiercest war, not against the principle of evil, but against ideals of good different from their own ; and even in human nature itself the cruellest conflicts are between higher and lower forms of good. A fight between Catholicism and Freemasonry would have been inevitable, and during the eighteenth century both sides prepared their weapons, in Spain as well as out of it.

But we cannot understand the position of Joseph Bonaparte in Spain till we consider European religion as a whole.   It was a time when the spirit of Christianity was smothered in conventionalism—as Godoy was smothered in his heavy mat at Aranjuez. The impulses of the sixteenth century had died away, and the habits of all sorts of Churches had become so formal and conservative that, except for occasional outbursts of fervour, chiefly on the evangelical side, the Christians seemed to have lost interest in the regeneration of mankind. On the other hand, a vast and important school had arisen which pointed to the intrinsic good in man and nature, and so discovered to the enthusiasm of men a realm of delight within the reach of all. The essential theories of the Church had no quarrel with that movement : they too held that creation was good, and that human nature had, in the order of outward creation, a superior dignity. But the unique theology of the Church explored another realm of which she spoke in a language that, in the mouth of many, and in the ears of more, had become stale ; for if one compared the gospel of the Redeemer with the social system which upheld His Church, the words of the preacher sounded in much of Europe like hollow brass.

There was, in fact, something so rotten in conservative society that in the centre of civilisation men could stand it no longer. All over Europe were great monarchs who lived in luxurious ostentation, surrounded by a privileged few. Below these were hereditary landowners who were invested with dignity and exercised immense power, and below these again were middle classes who were beginning to make themselves important with business and machinery. Ministering to all these were the large majority who made up the lower classes. These lived in servitude. Moving among all were the officials of the Church, of a Church which existed to see that all men should have a share of good things, both in this world and in that which was to come, and which, now with ruthless warnings, and now with radiant promises, asked how the love of God could dwell in men who, having this world's goods, had no compassion for those in need. But somehow the officials of Churches were able to disdain the actual sufferings of the poor. All they cared about was the maintenance of the prestige in which they, as officials, shared. This gave the Masons their chance ; for the masses knew instinctively that civilisation had become intolerable. They rose against Church and State in a bloody insurrection : there were, they said, such things as the rights of man.

It was the peculiarity of Spain—still is, and so will continue to be—to feel the rumbles of agitation or advance at the centre of Europe, and yet to live apart, as Africa and Asia live apart. In Spain the Church of the eighteenth century was still a great reality in which the clergy shared the life of the masses, and in which the claims of the Church were enforced by an almost universal faith in the Mass, by a fervid devotion to the Virgin Mother, and by intense enjoyment of the festivals and ceremonial of Catholicism ; where now in popular song, now in a sumptuous procession, the people, as we saw, warmed their hearts in fresh devotion to the altar and to the throne. For they accepted the idea of a consecrated central authority in the State as spontaneously as they accepted the Catholic hierarchy. In such a country Freemasonry

meant next to nothing. And with that fact Joseph
Bonaparte met his doom.

For the power and appeal of the Bonapartes was to
combine the Catholic tradition, and patriotism, with
the universal instincts shared by masonry and the
revolutionaries. The Spanish people, who had long
accepted the enlightened despotism of their monarchy,
had no more interest in revolution than they had distrust of the Church. They had as yet little of the
intelligent middle class to which the Bonapartes
offered the promises which they themselves astonish-
ingly exemplified. All that had happened in Spain
was that a faction had succeeded in changing a
monarch and a minister. It had no need of the
Emperor Napoleon. It looked at him merely with
a stupid admiration not unmixed with horror, as the
inhabitants of an oasis in the African sand might look
at a brilliant but menacing meteor across the undula-
tions of the desert.

3

The new King had got no farther than Vitoria
when he wrote to his brother that the Spanish enterprise was to be a failure. He repeated the warning
at Burgos ; he clinched it at Madrid, writing on
July 24 to the victorious Emperor, " Your glory will
be destroyed in Spain." If Napoleon thought that
Spain was won over, wrote Joseph, he was much
mistaken : everywhere the feeling was as bad as it
could be. " I have no need to tell Your Majesty,"
he wrote again on July 28, " that it needs a hundred
thousand men to conquer Spain. I repeat that we
have not a single supporter, and that the whole nation
is embittered and resolute to sustain with arms the
side which it has taken." It was all as he had
prophesied when on his way from Naples he had met

his old tutor, the Abbé Simon, then Bishop of Grenoble. The Bishop had congratulated him. But Joseph saw his horizon dark with clouds, which gave warning of a ghastly future. " Will my brother's star," he asked, " shine always luminous and clear in the sky ? I do not know, but sad presentiments assail me in spite of myself. They obsess me, they dominate me. I much fear that the Emperor, in giving me a crown finer than that which I lay down, has laid on my head a burden heavier than it could bear. So pity me, my dear Master, pity me, do not congratulate me." [1]

The King could neither apply the constitution of Bayonne nor win the hearts of the people. Like Murat, he was dependent on the French Army. And when the French were defeated by the Spaniards at the famous Battle of Bailen in Andalusia, Savary advised the King to retire to the Ebro, and apply for reinforcements from the Emperor. No sooner had he left the capital than a Provincial Council was called together by Godoy's predecessor, Floridablanca, and it looked as though Joseph's reign in Madrid was over.

But Napoleon decided himself to take the situation in hand. On October 25 he addressed the Legislative Assembly in Paris ; he told them that he would place himself at the head of his army, " to crown the King of Spain in Madrid, and plant his eagles on the forts of Lisbon."

His march was rapid and triumphant. On December 4 of that eventful year (it was still 1808), Napoleon camped on the high ground outside Madrid, known as Chamartín de las Rosas, sleeping in the palace of the Duke of the Infantado. From there he made several pronouncements to the Spanish people

[1] *Mémoires du Roi Joseph IV*, pp. 396–412.

announcements so moderate and so prudent that they
could not have failed to make an impression on any
reasonable people. "Your monarchy has grown
old," he said. "I will make it young again. I will
ameliorate all your institutions, and if you second me,
I will make you enjoy the benefits of reform without
a convulsion." [1] But the Spaniards were no longer
reasonable. Their gracious and kindly ways, their
cheerful patience, their charity and charm, were
exchanged for a bitterness as fierce as it was obstinate.
They could not hate King Joseph; but they could
see no good in the master of Murat. Their only
instinct was to avenge at any cost to themselves the
executions of May 2. Napoleon spoke of conserving
but moderating the religious orders, abolishing the
Inquisition, freeing the estates from the tyrannies of
landlords.[2] But Joseph, as well as his subjects, was
furious. "I shall always prefer honesty," he wrote
to Napoleon, "to a power bought at so high a price."[3]

The Emperor, who at once understood the power of
the Church in Spain, attempted to proclaim his conquest as a victory for the Catholic religion against the
interference of those foreign heretics which came from
England. Was he not, as the sovereign of France, the
elder son of the Church? But, somehow, the elder
son of the Church awoke no interest from the devotees
of His Catholic Majesty. As the conqueror of Europe
went from Chamartín to the Royal Palace, the people
of Madrid simply took no notice. No one stopped to
look at him. He admired his brother's home, but he
went back to Chamartin in a bad temper, and consoled himself with an inspection of his troops. "I
had rather see a soldier without his breeches than

[1] See Napoleon III : *Des Idées Napoléoniennes*, chap. iv.
[2] Geoffroy de Grandmaison : *L'Espagne et Napoléon*, i. 394, 395.
[3] *Mémoires du Roi Joseph*, v. 281.

without his bayonet," he used to say.[1]   And it was not long before he was again on the march.

As for King Joseph, it seemed that he had become almost as tiresome as his subjects.   He had always insisted that the Bonapartes were not wanted in Spain; he was no soldier, and he would neither give uncompromising orders nor accept them from his younger brother.   Though he owed everything to that brother, he could never forget that he was himself the elder, and was never far from a certain feeling of jealousy.   In all matters, his sense of his own personal dignity was extreme; and, what was more, he had a real desire to make himself one with the Spanish people, and to incarnate their interests.   From his point of view, the Emperor had gone too far.   The sovereign rights of the King had been impugned, and Joseph wrote to Napoleon on December 8, from the palace of El Pardo a few miles out of Madrid, a formal renunciation of the crown.   But the Emperor would not hear of it: he wanted to have his brother on the Spanish throne; he insisted on Joseph taking back his abdication, saying that Spain belonged to him (Napoleon) by right of conquest, and he could give the crown to whom he would.   The cession, however, was only formal, and Napoleon acted as though he were himself henceforth supreme, and his brother's kingdom a French province.[2]   With a people as proud as the Spaniards, the mistake was more fatal than imposing on them an unwanted king.

Napoleon had now to turn his attention to the English: crossing the Guadarrama in deep snow, he found that they had moved from Salamanca, and at the approach of the French troops they took to their ships at Corunna at dead of night, after they had

[1] Geoffroy de Grandmaison : *L'Espagne et Napoléon*.
[2] *Mémoires du Roi Joseph*, v. 281.

buried Sir John Moore. Napoleon meantime hastened north again, and King Joseph made his second entrance into Madrid on January 22, 1809. In the following autumn he made a triumphant campaign in Andalusia.   He then returned to model the administration of Spain on that which Napoleon had organised in France, and for a short time, in the autumn of 1809, it looked as though the crown of Spain was really his.   The municipalities seem to have welcomed him.   Bishops and Cathedral Chapters had greeted him with acclamation.   He himself lowered certain taxes and promulgated decrees to encourage agriculture and trade.   And though he was deter-mined to put down those who rebelled against him, he moved about as graciously as he could, and tried to make real improvements in the life of the people. He even sponsored a greater reform : he abolished the Inquisition ; the Cortes, it is true, imitated him in this ; though more than a third of its members were still in favour of the State domineering over conscience in the most sacred mysteries of the soul.

The Spaniards, however, though the kindest people on earth, are impossible to mollify if they once feel a grudge.   At such times, nothing will dislodge the rooted passion for revenge.   If King Joseph made open spaces in Madrid, they merely complained that he had pulled down a church, and called him King Bigsquares ; if he was hospitable and gracious, they said it was only because he was always drunk, and called him " Bottle Joe."   In more serious mood they called him King Intruder, a name he has kept in Spanish history.   Once he caressed a child dressed up by his father in the uniform of the Civic Guard which King Joseph had himself created.

" Ah, bravo, bravo, boy ! " he said in his curious mixture of French, Spanish, and Italian, the three

languages he had to learn in succession since he left
Corsica. "And why do you wear this sword?"

"To kill the Frenchmen."

"Excuse him, Your Majesty," said his father, "he
is only repeating what he hears from the servants
and people about." To shrewd ears the excuse only
deepened the unpleasantness.[1]

He then turned to arrange the etiquette of his
palaces. It was not the least striking characteristic
of Napoleon himself that he would return from the
campaigns, where in his grey cloak he had won the
worship of glory from his soldiers, to assume robes of
white velvet and of silk in which to elaborate the most
formal ceremonial of ancient Courts. In Joseph, who
was no warrior, the taste is perhaps easier to understand. He too worked out with great elaboration the
ceremonies and precedence of the royal palace,[2] for he
delighted both in the name and all the additions of a
king, while he disliked the responsibility of power, and
kept a taste for living quietly. His private life in
Madrid was lonely and uneventful, in spite of his
warmth of heart. Queen Julie did not join him.
But he found consolation with the Señora de
Montehermoso, who spoke four languages, the
Countess de Jaruco, and finally with Madame Nancy
Derrieux.[3]

4

Nothing could be stronger as an ingredient of drama
than the way in which the quarrels and scandals of
the Spanish Court involved the history of the country
and the politics of Europe. The intricacy with which
the personal relations of the Bonapartes are patterned

[1] Mesonero Romanos : *Memorias*, pp. 79–81.
[2] Villa-Urrutia : *El Rey José Bonaparte.*
[3] Geoffroy de Grandmaison : *Napoléon et l'Espagne*, ii. 328, 330.

out with their careers in history now turns the fate of Spain. As for King Joseph himself, the story of his heart is simple. When he was practising as a young barrister in Marseilles, he had wedded Julie Clary, the daughter of a wealthy merchant of the town. She had borne him two daughters, and reigned with him in Naples, and then his affectionate nature sought sympathy elsewhere, while she retired to Paris.

Napoleon's own marriages had an influence wider than historians are apt to realise. The fact that Josephine bore him no children did not at first disconcert him : he planned as heir, first Eugène Beauharnais, and then one or another of his brothers' children. It was only at the first approach of the megalomania which undermined his towering fortune that he thought of divorcing the Empress Josephine. It was to arrange that divorce that he hurried back from Spain in 1808 ; it was to settle the Austrian affair, which meant finally the marriage with Marie-Louise, that he returned in the January of 1809. His marriage to her consummated and sealed the pride which played havoc with his genius and glory. "The husband of the Archduchess Marie-Louise had no success in war. Crippled in 1812, driven off in 1813, dethroned in 1814, annihilated in 1815, that was the record of the son-in-law of the Emperor Francis." [1]

Spain and her king were to be the first to feel the fatal disease which impaired the judgment of the Emperor. With regard to Spain he had made at Bayonne a mistake which he afterwards admitted as the most fatal in his career. His treatment of Fernando, when Fernando was at the height of his unmerited popularity, made the young plotter into a martyr and the great administrator into a tyrant.

[1] Norwood Young: *Napoleon in Exile : Elba.*

" That wretched war broke me," were Napoleon's own words.[1] But that mistake, under the tactful influence of King Joseph, might have been gradually repaired. Year by year the ideas of the French Revolution were filtering into Spain ; year by year the idea of the Inquisition appeared more intolerable ; year by year the Spanish leaders leaned more to the idea of a Parliament, or as they called it, Cortes. In all these senses the administration of Joseph anticipated their instincts, and met their half-formed wishes. But the Emperor was unwilling to let the system grow. As an unskilful gardener, in an ill-judged attempt to force their growth, will kill his flowers by allowing manure to touch their roots, he decided to annex the most conservative and Catholic provinces of Spain into the French Empire. Those provinces, Biscay, Navarre, Aragon, and Catalonia, were the nearest to the Pyrenees. They were populated by manly peoples, who cultivated, and still cultivate, their traditions with uncompromising devotion ; and as they were fervid Catholics, they looked with more hostility on the Napoleonic compromise with the tendencies behind Freemasonry.

King Joseph did what he could to persuade his brother both of the injustice and of the foolishness of such an attempt upon the Spanish kingdom. He sent Ambassadors to Paris, he argued in letter after letter, he pleaded with his wife, and finally, taking advantage of the birth of the King of Rome, he went himself to Paris, arriving there on May 15, 1811. "My first duty," he argued, " is to Spain. I love France as my family, Spain as my religion. I am bound to the one by the feelings of my heart, to the other by my conscience." [2] Napoleon at last gave in, and in the summer Joseph

---

[1] *Mémorial de Sainte-Hélène.*
[2] *Mémoires du Roi Joseph,* ix. 433.

eturned, believing that he could come to a happy
greement with the Spanish Cortes, who, supported
by the English, had continued to meet at Cadiz for
three years, and regarded themselves as the representatives of Spain. To Joseph's advances they were
inexorable, and in a short time he was to discover that
his position was being made impossible by the military
progress of Lord Wellington.

5

The attitude of England to Spain was not the least
peculiar element of the complex drama of the Spanish
throne. Ever since the time of the Armada, even
back to the marriage of Mary with Philip II, the
English had felt a violent antipathy to Spain ; and
the many likenesses of the Spanish temperament to
their own made them the more severe where there
were differences. Both peoples were proud, insular,
virile, and restrained. Both had the same curious
alternations of independence with conventionalism,
and of roughness with kindness. But while the
Spanish were the more friendly, with a particular
predilection for foreigners, the English were in every
sense the better trained in the arts and discipline of
life. Their genius was that of braced enterprise.
The English were the more competent, the Spaniards
were the more charitable. Such differences threw
into sharper contrast the tempered Protestantism of
the English and the fervent Catholicism of the
Spaniards. And here again the likeness accentuated
the difference. For in the Protestantism of a hundred
years ago there was more likeness to Catholicism than
there is to the agnostic temper which in the present
day has mastered the Protestant denominations and
the Catholic countries alike.

6

It was therefore with no particular surprise that th
English found themselves fighting against the Spanis
when they fought against the French in 1805. The
were inclined to look on not only the French but th
Spaniards as hereditary enemies, whether Godoy wa
at the head of them or young Fernando. Indeed, i
1808 they intended to take advantage of Fernando'
foolery by making a raid on Spanish America, an
had a competent fleet prepared to compensate ther
in the Southern Continent of America for their losse
in the North. It was at this point that the Count o
Toreno arrived in England to seek their aid again:
Napoleon.

Canning's whole aim was to preserve England fror
the supremacy of Napoleon, and the English socia
system from that free course to natural talent int
which, as into a canal, the Napoleonic system ha
directed the devastating overflow from the meltin
snowslide of the Revolution. When he heard there
fore that not only the Portuguese but the Spanis
would be his allies against the French Empire, th
fleet which was to have attacked the dominions o
Spain was rapidly changed into a convoy for Spain'
defenders. Sir John Moore was no match fo
Napoleon, nor could his undisciplined troops meet th
Grand Army. It was always in Napoleon's absenc
that dangers would develop. If he could have move
about in a motor-car, he might have made sure of a
his conquests. And when the genius of Wellingto
began to change the face of affairs in the Peninsul
King Joseph's throne was again shaking beneath him
It was the Battle of Salamanca, on June 12, 1812, tha
made his position hopeless ; and while Goya painte
a wild-eyed Wellington, couriers galloped to Madri
with a message of doom. Masséna had been de
feated in Portugal ; now Marmont his successor was

and while King Joseph fled towards Valencia, joining
at Almansa Soult's army from Andalusia, Wellington
entered the capital—and the population went wild
with joy to acclaim the conquering hero. On the
other side of Europe, the fatal expedition to Moscow
was in the same year to menace all the Bonapartes,
and all that their success implied.

6

But King Joseph was not yet dethroned. Wellington, after advancing to Burgos, had prudently retired
to winter in Portugal, and Joseph once more came
back to Madrid. The population was colder than
ever, and he gave up the attempt to propitiate them.
He even constructed a tunnel so that he could pass to
his park across the Manzanares, the Casa del Campo,
without having to face the sullenness of the populace.
And if he was still in possession of the crown of Spain,
he had to face the fact that the Indies were no longer
in his possession. One by one the great vice-royalties
of America had refused to acknowledge his rights, and
declared either their loyalty to Fernando or their
independence. His Spanish kingdom, as much as
it was under his command, was ruled by decrees from
France : it became more and more wretched ; while
the rest, wretched also, welcomed other foreigners in
the effort to displace him.

7

That was a *pis aller*, for the feeling against the English as heretics, and their own impatience with the
Spanish lack of discipline and co-ordination, created
much distrust on one side and the other. The English
felt qualms in supporting the party of the Inquisition.

There were many Spaniards who felt that they were being made into pawns between two parties of invaders. The English knew this. And when it was suggested to the Foreign Secretary, Wellington's brother, Lord Wellesley, that the English should try to bring Fernando back to Spain, Wellesley agreed that his person would be valuable to the English cause. If the idea had really been tried, it would hardly have helped, for Fernando would have issued from his mist of romance.

The proposal came from Louis Collignon, a drum-major's son. After having been put in jail for theft, and pawned the jewels of a Genevan banker's wife, he now passed as the Baron de Kolli ; many times he had been employed by the English as a spy. He suggested that he should go to Valençay with letters from the King of England, and induce Fernando to escape to the coast, where he could board an English ship. The Duke of Kent was won over to the idea, and recommended it to George III. Before long, politicians and prince had worked out a plot. Kolli (his new name sounded like the Wellesleys' discarded name, Colley) was given, as proof of the powers behind him, the Latin letter in which Carlos IV had announced to George III the marriage of Fernando to Maria Antonia.[1] To this King George himself added a letter of his own for Fernando, and Lord Wellesley a false passport ; Kolli was also given heavy drafts on foreign bankers, and as additional support some valuable diamonds. A little convoy took him to land at Quibéron, and there awaited his return. But through the indiscretion of an underling, he was discovered in Paris,[2] arrested, and thrown into prison at Vincennes. Fouché was not satisfied merely to

[1] Geoffroy de Grandmaison : *Napoléon et L'Espagne*, ii. 32, 33.
[2] Vaya : *Fernando VII.*

frustrate the plot.   He found in Kolli's suite a certain
Richard ;   Richard, taking the papers and passports
of Kolli, was to impersonate him at Valençay, and
so sound the soul of Fernando, who so far had been
submissiveness itself.   He had petitioned King Joseph
to be admitted to the new order of knighthood that
Joseph had founded in Spain ;   he had continued
writing to both Bonapartes the humblest and most
fulsome letters, and after a special Te Deum in honour
of the marriage of Napoleon with Marie-Louise, he
had turned round in the church and, facing the con-
gregation, before going to toast " the great Napoleon
and   the   adorable   Marie-Louise,"   cried   " *Vive
l'Empereur ! "   Napoleon himself was impressed and
perhaps a little puzzled at such extreme enthusiasm
from a prince he had dethroned.   Here was a chance
to test it.[1]

Fernando's submissiveness survived the test.   When
the impersonator of Kolli arrived at Valençay, the
Spanish Prince at once wrote to complain to Napoleon
of the defenders of his rights in Spain.   " The
English," he wrote, " have taken my name in vain,
and caused great hurt to the Spanish people, and are
even now the cause of bloodshed there.   The English
Ministry, falsely persuaded that I am detained here
against my will, have proposed to me a means of
escape, and have sent an emissary who, under the
pretext of selling me some curiosities, came to bring
me a message from the King of England."   Such was
the gratitude of the hero, " the man we long for," as
his Spaniards called him, for whose honour heroic
men and women, year by year, were offering their
sustenance and their blood.[2]

In fact, through all that time, Fernando had

[1] Geoffroy de Grandmaison : *Napoléon et l'Espagne*, ii. 34.
[2] Vaya : *Fernando VII.*

cherished the scheme which he owed to old Escoiquiz of uniting himself with some daughter of the house of Bonaparte. At first he could find no one better than the cousins of Joséphine—Rose-Françoise, or Stephanie Tascher de la Pagerie. Then he had thought of Lolotte, the daughter of Lucien : he could hardly have waited for Princess Mathilde, but in 1810 his desires seem to have settled on Joseph's elder daughter, Zenaïda, who was then nine years old.

The resistance of Spain centred its obstinate loyalty on Fernando. At the beginning of 1810, therefore, Napoleon decided to publish in the *Moniteur* the abject and amazing letters in which the young man, as indeed his parents also, had placed themselves at the disposition of the Emperor. The letters (we have seen a little of them) were sensational enough to make an impression on the most devoted Spaniards and on Europe as a whole, letters which, as already shown, went so far as to congratulate Joseph on his succession, and to petition him for favours. But Fernando was unabashed. His passion for a Bonaparte bride was unabated. He did not even make so bold as now to suggest the Princess Zenaïda. He left the entire choice to the Emperor himself.

"My greatest desire," he wrote on April 4, after the publication of the letters, " is to be the adopted son of His Majesty the Emperor, our Sovereign. I believe that I merit this adoption, which would truly be the felicity of my life, as much for my love and affection to the sacred person of His Majesty as for my submission and entire obedience to his intentions and desires."

That was not all ; on May 3 he went considerably farther.

" The publicity," he wrote, " which Your Imperial Majesty has been kind enough to give to my letters, gives me confidence that you do not disapprove my sentiments nor the desire which I have formed ; and this hope raises me to the height of joy.

" Allow me, therefore, Sire, to pour into your heart the thoughts of a heart which, I do not hesitate to say, is willing to belong to it by the link of adoption. May Your Imperial Majesty deign to unite my destiny to that of a French princess of your choice, and fulfil the most ardent of my wishes. With this union, in addition to my personal advantage, will increase the sweet certitude that all Europe may be convinced of my unchangeable respect to the will of Your Imperial Majesty, and that Your Majesty may requite such sincere feelings with some return.

" I shall make bold to add that this union, and the publicity given to my statements, which, if Your Majesty permits, I shall make known to Europe, should exercise a salutary influence over the destiny of the Spains, and will rid a blind and furious people of the pretext of continuing to cover their country with blood in the name of a prince, the first-born of his ancient dynasty, who in a solemn treaty, by his own choice and the most glorious of adoptions, has changed himself into a French prince, and the son of Your Imperial and Royal Majesty."

A marriage with the Princess Zenaïda would have been a clever stroke : as King Joseph had no sons, it would ensure the crown both for his daughter and for Fernando, and everybody might have been pleased together, except Lord Wellington and the

English. Napoleon, however, had not yet pressed it, and in spite of being as keen a matchmaker as Maria Luisa, he could not make up his mind to sacrifice any daughter of his family to Don Fernando. When the match had been suggested to Lolotte, the daughter of Lucien, she had scornfully rejected it. And as for Zenaïda, at nine years old, could she not wait a little longer ? Napoleon had not yet made up his mind. The question was settled for him by the advance of Wellington.

8

Joseph's attempt to improve the condition of Spain had been a failure. The nation, which under Godoy had enjoyed a steady prosperity, was ruined by its own heroic struggles, and by the presence of the foreign armies of France and England. Agriculture had been abandoned ; trade was impossible. Starvation and disease invaded Madrid itself. Joseph had never been able to raise a revenue for himself, and the important sums sent year by year from his brother now began to fail him. As the terrible winter of 1812 passed, leaving in Madrid its thousands who had died of famine, Wellington stirred from his winter quarters in Portugal, and once again began his able man-œuvres against Jourdan. As he marched steadily northwards, Napoleon, who had now returned from Moscow with his ruined army, knew that all Europe was gathering against him. He gave orders to Joseph to leave Madrid for Valladolid. Heaping together from the robbery of churches and monasteries what treasure he could, taking from the Prado Raphaels, Titians, Velasquez, and Corregios, Joseph left Madrid for the last time on March 17, 1813. The month of April, the fifth from his succession, was passed quietly but in anxiety, while Wellington, who himself advanced up the valley of the Douro, completed his advances with encircling movements from Galicia on the one side and Estremadura on the other. They forced Joseph to retire from Valladolid, they pushed him over the Ebro. They caught him at Vitoria, where he was waiting for more French troops. Wellington knew it, and pressed an attack on June 21. Aided by timely reinforcements (for Wellington had no numbers to spare), and strong with the confidence in the genius of their advancing commander, the allied Spanish, English, and Portuguese troops soon forced the army of Joseph back into the city, while they advanced to the Bayonne road to cut off his retreat. At that danger the battle became a rout. Joseph abandoned the coach in which he had been travelling, and galloped away. The crown, the jewels, the paintings, the treasure, the wines, the delicacies which loaded his immense convoy fell into the hands of the conquerors. Jourdan had not even taken his baton. The families of Joseph's Spanish officials were left to be the victims of the wild excesses of the victorious army [1] ; for there is nothing which unchains the passions of lust and greed like victory in battle after months of hardship.

Joseph tried to make a stand at Pampelouna, and then in the Valley of Baztán. But the movements of Wellington were too much for him. Napoleon, furious with the defeat at Vitoria, said to Cambacérès : " It is long enough that I have allowed imbeciles to muddle my affairs," and replaced Jourdan by Soult.[2] The day that Soult arrived at St. Jean-du-Pied-de-Port in the Pyrenees, Joseph parted from Madame Nancy Derrieux and retired from his harassed kingdom to Bayonne.

[1] Toreno : *Historia de la Guerra.*
[2] Aguado : *Historia de España.*

During his years in Spain he had supped full with
horrors. His kindly heart was only too thankful to
have a fast from them. And he turned with a sense
of relief to the obscure life for which in time of trial
he had always hankered. He retired to Mortefontaine,
and from there he added a postscript to the little letter
his daughters wrote for their famous uncle's birthday.
Neither letter nor postscript was answered.

It was a strange company which gathered at Mortefontaine : the dethroned Joseph, the Queen of
Würtemberg, Madame Bernadotte (Princess of
Sweden), Queen Julie (her sister), and the daughters,
Zenaïda and Charlotte ; around them courtiers from
Spain, from France, from Germany, still hung,
although there was no court to pay. They gambled,
fished, picnicked, shot, waiting for the storm to burst
and scatter them. "*Et pour comble de singularité,*" [1]
wrote Miot, " *le patriarche des Indes, grand Inquisiteur
d'Espagne, nous disait, de temps en temps, la messe.*" [1]

At last the thunderbolt fell. Napoleon ordered
that His Majesty the King of Spain should become
once more Joseph Bonaparte ; for the Emperor could
never tolerate a failure. Joseph's behaviour, he had
said, " has never ceased to bring misfortune on my
army : it is time to make an end of it."

[1] Miot de Mélito : *Mémoires*, iii. 341.

IV

THE KING THEY LONGED FOR

" Les jardins y étaient beaux," said Talleyrand—of Valençay,
*" avant que les princes d'Espagne ne les eussent brulés par leur feux
d'artifice pour la Saint Napoléon.*

MADAME DE RÉMUSAT : *Mémoires.*

Where great addition swells, and virtue none
It is a dropsied honour.
All's Well That Ends Well, ii. 3.

I

WITH the victories of Wellington and the collapse of
Joseph, Napoleon had to decide what he would do in
regard to Spain. The country wanted Fernando,
there could be no further doubt of it, whether one
spoke of pride and obstinacy or loyalty and affection.
And the Emperor had Fernando in his possession.
The attempt with Joseph had proved to be a mistake
from every point of view : wrong in its original crude-
ness ; misguided in its fashion ; a failure finally
even in the things of war ; but if Fernando were now
to marry a Bonaparte princess, as he had appeared
for six whole years so hotly to desire, might not
Napoleon still secure an ally in the Pyrenees, an ally
who was not less than necessary in view of the increasing complications in the east and west and north ?
There was a chance to appeal to Fernando against the
extreme parliamentary system which, in alliance with
the English, had been developing at Cadiz. The
Emperor therefore wrote a letter to Fernando on
November 12, 1813, and sent it to Valençay by the
hand of the Count de Laforest.

" MY COUSIN," the letter began,—
    " The circumstances in which my Empire
and my politics find themselves at present awaken

in me the desire at once to finish with the affairs of Spain. England is fomenting in it anarchy and jacobinism, and is attempting to annihilate the monarchy and destroy the nobility, in fact to establish a republic. I cannot but feel in the deepest degree the destruction of a nation so near my states, and with which I have so many common interests on land and sea.

" I therefore desire to give no opportunities to the English influence, but to re-establish the bonds of friendship and neighbourliness which have so long existed between the two nations." [1]

When Laforest presented this letter, Fernando asked for time to think it over. His mind was far too cunning not to see that it came from the weakness of Napoleon. He realised that if the Emperor were to fall, it would be a crash from battlement to moat ; he knew that the English, not the French, were now masters in Spain. Next day he answered that he could not treat with the Sovereign of France without the consent of the Spanish nation represented by the Regency. Napoleon now smiled on the idea of a Bonaparte marriage for Fernando ; but he smiled too late. Fernando had already decided to wait and see.

Noting his hesitation, the Emperor remembered that the Duke of San Carlos, who had been put aside as a strategical reserve, was still in isolation at Lons-le-Saulnier at the western foot of the Juras. The Duke was not only a close ally of Fernando, but he hated anything of the nature of democracy. Napoleon now saw that the time had come to transfer him to Valençay. Fernando, in his own recoil from parliamentary government, needed only the Duke of San Carlos to

[1] Escoiquiz : *Idea Sencilla.*

make him distrust anything to do with those Cortes of
Cadiz to which, in his letter to Napoleon, he referred
as the Regency.   The Cortes, abrogating authority
to themselves, had indeed now gone much farther in
the direction of democracy than anything to do with
France or the Emperor—so far, that in the opinion
of a leading Spanish mason of the time, their attitude
to their king was hardly short of insulting.   They
simply ignored the doctrine of the divine right of
kings.   They also deprived the monarch of his
authority.   Although denouncing the innovations of
the Bonapartes, they had really gone far beyond them.
For it very often happens that in the course of a war
a nation cedes spontaneously to the idea which it is
combating ; for by a subtle law—not less inexorable
in masses than in the single heart—men grow
like the dominant object of their thought, not only
when it is what they love, but also when it is what
they hate.

Fernando, though he wrote to Napoleon that he
knew nothing of what was happening in Spain except
from the French newspapers, really knew perfectly
well what was happening ; with his ingrained astuteness he saw that he must keep both the Emperor
and the Regency in play while, in the familiar phrase,
he waited to see which way the cat would jump.
Accordingly, an extremely diplomatic letter was
again sent to Napoleon, while another equally diplomatic was sent to the Cortes.   And the Duke of San
Carlos, under an assumed name, went to Madrid to
sound the feeling of the people.

The Duke carried with him two letters : one for the
sight and cognisance of Napoleon, instructing the
Cortes to confirm the treaty Fernando had signed ;
the second secret, to see whether or not the people
had become Jacobins, and at the same time to take

such steps that Fernando could repudiate his signature
the moment he felt inclined.[1]

Although San Carlos was greeted at Madrid with
many an ironic cut in the papers as to his part in the
doings at Bayonne, he nevertheless went on to Cadiz.
There the Cortes delivered him an ultimatum for the
sovereign they hoped for, saying that they would not
allow him to exercise royal authority until he had
sworn to maintain the Constitution. They furthermore ordered the King to enter Spain unattended
by any foreigner or any Spaniard who had served
Joseph ; they prescribed what route he should follow,
and ordered him, as soon as he reached Madrid, to
swear to observe their Constitution. That was not
the way to deal with Don Fernando ; and without
him there was in Cadiz itself that large majority who
still believed in absolutism and the Inquisition. But
Napoleon, finding himself involved in fresh difficulties
in the spring of 1814, finally liberated his cringing
captive, who received the news of his freedom late in
the evening of March 7.

Six days later he drove out of Valençay with Don
Antonio and Don Carlos. The King, who was about
to receive the crown he had snatched from his parents
six years before, had passed those six years in developing the taste for self-indulgence and the arts of
trickery which were born in him. " We have seen,"
says the Spanish historian, " how without dignity to
bear misfortune he degraded himself with adulation
and flattery ; we have observed his supineness, his
hypocrisy, and his humiliation before the Sovereign of
France ; and finally, he has exhibited himself to us as
he was when, offering congratulations for the triumph
of the Imperial army, he seemed with this deed to
scoff at the blood which had been shed for his sake on

[1] Vaya : *Fernando VII*, i. 322–3.

Spanish soil.   Given up to feasting while his subjects
astounded the world with their constancy and zeal,
what can we add to what we have depicted ?   His
gallant adventures ?   They do not belong to history,
and we will not defile our pen in painting them.   We
shall only say that what the Spaniards called a prison
was not impenetrable to the beauties of Valençay." [1]

2

And was the crown of Spain to be at last firm on
the brows of Don Fernando ?   If guile could make it
so, it was.   When he crossed the frontier at Figueras in
Catalonia, he accepted the decree from the Cortes as
to the conditions of his return, while at the same time
he made a promise to Marshal Suchet that he would
set free any who for the French cause were in prison or
otherwise suffering.   Fernando could not keep both
engagements ; and as a matter of fact, he kept neither.
Napoleon, who had forced him to travel on the
Eastern side of the Pyrenees, lest he should meet
Wellington, was the first to learn the meaning of all
his extravagant protestations of adherence to the
Empire, but he eluded his emancipators almost as
quickly as he slipped through the fingers of his captors.
In the spring of 1814, Fernando toured on through
Gerona, Barcelona, and Tarragona to Saragossa.   It
was in that city that under Palafox the most heroic
fight of all had been continued in his cause.   "There,"
says Vaya, "every stone recalled an exploit, every
street a combat." [2]   "Never," wrote Sir Walter Scott,

> hath the harp of minstrel sung
> Of faith so fully proved, so firmly true.[3]

[1] Vaya : *Fernando VII*, i. 312, 313.
[2] Vaya : *Ibid.*, ii. 16.
[3] *Vision of Don Roderick.*

There, Palafox, offered generous terms by the French besieging, had answered with, " War to the knife." There the heroic Maid of Saragossa had " sung the loud song and dared the deed of war," leaping to take her leader's place, and to appease her lover's ghost by her fierce fighting in the shattered wall.

Leaving the virile people of Aragon, the restored Prince travelled down through Daroca, Teruel, and Segorbe to Valencia. As he toured on he became more clearly aware of the irksomeness of the Constitution, to which his private counsellors were advising him already not to swear. He was also coming to realise that he could count on the army's support against it. At Daroca, the Count of Montijo had again appeared, and offered his services. And remembering the part he had played at Aranjuez, Fernando sent him back to Madrid. His new mission was to undermine the work of the Cortes, foment faction, and if necessary work up another riot.

The struggle against the Constitution came to a head before the royal procession was approaching Valencia, where it was awaited by Cardinal Luis de Bourbon, the brother-in-law of the Prince of the Peace and head of the Council of Regency. He had come out some fifteen miles along the road to meet the King. As Fernando realised the import of that encounter, his heart distended and hardened in its strength. For in spite of his quailing treachery, he was still the embodied force of sacred kingship, and obstinacy has no small part in the mentality of those who will adopt any ruse to win their own way. When he saw the other coach approaching, he ordered his to stop and descended from it : the Cardinal, having done the same, found therefore that he had to walk on to where the King was waiting for him, though he had received orders to offer no sign of submission till

Fernando had accepted the Constitution. Fernando decided to put an end to that nonsense. The King's Majesty, reinforced by the prestige of a month of triumphal progresses, had assumed all the power of a dominant will. He raised his hand for the Cardinal to kiss : for six or seven seconds the Cardinal made efforts to press it down, while the King, still holding it up, grew pale with anger. He then held out his hand at the full length of his arm, and in the most imperious tone said, " Kiss it." So strong was the force in those words that the Cardinal inclined and made the sign of homage. So first came to an end parliamentary government in its struggle with Fernando VII.[1]

On May 13, 1814, Don Fernando entered his capital in the same triumph as he had entered it in 1808. The starving people of Madrid, after another dreadful winter, thought they saw the end of their sorrows. Nine days before, the King had said in Valencia, " I abhor and detest despotism : neither intelligence nor education will suffer it any longer in Europe ; nor were the kings of Spain ever despots, nor have the laws and constitution of the country ever allowed it." [2] But on May 11 he had published a decree in Madrid annulling " the so-called Cortes," the Constitution and all its decrees and orders, and commanding that all should return to the state of absolutism in 1808. Meanwhile, two or three hundred people of the lowest dregs of the *canaille* were gathered out of the taverns and slaughter-houses. They went through the streets describing the Parliamentarians as Freemasons and heretics. " Down with the Cortes," they cried. " Long live the Inquisition ! " " Long live Fernando VII ! " They rushed to the parliamentary

[1] Vaya : *Fernando VII.*
[2] Mesonero Romanos : *Memorias*, p. 143.

building, flung down the statues, invaded the chamber, and defaced it. They insulted every man who wore a black tie, and every woman in his company.[1] There can be little doubt that the Count of Montijo had been at work.

The Pope was against persecution, and was about to repudiate it. " The Divine Law," he said, " is not of the same nature as that of man, but a law of persuasion and gentleness ; persecution, exile, and imprisonment are suitable only to false prophets and the apostles of unsound doctrines."[2] But that vindictive, savage, sadistic element which is in human nature, was still to delight in Spain in watching not only the bull tear out the entrails of the horse, but also the tortures of the Inquisition, which along lines little differing from the old, Fernando re-established on July 14, 1814. " God does not pay on a Saturday," says the Italian proverb, and no doubt much of to-day's persecution of the Church can be traced back to the re-established Inquisition.[3]

When Fernando entered Madrid, with his brother and his uncle, he was to have driven along the Calle Fuencarral and the Calle del Desengaño, the Street of Disillusionment. But on arriving at the Puerta del Sol, he turned in the opposite direction from the Congreso and the Street of Disillusionment. He prayed before the Virgin of the Atocha in the Church of Santo Tomás, and then went on through the Plaza Mayor towards the Royal Palace.[4] But all seemed to the people to fulfil their wildest hopes. The reign of the king they longed for was to inaugurate a millen-

[1] Mesonero Romanos : *Op. cit.*, p. 145.
[2] *Gazette de France*, No. 41, May 22, 1816.
[3] Llorente : *History of the Inquisition*, Eng. ed., 1826, pp. 568, 573.
[4] Mesonero Romanos : *Op. cit.*, p. 147.

nium in Spain ; he was adored as a model of princes. A book was published celebrating the heroism of the new monarch (his heroism being proved by his virtuous life at Valençay), and the mood of the moment was expressed in another volume, *The Reciprocal Triumphs of God and Fernando VII.*[1]

3   42820

While Fernando was outwitting his defenders in Spain, he had another task to which he lent his talent for intrigue with equal vigour, though with less success. This was the persecution of his parents. He feared lest they should contrive either with Napoleon or with the Congress of Vienna to dispossess him of the throne he had unified.[2]

When Napoleon sent them to Compiègne after the affairs of Bayonne, they did not stay there long. There was little to amuse old Carlos, and once the summer was over the climate showed itself too miserable for people who had spent their days in sun and light ; for whom the night had been starry and the days a lambent blue. Napoleon allowed the captive royalties to move to Provence. Carlos was at first attracted by the provincial dignity of Aix : the space and amplitude of its old churches and palaces, the green of its quiet avenues, the Tuscan charm of its surroundings, its Roman monuments, and even its rustic aristocracy (of whom the flower had been Vauvenargues) seemed to harmonise with the temper of sovereigns in misfortune. But the one palace on which they set their hearts could be obtained only at too high a price, and they went over the hills to the sea.

On October 18, 1809, the sovereigns entered

---

[1] Villa-Urrutia : *Fernando VII.*
[2] Villa-Urrutia : *Ibid.*

Marseilles in a gilded coach. It was drawn by six white mules ridden by lackeys in scarlet and gold. The Queen, in a splendid toilet, irradiated the dazzling charm which in other years the great palaces of Castile so well became, and the people of Marseilles, who were a little restive under the Bonaparte dictatorship, were glad of an excuse to shout " *Vive le Roi* ! "

To indulge the King's pleasure in shooting, another property was acquired in Mazargues, and between the two places he and Maria Luisa passed their lives for nearly three years.

The impression which King Carlos left behind him in Marseilles was that he had not been born to govern a great nation.[1] But his private life was blameless. Good without being pious, he was a little choleric but easily pacified, especially if the Queen were present. He had perhaps an exaggerated idea of the formal respect which is paid to a king, was served by kneeling attendants, and kept his enormous appetite ; but he was full of kindness of heart ; and believing that almsgiving was the duty of a king and a Christian, he visited the poor, and distributed to their necessities with his own hand. After his heavy dinner came the siesta, and then he played a game of cards or took a violin lesson, in which he showed less aptitude than good will.[2] When the hour came for the outing, or *paseo*, which is so universal a habit in Spain, he and the Queen, if the weather were fine enough, entered a royal carriage, and followed by the functionaries of their little Court, would gallop through a cloud of dust for about an hour on the road to Aix. Then he

[1] Villa-Urrutia : *La Reina María Luisa*, 2nd ed., p. 138. *Notice sur le Séjour à Marseille du roi d'Espagne Charles IV par un vieux Marseillais.* Marseilles, 1826.

[2] Geoffroy de Grandmaison : *L'Espagne et Napoléon*, iii. 390.

would descend, and receive the homage of those presented to him.

At Mazargues the Queen would give little balls, to which she invited the young people of the neighbouring states. She too was charitable, but as she did not investigate the cases herself, and was liable to be exploited, she finally handed over her charities to the Curé of Mazargues. She had always had a taste for religious ceremony, and she elaborated the details of the worship in her chapel with assiduous care.

And so the life of exile might have been happily continued if it had not been disturbed in two different ways : the first was Napoleon's economy. It deprived this Court of its due allowance, so that it would have been in difficulty if Godoy and his brother-in-law, Brancimonte, had not come to its aid. But the greater difficulty was with their daughter, the Queen of Etruria. In spite of the letters she had written to Murat from Aranjuez, she had soon lost patience with Napoleon, whom she regarded—not unnaturally—as the author of the family's woes. She did not hide the feeling, and Napoleon, who was careful to be informed of everything, expelled her from France. Her father, who felt a great affection for her, did not forgive the Emperor for that.

Nor was the lessened allowance the only other cause of a change of feeling. Carlos, month by month, became aware of the grievous sufferings of Spain : he saw that he had been led by Napoleon to betray the cause of the subjects he had always loved with such fatherly simplicity. When the trust of Carlos was deceived, as we have seen in the case of his son, his bitterness was great, and Maria Luisa, with her temperamental violence, gave a sharp edge to the change from admiration to disgust. There was some idea of the English fleet helping him to escape, but when the Admiral refused to take Godoy with the party, King Carlos said that he would rather stay with the Emperor, whom, however, he now described as the " tyrant who oppressed " him.[1]

But at the instance of King Joseph, the dethroned sovereigns were allowed to move on to Rome, and there they arrived by way of Turin and Florence in the spring of 1812. Everywhere they were accorded the same honours as the Emperor himself. They were to have been lodged in the Quirinal. But as it was in the hands of workmen, they were given first the Palazzo Borghese, and then the Palazzo Barberini.

Here, when the royal music continued, somehow the Italian musicians could not keep tune with the fiddling monarch ; but if he were a few bars ahead, that was their fault. " Kings never wait," said His Majesty.[2]

Once he tried to execute with four Italians the famous Boccherini quintet : but the din was frightful. After a few minutes he came back to the Queen and Godoy, with his violin under his arm, his bow in his hand, and wiping his brow with his red cotton handkerchief. " You see, you see, you hear," he said. " They can't follow me. Ah, if I had my 'cellist Dupont with me ! *He* used to follow me. But these Romans can't manage it : it is too much for them." [3]

It was in this new environment, and amid such mild distractions, that their son now harassed them. The ungracious task of complying with his demands fell upon his Ambassadors, and especially Campo Alange in Rome. This man, who owed everything to the Prince of the Peace, and who had been re-

---

[1] Villa-Urrutia : *María Luisa*, 2nd ed., p. 143.
[2] D'Auvergne : *Godoy : the Queen's Favourite*.
[3] Beausset : *Mémoires*, 3rd ed., vol. iv.

warded with the title of Marquis de la Constancia, now became his most pitiless enemy. There was nothing Fernando had more at heart than the ruin of Godoy, whom he succeeded for a time in dividing from his parents. But while malice made him spiteful, anxiety played upon his fears : trembling lest they should either at Vienna or elsewhere represent their rights to the crown, he instituted a system of spying on all their doings. Made still more restless by the stings of greed, he prosecuted a search for certain crown jewels, which he insinuated that his mother had stolen from Madrid.[1]

The Marquis de la Constancia therefore tried to set the King and the Queen against the Prince, and also Godoy's own daughter ; he even plotted to persecute Godoy through the sister of the Countess of Castillo Fiel. No means of pressure were too contemptible for him to employ—anonymous and even forged letters, menace, blackmail. " The letters of Vargas Laguna are shameful to read. . . . The double-dealing, the deceit, the vileness of the master are reflected," says the Marquis de Villa-Urrutia, " in the correspondence and the work of his representative in Rome." [2]

4

Yet none of Fernando's mean motives tormented him so cruelly as that his parents, which also meant Godoy, would find a means to represent their claims at the Congress of Vienna. Both sides of the Spanish family had felt relieved when in 1814 Napoleon,

[1] Pérez de Guzmán : *Estudios de la vida, proscripción y muerte de Carlos IV y María Luisa.*
[2] Villa-Urrutia : *María Luisa*, 2nd ed., p. 149.

though still Emperor and King, found his Imperial dominions reduced to an island five miles long and two broad. They had survived the disquiet of the hundred days of the Emperor's return, though Carlos and Maria had retired temporarily to Bologna. But if Godoy represented the elder sovereigns at Vienna— and there is no doubt that that is what he intended— the result would be awkward. And even if he were formally to abdicate, that act alone would advertise to Europe the treason and violence by which Fernando originally obtained the crown at Aranjuez. Godoy, in his Memoirs, has given us the fullest account of what happened, though, to be sure, in some of its particulars his account is contradicted by Castlereagh. Castlereagh received a messenger from Carlos with letters for the Prince Regent, one asking to be repre- sented in the Congress, and another claiming to be the lawful King of Spain, so that if he could not have that crown, he should have another.

Godoy's story is that King Louis XVIII wrote from Paris saying that he doubted whether Fernando was in lawful possession of the crown which he had taken at Aranjuez ; that his reactionary policy was a danger also in France ; and finally, that it might be advisable for Carlos to reclaim the crown. To this, according to Godoy, Carlos answered that he would pass over the affair of Aranjuez ; that he was ready to sign a new act of abdication ; but that he must be confirmed in all his rights and prerogatives.

It was at this point that Fernando decided that he must be rid at any price of Godoy, he attempted to induce the Pope to exile him, and for a while Godoy was sent to Pesaro. But through the Congress of Vienna, after many complications of intrigue, Fer- nando was confirmed in all his rights ; his petty per- secutions of the party at Rome still continued.

' From Madrid," said Metternich, " all they want
rom friendly Courts are savourous fabrications, while
nterests of the highest moment are shamefully neg-
ected." [1]

<h1 style="text-align:center">5</h1>

Metternich was thinking of America. Fernando's
estoration had not restored the Indies to Spain. The
ise of Bolivar made it impossible for him to regain
he northern Vice-royalties, and he finally assented to
he independence of Venezuela, Colombia, and Peru.
Chile's independence was won in 1818 at the Battle of
Maipo, and at Angostura Bolivar proclaimed a union
f South American Republics. In 1821 the royalists
vacuated Lima. The Battle of Ayacucho in 1824
was Bolivar's final victory. Paraguay, since 1810,
ad been the fief of a tyrant. The Argentine had
een declared independent as early as 1816. Espoz
Mina lost his life in Mexico in a vain attempt to win
t back. Iturbide proclaimed himself an independent
Emperor in 1821. There was little left to Spain of the
ndies except Cuba, the Philippines, and California. [2]
But for what happened in America Fernando cared
ttle. He was determined on nothing but reaction in
pain. The members of the Cortes de Cadiz were
xiled or thrown into prison. The Inquisition was re-
stablished ; the Jesuits who, after fifty years of sup-
ression by the Holy See, had been redintegrated,
were summoned back to Spain, and Fernando and his
ourtiers combined to throw Spain back into a state of
bsolute submission to the monarchy and the priestly
uthorities. All over Spain the leaders of the fight for

---

[1] Villa-Urrutia : *Maria Luisa.*
[2] *Cambridge Modern History,* x., chaps. viii, ix, x.

freedom revolted, and first among them Espoz y Mina
who as " the boy king of Navarre " had fought s
gallantly for the cause of Fernando. Porlier of Co:
unna was imprisoned, his friend López Alia hanged
Lacy headed a movement in Catalonia and was sho'
Vidal and Beltran de Lis in Valencia also were exe
cuted. There was a formidable revolt which went a
far as aiming at the King's life. Richard, who led i
was hanged, and his ally Yandiola was put to th
torture.[1]

The plan of the Madrid conspiracy had been t
capture and kill Fernando in the house of a beautifu
Andalusian, Pepa la Malagueña, whom he was accus
tomed to visit nightly in the company of the Duke o
Alagon.[2] These perambulations on which Fernand
would go out, disguised but not unrecognisabl
to prosecute his amorous intrigues gave rise t
many scandals ; but he persevered in them as
means of obtaining compensation for the loss o
opportunities offered by constitutional government
he kept himself in close touch with the lowe
elements of the people, so that he could, at th
same time, explore their opinions, and persuad
them that in spite of everything he was one o
themselves.

Nevertheless, he could not dismiss the idea o
marriage. It was not every princess who, like Lolot
Bonaparte, had the spirit to refuse him. In 181(
therefore, a double marriage was arranged with th
House of Braganza. He was to marry the elde
Princess, Isabel, while his brother Carlos married th
younger sister Francisca. The two Princesses arrive
at Cadiz in August 1816, and entered Madrid o

[1] Vaya : *Fernando VII*, ii. 52, 53. Clarke : *Modern Spain*, p
38, 39.
[2] Villa-Urrutia : *Mujeres*, p. 99.

September 27. On the gate of the Atocha was written a verse of welcome :

> You will see the King's passionate zeal
>   To maintain our laws and our rights,
> And a people who in an ideal
>   Of loyal love always delights.[1]

These lines were not written in mockery. There was something about this man which, in spite of everything, attracted loyalty and kindled affection in Spanish hearts. He at least kept himself central as their king ; thus he was popular, and remained so to the end ; and as for his policy, the large mass of the people were still so conservative that they preferred reaction to civil liberty.

As for Isabella, she had beauty of neither face nor figure. But the eye that searches for goodness of heart could detect the more important signs : could see from her well-shaped hands that she had a natural fineness of character, and from the expression in her eyes that she was mild and kind. She and the King lived amicably together, and gossip was no longer noisy, though there is evidence that with the Duke of Alagon he continued his nightly prowls in search of amusements, and did not break off his relations with the Andalusian lady in whose house he was to have been murdered. After two years, however, the Queen died, without having a child, while on a visit to Rome. And within a few weeks both the parents of Fernando followed her.[2]

---

[1] *Veras del Rey el anhelo*
      Por guardar justicia y leyes,
   Y un pueblo que es el modelo
      De como se ama á los reyes.
          Quoted in Villa-Urrutia : *Mujeres*, p. 97.

[2] Villa-Urrutia : *María Luisa*, p. 171.

6

The marriage with Isabel made Fernando mor
eager than ever to make his mother give up her jewels
he wanted not only Maria Luisa's, but even those c
the Countess of Castillo-Fiel, who, by dint of pressur
and menace, sent hers to Rome to the old sovereign'
hands from whom Godoy was supposed to hav
obtained them. But both Carlos and Luisa denie
the story, and the old King insisted on their being sen
back to their lawful owner.

When this plan failed, the Marquis de la Constanci
received orders to proceed directly against the Queen
Mother and her " creature," so that her private jewel
should be seized and an inventory made of them ; fo
they feared lest she should bequeath or give them t
the Prince. But this again the old King, steppin
in, flatly refused to allow. " This blow," he saic
" would kill the Queen, and I neither want to be he
executioner nor agree to anyone else killing her."

And yet so outrageous was the insistence of their so:
and his envoy that the sovereigns did at last give i.
so far as to make the inventory.   " Now I know," sai
Maria Luisa to Carlos as he signed it, " that they ar
flattering and deceiving you, so that, when they hav
done with me, they can do with you what they ar
doing with me now. I see well what people our son
have turned. Never in the world were there parent
so wretched as we are."

King Carlos sent for Godoy, and in the presence c
the Queen told him what had happened, and said
" When the Queen and I doubted that my son
Fernando would allow you to return and join us, ane
before you came back from Pesaro, the Queen aske
me to authorise a will in your favour of the little w
have left, in remuneration for your services, and as :

nall indemnity from us of what you have sacrificed
r our sakes. And I have authorised it. The will
as been made and signed by me. I hand it over to
ou in these papers. Keep it, perhaps as the last
vidence of the love which we have felt for you, and
f the appreciation you deserve. Things are so turn-
ıg out, Manuel, that I do not know if the Queen and
 can survive such outrages."

Indeed, the health of both was breaking. Carlos
ıffered more and more from gout, and Maria Luisa
rew weak and dispirited. "It does not stop rain-
ıg," she wrote on October 22, 1817. "I live in the
reatest solitude. Old and worn out, my nerves tor-
ıent me, and I see that my days are to be very short."
ınd six days later : " It is so lonely, so silent, so cold
nd melancholy that it seems the antechamber of
eath." [1]   A year or two before she had enjoyed row-
ıg on a lake in the Villa Mattei with Godoy, while
he King watched them benevolently from the bank.[2]
)ne day, while they were still in the Palazzo Borghese,
vhere Godoy with his mistress occupied an upper
partment, they were visited by a French nobleman.
' Caballero," said the Queen, " have you ever seen
he Prince of the Peace in his fine clothes ? "

" No, Madame, I have never seen him except in the
ılack suit which he is wearing now."

" Oh, you must see him in his fine clothes : you will
ee how they suit him ! "

" Yes, yes," said the King, who was delighted at
he idea. So the uniforms were brought in, and the
'rince, unabashed in the presence of Their Majesties,
lonned his uniform as Prime Minister—a uniform
tiff with embroideries and decorations.

" Walk up and down, Manuel," said the Queen.

[1] Villa-Urrutia : *María Luisa*, p. 174.
[2] Stendhal : *Promenades dans Rome*.

" Yes," repeated the King, "walk up and down."
And the Prince paraded himself proudly.

" *Qu'il est beau !* " said the Queen.

" *Qu'il est beau !* " repeated the King.

" *Mon Dieu, qu'il est beau !* " echoed the attendant.
And then he was dressed up in turns as Gran
Admiral, as Generalissimo, as Captain-General, an
no one could tell which enjoyed it all most, the King
the Queen, or the Prince himself.[1]

But those days were past. The Queen beneat
the jewels, the feathers, and the flowers which she wor
in her curls had grown sallow and wrinkled ; abov
a double chin her features had the hard expressio
of a woman ambitious but disillusioned. And th
weather depressed her more and more. Her sequine
life, if she looked back on it, was like a rajah's journe
through hill jungle in Mysore. Passing from on
durbar to another, one sees the cloud from the mon
soon downpour, then in the succeeding sun an
vapour the drenched poinciana is seen blooming i
scarlet and ochre ; one hears the tom-tom beating u
the tiger or the scared runner shaking his iron ring
as his ear catches the howl of the hyena ; one watche
for the spotted snake which basks in the sun or rustle
in the grass. And, in the end, after her long pro
gress of jewels and fury, where had Maria Luisa come
The sumptuous sacredness of Rome became as fearfu
and as comfortless as, to the traveller, the fall of evenin
in the forest, or lightning among the precipices abov
his slippery track. It was an icy winter, and the grea
salons of the Palazzo Barberini were impossible t
heat. The Tramontana, that harsh wind, whic
Shelley was even then comparing to a wolf which ha
smelt a dead child out, would pierce even the yellov
damask of the Queen's bed-curtains. Finally pneu

---

[1] Beausset ; *Mémoires*, 3rd ed., iv.

monia, which is as rapid and treacherous in Rome as in Madrid, robbed her of her last strength. On January 2, 1819, she died.[1]

Only Godoy was with her. On November 6 the King had gone back with his brother Fernando to Naples. As the Queen's physical health gave way, so also weakened her mesmeric power over the King, and his healthy brother influenced him as she had done, so that at last he began to free himself from his fifty years' dependence. On December 30 it was known that she was dying, but Carlos did not know. He had left her with the Prince of the Peace. " I hope the King will come," wrote Godoy on January 2, for in the second letter Carlos had been warned that she was sinking. Indeed, the Queen had already made her confession and received the Blessed Sacrament. " I have fulfilled the duties of friend-ship," wrote Godoy at the last, " and she has made her peace with our Redeemer." She died the same even-ing. Though she may not have kept innocency, her last end was that of the righteous.

The death in Rome of one who enjoyed all the honours of a reigning queen, and who had never failed in outward acts of piety, occasioned the full splendour with which the Church loves to ordain its offices on the margins of eternity. As her body lay clothed in white and wearing the insignia of the Order of Saint Isabel of Portugal and the Starry Cross of Austria, the hands were clasped upon a golden crucifix. In the throne-room, where the body was laid, eleven altars were raised, and at these, one after another, more than a hundred priests celebrated the Mass of the Departed. On January 6 her coffin, beneath a royal mantle of scarlet velvet bordered with ermine, rested in the Sacristy of Santa Maria Maggiore, where next morn-

[1] Villa-Urrutia : *María Luisa.*

ing twenty-one Princes of the Church attended the funeral ceremonies. Finally the body was placed, by the orders of the Holy Father, in the crypt of St. Peter's, to await its translation to the Escorial. So alone among the women of the ages, Maria Luisa slept her last sleep in the crypt of St. Peter's, with the Vicars of Christ on earth. She had died a holy death, and who in Rome could be so unchristian as to pass judgment on her? On the contrary, the official preachers of the Church went to the utmost length in panegyric, and exalted her as a saint—she who all her married life had borne, as Hester Prynne bore the Scarlet Letter, the stigma of an adulteress, and who was persecuted, if not prosecuted, by her own son as the thief of jewels belonging to the State.[1]

When Carlos heard the news, on January 4, just after leaving Naples, he was so prostrated that he felt he could not continue his journey. Three days later he wrote to Godoy:

" FRIEND MANUEL,—

" I cannot describe to you how I have survived the terrible blow of the loss of my beloved wife, after fifty-three years of happy married life. I was rather overcome ; but, thank God, I am much better. I do not doubt that in the illness you have helped with all possible care ; but the Queen having passed away, it is not decent that Carlota [2] lives in my house. I have assured her a thousand dollars a month, and so take her away to live with you, and you will do well to carry this out before I go to Rome. This does

[1] See Pérez de Guzmán : *Carlos IV y María Luisa*, p. 224. His statement, that the Pope himself preached her panegyric, is incorrect. See Villa-Urrutia : *María Luisa*.

[2] Carlota was Godoy's daughter, the god-daughter of Maria Luisa, and had accompanied the sovereigns in all their travels.

not mean that you are not to come and see me whenever you wish, and that I remain, as always, the same   " CARLOS."

The widowed King, after recovering from the shock, had planned to set out from Naples on January 14. But that very day he had an attack of fever, which greatly prostrated him. He sent for his brother, who was out shooting. " Curse it, the King of Spain's pretty bad," said the King of Naples ; but, later, thinking better of it, he said, " I think these reports are exaggerated : let's shoot first, and then we'll see." But at this point fresh messengers arrived, saying that he was dying. At this the King of Naples gave orders that no more messages should be opened. " My brother," he said, " will either die or get better ; in the first case, what can it matter to him whether or not I have amused myself shooting, and in the second, he, who is such a good shot himself, will be delighted to see me coming back with a big bag to celebrate his convalescence." So they spent a couple of days shooting. Then they opened the last despatch, which said that the King of Spain had died, and with his brother's name upon his lips. But since nothing more could be done, the King of Naples finished those days he had planned for his shoot. He then returned to Naples, and the Court went into official mourning.[1]

7

At the death of his parents, Fernando insisted that everything in their possession should be brought back to Spain. He seized it all. He refused to carry out their wills, and Godoy, after ten years of exile, was ruined.

[1] Villa-Urrutia : *María Luisa*, pp. 189, 190.

He was forced to return to Paris, where King Louis, in view of his Bourbon marriage, made him a small allowance. He took a flat on the second floor of 20 Rue Michaudière, and there he lived for over thirty years, tended by two women servants. His great amusement was to sit on a bench in the gardens of the Palais Royal.[1] And there the children of the poor would ask M. Manuel to umpire their games, not knowing that he who watched them had given absolute decisions for the administration of one of the widest empires that history has seen, that he was Grand Admiral of the Fleet which engaged with Nelson at Trafalgar, and treated, as the head of a great power, with the invincible Emperor of the French. They did not know that the mild old man who lived two floors up in the mean street close by had lived supreme among the oldest names of Spain, that he had been, like Wellington, Señor del Soto de Roma and Knight of the Golden Fleece, that the Queen of Portugal had made him Count of Evoramonte, and the sovereigns of Spain Duke of Alcudia, Prince of the Peace, and Universal Minister of Spain and the Indies. The ring which still glittered on his finger had been placed there on his wedding-day by a Bourbon princess, whose father was a descendant of the Grand Monarque himself.[2]

When he died in 1852—to be buried in Père Lachaise—Wellington too was dead, and as for Fernando VII, his bones had been resting for nearly twenty years in a sarcophagus of porphyry, while year by year at the stately altar overhead monks sang their solemn office for his soul.

[1] Mesonero Romanos : *Memorias.*
[2] Mesonero Romanos : *Op. cit.*

8

But in 1819 Fernando had few thoughts of death.
e was just thirty-five years old, and neither his wife's
eath nor his parents' coming all within a month
pt him a moment from thinking of a third marriage.
n the contrary, the seizure of his mother's jewels
moved one indignity from his suit.   This time his
oice fell upon Maria Amalia, daughter of the King
` Saxony, a niece of the rich Princess Augusta, who
ad been considered for him eighteen years before.
he was also a niece of the Emperor of Austria.   The
[arquis of Cerralbo was sent to Dresden to sue for
er hand ;   and no one having the scruples of Lolotte
onaparte against a marriage with King Fernando,
e young Princess started immediately for Spain.
he only incident was at the frontier.   Fontarabia
sputed with Irun the right to provide the boat in
hich she was to be rowed across the Bidassoa, while
e bride was kept waiting on the French side.   But
is delay, which might have been protracted, was
ercome by the documents in support of Fontarabia,
d in due course the Princess arrived in Madrid.[1]
She was, says the Marquis de Villa-Urrutia, a pretty,
mid, innocent creature, strictly educated at a convent
the banks of the Elbe.   Her mother had died while
e was yet a baby, and all her ambitions had been
odelled on nuns' ideals.   She sought therefore to
e in the Royal Palace more as though it were a
onvent of the Sisters of St. Vincent de Paul.   She
dicated herself to good works ;   in her lighter
oments, as a relaxation, she composed hymns, which
ay be read in an anthology of lyric poetry published
Madrid in 1915.   Although these lyrics have

[1] Villa-Urrutia : *Mujeres*, p. 101.

received the praise of certain Spanish scholars, the
will strike the foreigner as of unequal value.   Th
lines—

Busco en mi solicitud
La pública convenienza,[1]

were written no doubt as the sincere expression of
charitable intention, but it is not all whom they wi
raise into that dream-world of poetry which is on
with our sense of the supernal.

But though no one could fail to appreciate he
charitable aims as queen, she failed Fernando in th
central particular.   He had still no heir.   And th
conventual ideas of the Queen, or some essential di
equilibrium in her temperament, made her utterl
unable to realise that the Church requires of a wi
something very different from the celibate attitud
proper to the vocation of the nun.   The point is plai
and the very existence of human lives depends on i
But, somehow, the new Queen failed to understand i
She continued through the years to mock the marriag
ties' essential nature, as Fernando had begun by doin
with Maria Antonia.   No doubt he consulted priest
but evidently in vain.   At last he addressed a lett
to the Pope.[2]

But even this seemed to have no effect ; for if a
answer exists, it has not yet been found, and the Quee
remained childless year by year.

9

That was not Fernando's only difficulty.   In spi
of the torture and execution of the constitution
leaders, in spite of the re-established Inquisition, i

---

[1] I seek with anxious care
The public convenience,

[2] Marqués de Lema : *Estudios Históricos.*

pite of the return of the Jesuits, the Parliamentarians gained power. There might be in the Court a reactionary party who wanted nothing changed from what it had been fifty years before ; but there was another movement which insisted that Spain should share material advantages with Europe, and that the unity of peoples should vanquish the separation of distance. " A party fanatical, ignorant, and stupid," says the Marquis de Miraflores, " though it had an absolute and exclusive command of the country, had yet a great energy to combat. . . . For there were other causes and combinations than those of the political parties and factions of Spain. There was *the irresistible force of the age*, an immense force, a force which was opposed to the idea of an inquisition in Spain and which prevented it, a force which penetrated all the pores of government, a force which gave an impulse to facilitate the means of communication, to establish coach services and companies, and to make use of gas and steam, a force, in short, which was penetrating the country in spite of every obstacle. Influences rooted in the demands of the age were escaping from their trammels, creating necessities of progress, demands, and means of development, and chairs of natural sciences." [1] The remainder of Fernando's reign was to be an open struggle between those and the rooted instinct to leave things as they were. The question was, which would find the men, and soon after the marriage of Maria Amalia, the progressive party, which in this case was identified with the masons, found leaders who have left a name in Spanish history. Fernando had foreseen what was coming, and was not surprised when, at the opening of 1820, there was a great movement of the people to demand the Constitution which he had found it easy to

[1] Miraflores : *Memorias*, i. 27.

deny them on his return. And in the autumn, when he returned from the Escorial, he was made the subject of such gross insults, and in this movement the masons, though they had received no orders to do it, made themselves so prominent that they offended the feeling of Madrid.[1]

But meanwhile their organisation in Andalusia was complete, and there they found their men.[2] The occasion was the departure of an expedition for America. Two army officers, Quiroga and Riego, had agreed to lead a revolutionary movement at the beginning of the year. Of these Riego was the more attractive and enthusiastic figure. Rather than not leave the General to whom he was attached as A.D.C., he had passed most of the Peninsular War in a French prison. He had become a mason. His education had been superficial. He had neither a great mind nor a power of speaking, but what he lacked in ability he indemnified in fire. Glory he craved, and this gave him in danger an impetuous valour. Consumed with his passion, he would engage in deeds sometimes of selfless sacrifice, and sometimes of childish vanity. Such a man soon had a hero's prestige, and with Quiroga focused at once the fear of the Court party and the enthusiasm of the rest.

During the whole of the months of January and February the demonstration of public feeling was so strong that the King felt obliged to give way, and on March 9 he signed a Constitution : he published a proclamation to the people ending with words which were soon to pass into a classic statement of insincerity known even to this day to every educated Spaniard " Let us walk frankly, and I the first, in the con

[1] Alcalá Galiano : *Memorias*, ii. 151, 152.
[2] Menéndez Pelayo : *Heterodoxos*, iii. 498.
[3] Alcalá Galiano : *Memorias*, ii. 179.

stitutional path." The monarch who had conspired
against his parents and dethroned them, who had
repudiated his defenders, who had cringed for five
years in abject flattery to his enemies, was not the
man to hesitate when it came to an oath to democrats.
But the Constitution was hardly signed when his
party were attempting to arrest the popular leaders.
In fact, at the very moment that Fernando was signing the Constitution, his agents in Andalusia were
attempting to lead Quiroga and Riego to prison.
But as they were being taken towards the prison of
Seville, the people were crowding through the streets
to celebrate the newly proclaimed Constitution [1] and
the triumph of reform.   The reformers were therefore set free.   On March 10 the troops had fired on
the mob in Seville.   Then the people, in the words of
an English newspaper, "in a state of frantic fury,"
rushed on the troops, "and the officers were literally
torn to pieces."   At this news apparently, Fernando
shrewdly decided that he would be wiser to change
his advisers.   Those "servile men" who were "trembling" at the fear of being "brought to account for
their past crimes" perhaps themselves judged it wiser
to escape.   But the people of London were assured
that the Peninsular War had not left Spain in the
toils of inquisitors and "galling parasites" : nobly
indignant, the *Morning Chronicle* declared, in one of the
gorgeous phrases in which the journalism of the time
sought to outdo the diatribes of Burke, that "the
palace has been cleansed from the vile reptiles which
so lately crawled within its tainted purlieus." [2]   In
other words, Spain's first experiment in parliamentary
government had begun.

[1] *Journal des Débats*, Paris, March 19, 1820.
[2] *Morning Chronicle*, April 5, 1820.

It was not an encouraging affair. The Parliament was a masonic creation, and represented the revolt not of the whole country but of energetic reformers who felt less hostile to the King's ministers than to the religious traditions of the country, and especially to the religious orders. There was a very general feeling at that time among the aspirants to universal freedom that religion should not be free : religion as a department of life could be allowed, but if men, or women, grouped themselves together in communities, with vows to give up personal possessions and even the claims of sex, to devote themselves in entire obedience to the rules and ideals of their community, whether that was the worship of God, the assistance of the clergy, the education of youth, the care of the sick and aged, or the pursuit of sacred and profane learning, it was felt that it must be stopped. Whether the enormous lands they had in their possession (in Spain these were said to be a third of the entire area) were a real obstacle to individual enterprise, whether there was an instinctive recoil against the example of such spiritual self-sacrifice, whether individuals coveted the accumulating wealth of the communities, it was one of the first demands of the masonic instinct that the religious orders should be abolished.

Now, if in Fernando's disordered and treacherous nature there remained one redeeming loyalty, it was the sense of his responsibility as a Catholic king. Two things at least he did seem to incarnate in Spain, the Church and Monarchy, the two great institutions which, in their different ways, safeguarded life in the realm, both in order and in administration. When the reforming party began with its attack on the religious orders, Fernando naturally refused to sign

the decree they asked, and naturally he had behind
his refusal the support of the Pope and his Nuncio.
At this the reforming party prepared a mutiny.   The
King then saw that he must give way.   Obviously
monarchies, including the spiritual monarchy of the
Vatican, must always escape somehow from open conflict in their own defence.   Unless they are identified
with the interests they represent, there is no place
for them.

Nevertheless, the King had his own adherents,
both in the country and outside it ; these had little
patience with Parliament, and none with masonry.
But without the authority of the King, what authority
was there ?   Ministry succeeded ministry, and each
was ineffective.   The country suffered ; the foreign
powers, and especially Metternich, became alarmed.
Metternich was arranging a Council in Verona for
the autumn of 1822.   To it went Wellington, Londonderry, Chateaubriand, Nesselrode, Lieven, and Pozzo
di Borgo.   It was a time when Europe was still so
united that ideals of government were felt to be of
universal interest, and when one country concerned
itself individually with the constitution of another.
The Liberal masonic movement in Spain, which was
represented as the violence of a minority over the
King and his people as a whole (and perhaps it was
so), was condemned by Metternich and his allies.
England, even under the Duke of Wellington, would
not commit herself, but Chateaubriand went so far
as to pledge a French army, if necessary, in support
of the King of Spain.

Next spring, this army, known as the Hundred
Thousand Sons of Saint Louis, and commanded by
the Duke d'Angoulême, passed the Pyrenees.   It was
received with enthusiasm in Biscay and Navarre, where
masonry was odious.   The Parliament could not

engage in civil war against it, for it had neither money
nor executive power ; it dare not, for it knew that the
masses were with the King and the Catholics. The
Duke d'Angoulême proceeded from the Pyrenees to
the Sierra Nevada in a triumphal march. All that
the Parliamentarians could do was to seize the person
of the King and march him to Seville. But as the
French army approached Seville, it was thought
advisable to translate him to Cadiz. But somehow the
King, in spite of Liberal persuasions, seemed to prefer
the foreign invaders to his own Parliamentarians.
Better a foreign absolutist than a Spanish mason !
And so, when he had given his answer, he told them,
" I have no more to say," and turned his shoulder.

But at this point Alcalá Galiano took up the argument ; he urged that a king who would prefer reactionary soldiers to advanced Liberals was evidently
deranged. He quoted an article of the Constitution
which declared that a Council of Regency should act
for an insane king ; thereupon the Cortes, who
were content with themselves as medical authorities,
declared him insane ; they appointed their regents,
and in the violent heat of Andalusian June, they
carried their royal lunatic off to Cadiz, to all intents
and purposes dethroned.

Never was a dethronement shorter, or a treatment
of insanity so rapidly successful. When they saw the
white walls of Cadiz rise from its cobalt sea, the
parliamentary psychiatrists found their patient perfectly cured, and able to perform such functions as
they required of him. But they could not hold
back the army of the Duke d'Angoulême, who, on
August 17, took command of the troops besieging
Cadiz. After a courteous exchange of letters with the
King, the Duke prepared to receive his royal cousin
in his camp. The Cortes had abandoned their pre-

rogatives, and all they asked from the King was mercy.
The King of course promised them all that they
wanted—what's in a promise ?—and the royal cousins
dined together in perfect amity on September 29.
On October 1 the King and Queen sailed from Cadiz
in a warship flying the royal standard.   As Fernando
VII looked for the last time on the city of the Cortes,
his eyes blazed with fury.[1]

In the meantime, his most flamboyant subject had
been captured and thrown into prison.   Rafael del
Riego was not made of strong stuff : he made every
sort of effort to save himself, but the powers of reaction
were determined on his execution.   His end was
abject : he not only gave in wholly to the Church he
had scorned, but asked the Supreme Being to pardon
his crimes, and asked his fellow-countrymen to pray
for his soul to be purged of its excesses.   On the
scaffold he repudiated his cause.   Such was the end
of the hero of Spanish revolutionaries, of the man
whose words are now the National Anthem of the
" Republic of Workers."

Democracy, meanwhile, was admitted to be a
failure.   The King regained his absolutism ;   the
people of Spain, left with a choice of compromising
their sacred system of a life in participation of heavenly
mysteries, or the claims of human opinions, found that
if liberty was not yet available for all, they preferred
the supremacy of the Church to the supremacy of
masonry.   They thought their monarchy, with all its
faults, less disturbing than the ministries of Arguelles,
or Feliú-Bardaxi, or Martínez de la Rosa.   And the
ingenuous Fernando finally gave up the pretence of
keeping any promises to reign as a constitutional
sovereign.   At one crisis, Martínez de la Rosa had

---

[1] Vaya : *Fernando VII*, iii. 140–55.   Butler Clarke : *Modern Spain*, p. 70.

suggested the creation of a second chamber. "A second chamber!" exclaimed the King, "when we are paralysed as it is with one. Never!"

II

That was in 1823. The King was nearly forty, but such had been his life that he seemed a much older man. From that time on he pursued a policy of harsh repression, the rigours applied by his Minister of Justice, Tadeo Calomarde, being so severe that the period was known by Calomarde's name.

"The head of King Ferdinand," writes Miraflores, "was from his first years affected by one fixed idea, due to his family position, and that was never to have a favourite. Whoever approached him with evidences of capacity in any way distinguished awoke his distrust. Neither his favour nor an influence over his mind could be acquired except on the basis that the monarch was assured of the superiority of his own capacity and talent. He could not endure the idea that anyone knew more than he, fearing always that in the end the superior knowledge would be used to quench his own rights. No one was farther from inspiring such doubts than his favourite minister. A low and mean flatterer, he never allowed the possibility of the remotest contradiction to the King to enter his head. If at any time he appeared to contradict the monarch, whom he called his master, it was a new stratagem of adulation. Appearing to give way to the force of his argument, he would have another reason for exalting to the clouds the penetration and wisdom of his sovereign, and confessing his own ignorance."

The minister's only idea was to keep his post. "He was the blind and servile instrument of the King's

will, in whatever way that should show itself," and for
the most part it showed itself in ruthless persecution.
Anything of the nature of parliamentary movements,
or of masonry, was hunted out and exterminated.   It
was a system, not of enlightened despotism, but of
terrorism.   And this reached its culmination in 1831,
after the revolt of Torrijos in Andalusia.   A General
of Liberal views, and so kind and good that even his
enemies loved him,[1] had landed on the coast of
Malaga only to be captured, and, with all his companions, shot.   In the same year a sempstress at
Granada, for nothing more than embroidering the
words Liberty, Equality, and Fraternity, suffered
execution.[2]

After the final revolt of Mexico, and its declaration
of independence under the Emperor Agustín Iturbide,
after the protests received not only from Canning in
England but from the powers in France who had just
saved him, Fernando judged it more prudent to hold
back from the last extreme : he did not re-establish
the Inquisition.   And, indeed, though Calomarde
was a terrorist, he was not the last word in reaction.
He followed a system which Fernando called a stick
for the white donkey, and a stick for the black donkey.[3]
There was another party which went farther still.

12

The true function of the Church in human society
(is it not ?) is to aim at bringing peace and well-being
to all, and assisting them to obtain spiritual perfection
as they fulfil the duties of their state, while it reserves
to some the special vocation to the life of sacrifice

[1] Alcalá Galiano : *Recuerdos.*
[2] Butler Clarke : *Modern Spain.*
[3] Aguado : *Historia de España*, ii.

which, now in works of charity and now in sacred learning or mystic discipline, pierces the secrets of the life which is hid in the heavenly heights. This function was completely misunderstood in Spain. As early as in 1823, a party of fanatical reaction had been formed. It called itself the *Apostolica Junta*, and aimed at killing the grass of free opinion at the root. Instead of allowing holy influences to win the human will and exalt the life of man into a realm higher than its own, the Apostolic Party aimed at enforcing a uniformity of observance. The great apostle of the New Testament wrote that he laboured not as one having lordship of the faith of Christians, but as one who shared in their joy. The Apostolics, however, were different men from the Apostle.

His conception, in any case, does not always come easily to the priest of Rome, and there was a certain violent element in the Spanish layman's character which, out of open-heartedness and almost excessive *laissez-faire*, burst suddenly out into ruthlessness. That element, a part of Spain's inheritance from the Moors, could then be exploited, as now it can no longer, by a few fanatics. And these, in 1825, under Bessières, formed together into what called itself an Apostolic and was an Absolutist Party. They wanted the Inquisition back, the Universities closed, and the Press chained. The educational programme was summed up by the University of Cervera : *Far from us be the perilous novelty of discussion.*[1] Everything was to be hammered down to the flat level of the narrowest and most unenlightened Catholicism. It found its head in the King's brother Carlos. In 1827 the Carlists were definitely recognised as a political force in Catalonia to cope with the policy of Calomarde, which to these reactionaries looked sinister and liberal !

[1] Mesonero Romanos : *Memorias*, i. 336.

The part of Carlos in the history of Spain through all these noisy years was to remain the devoted ally of Fernando. Carlos had no doubt sympathised with his brother in the conspiracies of the Escorial and Aranjuez, for he went with him to Madrid and then to Bayonne. He remained steadily with him at Valençay. He returned with him in 1814. With him he made the second triumphal entry into Madrid. And, as we have seen, when Fernando married a second time, Carlos married on the same day Francisca, the sister of Fernando's bride. Such a marriage did not at first lessen the devoted loyalty of the brothers. But no doubt, as time went on, and Fernando took to himself a third wife, the strong character of Francisca began to give a different tinge to the brothers' intimacy, as difference in temperature will alter the flavour of bottles of old wine. Doña Francisca, an impressively ripe matron of strong features though soft flesh, was an ambitious and high-tempered woman, *très princesse*. She took a great interest in politics. As the years had gone, and the wives had succeeded one another, each leaving the King childless, she naturally looked on herself as the future Queen of Spain. And she was determined that the next reign should preserve the monarchy absolute.

Fernando, however—it was natural—still hankered for a son. Recourse was taken to *novenas*, rosaries, *exvotos*—the classic devices with which Catholics strengthen their supplications to bend the will of heaven to their own designs, but the recourse was vain. Whether the Queen had yielded to the counsels of orthodoxy with regard to the duties of the married state, or whether she still maintained the false scruples of her pious temperament, which fell in so well with the ambitions of her sister-in-law, no one

knew. The Liberals knew that if the King had nc
son, their cause was lost. Whether they prayed oi
not, they have not told us. The Carlists, fearing them
attempted an insurrection in 1827 in the mountain
of Catalonia. But it was enough for the King tc
travel in person to Tarragona : they loved him stil
so warmly, and deferred so wholly to his prestige, tha
when he was near, the rebel cause was lost. But wha
difference did it make either way when the King wa
growing weak, and Don Carlos, married to Francisca
remained his heir ? How was the irresistible force o
the age, as the Marquis de Miraflores called it, tc
express itself? No one could see how to loosen the
tangle.

"Divine Providence, however, in His inscrutable
designs," so Mesonero Romanos writes, " found the
solution of the knot in calling to Himself the angelica
Lady who was the involuntary obstacle to the desire
of the King and the whole nation." (To this writer
evidently, the Apostolics and their leaders were nc
part of the nation.) On May 17, 1829, Queen Maria
Amalia suddenly died in Madrid ; as people looked
at her face in the coffin, and saw that it had turned
black, it occurred to them that a little poison migh
have assisted in the consummation so devoutly
wished.[1] However that may be, the fate of the crown
became more of a drama than ever.

[1] E. d'Auvergne : *A Queen at Bay*, p. 2.

V

THE LEOPARD CHANGES HIS SPOTS

> Authority, though it err like others,
> Hath yet a kind of medicine in itself
> That skins the vice o' the top.
> *Measure for Measure*, ii. 2.

I

To Don Carlos and Doña Francisca the death of
the Queen was devastation, for the King at once
announced his intention of marrying again. All they
could now hope was to dictate his choice : he had
always had a great respect for Francisca, and still
deferred to her judgment. As the wife of the heir-
presumptive, however, she could not be accepted as
the sole authority. There was another Infanta at
hand to advise.

When Carlos and Maria Luisa had gone from
Bayonne to Compiègne, from Compiègne to Marseilles, and Marseilles to Rome, they kept with them
their youngest son, Francisco de Paula, in whom
mischievous Lady Holland detected, or thought she
detected, " a most indecent likeness to the P. of the
Peace." [1] There is nothing to show whether it was
indeed a fear of an incestuous complication which
held Don Francisco de Paula back from marriage
with Godoy's daughter—which was what his mother
urged. But if there were qualms about marrying a
possible half-sister, there was none apparently about
marrying a niece. Don Francisco de Paula wedded
early in 1819 the Princess Carlota of Naples,

[1] Lady Holland : *Spanish Journal.*

whose mother was his sister, and whose father wa
his uncle.

Doña Carlota was a woman of hardly less powerfu
character than Doña Francisca. Of a strong mascu
line type, she had the kind of energy that would giv
way to no obstacle.[1] She had a passion for intrigue
and she was no lover of her sister-in-law. As th
younger brother's wife, she had had to accept in th
Court an inferior position, which greatly irked her
and nothing obviously would give her greater satis
faction than to intrigue against the lady whom sh
had most to envy and most to fear. Besides that, sh
had in her younger sister Cristina a talented, pas
sionate, and beautiful princess who was waiting for a
crown. Between the two Infantas a duel began : fo
Fernando was disposed to leave it to them to choose
his bride.[2] The suggestion that he should marry
another German princess had been dismissed with th
three words : " No more rosaries ! "[3]

The duel of Carlos and Francisca against Francisco
and Carlota grew more desperate. Carlota had, o
course, the Liberals on her side. They saw in her the
only means to free themselves from the Apostolic Party
It was obviously congenial to these to denounce
Cristina, and to attempt to disqualify her as a Liberal.
though on what grounds a Bourbon of Naples was
accused of being a Liberal it would be hard to tell.
The very accusation naturally made the Spanish
Liberals her enthusiastic supporters. The argument,
however, was settled not by politicians but by an
artist. Carlota produced a miniature of her sister.
It showed a young girl of winning loveliness. Her

[1] F. Fernández de Córdova : *Memorias*, i. 113. Guizot :
Mémoires, viii. 184.

[2] *Cambridge Modern History*, x. 231, 232, 233.

[3] Villa-Urrutia : *Mujeres*.

QUEEN MARIA CRISTINA DE BOURBON
After the portrait by López in the Prado, Madrid.

" The heavy, gouty, susceptible uncle decided that his niece
was irresistibly seductive."

eyes, which looked black at a little distance, had a sweet expression, and as Princess Clémentine of Belgium said, they thirsted for pleasure [1] ; her skin was of a pearly whiteness which, at her cheeks, flushed delicately rose ; her lips, which were finely cut, were ever curving into a smile, which made her whole face radiant with sweetness [2] ; she had chestnut hair, and her ears were such that a little later they struck an American gallant who saw her as the first to which he could really give the name of beautiful. [3] When the King saw the miniature, there was no need for further discussion. The heavy, gouty, susceptible uncle decided that his niece was irresistibly seductive. He immediately sent an embassy to Naples to seek her for his bride.

She set out on an interesting journey. From Naples of course she went to Rome. When at Albano she received the blessing of the Pope, who had already dispensed her from the impediment of consanguinity. At Turin she was the guest of the Sardinian Court, and met Prince Victor Emmanuel. She crossed the Alps to Grenoble, where she was met by another important person, Louis Philippe, who was still the Duke of Orleans, and who had married her aunt ; there also she met her sister Carlota, Francisco de Paula, and one or two Spanish Liberals. At the frontier of Spain, and in the northern cities of Catalonia, her tour was a triumph. It was during her stay in Barcelona that she showed that she had in the highest degree the grace and talent of one who was to make a remarkable queen.

The people received her there with immense enthusiasm : her beauty won them from the first.

[1] E. d'Auvergne : *A Queen at Bay*, p. 219.
[2] Washington Irving : *Life and Letters*.
[3] Slidell Mackenzie : *A Year in Spain*.

They celebrated her arrival with balls, with function
in the theatre, and with popular rejoicings. She
lodged in the palace, and watched from a balcony a
peasant dance in the plaza below. To save the
soldiers from the cold of the night, the Princess gave
orders that they should wear their cloaks ; they held
their arms at the salute, and she gave orders that they
should stand at ease ; the officers stood with their hats
in their hands, and she gave orders that they should
put them on. At seeing so much interest in their
comfort, the soldiers were filled with enthusiasm ; and
the people, who had also received signs of her care and
attention, compared her thoughtfulness with the disdain and neglect to which they were accustomed, not
only from the Court, but from the authorities and
nobles. " I have never seen," wrote the Marquis de
Mendigorria, " so much enthusiasm in the people or
in the army. If kings understood how much they gain
when they withdraw from the adulation of the powerful and give these and other simple attentions to the
people and to the army, their enemies would find them
invincible in the great tempests which pass by." [1] In
the *Lonja,* or Exchange at Barcelona, Cristina danced
quadrilles and valses, not only with the members of the
aristocracy, but also with the merchants.

" Without exaggeration one may say that Cristina
awoke the enthusiasm of all that saw her," continued
Mendigorria. " In addition to her enchanting beauty
and grace, she was so pleasant with everybody, and
looked and smiled so kindly at those to whom she did
not speak. Her form was slim and elegant, and she
was dressed in a style that was at once both rich and
simple. Even her enemies were overcome by her,
and if the partisans of Don Carlos had had much to do
with her, very few would have deserted her flag."

[1] Fernández de Córdova : *Memorias,* i. 115.

She united with an extreme beauty which won all
hearts an especial talent for politics and discussion. . . .
As she left Barcelona, she attracted the sympathy of
everybody, and gave the throne a power which neither
shootings, imprisonments, nor deportations could
give it.

She went next to Valencia, arriving at Aranjuez in
the first week of December. On the eleventh, at half-
past eleven in the morning, the King arrived to visit
her and remained to luncheon, driving back in the
afternoon, more than satisfied with Carlota's choice.
Next day (it was a cold but brilliant morning) she
made her entry into Madrid in a robe of brilliant blue,
the intense and lovely blue of the waters of her native
coasts, which ever after was taken as the colour of the
Liberal Party. On the 12th, the Church blessed her
union with Fernando, and made her Queen of Spain.

She had changed her scene from the Bay of Naples,
from the velvet outlines of Vesuvius and Ischia, from
the charm of Castellamare and Sorrento, to the
sumptuous austerity of a palace looking through dry
rare air over a bare plain to the snows and declivities
of the Guadarrama. Her sister had doubtless made
it plain to her that in doing so she was not only to
wear the crown of Catholic Majesty, but to engage in
a high political adventure. In a short time she found
herself, if not the arbitress of Spain, at least the central
eminence among the disordered factions which kept
shooting up like geysers out of the boiling hole of mud
which broke the volcanic crust of Spanish politics.
The insurrection of Torrijos and the hanging of
Riego were among the first political incidents of her
life as Queen. And the Liberals turned to her as
their defender. Compelled to find allies where she
could against the reactionaries, who were still grouped
around the heir-presumptive, she herself became a

Liberal. Had she no heir, this would make her future
position impossible, for the Apostolics would no doubt
hunt her from the country. But for the present she
was the King's most powerful adviser. Not only so.
The Court very soon knew that she was with child.
Fernando's life had become precarious, and she might
be at any moment, as the widowed mother of his heir,
a Regent endowed with almost absolute power. The
most curious adventures were before her, and she
entered upon the scene of what we know to have been
already a school for scandal. She rapidly passed
through it with the highest honours.

2

It was almost exactly ten months from her wedding-
day that she gave birth to her eldest child. Fifteen
months later another child was born. In each case
the Carlists had feared that their cause was lost : each
time they had learnt that the child was a daughter
This did not save them ; but it filled them with hope,
because no one had finally decided whether the Salic
Law was in force or not. Philip V, reversing the tradition of the country, had brought in the Salic Law
which, as everyone knew, forbade queens to reign
But in 1789 Charles IV, guided by Godoy, had
reversed it by an enactment called the " Pragmatic
Sanction," which restored to the King's daughter a
right, as in England, not above her brothers, but
above her uncles. For some curious reason, this
"Pragmatic Sanction" had not been published. Don
Carlos claimed to know nothing about it, and even
when he did know, he argued that it was not in force
at the time of his birth, and that he could not be
robbed by an arbitrary enactment of the rights to
succession with which he was born.

Such was the state of affairs when Isabel, Cristina's first daughter, was born on October 10, 1830 ; such it still remained when her second daughter, Luisa Fernanda, was born on January 30, 1832. The position was so uncertain, Fernando's health had grown so weak, the reactionaries seemed so firmly in power, that the Carlists counted on the throne. But to make assurance doubly sure, they induced Fernando, when in a state of exhaustion, to sign an edict, revoking the "Pragmatic Sanction." Cristina was persuaded to strengthen their persuasion by the threat that otherwise there would simply be civil war. And Calomarde, who was practically a dictator, went over to what he believed was the winning side, and in which, in any case, he felt far more comfortable than with the Liberals. For fear of trouble, however, the new decree was to be kept secret till the King's death, for that seemed very near. Fernando grew weaker, and he sank into a lethargy from which the doctors were sure he would never recover ; and Don Carlos went about the Court as though he were already its master, while the disconsolate Cristina, thinking that her days as Queen of Spain were nearly done, devoted herself entirely in sad and anxious care to nursing her dying King.

Carlos, however, had reckoned without Carlota. She had been away in Andalusia for her health that autumn, but hearing that the King was dangerously ill, she summoned the phenomenal powers of her energy and came quickly back. In the meantime, as the King's death seemed so certain and so near, the news of the edict he had signed had been allowed to leak out in Madrid. Carlota heard it as soon as she arrived : she had won one battle for her sister ; the strong enterprise of her character did not fail her now. She went to the Queen, and told her in uncompromising phrases that she should be ashamed of the weakness she had shown. She called for Calomarde, she denounced him as treacherous and mean, and slapped him in the face. Whether or not, like the sentry who was slapped by the Empress Eugénie, he felt the touch of a princess in any circumstances to be flattering ; whether he felt hers was a mild blow compared to that he had received not long before from a military officer, he received the sign of Carlota's anger with extreme mildness. " Señora," he said, quoting the title of one of Calderon's plays, " white hands do not offend." But, before long, she was to convince him to take her more seriously than he had taken the slapping soldier. She induced the Duke of San Fernando to obtain from the Secretary, or as he was called, the Keeper of the Council, the actual text of the decree. She took it in her own hands, and tore it to small pieces.[1]

It happens not seldom that, when persons master the hazards of earth by the force of their temper, events beyond their action yield also to their designs, as though they and the stars were alike ministers of an overwhelming will. At the advent of Carlota, Fernando, to the amazement of his doctors, stirred from his coma. His pulse regained strength. His wits returned. And when by the laws of nature, as far as doctors understand them, he should have been dead, he again assumed the power to reign. His first act was to repudiate the designs of his brother. He dismissed Calomarde, who, after ten years of confidential power, was sent to exile in his native province ; but by his own choice Calomarde crossed the frontier, taking as an example in his flight those who—

> Dying put on the robes of Dominic
> Or in Franciscan think to pass disguised.

[1] Vaya : *Fernando VII*, iii. 365.

He had escaped not from life but from Spain in the garb of a friar.

By October 6 the King was well enough to sign a document making Cristina regent for the period of his illness. The next day she issued a decree of general amnesty and reopened the Universities. She gave freedom to the Press. She dismissed reactionary generals, and three hundred Carlists who were in the bodyguard. A week later, Fernando himself published another and wider amnesty, pardoning in fact everyone accused of political disloyalties, except those who had borne arms against him personally in 1823 : for these, though against his will, he was still forced to apply the penalties of the law. This decree of amnesty meant the end of the reign of terror : Calomarde and his band had fled, never to return, and a party of Liberals took their place. Zea Bermúdez, formerly Ambassador in London, was the most remarkable among them.[1]

On October 18, as the autumn weather sharpened in the high air of La Granja, Fernando and Cristina drove up through the pine-woods to cross the Guadarrama on their way back to Madrid. Though they drove in a closed coach and he was still desperately ill (his face looked livid), he could soon see that the greater acclamation was made for the radiant creature beside him. To her therefore he turned now, and though he knew the Carlists were obstinate and strong : " Spain," he kept on saying through his bout of suffering, " is a bottle of beer, and I am the cork ; as soon as that comes out, all the liquid inside will pour out, God knows in what direction." [2]

But no matter what his anxieties, the King could not but put a fuller confidence in his devoted Queen.

---

[1] Vaya : *Fernando VII*, iii. 370–8.
[2] Mesonero Romanos : *Memorias*, pp. 399, 400.

" I never opened my eyes," he said, " but that I saw you at my side, and found in your expression and your words something to heal my pain. I never received assistance except from your hand. I owe you counsels in my affliction, and alleviation in my pain. Weakened by suffering so long, and obliged by a long and feeble convalescence, I confide to you henceforth the reins of government, and I have been rejoiced to see the singular diligence and prudence with which you have held them, and far more than satisfied my trust. All the decrees you have promulgated, whether to assist public instruction or to alleviate the sufferings of the unfortunate, or to increase public wealth and my own revenues ; in fact, all your decisions, without exception, have given me the greatest satisfaction, as they have been the most prudent and timely for the welfare of the people." [1]

By the end of the year, therefore, he had established everything possible in her favour, and on the last day of the year he gathered together the powers of the nation to announce his royal will.

" The tumult and anguish," he began, " of a state in which at times I seemed to be dying, are final proof of the act not being done by my own will, even if that were not shown by its nature and its effects. Neither as a king could I destroy fundamental laws of my kingdom which had been openly promulgated as being in force, nor as a father could I deliberately rob my descendants of their august and lawful rights. Disloyal and deceiving men surrounded my bed, and by taking advantage of the love which I and my dear wife bear to the people of Spain, they

[1] Mesonero Romanos : *Memorias*, pp. 399, 400.

increased the bitterness and affliction of my estate, asserting that the entire kingdom was against the 'Pragmatic Sanction,' and that unless it was withdrawn, it would be the reason for torrents of blood and universal desolation. This atrocious statement, made in circumstances when the truth was more than ever a duty of persons who had the obligation of telling it to me, when I was given neither time nor decision to enquire the certainty of it, threw my tired mind into consternation, and absorbed what remained to me of intelligence ; that I should think of nothing else but the peace and welfare of my peoples, as I said in the decree, I made, for the peace of the Spanish nation, as far as I could, this great sacrifice. What perfidy led this horrible plot to the end which sedition had begun ; and in that day, certificates of what had been done, with the decree attached, were published abroad, treacherously breaking the seal which, at my orders and according to the very decree, was to be kept over this document till my decease. Now, informed of the false calumny against the loyalty of beloved Spaniards, who are always faithful to their kings ; persuaded that it is neither in my power nor in my desire to derogate the immemorial custom of the succession established by the laws, sanctioned by the law, pledged by the illustrious heroines who preceded me on the throne, and desired by the unanimous vote of the kingdoms ; and free to-day of the influence and compulsion of those fatal circumstances, I solemnly declare of my own free unfettered will that *the decree torn from me in the sufferings of my illness was wrenched from me by surprise ;* that it was an effect of the false terrors which overwhelmed my soul, and that it is null and void, being opposed to the fundamental law of the monarchy and to the obligations which as king and father I owe to my august descendants."

This time, there should be no question of a secret act. The highest officers of the State were called as witnesses. The wiles of Calomarde were openly repudiated ; the claims of Carlos dismissed. Even before the death of Amalia, Fernando had thought of declaring the "Pragmatic Sanction" : he had at once done so at the birth of his elder daughter, Isabel ; and nothing, he said, but the fact that he did not know what he was doing would have induced him to revoke it.

That was a document which it was impossible to gainsay. But Don Carlos was by no means at the end of his resources. The Liberals had certainly not enough of the confidence of Spain to make their position certain, and reaction was a strong instinct among the people, supported very generously in city and in the country village by the one man of education, the priest, and in the seats of power by the bishops and the Nuncio, and all those Catholics who felt that all was well as long as there were regular offices of prayer. On those Don Carlos built his hopes, and on them he modelled his ways. Every morning he assisted at the Celebration of the Mass ; every evening his little Court assembled to say the Rosary.

The reaction on his royal brother was one of life's little ironies : the King, who had for eighteen years adopted every means possible to cheat his subjects of constitutional rights, who had perjured his solemn oath not to assume the powers of an absolute monarch, who for nine years had reigned by terror, became at his end the darling of the Liberals. Through all

those years he had never lost the love of the people :
he had been, says Miraflores, not so much a man as an
idol who symbolised the moral force of the nation.
The function of the King's Majesty after all is essentially to symbolise the nation's unity, and it is a source
of strength and happiness to the people who can force
the King so to serve by means of their loyalty.   The
workings of the powers of the spirit are stronger than
the deliberate designs of the most able men ; and in
the end Fernando was subjected to the cause of
Liberal institutions.   Once again it was proved that
in the cause of freedom loyalty is a stronger weapon
than revolt.

3

The long partnership in intrigue between Don
Fernando and Don Carlos had come to an end.   The
egoism inherent in absolutism had killed it.   Carlos
wanted it for his family : Fernando determined to
reserve it for his babies.   While they struggled, it was
quickly transformed into a constitution.

Carlos fought hard and skilfully.   When he became
aware that Fernando was about to call together the
leaders of the nation to swear fealty to his daughter
Isabel, Carlos asked for permission to retire to
Portugal.   In order to avoid too open a conflict, the
King allowed him this permission.   But that was soon
proved a mistake.   Portugal was so close to Spain
that Carlos was able to organise powers of resistance,
and he found support in Lisbon, because a similar
problem of succession had created a similar conflict,
and there also there was a powerful element in favour
of the Salic Law.

King John of Portugal, who died in 1826, was one
of the sovereigns whom Maria Luisa secured as a son-

in-law. He had two sons, Pedro and Miguel. Pedro could not succeed, for he was Emperor of Brazil ; the question was between his only daughter, Maria da Gloria, and Miguel, who like Carlos was a reactionary. Miguel, as an absolutist, had obtained the sympathy of Metternich and the armed support of Fernando ; France, however, did not approve of his intervention, and England liked it so little that she landed an army in the Tagus.[1]

But Miguel's position was strong. Don Pedro must nominate a regent for his daughter, and whom could he choose except his brother? To be regent meant to Miguel, however, only one thing, and that was to gather the munitions for his campaign. He soon felt assured of his strength, tore up the Constitution, and exiled his infant niece.

But this was more than the Emperor Pedro could tolerate. He abdicated the throne of Brazil, and landed in Portugal to fight for his daughter's claims. That was on July 8, 1832. But he could do little ; in fact, he was besieged in Oporto until the next year. Sir Charles Napier, commanding a fleet prepared in England by the partisans of Maria da Gloria, defeated the ships of Dom Miguel, and landed a force in the Algarve. At this point Dom Miguel was between two fires, and Lisbon fell to the Liberals, who proclaimed Maria da Gloria to be again their Queen.[2]

But that was not until September of 1833. And it was in the spring of that year, while Miguel was still reigning in Lisbon, that Carlos arrived there with Francisca, to make common cause with Miguel against the " Pragmatic Sanction." On April 21, Fernando addressed an affectionate letter to his brother, and

[1] Butler Clarke : *Modern Spain.*
[2] Butler Clarke : *Op. cit.* J. R. Hall : *England and the Orleans Monarchy*, p. 80.

entrusted it to one of his most devoted officers, Luis Fernández de Córdova. It asked him frankly to declare his feelings. With equally warm affection, and with equal frankness, Carlos reasserted his claim to the succession. "What you wish to know," he wrote, "is whether or not I intend to swear allegiance to your daughter, as Princess of Asturias. How I wish I could! You must believe me, for you know me, and I speak from my heart that nothing would give me greater pleasure than to be the first to swear, and not to give you this annoyance, and the others which ensue from it, but neither my conscience nor my honour allows it. I have certain rights to the crown so legitimate that—if I survive you and you have no son—I cannot give them up : rights which God gave me when He willed my birth, and only God can take them from me by granting you a son, which I much desire, possibly even more than you." How Carlos had been able so long to tolerate the perfidies of Fernando one can hardly explain, for Carlos was a loyal and honest man.

He was so loyal and honest that he compelled even Fernando to be so. His honesty had shown his brother that the sooner he left Portugal the better. So the King wrote on May 6—in the same terms of warm brotherly love :

"I believe that you feel the affection that you say ; but I am a father and a king, and must regard my rights and those of my daughters, and also those of my crown. Nor do I wish to do violence to your conscience, nor can I hope to dissuade you of the rights you claim, which you think that only God can derogate, though they are founded on the choice of men. But the brotherly love which has always been mine impels me to save you from the unpleasantness of being in a country where the rights you claim are not recognised ; and my kingly duties oblige me to keep away a prince whose claim could be made by malcontents a pretext for disorder. Therefore, on account of the highest reasons of State, of the laws of the kingdom which expressly so ordain, and for your own peace, which I desire as much as the well-being of my people, I give you permission to travel henceforth with your family in the Papal states, informing me of your destination and of your place of abode. One of my warships will shortly arrive at the port of Lisbon to conduct you thither." [1]

And very soon after a warship, the *Loyalty*, arrived in the Tagus.

Carlos, without the slightest change of tone, answered that he had been most happy and peaceful in Portugal—and that he saw no reason why he should leave it—the *Loyalty* had no attractions for him. And how could his brother ask him to go to Lisbon, when they had fled from it on account of an epidemic of cholera ?

That was all very well ; but Fernando did not quite see the point. There had already been Carlist risings in Spain, and the very person of Carlos was a centre of disaffection. Therefore he could not wish him within reach of the frontier. " And when I suggested for your residence the beautiful scenery and the benign climate of the Papal states," he added, " it is strange that you should prefer Portugal as more adapted to your peace when a bloody war is being fought over its very soil, or more adapted to your health when it is suffering from a cruel epidemic which made you anxious lest all your family should perish."

[1] Vaya : *Fernando VII*, iii. 397–404.

And as for embarking in Lisbon, there was no need to touch it. The *Loyalty*, for fear of contagion, had no communication with it, and could pick up Don Carlos at any point he wished.

Carlos received this letter on May 25, and answered it two days later. He did not alter the expression of affection, but the letter began by showing a little irritation in its tone. Nevertheless, he would agree. " I shall do your pleasure and obey you in all ; I shall start as soon as I can for the Papal states, not for the beauty, delight, and attraction of the scenery, on which I put little store, but because you wish it, as my King and Lord, whom I will obey as far as my conscience allows. But now the Feast of Corpus Christi is at hand." Where could he keep it so well as among the monks of Mafra ? " I did not say," he added, " that I was afraid of all my family perishing, but that we were going to embark there no matter what danger there is in its pestiferous air, or what disease anyone might contract on the ship, where we might all perish. But now that we have your permission to start from any other point, I hope to see Guruceta." [1] But just as he was about to embark on the *Loyalty*, he suddenly changed his mind, and retreated hurriedly to Coimbra, a pleasant, quiet, old city towards Oporto, where Dom Miguel was holding his summer Court. They could not start, he said, till his wife had taken leave of her brother, and all had exchanged a last embrace.

Now, the return of Carlos to the Court of Miguel at such a time was not only annoying in itself, but it was extremely compromising to Fernando's own position. Fernando could no longer support Miguel, for he could no longer support the Salic Law. And besides, Miguel was a reactionary, and had not Fer-

[1] Guruceta was the captain of the *Loyalty*.

nando become a Liberal ? " You ought to know,"
he wrote, " that the high reasons of State which are
opposed to this journey are of equal moment to both
nations, and that your exalted rank demands that
these family affections and courtesy should cede to
great political considerations." Two more letters
were sent from Coimbra by Carlos : they made it too
obvious that the King was being fooled. How was
it, he asked, that, when Carlos had remained in
Portugal to keep the feast of Corpus Christi at Mafra,
the very next day he had started for Coimbra ? " A
man who speaks with sincerity," Fernando wrote
later, " does not answer with such cunning subterfuges.
. . . I cannot consent, nor do I any longer consent,
that you resist my orders with such frivolous pre-
texts." " I shall show you as I judge convenient," he
wrote finally, " that an Infante of Spain is not free to
disobey his King." [1]

But it was no use : Carlos did not move ; the
Loyalty remained at his disposition, but he refused to
set foot on her deck, and in a foreign kingdom Fernando
had no means to force him. His only agents were Luis
Fernández de Córdova and his brother Fernando,
who kept close watch on him, and reported his every
movement. Early in the summer, Carlos had started
out without saying where he was going. The younger
Córdova rode after him, and hearing that he had slept
at Mafra followed him to Coimbra.

" Hullo ! " said Carlos. " Are you doing policeman ? "

" No, sir," said young Córdova. " I follow Your
Highness in case you need my services."

" Many thanks. I do not need them, and I do not
want them."

He might be forced to endure surveillance, but i

[1] Vaya : *Fernando VII*, p. 424.

was another thing to go to Rome. Meanwhile,
officers and leaders of the Carlist Party kept making
pilgrimages to Portugal.[1] And no one went on board
the good ship *Loyalty*.

4

Fernando saw that there was to be trouble. However, all he could do was to persevere in his plan to
attach the allegiances of Spain to his baby daughter.
Carlos might be disobedient ; but that was the better
reason for celebrating the great ceremony of homage.
Fernando still retained an immense moral force : " A
force," says Miraflores, " which history has not even
defined : the power of the Spanish throne invested
with its prestige and its traditions ; an idea still identified with religious faith, with public use and custom,
and kept vigorous and robust in the midst of events in
which England and France had stained their traditions, sprinkling the pages of history with the blood of
kings." [2] Sacred, beloved, and now the pledge of
liberty, the person of Fernando, in spite of everything,
was still invested with majesty ; still commanded un-
swerving fealty ; still attracted love. And all that
power he determined to enlist in favour of his
daughter.

On June 20, 1833, the Cortes were summoned to
take their oath of allegiance to the Princess of
Asturias.

The great ceremony took place, with all the splendour of the *ancien régime*, in the Church of San Jerónimo, which had been draped with velvet and cloth
of gold. There the cardinals, archbishop, and

---

[1] Fernández de Córdova : *Memorias*, i. 4, 5.
[2] Miraflores : *Memorias*, Introduction.

bishops were gathered in copes and mitres ; facing
them were the nobility in robes of State, and the provincial deputies with their three-cornered hats and
ancient robes. The Patriarch of the Indies sang a
Pontifical Mass ; the royal choir sang the *Veni
Creator*, and the sovereigns retired while a table
covered in crimson velvet was placed before the altar.
There sat the Patriarch to receive the oath. Then
the King-at-Arms summoned in due order all who
were to swear, who, having taken their oath on the
gospels, advanced to kiss the hands of the sovereigns
and the little princess.

She who was the object of this great ovation was
not yet two years old, and as she saw the bishops and
grandees come up to kiss her hand, hid it, and her
face too, and burst out crying, only to be drawn back
to her duty by the coaxing of her parents. Then the
Te Deum was sung, the royalties retired to their
palace in El Retiro, and from there made a public
entry into Madrid, which was lined with troops.
They reached the Royal Palace at sunset in the
gorgeous summer evening.[1]

While the royal party went back to their rest,
Madrid gave itself to celebrations till a late hour.
Rockets shot into the sky and burst in stars ; the
streets were splendidly illuminated, and there were
processions of maskers in the streets. Next day there
was a great bull-fight in the Plaza Mayor, while
armies manoeuvred as though in attack and defence
of Madrid. Through the whole ceremony Madrid
received an impression of oriental sumptuousness
both in the costumes and processions, and, as though
to complete the gorgeousness of kingly state, large
sums were spent in providing comforts for the poor
and needy.

[1] Mesonero Romanos : *Memorias*.

5

But no matter what was done the populace, and especially the army, remained unquiet. The royal guard itself mutinied on July 30. The collapse of Absolutism released the forces of disorder ; and the clergy perhaps not unnaturally believed that the only way to guarantee order was to turn their eyes to Don Carlos, in whom, on the other hand, the Liberals saw a monster of fanaticism, ambition, and hypocrisy. Anxious and restless, the country waited for the invalid King to die. On July 19 he had complained of a pain in the thigh which prevented him from walking ; his sleep failed him ; he lost his appetite, and though he was no longer in great pain, there could be no doubt that he was failing. On September 29 he was much weaker, and the doctors kept close watch and applied poultices of cantharides ; but he ate his food as usual, and as usual they left him with the Queen to amuse him. Then suddenly, at a quarter to four in the afternoon, he had an attack of apoplexy. It was so violent that in five minutes he was dead.

Three days later his will was read. In it, as was to be expected, his daughter Isabel was declared Queen, and her mother Guardian and Regent : he also named a Council of State. He left his widow a fifth part of all his property, of which in the Bank of England alone were twenty-five million pesos. He left five thousand pesos to the poor of Madrid, and one thousand to the poor of each of the towns where he had been accustomed to sojourn. Finally, he left instructions that priests should say Masses for his soul to the number of twenty thousand.

On October 4 they buried him. It was part of the funeral ceremonies of the Escorial that the

outer coffin should be opened with two golden keys
while men looked through a glass window so as to
guarantee that the corpse which was to be received
into the royal resting-place was indeed the King's
After this observance, the Duke of Alagon, who had
accompanied his master in so many secret places
called aloud three times at short intervals: *Señor*
Señor, Señor ! But Alagon knew the King was explor
ing secrets far more arcane than those to which any
duke could guide him. The ritual was completed
" Since His Majesty does not answer, he is truly
dead," cried the Captain of the Bodyguard. And
then they closed the coffin, and left its golden key
with the Prior of the Escorial.[1]

At this funeral there were two circumstances which
were felt to be significant. The one was that as they
carried the coffin down to the tomb, one of the stone
steps was broken. And this was taken as a portent o
ruin. The second, and the more unpleasant, wa
that when the coffin was opened, the odour of corrup
tion was so foul that some who were present fainted.

[1] Vaya: *Fernando VII*, iii. 436, 437.

PART II

VI

THE PASSIONATE REGENT

Nous ne sommes qu'un sang et qu'un peuple en deux villes,
Pourquoi nous déchirer par des guerres civiles,
Où la mort des vaincus affaiblit les vainqueurs
Et le plus beau triomphe est arrosé de pleurs ?
                    CORNEILLE : *Horace*, I. iii.

What would the world be, once bereft
Of wet and wildness ? Let them be left,
O let them be left, wildness and wet,
Long live the weeds and the wilderness yet !
                    GERARD MANLEY HOPKINS.

I

THE body of Fernando was not cold when Cristina
received the Liberal leaders, and entrusted her
interests to the care of Zea Bermúdez.   He was hardly
gone when Miraflores came with other counsels :
what was the young Queen to do?   "I want nothing
more than the happiness of the Spaniards," she said to
him, sobbing ; "for that I will do all I can : what I
don't do will be only what is beyond my powers." [1]
Zea Bermúdez, as he had shown in a manifesto signed
by the Queen a year before, was no real Parliamentarian : he believed that the Crown should be absolute.   Miraflores said quite rightly that this would not
content the Liberals ; and it was, of course, Liberal
support that Cristina needed against Carlos.

[1] Mendigorria : *Memorias*, ii. 141.

151

Meanwhile, the news of Fernando's death was given to Carlos at Coimbra by Luis Fernández de Córdova, and with the news Cordova once more pressed on the Pretender the royal order that he should leave the Peninsula.

" Now I am the King," said Carlos, " and you, if you like, my Minister in Portugal."

" No, *señor*," answered Cordova ; " I am a Minister of the Queen. To her I owe obedience and loyalty."

" Then get away ; for I neither recognise you nor want you."

When, a little later, Córdova's younger brother came to announce that if Carlos crossed the frontier he would be arrested as a rebel, he was told that he was in the house not of an Infante but of the King of Spain. " I also have rights," said Carlos, " and I shall use them."

Meanwhile, the Courts of Europe were in some doubt which claimant to recognise. Isabel was at once accepted by England and by France. Louis Philippe was now King, reigning by Liberal principles, and even without them he was naturally disposed in favour of his niece. Miraflores was sent to England, and with the help of Lord Palmerston, of whom we shall hear more, what was called the Quadruple Alliance was negotiated—England, France, Spain, and Portugal uniting to recognise the sovereign on the side of Liberalism. " I carried it through the Cabinet," said Palmerston, " by a *coup de main*." [1] But the autocratic monarchies of Russia, Prussia, and Austria, having no Palmerston in them, refused to acknowledge Isabel. And with them also was the Holy See.

The home of reaction was still Navarre. And there, after a visit to England, Carlos arrived on July 12,

[1] Maxwell : *Lord Clarendon*, i. 71.

1834, to join with the head of the revolutionary army, Zumalacarregui. Cristina meantime had appointed as head of her own forces another romantic figure, Bartolomé Espartero. In his hand was soon to be her fate.

Carlos had hardly arrived in Navarre to encourage the Catholic Diehards, when the anti-clericals rose in revolt in Madrid. The cholera which had driven Carlos out of Lisbon was now rife in Spain, and while the more superstitious of the Catholics believed it to be a visitation on Liberalism, those at the other extreme said that the friars had poisoned the water. On July 17 a priest was supposed to have been caught in the act at Madrid. The accusation was made the signal for an attack on the religious houses, and more than eighty priests were murdered, some at the very altar. The next summer there was mutiny and violence in Barcelona. At the same period there was intense excitement about a nun in Madrid, Sor Patrocinio, who was said to have received, like St. Francis, the sacred stigmata in hands and feet and side. Everywhere Spain was in a state of uproar, made more terrible by the swift and agonising attack of cholera in city after city. And month after month civil warfare was being carried on in Northern Spain, renewing the horrors of twenty-five years before.

2

Yet all these complications were as nothing to Cristina in comparison with her strongest feelings as a woman. It was not for nothing that the Queen-Regent was a granddaughter of Maria Luisa. Though her character was so winning and attractive, the heart of flesh within her beat with the same impetuous blood. There is no record of the feelings of this ardent and voluptuous girl at the sight of the unpleasant uncle she married ; but obviously the glitter of the crown, which is apt to mesmerise and fascinate those living on or near a throne, had subjugated her so wholly as to leave natural attraction out of all account. Her position as queen mastered in overpowering embrace all question of her inclinations as a wife. She had married the Bluebeard of Spain. Each of his wives had sickened when she married him. But here was one who could survive.

That very fact suggested another question : how could a nature like hers, so ardent, so generous, so youthful, so rich in health and animal spirits know nothing of the allurements of the blood? Her marriage had awakened her capacities of experience in love, but it was impossible to satisfy them with an ageing, heavy, melancholy invalid, even if he wore a crown. And did not the keen winter of high Madrid set her pulses tingling as they had never tingled in the soft air of Sicily or Naples? Did not her brilliant position in the Court fill her from day to day with a sense of the intensity of her personal radiance? No sooner was Fernando dead than the young Queen knew that in the most romantic sense she also was a woman. Young Spaniards of both sexes have very generally a robust beauty and a warmth of approach which no susceptible foreigner could fail to observe. With her grandmother's example before her the Queen could not be an exception, and the King was hardly buried before she found herself desperately in love with a corporal in her bodyguard.

What was she to do? Although she was, in her own words, a woman of short prayers,[1] she was, in spite of her temperament and her environment, an extremely moral woman. She was, moreover, the

_____
[1] Palacio de Liria : *Archivos, Condesa de Montijo.*

Queen-Regent, endued still with almost absolute power. The man she loved was the son of an hidalgo : he had classical features, a pale complexion which threw out in strong contrast his neat black moustache ; yet more remarkable were his eyes : they rested languidly within the lids, but were full and dark, and could flame with excitement ; altogether he was " a very noble-looking man." [1] And yet he was no more than a corporal, and his father had come down so low in the world that he kept a little tobacco shop. [2] And if she were actually to marry him, she would forgo her position as regent, her emoluments, her guardianship of her babies. It was a mad idea ; but what is a mad idea to one madly in love ? As the winter weather sharpened in Madrid in the autumn of 1833, the lovely young Neapolitan felt an intense and yet an intenser craving for the Spanish corporal's heart.

The King, as we saw, died on September 29. On December 17 the Queen-Regent, in spite of a snow-storm, set out from Madrid to cross the Guadarrama on her way to Quitapesares, her park near Segovia. Madrid is itself two thousand feet high, and the ground rises steadily towards the Sierra. The lowest pass over it touches on five thousand feet. At that time of the year it was covered in snow, deepened by the cold weather which met her escapade. She found the road impassable, and was forced to come back while some villagers were sent to clear it. [3] Next day they set out again. There was no woman in her suite ; only two officers, Arteaga Palafox and Carbonell, and with them the corporal, Fernando Muñoz, who sat opposite to her. As they drove over the frozen ground, the royal carriage, skidding, collided with a peasant's

---

[1] Slidell Mackenzie : *A Year in Spain.*
[2] Villa-Urrutia : *Reina Gobernadora*, p. 156.
[3] Biblioteca Nacional, Madrid : *Fondo X*, F. 89.

cart.   It broke the window in the royal carriage, and
the Queen's arm was cut by the broken glass.   Her
hurt was bound up with the handkerchief of her
lover.[1]   When they arrived at Quitapesares, she went
out for a walk, taking with her Arteaga and Muñoz.
Inventing an errand for Arteaga, she found herself
alone with the corporal.   At last her opportunity had
arrived : she told him of her love.

Next day they returned.   But Cristina had to
employ many devices to see her lover as she wished,
and she could employ none which did not look
scandalous.   And yet she felt she must have Muñoz
near ; so she appointed him *gentilhombre del interior*, or,
as it might be called, a groom of the bedchamber—
a post general in the service of the king, but hardly
applicable to a queen.[2]   In a few days they had become
foolhardy, and Muñoz wore on his breast the pins and
jewels of the late king ; he took his meals with the
Queen, and had an apartment in the palace.   When
she went out, she was never seen without him.

Her passion grew on her, but it could not compromise her sense of wifely virtue.   There was therefore only one thing for her to do ; and that was a
clandestine marriage, so as to save her position.   It is
true that if she married him secretly, she would be
receiving a stipend and exercising power on false
pretences ; but left with a choice between two kinds
of fault, she never hesitated.   Her love for Muñoz was
a natural passion, but in no sense an ignoble one : it
was the love of a generous and ardent nature, which
could contemplate nothing but the idea of being his
wife.   Neither could she bear to give up her children :
she felt she must be their guardian and their regent.
Who of us can withhold sympathy if the claims of a

[1] Bermejo : *Estafeta del Palacio.*
[2] Villa-Urrutia : *Reina Gobernadora*, p. 159.

warm heart blurred her sense of propriety in her relation to the government of Spain ?

It was no easy business to arrange the marriage. She dare not trust the chaplain of the Court, and her only confidante was a milliner, Teresa Valcarcel.[1] At last Muñoz found in Madrid a priest from his own village, Don Marcos Aniano González, in whom he felt he could confide. But no one was sure how González was to obtain a licence to administer the Sacrament. The Patriarch of the Indies refused to give him one, for he doubted his character. He then applied to the Bishop of Cuenca, but the Bishop did not trust him either. Why should so young a priest be so desperately anxious to bless a marriage ? But Cristina was in no mood for compromise, or even delay : she sent him to the Nuncio, who at last gave him his permission for one occasion only. That was on December 27. Next morning at seven o'clock the lovers were wedded ; another priest was found to assist, and two witnesses, López de Azevedo, who also had been in the bodyguard when he married above him, and the Marquis de Herrera. At last the Queen had her way, but in such circumstances marriage was only the beginning of complications. The first thing to do was to fight free of the witnesses. They were all in a very short time sent separately to remote parts of the country, and an eager watch was kept on gossip. This was in one case pushed to such an unscrupulous extreme that the editor of a newspaper, *La Crónica*, was exiled, and his newspaper suppressed, because on February 4 he referred to Muñoz, as one of the Queen's servants, driving her carriage.[2]

---

[1] For an account of this woman see Walton : *Revolutions of Spain*, ii. 50–55.
[2] Centon : *Epistolario de Domingo del Monte*. Habana, 1924.

Soon afterwards, Cristina found herself *enceinte*. This imperiously urged still greater ruses and precautions. On March 15 she went to Aranjuez; on the 28th to La Granja, and later to Riofrio. The cholera which drove so many people out of the capital was given as the excuse, and it was a very good one for the mother of two children, one of whom was the Queen, and on whose lives the safety of parliamentary government depended. But Parliament made its own claims, and with those the Regent, who was dependent on it, could not compromise. The Cortes had been convened, and were to be opened on July 24. How was she to disguise her state? In spite of the summer heat, she wore innumerable petticoats; but petticoats or no petticoats, observant eyes could not fail to detect that her figure, since her last appearance in Madrid, was curiously altered.

Guessing suspicion, she hurried back to Riofrio; and there she remained till August 16. Then she returned to her daughters at La Granja. But on the 29th there was an outbreak of cholera at Segovia, which is only a few miles away. She therefore hurried back to El Pardo, which is only nine miles from Madrid, and again she made the cholera her excuse for seeing no one. On November 17, a little before midnight, she gave birth to a daughter. That same night the baby was driven out of the palace in a closed carriage and handed over to Señora Castanedo, a widow whose husband had long been in the employment of the sovereigns as administrator at La Granja. Ten days later the Queen was on her feet, attending a review of troops who were leaving to fight for her eldest daughter's cause in the north.[1]

[1] Villa-Urrutia : *Reina Gobernadora,* p. 160.

3

The war continued through 1835, now swaying in
one direction, now in another, while ministry succeeded ministry in the capital, Toreno, and then
Mendizabal succeeding Zea as heads of the Government. While the Liberal movement was developing
at Madrid, it was in danger of being completely
extinguished by the fighting in the north. But at
last, on July 16, 1835, Luis Fernandez de Cordova,
who had taken command of the army, vanquished a
Carlist general at Mendigorria. Don Carlos himself
was present in the village, and remained quietly eating
his bread while the engagement was hottest. But at
last he saw Cristina's soldiers entering the village, and
at this he hurriedly mounted, just managing to cross
the bridge which gave him his retreat before it was
captured.[1]

But Carlos, troublesome as he was, and even the
unsettled Parliament, were still secondary considerations to the Regent. She had come from Aranjuez
to close the Cortes on May 29, but she returned the
same day. On July 8 she again passed through
Madrid, arriving at La Granja three days later.
She was expecting another child, and determined
this time to keep herself still more cautiously
from the public eye. On July 17, therefore, a
royal order was issued suppressing the customary
visits of homage. But to hide was hardly less pre-
judicial to Cristina than to be seen. If she kept out
of sight, there was not a single person in the Court
who did not guess the reason. The word went round
that she was secretly married and openly *enceinte*.
The vain devices which the Queen employed to
hide her pregnancy were rendered still more useless

[1] Mendigorria : *Memorias*.

by the demands made on her mother's heart by th
baby already born.   Every evening that the Cour
was at La Granja, Cristina and Muñoz left the palac
for Quitapesares.   Every evening the nurse Cas
tanedo came with her charge from Segovia.   Th
sumptuousness in which the nurse lived, the guard
who went out to explore the road before she started
and a thousand other little indications, ill-disguised
made it so plain to whom the baby belonged, that th
very street boys of Segovia called out as she went b
that she was the daughter of the Queen.

Little as the Queen liked it, considering her con
dition, she was forced by Toreno, then Prime
Minister, to move from La Granja to Madrid in orde
to be present at a great function on August 12.   Ther
again she immediately retired to El Pardo, and
waited again in secret for her delivery.   The new
baby, a daughter also, was born likewise at El Pardo
on November 8, 1835.[1]   A third child, a son, wa:
born in 1838, and another daughter in 1840.

Meanwhile political schemes were ripening in
Madrid.   Mendizábal, anxious to raise money agains
the Carlists, suppressed the religious houses and confis-
cated their property—making, however, an exception
in favour of those whose object was to teach the poor
or to tend their sick.   But the measure brought in
only a small sum ;   for, as is not unusual in such
cases, private rapacity left little for the State,[2] and
the next year Mendizábal fell from power, handing
over the ministry to a moderate called Isturiz.   No
sooner had Mendizábal fallen than he began an
unscrupulous intrigue which led to a sensational attack
upon the Regent and her man.

[1] According to the *Guía de Grandeza.*
[2] Pedro Aguado : *Historia de España.*

4

In July, when she arrived at La Granja, she began to receive anonymous letters which made her fear that an attempt would be made to kidnap her daughters.[1] The plan, however, was a subtler one. Making use of the Masonic Lodges and an agent called Barrios, Mendizábal succeeded in corrupting the sergeants of the bodyguard, so that they should force their way into her presence, and compel her to sign a new Constitution.

A trumpet sounded, and the guard entered the palace. The Regent, with the Duke of Alagon and some ladies-in-waiting, hearing an uproar, cried out, "What is the matter? What is happening? What do these people want?"

Someone answered, "The guard is coming up to capture the Queen."

"Open the door and let them come in," said she.

After this no one knows exactly what happened. The stories conflict. According to one, two or three men entered. They found themselves in a room where the ceiling was being repaired. They saw Her Majesty, sitting at a marble-topped table with candlesticks, in a dress of simple white. One sergeant came forward and said, "*Señora*. It is the will of the nation that Your Majesty signs the adjoined decree which re-establishes the Constitution of the year 1812." The Queen naturally demurred. One sergeant threatened to cut her hand off; another threatened the life of Muñoz.[2]

The other account says that the sergeants found the Queen with the Minister of Justice and several courtiers. She asked the intruders what they wanted.

[1] Villa-Urrutia : *Reina Gobernadora*, p. 260.
[2] *Los sucesos de la Granja*. Madrid, 1864.

One of them, Gómez, answered, " That for which we have been fighting for three years in the Basque Provinces."

" You were fighting," said the Queen, " for the rights of my daughter."

" And for liberty," said Gómez.

" Yes, my men," said the Regent, " for liberty, for liberty."

The sergeant questioned whether they had got it.

" Do you know what liberty is ? " asked Cristina. " Liberty is that the laws should be applied, and respect and obedience given to constituted authority."

Gómez began a political argument as to whether or not the policy of Isturiz meant liberty. The Regent asked him if he had read the Constitution. He cited a clause which insisted that in the case of a Royal minority there should be five regents. The wrangle continued, and at last they threatened to shoot Muñoz before her face.

Where was he ? As they well knew the strength of the feeling against him, it must be supposed that the sergeants' mutiny was directed at him, and that he had fled from the Regent's presence. But how was he to escape ? He managed to hide himself in the great underground passages which bring the water to the famous fountains, and to pass along them into safety in the woods above. For the Palace of La Granja opens immediately on a heavily wooded park, surrounded by a high wall which it is not impossible to scale. On the other side of this wall is the open forest leading to the heights of the mountain.

But whether Muñoz was safe or not, the Queen could not yet know. And the threat was too much for her. The soldiers were entirely out of hand, and there was an ugly spirit in them which might lead to general massacre at any moment.[1]   She signed at last the following decree :

> " As the Regent of Spain, I ordain and command that the Constitution of 1812 should be promulgated until the nation is united in the Cortes to manifest its will, or enacts another Constitution.   San Ildefonso, August 13.
> " I THE REGENT."

Cristina was by no means vanquished.   She soon had Muñoz back, though from that time forward he did not dare to appear with her in public.   In fact, he hardly ventured out of his rooms in the palace, which were known henceforth as the attics of Muñoz. As for their two daughters, these to avoid public scandal had been sent away to Paris at the beginning of 1836.[2]   The next year was to see Spain served with one of its new Constitutions, which is always a dainty dish to set before a Spanish king or queen.   To prepare it this time, as we have seen, history had thrown in such strong ingredients as a dynastic war, a queen's clandestine marriage, the concealment of her children's births, an embittered minister, a plot ripened in the lodges of a secret society, a mutiny in the royal palace, and a signature obtained by violence and menace.   The system which allowed great affairs of State to hang on emotional episodes in the life of royal persons was still to centre on the Spanish throne the political intrigues of Europe.

5

From 1836 to 1839 all questions in Spain hung on the Carlist war.   Córdova and another General,

---

[1] Sir H. Maxwell : *Earl of Clarendon.*
[2] Villa-Urrutia : *Op. cit.*, p. 271.

Narváez, high in royal favour, disputed the leadership with Espartero on Cristina's side, and carried on such a violent intrigue that, when Espartero got the upper hand, she was forced to exile the other two. At the moment of Espartero's weakness, the Carlists became so strong that on September 12, 1837, they actually got to within twelve miles of Madrid. At this point Don Carlos issued a proclamation, in which he returned to an idea already canvassed, that his eldest son should marry the girl queen—an idea which in his obstinacy the year before he had contemptuously refused. " The hour has rung," said the proclamation, " when the conquering arm of the invincible Don Carlos will break the yoke of a handful of ambitious cowards steeped in all the most horrible crimes. The first general of the age, the victor of Morella, will soon occupy the capital ; and there is nothing to fear. All has been carefully arranged by the Northern Powers. The Prince of Asturias will occupy the throne of Spain which his father cedes to him ; the daughter of Fernando VII will be his wife ; and the august widow will return to Italy to enjoy what is rightfully hers." [1]

The august widow, however, was able to answer for herself. Madrid stood firm by her. Espartero hurried to her defence, and the Carlist army fled in disorder. It was in the next year that Espartero overcame his rivals. In 1839 his army invaded the Carlist provinces, and at last, on August 1, 1839, the Carlists came to his camp at Vergára and fraternised with his soldiers, finally signing a treaty of peace. Espartero, meanwhile, had been made first a count, and then a duke—the Duke of the Victory.

But though he was victorious in arms, the political interests of the country were with politics less radical

[1] Butler Clarke : *Modern Spain.*

than those of the new duke.   Another party, calling
itself the Moderates because it stood between Carlism
and Democracy, had won the upper hand at Madrid,
and enjoyed the favour of the Regent.   Narváez was
gradually recognised as the leader of this party, and
so he remained for nearly thirty years.   The history
of Spain is the history of his rivalry, first with Espartero, and then with another general, O'Donnell.
For so incapable were the civil ministers of Parliament
that Spain, in the interests of order, inevitably gave the
power to the only efficient organisers, and these in
such a great majority of cases were generals that
parliamentary government was not to be distinguished
from military dictatorship.   On them not only the
Parliament but the Crown depended.   Cristina was
soon to find that the saviour of her cause was her most
dangerous enemy.   She had now to pit all her
strength against the man she had perforce endued
with such high privileges and powers.   The Moderates
complained that she had been foolish in doing so.
But the fact was that she could not help it.   It was
the fault, not of her gratitude, but of his disloyal ambition, which made him so dangerous to her.   " I have
made you a count," she afterwards said to him.   " I
have made you a duke, but I could not make you a
gentleman." [1]

6

The son of a cart-driver in Ciudad Real, Espartero
had been born in 1793.   At the age of thirteen he
prepared to serve against the French, and at the age
of eighteen was a Lieutenant of Engineers.   In 1815
he went to South America, and stayed there till 1823,
receiving many wounds and amassing a considerable
fortune.

[1] Opisso : *Historia de España*, xxv. 9.

The *ayacuchos*, as the soldiers returned from America were called, were not altogether approved by the Spanish army. They formed themselves into a group with Espartero at their head.

He had been sufficiently prominent to receive command in Biscay at the death of Fernando in 1833; and firmness was the secret of his power. When he heard that General Escalera had been assassinated by his own troops, Espartero went to the place of mutiny. " Here is the general's grave," he said. " Here are the murderers ! " and one by one he had them shot.

It was at the same time that he entered political life as a Progressist or Liberal. His party had obtained control of the municipalities, and these in turn control the general elections even to this day. The idea of a free vote is not one which any Spaniard seriously considers. If the Liberals had control of the municipalities therefore, the Conservatives' hope was gone. They therefore advised the Queen to sign a municipal law, which would make the Crown, or rather the Ministry of the Interior, responsible for naming the mayors and other municipal officers.

Espartero was bound to fight this law. Cristina, who was rather weary of her Government, turned to him for help : he asked for a little time, and then met her at Barcelona. He said that the law was an attack on the Constitution, and urged her not to sign it. But she had seen by this time that she was better off in the frying-pan of conservatism : she therefore did sign it, and sent it at once to Madrid. From that moment he was her ruthless enemy. He defied both her and the Government, and established himself in absolute power. She fled to Valencia. After a triumphal entry into Madrid he followed her there, and with the object of ridding himself of anyone who

ESPARTERO, DUKE OF THE VICTORY
From an old photograph.

" I have made you a Duke," said the Queen, " but I could
not make you a gentleman."

could cross, or even dispute, his will, he decided to deprive her of the regency and banish her from Spain. The affair of Muñoz made his plot only too easy. The increasing family of the Queen had involved so many that concealment had finally become impossible. She must either pretend to be living a scandalous life, or face the fact that a second marriage had deprived her of the privileges of the King's widow. At last the ministers themselves had felt bound to speak to her, and each tried to push the unpleasant interview on to another.

Meanwhile, the feeling of outrage spread. The Regent's own sister, to whom she owed so much, had deserted her, and was intriguing against her at the Court of Louis Philippe. Her courtiers were outraged by the prominence of the family of Muñoz : they spoke of an atmosphere of " sensuality " ; they said that the young Queen learnt nothing, and what was she not to lose by being thrown into intimacy with brothers and sisters of such an equivocal and low position ? And who were the Regent's own companions ? Only one qualification was needed to be in Her Majesty's favour, and that was to be involved in the affair of Muñoz.

Such was the gossip of which the Duke of the Victory now made cruel use. He could attempt to blackmail the Queen. He could not weaken her loyalty to her husband or shake her promises to the politicians who supported the throne. Coming back to Valencia, he invited her to meet her new ministers in council. There the most radical of the ministers, Cortina, asked her to give up the principal rights of the throne, beginning with the words : " There are some, *Señora*, who believe that Your Majesty cannot continue to govern the nation, whose confidence it is said you have lost, and for other reasons which must be known on account of the publicity which has been given them. . . ."

The Queen said nothing, but the habitually gracious expression of her face turned to one of disdain. She then sent for the Crucifix and the Gospels, that the ministers should take the oath in their accustomed form. These expected her immediately to discuss their proposal. She told them she would give her answer the following day. The Duke of the Victory was commanded to remain with her. She told him that she had decided to abdicate the regency and leave Spain. There was a hot debate. " Let us have done, Espartero," said Cristina at the end. " My decision is irrevocable : I entrust to you the care of my daughters, and the defence of the throne. I trust in you to be religiously faithful to them, both as a general and as a Spaniard."

Next day she met the Council. Taking from a case a paper, she handed it to Cortina. " Take it," she said, " I much liked your manner of reading yesterday. This is my resignation : read it to your colleagues." He did so. The Council argued against the terms in which it was expressed : the writing, they saw, was not the Regent's. They induced her to modify the expressions. And they begged her to remain, Espartero even going down on his knees. Her resolution, however, appeared unchanged. But what reason was to be given ? " *Señora*," said Cortina, " as we cannot find any becoming reason to give for Your Majesty's resignation, I would wish that there was something definite about a matter which is discussed openly enough, and which in other circumstances I would deeply regret ; but to-day it would bring to an end the discussion we are carrying on." The Queen seemed not to recognise the allusion. " I am speaking of Your Majesty's marriage," went on Cortina. " Oh no," she said at once ; " that is not certain !" and succeeded in changing the subject. In the act she signed she began : " Considering the present state of the nation and the delicate state of my health," but the cause she gave was still loyalty to her political convictions : she could not concede to her ministers' proposals.

Finding herself alone, however, with her intimate friends, she showed them cuttings and printed papers with insulting references to her private life. There were those among her ministers who argued that if she was not certainly married, it was time she was. She allowed no abuse of Espartero, with whom she had amicably discussed the guardianship of her royal daughters. Of them she had now to take farewell.[1]

At night, before the children went to bed, she called them to her and told them that next day she was going away, and would not see them for some time. And then all burst into tears. Her health, she said, obliged her to try a change of air. Then, taking the little Queen in her arms, she spoke to her of the gratitude she should always feel to her subjects for the sacrifices they had made. She kissed and embraced the children many times.

" Mama," said the Princess, " we will go with you ; if not, shall we be left alone, and when will you come back to see us ? " The mother answered that she would soon return, and that those to whom she had left them deserved all their trust, and that while she was away they should obey and respect these persons as if they were herself.

Then, as she tried to tear herself away from them, she fainted. She turned back to look at them while

[1] Villa-Urrutia : *Op. cit.*, p. 505.

they slept, and gazed at them for some moments, weeping.[1]

Next morning, accompanied by the Duchess of the Victory, she went down to the harbour of Valencia, and in the company of Muñoz sailed for Port Vendres. Though she struck an English traveller as being just as " gay and *dégagée* " as when he had seen her at Florence eleven years before,[2] she found the opportunity in Marseilles to address a moving letter to the people of Spain.

> " My constancy in resisting what neither my duty, my oaths, nor the dearest interests of the monarchy allowed me to accept, has brought on the head of the frail woman, who to-day turns her voice to you, a wealth of tribulations such as the words of no human tongue can speak. Well do you remember them, people of Spain. I have borne my misfortune from city to city, receiving affront and scorn ; for God, by one of those decrees which men cannot search, has allowed that iniquity and injustice should prevail. Therefore, without doubt, the few who hated me have gone so far as to take the very flesh from my bones, and have cowed the many who loved me to offer as pledges of their love at the most a sympathetic silence. There were some indeed who offered me their swords, but I refused their offer, preferring to be myself the only martyr rather than to be condemned to read a new

[1] Biblioteca Nacional, Madrid : *Fondo X*, F. 89. Bermejo quotes the story in his *Estafeta*, and the Marquis de Villa-Urrutia introduces the quotation with a doubt in his *Reina Gobernadora* ; but the paper in the Biblioteca Nacional is confirmation enough, if any were needed.

[2] *The Times*, Oct. 28, 1840.

martyrology of the loyalty of Spain. I might have kindled a civil war, but it was not for her who had given you a peace such as her heart desired, a peace cemented by oblivion of the past, to kindle war ; therefore I turned the eyes of a mother from so horrible a thought, telling myself that when the sons are ungrateful, a mother should suffer unto death ; but she should not kindle war against her sons.

" So, passing my days in this fearful condition, I came to see my sceptre changed into a useless stick, and my diadem into a crown of thorns. At last I could bear no more ; and I put down this sceptre, and took off this diadem, to breathe free air, unfortunate, yes, but with an untroubled brow, with a tranquil conscience, and in my soul no feeling of remorse.

" Such has been my conduct, people of Spain. In explaining it to you, that calumny might not defile it, I have fulfilled my last duty. She who has been your Queen asks of you nothing more than that you should love her daughters and respect her memory." [1]

7

On July 19, 1841, Maria Cristina had changed her point of view : she then sent an emphatic protest to Espartero to be published in the national gazette. She declared :

" That the decision of the Cortes is a forced and violent usurpation of powers to which I neither can nor should consent ; that those powers continue ; that I do not lose nor renounce the rights,

[1] Donoso Cortes : *Colección Escojida,* pp. 266–70.

jurisdiction, and prerogatives which belong to me as Queen Mother, and the only guardian by will and law of my beloved daughters, Queen Isabel and Infanta Maria Luisa ; rights, jurisdiction, and prerogatives which exist and will exist in all their power, even though in fact, through violence, I am suspended and impeded in their exercise."

This was published in the *Gaceta de Madrid* on March 5, with a long answer from Espartero, pointing out that in her pronouncements, both from Valencia and Marseilles, Queen Cristina had given up her rights.[1]

But meanwhile, Cristina's champions had been at work in Spain. Recognising that it was to the possession of Queen Isabel that Espartero owed his position, they made up their minds to kidnap the little girl, and their attempt is one of the fiercest episodes in Spanish history.

When Cristina sailed from Valencia, Queen Isabel had been placed in charge of Quintana. He had appointed the Marquesa de Belgida to supervise her life. This Marquesa was actually a sister of the troublesome old Count de Montijo. The Marquesa de Belgida was a widow, and Montijo had died in 1836, after marrying a *cigarrera*. The new Countess de Montijo, though a friend of all the politicians, had given her allegiance to Narváez, and was therefore on Cristina's side. But the person immediately responsible for Isabel was the widow of Espoz y Mina, who won his fame against the French as the boy king of Navarre, and who had died in the Carlist war.

Cristina's champion was a young general, Don Diego de León. On October 7, 1841, he commenced his attack upon the palace. It was a rainy evening.

[1] Biblioteca Nacional, Madrid : *Fondo X*, F. 89.

Colonel Domingo Dulce, who was commanding the guard, heard an uproar in the courtyard. Balancing on the balustrade of the main staircase, he was shouting to the troops to come to the defence of the little Queen against her mother's champions. Below all was in confusion. Shouts of command, screams, curses, groans mingled in a wild clamour. What actually happened in the palace we know from the governess, who gives in her diary the most graphic story.

" At a quarter-past eight," wrote Doña Luisa Maria Vega, Countess Espoz y Mina, " when I was preparing to descend to Her Majesty's room, I heard a number of voices shouting ' *Viva !* ' as from the courtyard of the palace. As soon as I heard it, I ran to the Ladies' Staircase, and rushed down it, and, entering into the *galeria de cristales*, I found the sentinel of halberdiers, who asked me what it was. I did not stop to answer ; and still running as hard as I could, I arrived at the Great Staircase, where I at once saw that there was a rather large group of armed men in the waiting-room of the Leones, and that a guard of halberdiers was placed at the banister of landing with their swords drawn, receiving the first charge of the insurgents at the very moment that I passed behind them.

" Happily saved from that first peril, I went on my way, still running, and entered the gallery, called Camon, so as to reach the maids-in-waiting at the quarters of Her Majesty ; but before arriving at the door, I heard another volley, which was so close as to break some of the windows in the gallery. Reaching the door as best I could, I pushed it with the anxiety of one who might

well be killed, or wounded in the place I was
and found it locked. Two more volleys wer
fired while I was still hammering at the door.

"At last it was opened by the assistan
governess, who asked me what was the matter
and not being able to tell her more than I had
seen, we both moved into Her Majesty's room.'
There they found the two princesses, surrounded
by four ladies, some maids of honour, and
singing-master. "As soon as the little Queen saw
her governess, she rushed to her arms, asking in
great alarm, ' *Aya mia,* are they rebels ? ' ' Nc
Señora, they are not rebels.' ' Then who ar
they ? Do they want me ? Is that for us ?
All I could tell her was what was happening
on the staircase where I saw them fighting.

"This answer, not unnaturally, did not calm
either the Princess or her sister, whose state was
if possible, even more alarming than the Queen's
for she was shuddering in the arms of the assistan
governess, screaming, ' I want to know what i
happening ; I shall be quiet if they tell me.' I
was a sight to move the hardest hearts.

"I then heard from my assistant and the other
that the Princess had begun her singing-lesson
when she heard the first cries which alarmed me
and without realising that it was so great a
uproar, they immediately rushed to the window
and doors to lock and bolt them, rushing all t
the one room, where the governess had found
them. They gave the Princesses drinks of wate
to help them to recover from their terror. And
since the persons who surrounded them were con
vinced that their safety, and perhaps their live
depended on our remaining firm and quiet, m
assistant and I began to exhort them to overcom

their fear, and quietly to await the conclusion of the matter which, however terrible it seemed, we could all hope would end well ; and that in any case the peril would not be lessened by cries and screams. Our warnings, aided by the example of all those there, who were apparently calm, did to some extent quieten them, and we were able to get them to sit down by the wall between the two windows of the salon.

" Among the various scenes which took place before this time, the most touching was one of the little Princess's suffering. Tremulous and grieved, she went to the assistant and said, ' Inés, I want to tell you something, Inés ; I want to say my prayers.' And this she went on repeating between her sobs and screams. Then we all went into the Queen's bedroom, and I could not help feeling consoled by the tears I shed as I looked at those two innocent creatures who, full of fervour, begged Heaven that they might be protected and saved from a danger, the extent of which they did not know or apprehend as I did."

Yet why should the children apprehend their mother's return ? Diego de León, after all, was fighting in the interests of the Crown.

" After a little, one of the maids-in-waiting, who was waiting at the door of the salon, heard some knocks." So the governess's narrative goes on. " We listened carefully, and found that they were coming from the first story. We understood that the mutineers had obtained possession of those rooms, and that the blows proceeded from the breaking down of a partition, the wood of which we could clearly hear them sawing.

" It did not need much time to realise why
they were doing it, for it could be nothing else
than to find the entrance of the staircase which
led up to the State-rooms on the next floor. We
were full of apprehension that they would succeed
and that, except for two bolted doors, there would
be nothing to prevent them getting into the
Queen's rooms ; we thought it so likely that we
thought it best to warn the Princesses. I told
Her Majesty that the blows they heard showed
that they were breaking down a partition so as
to reach the staircase ; and if, as was likely, they
found it, we should have to let them through the
inner door, and that we should beg them not to
be violent if we opened it. And that if this did
happen, Her Majesty should ask them as quietly
as she could what they wanted, and that when she
heard the answer then it must be decided what to do

" At half-past ten it was possible to persuade
the Princesses to lie down, although it was
thought wiser for them not to undress, so as to be
ready for whatever happened ; and so as to keep
all together, another bed was placed in the little
Queen's room for her sister.

" But the children had not long been put to
bed when a bullet came through the window of
the bedroom itself, breaking the glass, and tear
ing out the hinge, remaining embedded in the
inner shutters. So that, if in the inevitable con
fusion which so sudden an attack caused to the
suite of the Princesses, they had omitted to close
the inner shutters, the ball would have reached
the little Princesses' bed, and perhaps wounded
or even killed them. The noise of the shot
terrified the children, who immediately returned
to the salon. But since they did not feel safe

there either, I remembered that I had seen a walled-up door in the Princess's bedroom, which they said communicated with the room which Don Francisco used to use. I went with my assistant to examine it, to see if it would be possible to get the Princesses through to that place, but we could find no tools ; and even if we had, and could have opened an entrance, we would have gained nothing except to get them a little farther from the staircase which they were so stubbornly attempting to reach.

" Meanwhile, the firing continued in various places, and from time to time one could hear a *Qui vive !* cried to the sentinels, and often a volley following the answer. So it went on till midnight. And by that time, the ladies-in-waiting had decided to take the Princesses over to a bedroom or passage, where the thickness of the walls could offer more security than windows opening on to the courtyard. The Princesses were no longer paying great attention to the shots being fired. They were more occupied with the idea that they had no dinner ; but indeed, there was no possibility of getting them anything to eat.

" At half-past one the two Princesses lay down on mattresses, and slept. ' *Aya*,' the Queen had said, ' send a message to the Duke of the Victory to come.' But the governess had shown her that that was impossible.

" At two o'clock a bullet from the *salon del teatro* broke the glass of the window. That room was so close to the one they occupied that they thought the bullet had come from their own windows ; and though the Princesses were safe from bullets coming in there, they might have wounded some of the suite. Then a suggestion was made. The Mistress of the Robes, looking through a keyhole, had seen two sentinels; thinking that they belonged to the mutineers, they intended to send by them a warning that a continuance of the battle might cost the lives of the royal children. The sentinels, in answer, asked them what they wanted.

" ' Tell the persons responsible that the bullets have come into the Queen's room. That she and the Princess are in great danger, and that I am acting as I am to cover my responsibility in the case of an accident ! '

" ' And to whom do you want me to say that ? ' said the sentinel, ' if I am shut up in these rooms defending the palace ?   I bitterly feel the position of Her Majesty.   I have wasted half a case of ammunition firing from these windows. *Señora,* the palace has been betrayed by the outer guard, and I have kept to my post here.   Where is Her Majesty ? '

" ' In her room.'

" ' And who is with her ? '

" ' The ladies of her suite.'

" ' And who has the key of this door ? '

" To this the Mistress of the Robes gave an uncertain answer ; but when he insisted on knowing who had it, I answered that it was in my power.   He then asked who I was, and knowing my name owing to the position he had the honour to occupy, he told me that he was sorry for the difficult position I was in.

" ' I do not feel my own difficult position,' I answered.   ' I grieve for that of the nation and of the Queen, which are most serious.'

" ' I feel the same,' he answered.   ' And for heaven's sake open me the door that I, defending

Her Majesty, can die with my companions at her side.'

" My first impulse was to accept this generous offer, but an observation which the Mistress of the Robes made to me caused me to reflect that the critical position of the Princesses would only be complicated if there was a fight to defend them in their own room. So I refused his proposal, and also that of the Commandant, that the Princesses should move to the rooms occupied by their defenders ; and promising to tell the Princesses of their loyal sentiments, we parted, and I returned with the Mistress of the Robes to take my place beside the Princesses, who were still asleep. The doctor who had visited them found them so little perturbed that he had contented himself with giving them a dose of antispasmodic medicine.

" From that time nothing particular happened till a quarter-past six in the morning, which was the time at which we discovered that the firing had entirely ceased. And we noticed only that the rebels had taken possession of the whole of the Galeria de Cristales, whom, by a little inner window, we could see passing from time to time, the most wearing their cloaks. At that hour the servants came, saying that all was over and that we should open the doors. But I did not consent, although I knew the voice of the man speaking, for fear it might be a stratagem of the rebels to enter Her Majesty's room. But a few minutes later the Guardian of the Palace arrived on the other side, and recognising his voice, the doors were opened, and we knew the happy end to this unforeseen and lamentable event." [1]

[1] Countess Espoz y Mina : *Memorias*.

The man responsible for the rising was General
Diego de León, a man of thirty-one. Though his
motive was loyalty to the reigning house, he was found
guilty and condemned to death. A company of
nobles surrounded the little Queen as she was taken
out for a walk, and begged her to intercede for his
life with the Duke of the Victory, now Regent. But
here the Countess Espoz y Mina intervened.

" Your Majesty," she said, " is a minor, and
because you are not recognised in law, you have a
guardian. What Your Majesty does without his consent is illegal. Call your guardian and tell him what
has happened. The tutor came forward, but Espartero persuaded himself that the state of feeling in the
people did not allow him to grant a pardon ; in a
few days, Diego de León was shot at the Toledo Gate.
And the young Queen of Portugal wrote from Lisbon
to commiserate with her sister in Madrid on the
truculence of anarchists.

A little later, Espartero led the child, now eleven
years old, to open Parliament. On November 8,
1843, she was taken to the Senate and seated on
the throne. The President and the Secretaries
approached, placing the Gospels at her right hand,
and the formula of the oath before her eyes. The
child arose, and placing her right hand on the book,
she lifted up her voice and swore, by God and His holy
Gospel, that she would maintain the Constitution of
1837, with eyes for nothing but the good and advantage of the nation. She was invested with the full
powers to rule. Her thirteenth birthday had been
the month before.

It did not take her long to learn her constitutional
position, for the warnings of Countess Espoz were not
lost on her. In the next year, 1844, the darling son
of the Carlist, Zurbano, had been shot. The boy's

QUEEN ISABEL II ON ASSUMING POWER
After a portrait in the possession of the Facoltád de Medicina, Madrid.

" After her thirteenth birthday she was invested with full powers to rule."

mother, and a deputation from her province, flew to Madrid. Followed by a crowd of sympathisers which filled the great courtyard, the mother threw herself on her knees at the foot of the grand staircase as the little Queen passed out. The cry of *Pardon, Pardon,* rang through the whole palace. But little Isabel was unmoved. " This is a thing for the ministers," she said coldly.

Her mother, who was with her, wept aloud.[1] For Doña Maria Cristina had returned to Madrid. We shall see how.

[1] Maxwell : *Clarendon,* i. 257.

VII

THE GREAT MARRIAGE INTRIGUE

> Redeem
> The time.   Redeem
> The unread vision in the higher dream,
> While jewelled unicorns draw by the gilded hearse.
> T. S. ELIOT : *Ash Wednesday.*

I

To change from the beautiful and brilliant Cristina to a spoilt child of ten years old was to dive into a shallow backwater.   Espartero could thank only his own rashness, if in a short time he was stunned by a collision with one of its hidden snags, or if in the slime on its edge leeches were waiting to suck his blood. The mood of the Spanish people is so swift and mysterious in its changes from patience to uproar, that to let loose into politics at such a moment a capricious little girl was to nullify the skill of politicians as completely as a covering of ice on the ground would nullify that of a torero who had just let a raw young bull into the arena.   It is difficult to see how the Regent could have gone over to the party which was hostile to the sovereign's power : it is equally difficult to see how the Duke of the Victory could acquiesce in a law which snatched success out of his party's hand.   But as Spain has continued to show, intrigue is more dangerous than compromise, and the little Isabel was a symbol of her country's heart both in its warmth and in its lack of discipline.

The little Princesses were both simple and affectionate ; they had a confiding openness which one often finds in children of the highest rank. When the Countess Espoz y Mina had been appointed governess, they would hardly let her out of their sight ; she was soon to be aware both that this was caprice, and that caprice, with extreme indolence, determined their moods from hour to hour. They were not stupid, but as Quintana wrote of them after Cristina's departure, they were young for their age, because nothing had ever occurred to train their attention. The slightest thing distracted it. "They can read and write," observed Quintana, "and know a little arithmetic ; they pronounce French well, speak it, translate it, and write it ; can conjugate a verb, know a little music and geography." [1]

This for ten years old was surely something. "Their understanding is clear and unimpeded," went on the tutor, "without any vice or fault in their faculties ; so that when they seek to fix attention, and give their interest to showing what they have really learnt, there is no exercise in which they do not succeed marvellously. But the lack of attention and interest is a grave inconvenience with which we have to struggle at all times." [2] Clever little girls, in a word, who had never done a thing for which they did not feel inclined.

Nothing obviously could have been worse for them than to remove them from their mother. But the Liberals were not content with that. They put them in charge of the Marquesa de Belgida, a sister of the turbulent Count of Montijo. They removed their earlier governess, the Marquesa de Santa Cruz, and not only removed her, they put her in jail. And then there came the execution of Diego de León, who

[1] Countess Espoz y Mina : *Memorias*, Introduction.
[2] *Op. cit.*

was acting on their mother's behalf. All this might have disturbed any little girl, let alone one who wore a diamond coronet while two duchesses held up her long train of crimson velvet.[1] And the Liberals could not keep the Queen and her sister even under the steady control of their own party : the children inevitably met aristocrats, and courtiers, of whom most, naturally, were on the Conservative side, and who soon produced an extraordinary complication in the relation of the Queen with her ministers.

After the fall of Espartero, the Conservatives allowed other Liberals to head a temporary coalition. The first of these was Gómez ; the second and the more important was Olózaga, a man who was the son of a doctor in Oyón, and who owed his rise to his brilliant gifts as a speaker. He had made his name in the patriotic societies of 1820. In 1830 he had been arrested as a conspirator and condemned to death. But he was not the only Spaniard who moved from prison to the premiership. From his prison he was actually helped to escape by the sister-in-law, afterwards the wife, of Don Carlos, the Princess de la Beira. She was won over by his handsome face and his romantic bearing ; and the way she helped him to escape furnishes one of the liveliest episodes of that sensational time. After Cristina's amnesty in 1833 he returned. Then his power as an orator rapidly placed him in the front rank. He spoke with immense power. Correct, sober, majestic, yet inspired, his harangues were listened to with such eager attention that at times his phrases changed the situation, or altered the government. His splendid black hair, naturally curly, outlined a face which in the excitement of his speeches was lit by passion.[2]

[1] Washington Irving : *Letters from Spain*, p. 75.
[2] Mendigorria : *Memorias*.

But Olózaga's gifts, phenomenal as they were, were soon to be brought to derision by young Isabel. On November 28, 1843, he secretly prepared a decree for the dissolution of the Cortes; in a private audience with the Queen he obtained her signature, and left the palace triumphant in the feeling that he could outwit the Court faction whenever he would. Next morning he received a shock. Isabel, who had evidently discussed his action with his enemies, complained that he had obtained her signature by assault. The ugliest insinuations were made against his behaviour. He denied the accusation, of course; but the girl insisted, and three weeks later her solemn declaration was read before the Cortes : " On the 28th of last month, Olózaga presented himself before me, and proposed that I should sign a decree dissolving the Cortes. I answered that I was unwilling to sign it, among other reasons because the Cortes had declared me of age. Olózaga insisted, and I again refused to sign the decree. I rose and turned to the door, which is on the left of my desk. Olózaga placed himself in front of me, and bolted that door. I turned to the opposite door : Olózaga again came before me, and bolted that door also. He caught hold of my dress and obliged me to sit down. He seized my hands and forced me to sign. After that he left, and I withdrew to my apartments." [1]

Olózaga's supporters said roundly that the child was lying. They said that when a commission of enquiry came into the room, Narváez whispered to an attendant : " Stand in front of the door so that they cannot see there is no bolt there." Domingo Dulce swore that when Olózaga withdrew, Isabel followed with some sweets for his daughter. But nothing could shake the Queen's statement, and Olózaga's enemies

[1] Ortega Rubio : *Historia de España.*

soon saw to it that he was forced to flee the country. A cry arose that Queen Cristina must come back.[1]

Her party had been adroit enough to win their battles, and in a short time Narváez, Duke of Valencia, was endued with a power that became virtually absolute. He had chosen as the instrument of his policy González Bravo, who at one time had been Cristina's worst enemy. It was another sign of cleverness to enlist so unscrupulous a warrior in her ranks ; and cleverest of all to reward and silence that unscrupulousness by sending González Bravo as Ambassador to Lisbon. On the afternoon of October 10, 1844, Narváez being Prime Minister, two impressive processions passed in different directions through the gate of the Atocha. The one which passed out followed the dead body of the Liberal tutor, Arguëlles ; the one which came in was the sumptuous escort of Queen Cristina, who in March had returned in triumph to her daughter. Doña Isabel was so anxious to see her mother, that when she knew the procession was drawing near, she left her pavilion, ran out into the road,[2] and pressed on to the very step of her carriage. The Queen folded her children in her arms and covered them with caresses. It was a scene which affected all who saw it, and brought tears to many eyes. Many of the ladies kissed the hand, the shawl, the robe of the Queen Mother : others clasped her round the knees. On every side there was an echo of joyous acclamation : " Long live Spain's guardian angel " ; " Long live the Queen of Heaven, Long live our Queen on earth." The demeanour of the mother was warm and tender ; Doña Isabel trembled as she moved ; her sister was struggling with forgotten feelings which

---

[1] Guizot : *Mémoires*, viii. 162.
[2] Washington Irving : *Life and Letters*, iii. 268.

renewed themselves in her young heart.[1]   With Doña
Cristina was Fernando Muñoz, who a few months
before had been raised to dignity as the Duke of
Riansares.   The Municipal Law which gave the
Liberals power had been annulled.   Cristina went
everywhere she would, with Riansares at her side, and
wearing on her wrist a bracelet that contained a
miniature of the King and Queen of the French.[2]

2

During the four years which Cristina had spent in
Paris, she had not been idle.   She had had Don
Carlos carefully watched at Bourges.[3]   She had added
two children to the four she had already borne since
she united to Muñoz ; but then a terrible fact had
assailed her.   She had, after all, not cheated the
Government in that affair : a marriage was not valid,
either in the eyes of the Church or of the Spanish
State, unless it met with the requirements of the
Council of Trent ; now, the Council of Trent did not
recognise a marriage where there was no authority
from a priest of the parish in which one of the contract-
ing parties lived.   When Cristina had said, " Oh no,
that is not certain," to the enemies who accused her
at Valencia of a second marriage, it had been therefore
the literal truth.   Devoted wife and devoted daughter
of the Church, what was she to do now ?   Her
Church did not fail her : she rushed penitently to
Rome, and the Pope relieved her conscience with a
dispensation.   She was then married in the eyes of
the Church ; though, since she did not mean to forgo

---

[1] Bresson to Guizot : *Archives du Quai d'Orsay*, March 22, 1844,
Espagne, 820.

[2] *Ibid.*, 1846, Espagne, 820.

[3] *Ibid.*

her interest in her daughters until they came of age, she managed to remain a widow to the law of the State. For without her daughter's permission she could not legally declare herself the bride of Riansares. The young Isabel withheld it from her accordingly till 1844.

Although Cristina's now hostile sister Carlota had been living in Paris with Don Francisco de Paula since they left Spain, they had not induced Louis Philippe to change his benevolent attitude towards Cristina. The King of France and the Queen Mother of Spain, uncle and niece, completely understood each other. The politics, on which they both depended, were in agreement. Louis Philippe had no sympathy with Carlist reactionaries ; neither had he any with such extreme Liberals as Espartero. The King's interests were with Cristina : he saw that she would have time on her side, he had no particular objection to Muñoz, and was she not through everything the mother of royal daughters ?

She had had her own tussles with Olózaga. As Espartero's Ambassador in Paris he had written to tell her of the horror which he felt, and which he expected her to feel, at the attempt of Diego de León. "I am assured," he wrote, "that Your Majesty cannot consent even a moment more that your name should serve as a banner to those who, profaning the immunity of the palace, have imperilled the life of the Queen and the Infanta ; and that it is my duty, without prejudice to others, to urge Your Majesty, on this occasion and with regard to such an unheard-of outrage, to make an announcement to the Spanish nation so that they may see the falsity of those who, attributing to Your Majesty the design of recovering the regency, take your name in vain to destroy by force of arms the government lawfully established."

To this one of Cristina's attendants immediately answered : "The Sovereign Lady, Queen Maria Cristina de Bourbon, commands me to inform Your Excellency that she sees no need to reply to your strange communication of the 12th instant, in which the facts are misrepresented, and the words of Her Majesty are falsified."

When Olózaga was appointed Prime Minister in Madrid, he attempted to influence the French Government against her. On October 12, 1843, he complained that she was in direct touch with rebels against the Spanish Government. Would the Government of France therefore expel her from French territory as soon as possible, but preferably not on the Pyrenean frontier ? [1]

"The Government of the King," answered Guizot, "is aware of its obligations towards the Governments with which it is at peace. It has always scrupulously fulfilled them, especially towards the Spanish Government. But it has other obligations to fulfil, above all to its own honour. Queen Cristina, when she left Spain, sought refuge in France with her closest kinsman—the surest friend of the Queen her daughter. We cannot refuse hospitality to the niece of the King, the mother of Queen Isabel. This hospitality will be maintained. The King after consulting his Council commands me to send you this answer."

3

But Cristina, apart from the question of Muñoz, and the intrigues of the politicians, had had another enemy hardly less redoubtable. This was her virile sister Carlota.

Carlota, finding that she could do nothing against

[1] Bermejo : *Estafeta del Palacio,* ii. 180.

Cristina at the Court of Louis Philippe, determined to see what she could do at the Court of Madrid.[1] Cristina, knowing that she had started, applied to Louis Philippe to prevent her crossing the frontier, and guards held up the carriage at the Pyrenees. She spoke to them with her accustomed force, but the carriage did not move. Then, said Carlota, in her strong voice : " We will not be held back by this new outrage. Let us walk." The soldiers dare not offer personal violence to the King's niece. And so, in accordance with the Eastern proverb, " Though the dogs bark, the caravan moves on," this redoubtable woman forced her way back to Spain.

Her object was to arrange for the Queen, and perhaps the Queen's sister too, to marry one of her own sons. Was not Doña Isabel now twelve years old ? In that very year, Louis Philippe, accompanied by Guizot, met Victoria, accompanied by Lord Aberdeen, at the Château d'Eu ; they had already discussed Isabel's marriage, and Carlota naturally thought that no better plan could be made than for the young Queen to meet her cousins often.

Queen Cristina, who had her own agents in the palace, knew what was happening. She could not communicate with Madrid openly ; but she knew that her daughter received fashion plates from Paris. Into one of these she inserted a letter for her daughter which Maria Luisa might have written to the Prince of the Peace. " My sister Carlota," said the letter, " is a real mischief-maker : there has been no conspiracy in which she has not taken part ; no intrigue but she has been at the bottom of it ; no act of my Government which she has not fought. Don't trust that woman ! She brings in her train misfortune and ruin ; her words are lies ; her protests of

---

[1] Bermejo : *Estafeta del Palacio*, ii. 180.

friendship are snares ; her presence is a danger. Ah, my daughter, hold in mind what you should hold in mind when your Aunt Carlota wants to win your soul and your heart ; when she insinuates herself into your confidence to deceive you ; when she claims from you an affection you ought not to feel ! " [1] Carlota's plan was checked. " I am in a rage always and everywhere," she confessed.[2] Yet, in spite of everything, the time was not far off when Cristina was to devote herself to her sister's plan. For just before Cristina's return, Carlota had died of measles, after two days' illness. She also was buried in the Escorial ; and never, wrote the French Ambassador to Guizot, was a coffin followed with less regret.[3]

4

Louis Philippe and Victoria, we said, had met at Eu in 1843. One morning after they had breakfasted in tents, the King of France and the Queen of England, each flanked by an advising minister, walked around the gardens of the Château. The King paused as if from weariness, and the four found themselves seated at a table. So had the King arranged the time to talk of Queen Isabel's affairs. She couldn't marry the son of Don Carlos ; but might she perhaps have the Duke d'Aumale ? On riper review he decided that that would be aspiring to too much, and so did Victoria. " *We* could *never allow that*," she wrote. The King did feel, however, that Isabel's husband should be a Bourbon of some sort.

" But why not a prince of Germany ? " said the Queen at this point ; and she breathed the name of Prince Leopold of Coburg.

[1] Guizot : *Mémoires*, viii. 182. Bermejo : *Estafeta*, ii. 181.
[2] E. d'Auvergne : *A Queen at Bay*.
[3] *Archives du Quai d'Orsay*. Bresson to Guizot, March 25, 1843.

The King answered her with " his ineffable smile.'
A Coburg, yes ; an excellent remedy. The Queen
had *taken it herself*, and it had *done her good*, he said
what more fit than that she should recommend it to
her sisters in Spain ! But there was a Coburg in
Belgium, a Coburg in England, a Coburg in Portugal
If there were a Coburg in Spain, France would be
almost in a ring of them. No, it would not do. The
Queen must really allow him to choose a Bourbon
that was all he claimed, and provided the Bourbon
was not his own son, Victoria came to entire agree
ment.[1] The contract seemed straightforwardness
itself ; though a caprice of nature was to make it
possible to evade the application even while exactly
keeping to the letter of the engagement.

Since therefore the suitor must be neither French
nor German, who should he be ? Not English, for as
yet no English royalty, even if one were available
would contemplate Catholicism. Not Austrian, no
Russian, for these Courts were still supporters of Don
Carlos. But what of the Carlist pretender, the Count
of Montemolin ? He had ruined his chance by
saying that he would marry Isabel only if he wer
acknowledged the rightful heir, in accordance with
the proposal of seven years before. But to that no
party in Spain could consent except his own. Nar
váez was determined that any move in that direction
must be absolutely suppressed. " If they hoax us,'
he said, " as they would, there is nothing for us to do
but throw up our hands." [2] There was still the
Crown Prince of Portugal. But much as the Spaniard
would have liked it, neither England nor Portugal
itself would tolerate Spain absorbing the whole penin
sula.

[1] Sir H. Maxwell : *Life of Lord Clarendon*, i. 254, 255.
[2] Fernández de Córdova : *Memorias*, iii. 108.

Then Queen Cristina, although she hankered after a French prince,[1] produced a candidate from her own family. It was her young brother, the Count of Trápani. It would be a moderate satisfaction to entrust her daughter to the care of that brother. If she had married her own uncle, why should not her daughter do likewise? The Court of Naples, it is true, was so much under the influence of Metternich that it had not yet acknowledged the accession of Isabel, but it would be a different matter if a crown was the game. Metternich might say what he would, but after all, it was not for Austria to dictate every marriage of a Neapolitan Prince, still less of a Queen whom he had not acknowledged. King Louis Philippe was delighted with Count Trápani ; Queen Victoria, and Lord Aberdeen, her Foreign Secretary, if they offered no support, raised also no objection. So suddenly an embassy was despatched from Naples to Madrid, with the double object of acknowledging the young Queen's accession, and obtaining her hand.[2]

The Court of the Two Sicilies regarded the matter as settled. Then for reasons they did not avow, the politicians of Spain, with Narváez at their head, assailed the innocent young Prince with calumnies. There had been from the first a most grave impediment to his candidature. He had been " bred up a Jesuit." [3] Now at that time, all the religious orders were banished from Spain, and everyone knew that the Jesuits were deemed the most insidious of them all. Louis Philippe had seen the impediment from the first. " But the way to make him popular in Spain," said His Majesty, " will be to *make him run away from the*

---

[1] Guizot : *Mémoires*, viii. 181.
[2] Miraflores : *La cuestión de la sucesión.*
[3] Lord Dalling : *Life of Lord Palmerston*, i.

*College and give out that he swears that he will have nothing
to do with the Jesuits.*"

" L. P. all over." So did George Southern, writing
to Lord Clarendon, sum up this little plan.[1] But the
playful King did not quite bring off the night escape.
The Spanish suspicions were deep, the calumnies
fierce. A Trápani for king, when a *trapo* was a dish
clout? A Neapolitan, when the Spaniards loathed
everything to do with Naples? A *Jesuit* on the throne
of Spain? " A Neapolitan boy, brought up in a
Jesuit College in Rome ! " (so Bulwer summed him
up).[2] Impossible ! The feeling was so violent that
the highest powers of Naples, France, England, the
Court and the Government in Spain could not combat their effects. Narváez told Fernández de Córdova to deny any rumours of the engagement so
openly that no one could think any more about it.
The pleasures of marriage were even described to
Doña Isabel, and Trápani was said to be utterly incapable of contributing to them.[3] So Queen Cristina,
with the rest, was baffled ; and there were no princes
eligible except the sons of her late sister Carlota.
Those princes were now intriguing with the aid of their
father. If they could rid the list of Trápani, their
success was ensured : the process of elimination was
complete.

But at this point Narváez fell and was replaced by
Miraflores. Miraflores, however, fell within the
month. Narváez returned to power, but only for
nine days. Then, in consequence of his suppressing
the newspapers, he in turn was forced to give way to
Isturiz, and fled to Paris. His final altercation with
Queen Cristina had been so violent that in the course

[1] Sir H. Maxwell : *Lord Clarendon*, i. 256.
[2] *Record Office F.O. Spain*, No. 698, July 8, 1846.
[3] Hon. F. H. Wellesley : *Lord Cowley's Papers*, p. 314.

it he had in his temper smashed a chair to pieces.[1]
ut no matter what ministers were in power, Queen
ristina could do nothing.   In spite of both her
ishes and her daughter's, Count Trâpani was de-
ared impossible.

Queen Cristina, however, was not yet prepared to
ave the way clear for either of her sister's sons.   She
ould above all have liked a son of Louis Philippe ;
ut that the King, in view of what he had said at
u, could not even allow her to propose.   Then she
ad fought hard for her brother, as we saw.   If she
uld not have him, she would go back and advise
e candidature of Prince Leopold of Coburg, a cousin
the King of the Belgians and of the Queen of
ngland.   That was what was urged by the British
inister, and Leopold's claims were energetically
ushed also at Lisbon, which he had arranged to
sit at this moment, and where his brother was
ready Consort.   On March 4 Guizot complained to
ord Aberdeen that Leopold had left Portugal, and
as contemplating a visit, perhaps a secret one, to
[M]adrid.   Meanwhile, Queen Cristina wrote direct to
e Duke of Saxe-Coburg Gotha, and asked for
[P]rince Leopold.   The Duke answered that in such a
[m]atter he could not run counter to King Louis
[P]hilippe, and sent a copy of Cristina's letter to Lord
[A]berdeen.   Lord Aberdeen showed it to the French
[a]mbassador, who communicated it to Paris.[2]

This had a double effect.   In the first place, Louis
[P]hilippe complained that he was being most unfairly
[tr]eated by Cristina ; that he had done all he could
[to] strengthen her brother's candidature, and that he
[d]eserved her confidence.   But then another and a
[su]btler suggestion presented itself.   Was it not implied

---

[1] Hon. F. H. Wellesley : *Lord Cowley's Papers*, p. 13.
[2] Bermejo : *Estafeta del Palacio*, ii. 664.

by the agreement with Victoria at Eu that if a Germa
Prince were proposed, the pact was broken ? If
German prince could be proposed, then a Frenc
prince could be proposed. Perhaps the way wa
open for the Duke de Montpensier to marry the youn
Queen.[1] But no ; England had done nothing t
support Leopold ; on the contrary, Lord Aberdee
had disclosed what he knew of Cristina's suggestior
So then a subtler plan was concocted. The Frenc
Ambassador in Madrid was able to suggest to Cristin
that if Isabel would marry one of her Spanis
cousins, *Montpensier might marry her sister Luis
Fernanda ;* and the Duke of Riansares, dining at th
French Embassy next day, was able to report tha
the two Spanish queens were delighted with th
suggestion, and agreed to keep it a secret.
Cristina could have that bond with the Court c
Paris, she would not be obstinate with regard to he
sister's sons.[2]

The French Ambassador in Madrid, the Count d
Bresson, did not write about this openly to the Qua
d'Orsay : he kept all record of what he did hidde
from everyone, except his King ; and certainly non
could expect him to mention his little plan to M.
Bulwer, his colleague from Her Britannic Majesty
the vagne colleague who, when he arrived in Madrid
had kept the Queen waiting while he went back t
the Embassy for the letters of credence he ha
forgotten.[3] Bresson did not like the British ministe
who looked so sleepy and who seemed so sly. Th
Frenchman complained that Mr. Bulwer's manner
were familiar, and familiarity breeds contemp
Besides, he mixed with the wrong people. " *S*

[1] Miraflores : *La cuestión de la sucesión*, p. 347.
[2] Bermejo : *Estafeta del Palacio*, ii.
[3] See *Archives Diplomatiques, Paris.* Espagne, Nos. 820, 82

alons sont mal peuplés." [1] But what did Mr. Bulwer say of M. de Bresson ? Mr. Bulwer said a dreadful thing for one Ambassador to say about another : that his French colleague was *middle class* ; and that like middle-class people raised above themselves was much inclined to be pompous ; that he was " given to play the *grand seigneur* with the punctilious pretensions which no real *grand seigneur* ever displays." [2] And more than that : " Take him for all in all, he was precisely the man whom an unscrupulous and able minister would choose as an able and unscrupulous agent, in a difficult affair." [3] The affair was difficult, was delicate in the highest degree.

For between the two sons of Carlota there was a distinction. The younger, Enrique, Duke of Seville, was gifted with the qualities which usually please an Englishman, and please a bride : his trouble was that he was a little too enterprising. Since his return in 1842 he had allied himself with the Liberal Party, which then, under Espartero, happened to be in power. Queen Cristina knew it, and regarded him as a danger—almost as a revolutionary ; and so naturally did her friends the Conservatives. They could not accept him on any account. Yet against his elder brother, Francisco de Asis, Duke of Cadiz, an even stronger disability was alleged : Queen Cristina, discussing him with the French Ambassador, had made the most pointed remarks about his rigid morality, and also about his voice and hips, and Isabel detested him [4] ; it was said, in fact, that he had not attained to being in the physical sense a man at

[1] Guizot : *Mémoires.*
[2] Dalling : *Life of Lord Palmerston.*
[3] Dalling : *Ibid.*, iii. 213.
[4] J. R. Hall : *England and Orleans Monarchy*, p. 369, quoting *Revue Rétrospective*, pp. 180, 181.

all, that *pour mettre les points sur les i*, he could no
consummate a marriage.

5

Yet Queen Isabel was very eager to be married
She had a temperament which even at that early age
was recognised as peculiarly warm and expansive
Guizot had even whispered to his king that there
was something in the physical exuberance of Spanish
princesses that made it possible for them to have an
heir before they had a husband. The Comte de
Bresson was keeping so close a watch that he was able
to send a message within two hours when the crisis
of potency had made itself apparent to Doña Isabel
and even to assure his master that she was not only
nubile, but that she was also *dans la meilleure condition de
nubilité*—whatever that may mean.[1] And negotiations were in still more urgent discussion when the
bargain between Victoria and Louis Philippe was
undermined on account of a change of government in
England. Lord Aberdeen left the Foreign Office ;
Lord Palmerston took his place.

Now, Lord Palmerston was not only a Whig. His
patriotism was impetuous, and furthermore there was
something about his methods which inclined foreigners
to feel that he was unscrupulous. This was the man
who, as soon as he came into office on July 6, 1846,
took up in a distinctly masterful manner the marriage
of the Queen of Spain. As a result of his enquiry,
he was assured that both Doña Isabel and her mother
preferred Prince Leopold of Coburg ; but that the
Tuileries and the Spanish Liberals were against him

[1] *La reine est nubile depuis deux heures*, F.O. France, Cowley to
Aberdeen, April 8, 1846.   Cf. Sir T. Martin : *Life of the Prince
Consort.*

The Liberals would prefer Don Enrique ; but the Tuileries appeared to be recommending Don Francisco. And so he wrote to Queen Victoria ten days after assuming office.[1]

Two days later, he had taken affairs into his own hands. In one of the most reckless letters ever signed by a Foreign Secretary, he denounced the " grinding tyranny " of the Conservatives of Spain ; and he went farther : he put Leopold of Coburg first among the candidates for the hand of Doña Isabel. He not only sent this letter of July 19 to Madrid to the British minister : he even thought it would be a tactful way of showing Paris what he felt if he handed a copy of it to Count Jarnac, the French Ambassador in London.[2]

Amazed at such effrontery, Jarnac hurried a copy over to Paris, where Guizot and his King, always deeply suspicious of Lord Palmerston, believed that he, in support of the party of Espartero, had seduced the Queen of England to break her promise. Victoria had never thought of such a thing : " *Neither she, nor her late, nor her present Government,*" as Lord Clarendon wrote to Lord Brougham, " *ever did or said a single thing to promote the marriage of a P. of Coburg with the Q. of Spain.*" [3] Victoria, at any time of her life, would have died sooner than depart a hair's breadth from any promise she had made. In fact, her feeling was that she herself had been duped. But Guizot and the King did not realise that : forgetting that they had promised not to marry Montpensier till Isabel had children, they thought they could give a French Roland for the English Oliver. They sent a copy of Palmerston's despatch to Queen Cristina, who felt

[1] *Queen Victoria's Letters*, 1st Series, ii. 90.
[2] Dalling : *Life of Lord Palmerston*, iii., chaps. vii, viii.
[3] Sir H. Maxwell : *Op. cit.*, i. 271.

even more strongly. When she saw that Lord
Palmerston had denounced her own supporters as
tyrants, she felt that it was time in her own interests
to abandon any thought of a Coburg. " *Les Anglais
et la Révolution nous ménacent,*" she said.[1] She summoned Bresson to the palace. She had already
hurried Miraflores to Paris to say that the marriage
could not possibly be delayed, and that Isabel must
have at once either an Orleans or a Coburg, for she
detested both her cousins.[2] Arriving there on July 20,
Miraflores saw the King just at the time when the
copy of Lord Palmerston's letter arrived from Jarnac.
Miraflores also saw Lord Cowley, who hurried back a
message to Lord P.[3]

That very English Minister was already thoroughly
aroused. The Spanish Liberals had him in their
hand, and he went from indiscretion to indiscretion.
He began by describing Don Francisco as a suitor
not to recommend ; and he hinted not obscurely at
the reason in stressing the manliness of Don Francisco's
brother, who was, he said, " the only Spanish Prince
who is fit by his personal qualities to be the Queen's
husband." He gave Bulwer instructions to press Don
Enrique's candidature in Madrid, and when Bulwer
answered that that was hopeless, sent back to the
minister a curt message that his business was not to
criticise but to obey.[4] He saw the Spanish Ambassador and openly asserted that Don Francisco neither
morally nor physically could satisfy a wife.

[1] Guizot : *Mémoires*, viii. 303.
[2] F.O. France : Cowley to Palmerston, July 20, 1846. Guizot
afterwards attempted to deny that Miraflores had spoken of the
marriage, but Palmerston answered that he happened to know
better.
[3] Miraflores : *La cuestión de la sucesión*, p. 349.
[4] Bermejo : *Estafeta del Palacio*, ii, 670. Dalling : *Lord
Palmerston.*

Now really this was too much. Was it for Lord Palmerston, asked the Spaniards, to pronounce as the sole authority on the responsibilities, the cares, the enjoyments of foreign queens in their most sacred privacy? They accused him of a shameless intrigue. They said that if he supported Don Enrique, it was because Enrique had entered into secret engagements in Brussels with Espartero and his party, and that England, personified in Palmerston, in giving him support, was cunningly exploiting him. The French police watching Enrique at Ostend saw him receive a great budget every day from England.[1] Espartero and Palmerston were believed to be in league : had not Espartero been received in London as a conquering hero when he was banished from Madrid? And how, asked Guizot, could anyone claim that the only prince fit to be the Queen's husband was one who was fatally compromised with the discredited party which had rebelled against the Queen and her mother?

Lord Palmerston had his counter-charge. He soon learnt the result of Miraflores' visit to Paris on July 20 : it was the arrangement—so consoling to Cristina, so promising to Louis Philippe—that, while Isabel should marry Don Francisco, her sister should marry the Duke de Montpensier. Thus, if Isabel had no children, Luisa Fernanda or her children would inherit. First cousins, if not actually brothers, might at the same time be kings in France and in Spain. The French, when they heard of the Coburg candidature, had naturally felt themselves free to push their own. It was certainly high-handed for Palmerston to dictate the marriage of any Spanish princess, but nevertheless he insisted, and he ordered Bulwer to insist that Montpensier should not marry Luisa

[1] *Archives du Quai d'Orsay*, Espagne, 829.

Fernanda till Isabel had produced a family. Queen Victoria, knowing how Palmerston had urged the claims of Don Enrique, complained on August 17 that he little appreciated how poor that Prince's chance was, and that Palmerston in any case had gone too far. Palmerston answered that he was hoping to get the Tuileries to support Enrique.[1] As for the marriage of Luisa Fernanda, which was now the crux of the situation, he did not mention it.

He was soon to be discomfited. Busy as Mr. Bulwer had been in Madrid, Count Bresson, supported by the Duke de Cazes, had been busier still. There can be no question that the Queen Mother was irresistibly attracted by the prospect of marrying one of her daughters to the dear good Piat, as Queen Victoria called the Duke de Montpensier. One thing was uppermost in Cristina's mind : it was that she needed the support of a strong foreign Court against Espartero and the party which had driven her out of Spain. It was for this reason above all that she had wanted the support of Louis Philippe ; it was for this that she had oscillated towards the Coburg marriage to obtain, through Bulwer, Queen Victoria's support ; it was for this reason that, at the advent of Lord Palmerston, she swung back to the idea of marrying her younger daughter to Montpensier ; it was for this reason that she absolutely refused to consider for a moment the candidature of Don Enrique, and that she ignored the disabilities of Don Francisco de Asis.[2] Her reconciliation with Louis Philippe was now ungrudging ; so much so that she lent herself to the sinister plan of marrying her elder daughter, even against the daughter's wishes, to that " wretched, imbecile, sulky fanatic " (as

[1] *Queen Victoria's Letters*, 1st Series, ii. 96–8.
[2] Guizot : *Mémoires*.

Greville calls him), the Duke of Cadiz. She asked him often to the palace : she threw him and the Queen together. Sometimes Isabel seemed disposed towards him, sometimes she would withdraw.

Don Francisco had also been uncertain, but when he arrived from Pampeluna at Madrid on August 16, the rough places had apparently been smoothed ; it was noticed that the royal servants had suddenly become exceedingly deferential, and Bresson could report that ministers, diplomats, and officials all paid him particular attention.[1] On August 28 there was a midnight council at the palace, and *The Times* correspondent guessed that something quite extraordinary had happened. Some say that there was a wild supper party : others that Riansares entered the Queen's boudoir, bullied her in the roughest barrack-room manner, and led her forth red-eyed to give her hand to Cadiz.[2] At all events, it was at once announced that the Queen had accepted the Don Francisco, that she was to marry him on her birthday, and that, on the same day, her sister would marry the Duke de Montpensier. Lord Palmerston was beaten, and so was Mr. Bulwer, who had said he was ill, though at the French Embassy they did not think that he had much the matter. M. Bresson had won a sweeping victory for Guizot and Louis Philippe.

The Queen of the French, in a gracious letter, announced it to Victoria. Marie-Amélie hoped that she would find in her new daughter the goodness and kindness of her parents, a daughter who would increase their inward happiness at the Tuileries, that inward happiness on which, she said, Queen

---

[1] *The Times*, Oct. 5, 1846, and *Archives du Quai d'Orsay, Paris*, Espagne, 828, Bresson, Aug. 27, 1846.
[2] Lytton Strachey : "Queen Victoria," *Times Literary Supplement*, Oct. 10, 1912.

Victoria knew what value to set. But the Queen of England was not to be drugged into acquiescence by these chlorodyne phrases. The news, she said, had caused surprise and regret, and she preferred the standards of sincerity.[1]

At first she had been inclined to blame Guizot [2] ; but what she sincerely felt about " that old white fox," as she now called Louis Philippe, she found ample opportunity to express to His Majesty's son-in-law, the King of the Belgians. " This is *too* bad," she wrote, " for we were so honest as *almost to prevent* Leo's marriage (which *might* have been, and which Lord Palmerston as matters now stand regrets did not take place)." The Queen was certainly very far from being amused : " We are extremely indignant," she wrote. " Moreover, it was done in such a *dishonest* way." In fact, the word for it was " *infamous.*"

Undoubtedly Palmerston also was to blame. " Certainly at Madrid he mismanaged it, as Stockmar says, by forcing Don Enrique, in spite of all Bulwer could say. If our dear Aberdeen was still at his post, the whole thing would not have happened ; for he would not have forced Enriquito (which enraged Cristina), and secondly, Guizot would not have *escamoté* Aberdeen."

The French argued that the Montpensier marriage was simply an *affaire de famille*. Victoria insisted it was not, and remembered that Louis Philippe had volunteered that it should not take place till Isabel had children. " How can we ever feel at our ease with L. P. again? " she asked the King of the Belgians, " Guizot's conduct is beyond *all* belief shameful, and so *shabbily* dishonest." The whole thing, she felt, was " sudden," " secret," " unhandsome," to put it in a

---

[1] *Queen Victoria's Letters*, 1st Series, ii, 101.
[2] Lord J. Russell : *Correspondence*, i. 120.

word, " disgraceful." [1]   There was even talk of war ;
for as *The Times* put it, the shocks of Mars were less
dangerous than the stratagems of Hymen. " Tell
M. Guizot from me," wrote Metternich in Vienna,
" that one does not with impunity play little tricks
with great countries."

Yet when all is said, Queen Victoria's expressions
are not quite justified. Louis Philippe insisted that
the Duke of Cadiz was in the *meilleure condition de
virilité*. And on such a matter, where is the final
evidence ?   Besides, Victoria knew perfectly well
that Lord Palmerston's procedures had aroused in
Paris a not unnatural suspicion ; she knew equally
that Queen Cristina would not accept Enrique ;
she knew therefore that there was no one left
except the Duke of Cadiz. Of Isabel's marriage
to him in the face of their mutual repugnance,
which is the real horror of the situation, Victoria
said nothing ; Louis Philippe said nothing ; even
Cristina—Cristina, the wife of Muñoz !—no longer
made a stand.

An argument surged to and fro between the
Chanceries of Europe, but it was over the question
of Montpensier, whose children Bulwer was ordered
not to recognise as claimants to the Spanish
throne.[2]

Though it is true that Louis Philippe had given a
guarantee not to allow this marriage till Isabel had
issue—and in this he broke his word—history still
supports his argument that Montpensier's marriage
did not matter to politics.[3] It is plain from his
published correspondence with Guizot that his in-

[1] *Queen Victoria's Letters*, 1st Series, ii, 102, 108 ; and Merimée :
Lettres à la Comtesse de Montijo, i.
[2] *The Times*, Sept. 25, 1846.
[3] T. Martin : *Prince Consort*, i. 370, 371.

tentions were honourable.[1] What did matter was that
there should be order in Spain, and there could not
be order in Spain if, at the head of the country, was
a self-indulged and passionate girl whose marriage
was a mockery. And it looked very like a mockery.
For whatever may, or may not, be said about the
consort's *condition de virilité*, he was no success as
Isabel's husband. She soon saw into what situation
she had been forced on that unhappy midnight.
Jaunty Lord Palmerston, and he alone, had really
taken thought for her happiness—and perhaps even
he would not have done so if he had not been in
league with Espartero.

For a short time, it seemed that Montpensier's
seed would be kings. While Bulwer sulked at Aranjuez, Bresson appeared triumphant at the marriage,
and his baby, not a year old, was made a *grand
d'Espagne* and the Duke de Santa Isabel : on the
darkness of the wedding-night at Madrid, the French
Embassy shone like the planet Venus through a rift
of cloud ; and the Duke de Montpensier was delighted alike with the bride and with the dot. But
it was *breve gaudium.* In the following year Bresson
committed suicide at Naples. In 1848, the great
sovereigns of France, with the Montpensiers themselves, were fugitives to the mercy of Victoria.
Twenty years later, Montpensier was to kill Don
Enrique. On the throne of Marie-Amélie, one of
Isabel's maids of honour was to sit ; but Isabel
herself in being deposed was to uncrown that maid
of honour through the Franco-Prussian War, which
still envenoms Europe ; and in fact, the Spanish
marriages from beginning to end spell horror.

[1] Revue Rétrospective : *Archives secrètes du dernier gouvernement,*
Paris, 1848, pp. 179–87, 194–9. Cf. *Quarterly Review,* Jan.
1868, " Guizot " ; and Stockmar : *Memoirs,* ii.

6

Yet Doña Isabel had her own family after all.
Mérimée, like Louis Philippe, was sure she would,
though *The Times* had doubted whether nature had
not vetoed the possibility. As for all the talk about
the Duke of Cadiz, that sounded to the ears of
Mérimée like a story made up by Bulwer. It was
hardly likely that such a thing should happen to a
race so fertile as the Bourbons. " *D'ailleurs, la reine
a bien des sujets fidèles qui le remplaceraient au besoin.*" [1]
But no one ever decided, and no one ever can decide
whether it was to her subjects' devotion that Doña
Isabel owed her heir ; and her throne, being set on
the quicksands of that doubt, tottered and tilted her
out to take refuge in the realms of the Empress of the
French, her former subject, after many storms of
mutiny and scandal. Of these some record remains.

[1] Mérimée : *Lettres à la Comtesse de Montijo*, i. 191.

VIII

QUEEN ISABEL AND REVOLUTION

This world accounts it stablest that the soft
Be whipped to show the face repentance wears.
MEREDITH.

I

THERE was nothing feigned, says Mendigorria, in the enthusiasm with which Madrid greeted the young Queen. "You would have been charmed," Washington Irving had written already to his sister, " could you have seen the dignified yet simple grace with which the little sovereign conducted herself." [1] The Queen, at seventeen, had all the privileges of fortune, wealth, and power. Although she was already extremely fat, and sometimes looked puffy,[2] she had still a rather attractive figure. Her rosy complexion, her quick and searching glance, the lively grace of her manners and with them all the distinction of her great race combined to attract the hearts of all those who came near her. She began to employ dress-makers from Paris, a habit that imparts to any attractive personality its own attraction. The affability of her manners and her bearing were always peculiarly kind. As a young and happy girl she had constantly on her lips the sweetest smile.[3]

---

[1] Washington Irving : *Letters from Spain,* p. 75.

[2] J. M. Sanroma : *Mis Memorias.* Washington Irving : *Life and Letters,* iii. 275.

[3] This whole passage is a paraphrase of Fernández de Córdova, *Memorias,* iii. 126, 130.

But she was capricious. Of other people's time and convenience she recked not. Every day her meals were served at a different hour, her visitors and even her ministers were received as she felt inclined. They might be kept waiting about the palace from noon till seven or eight in the evening. The high society of Madrid would meet in the waiting-rooms of the palace and chatter in a perpetual *tertulia* ; and as they waited ministers, making a virtue of necessity, settled affairs of State.[1] There were few so bold as to cross Doña Isabel in her wishes, which were as keen as those of a child—wishes so lively and so joyous that those responsible for her felt distinctly uneasy.

The police had once required to intervene in an affray which threatened her when she was out riding incognito ; and at another time the police, themselves, had fired at her, as in the evening she rode back in the dark from the quinta of the Countess of Montijo at Carabanchel. She herself, of course, was not at all disconcerted : that was the sort of adventure she delighted to relate. But there were other adventures about which she was not so open.

For this gay life Don Francisco de Asis had neither taste nor aptitude. He tried to subdue his exuberant spouse to his own mouse-like ways, but Isabel, who had long since realised what it was to be the Queen, had no idea of being a rodent. She left her consort alone and went her own way.[2] And she soon found congenial company with a handsome and dashing young officer, Don Francisco Serrano.[3] While on January 28, 1847, the Duke of Sotomayor became her Prime Minister, her mother, who disapproved of what was happening in the palace, went back to

---

[1] Fernández de Córdova : *Memorias.*
[2] Comtesse d'Avila : *J'ai voulu vivre ma vie.*
[3] M. Hume : *Modern Spain,* p. 396.

14

Louis Philippe, in whose Court Narváez was now Ambassador.

Meanwhile, political intrigue was hard at work. The Liberals naturally plotted to win back the power and behind them was the British minister. Mr Bulwer, furious at his discomfiture in the matter of the marriage, thought he might retrieve his position if he could make bad blood between the bride and bridegroom. There was certainly no love lost on either side ; and in Isabel's repugnance to Francisco, the British minister believed he had an opportunity, for he, holding it essential to his diplomacy that the Queen should have an heir, set all his hopes upon her intimacy with Serrano.[1]

In London, Lord Palmerston had Lord Clarendon at his side : impatient with Bulwer's blunders, they thought of replacing him by a younger and more handsome man, who would have more influence with the Queen. Lord John Russell, however, thought it would be more becoming if the new Ambassador were a married man with daughters of the Queen's age. Meanwhile Bulwer remained. And with Francisco de Paula and the Liberals, he intrigued inside the palace. When that plan failed, the Queen ordered her father-in-law to find quarters elsewhere.

In the summer of 1847 the Queen went to La Granja, while her husband still stayed in retirement at El Pardo. The bracing air made her spirits keener. Serrano and Bulwer kept her company, while she made excursions to Quitapesares and Rio Frio. Did she whisper of love to Serrano in the same garden where her mother had proposed to Muñoz ? At least there was talk of scandal.[2] They said she had loved Serrano

[1] Bermejo : *Estafeta del Palacio*, ii. 796. Villa-Urrutia *Serrano*, p. 69.
[2] Villa-Urrutia : *Serrano*.

nce she was first a budding maiden.[1] And Gonzalez
ravo challenged the handsome favourite to a duel.
ut duels are against the law, and their issue is un-
ertain.[2] So the plan which ultimately struck them
s sounder was to bring back Maria Cristina, who
uring her stay in Paris had made peace with Narváez.
arváez therefore returned and, breaking in upon
 meeting of ministers, told them they had been
ismissed. They answered him with such energy,
owever, that he compromised so far as to allow them
 resign.

As for Bulwer, Narváez said that he would have him
emoved from Spain, while he would have Serrano
 ot. But Serrano made his plans in time. He with-
rew his support from Salamanca, the rich Jew whom
 e Queen had made Prime Minister, and plotted for
arváez. Narváez, admitting that Serrano was an
lly worth having, retained him as a minister, with
 s friend Ros de Olano. As for Bulwer, Narváez
 pported him for a year. Then in a just fury at the
 inister's endless meddling at Palmerston's behest[3] in
 vour of the Liberals, Narváez approached the
 inister from behind, lifted him into the air with a
 ell-placed kick, and immediately sent him his pass-
orts. So fitly ended the Spanish career of this
 rvant of Lord Palmerston.[4]

Convinced in his turn that Narváez sought office
 r the sole purpose of speculating in the funds,[5]
 ulwer had done all he could to prevent the return
 f Narváez. He had had long talks with Salamanca :
 e even saw the Queen, and told her to have nothing

---

[1] Hon. F. H. Wellesley : *Lord Cowley's Papers*, p. 250.
[2] Villa-Urrutia : *Serrano*.
[3] Greville : *Journal of the Reign of Queen Victoria*, iii. 180, 181.
[4] Villa-Urrutia : *Serrano*, pp. 71, 72. Mendigorria : *Memorias*.
[5] F. O. Spain, 72, No. 698, July 8, 1846.

to do with Narváez. But Isabel was sufficient
mistress of herself to answer that she knew as well
he did what was becoming to her country.

And yet so far he had succeeded in his plan of kee
ing her and her husband separate, in spite of ever
thing. Queen Cristina had herself written intima
advice, more telling because it was salted with co
fession. " Perhaps I was weak," she wrote. " But
am not ashamed to confess a sin which repentance h
buried, but I never offended the husband whic
Providence gave me, and only when I was freed fro
all bonds of wifely duty did I allow my heart
cherish a love which I made lawful before God th
He might forgive me the secret which I kept from
warm-hearted people, for whose felicity I have ma
so many sacrifices. But I do not regard it as a
offence to have sought to level my high position to a
honest lowliness. In obeying my modest instincts,
sought that God should take them under His prote
tion, that the Spanish people should never speak ev
of my inclinations. I say these things, because rel
tions founded on caprice or other unworthy motiv
neither shield nor authorise doubts which invi
enquiry.

" It is not my intention to be inquisitive about yo
separation. I hear what both of you say, and since
know the one and have rocked the other in her crad
I believe that both should pass over quarrels, an
embark on a peaceful life which is as advisable for yo
as it is fitting for the Spanish people ; and you wi
avoid hard criticism and severe censure in the counc
of the leading nations of Europe. . . . I am n
hurrying to Madrid, because my presence might gi
place to incidents which would make things wor
instead of better : to me, as to most others, many a
ungrateful. I beg you, as your loving mother, that

iew both of your own good and of the peaceful order
of the Spanish people, you should return to your
husband's side, to whom also I am writing in the same
ense, while I am begging Heaven to grant you
happiness, that God may inspire the men who give
ou bad advice with more patriotism and common
ense." [1]

Patriotism and common sense so far prevailed that
he ministers sent an emissary, Benavides, to Don
Francisco de Asis. " This separation cannot go on
ndefinitely," said Benavides, " for it is of advantage
neither to the Queen nor to Your Majesty."

" I know," answered the King Consort, " but they
have sought to outrage my position as a husband,
which is all the worse, because I did not make great
demands ; I know Isabelita does not love me, and I
forgive her ; because it was reasons of State, and not
nclination which made our marriage ; and I am all
he more tolerant because I have no love for her
either.[2] I did not mind taking the road of dissimula-
ion. I have always been inclined to keep up appearances to avoid this disagreeable break ; but Isabelita,
either because she was franker or more passionate, was
unable to fulfil this hypocritical duty as a sacrifice for
he good of the nation. I married because I ought to
marry, and because I was flattered with the idea of
being King. I went into the thing for what I could
get out of it, and I ought not to spit in the face of the
fortune which came my way : I went into it meaning
o be tolerant, that others should be tolerant with me.
would never have been put out by the presence of a
favourite."

[1] Bermejo : *Estafeta del Palacio*, ii. 800.
[2] Greville, however, says that Don Francisco wanted Pacheco
o summon a council to which he, the Consort, could accuse his
Queen of infidelity. *Op. cit.*, iii. 78.

"Will Your Majesty allow me to observe one thing?" said Benavides. "What has just been said abou tolerating a favourite is obviously in contradictio with your stand to-day ; because, as far as I can see there is no obstacle so great in the way of the under standing we desire than the presence of Genera Serrano."

" That I do not deny," said the King frankly ; " bu it is because Serrano has insulted me. He is a littl Godoy ; but Godoy at least did first make advance to Carlos IV so that he might enjoy the favour of m grandmother. I was not born for Isabelita nor sh for me ; but the people must not be given tha impression. I will be tolerant, and I am ready t agree as soon as Serrano's influence ceases." [1]

And so it appears were things arranged. At leas Isabel had several children, though she and the Kin Consort were never much together ; and lived indeed, even when in the same palace, in differen wings of it. The first of these children died three day after he was born ; and it was believed that he wa strangled.[2] When the Queen's second child, Doñ Isabel, was born in 1851, the Queen would not let th baby out of her sight. The child was presented to th Virgin of the Atocha. As the Queen left the church a priest presented a petition. As she stooped to tak it, he stabbed her with a dagger in the breast. Th Queen, fainting, cried : "My child, care for m child ! " But this time the child was safe, and thoug the Queen pleaded for the assassin's life, he wa garrotted a few days later.[3]

Six more years passed before Isabel bore her sor His birth was greeted with national rejoicings, an

[1] Bermejo : *loc. cit.*
[2] Butler Clark : *Modern Spain.*
[3] Hume : *Modern Spain*, pp. 408, 409.

seemed to restore the Queen's popularity. Yet gossip was even fiercer than ever ; and the officer, Puig Moltó, on whom the Queen had been smiling, was hurried into exile, but not it appears before his work was done. Two more children were born, both daughters. And about all these there was as much gossip as over the children Cristina had borne to Muñoz.

2

As for the fortunes of the throne, these were for the present safe in the hands of the Duke of Valencia ; and, indeed, it was well for the throne that a man as strong as he was then in power. It was a time for a man who spat fire like a machine-gun ; for otherwise Spain would have been overwhelmed by the tumult of revolution which in 1848 crowded over Europe. England had her Chartist revolt. Metternich was removed in Austria, Louis Philippe was dethroned, the soldiers of Frederick William were attacked by the mob in Berlin, and he himself forced to make unexpected concessions. Sicily separated from Naples, calling to her throne Carlo Alberto. King Bomba accepted a constitution in Naples. Savoy made war on Austria. The Pope fled from Rome. And on March 26 a revolution was attempted in Madrid.

Thinking that all was well, the Queen had gone for her customary outing in the Prado, when, suddenly at six in the evening, there was a great confusion. Big black clouds had taken the light from the sky. Carriages drove past, some at a smart trot, some at a gallop. Women screamed ; men shouted to them to keep calm ; others came up with news that increased the fright ; ladies who stumbled as they started to flee were knocked and trampled down, and in ten minutes all that was left of the fashionable parade in the Prado were sticks, umbrellas, and hats.

Somehow the Queen found her way back to the palace. Narváez, as he passed down the Calle de Jacometrezo just escaped assassination : but he held firm and saved the situation ; he had, in his own words, " been given a free hand to hold the stick and strike hard."

Narváez was a man of impetuous courage in the face of all sorts of risks : at the Battle of Arlabán he had ridden almost on to the muskets of the enemy ; yet he was suspicious and distrustful to the last degree. When he entered the palace—and he began to spend much of his time there—he would gaze full into the faces of the servants, and look them up and down as though to read their most secret thoughts. As for those who waited on the Queen, he had a list made of them, women as well as men, down to the very humblest : he demanded from the police an exact account of the antecedents of every one of them, and ordered watch to be kept on all. He was particularly annoyed at the nun, Sor Patrocinio, who talked to the Queen rather platitudinous pieties [1] which many thought to be political plots ; Narváez was equally suspicious of Padre Fulgencio, in whom, after the same fashion, the King Consort put his trust. Hearing that the King was interfering with the army, Narváez sent Fernández de Córdova to arrest him. When this officer refused and resigned, Narváez himself, who was as uncompromising with kings as with ambassadors, went to the palace and placed the Consort under arrest in his own apartments, leaving a sentinel with fixed bayonet at the door. [2]

The Duke had a special aptitude for presiding at

[1] Ortega Rubio : *op. cit.*
[2] *Enciclopédia Universal*, xxxvii. 1124.

NARVÁEZ, DUKE OF VALENCIA

" Narváez was as uncompromising with kings as with ambassadors."

Councils of Ministers. His demeanour was habitually solemn, yet at times the gravity of his " fiercely expressive countenance," as Bulwer called it, would suddenly dissolve in a violent outbreak. No minister ever dared to interrupt him while he was speaking ; but if the discussion wandered from the subject, he would take steps—and always with much skill—to bring it back to the point. Sometimes, when his Andalusian temper came out, he would light on some characteristic witticism, more eloquent and more decisive at such times than the best of formal speeches. He particularly disliked the criticism of the newspapers. And conspiracy remained his bugbear.[1]

He did indeed preserve the country from the uproar of revolution. But he was impressionable, unscrupulous, and arbitrary ; and his distrust begat distrust, so that in the end his own party dissolved in discord. Yet through all the uproar of the time, it was he who propped the throne and so gave Spain stability.

His position in Madrid was immense. He married Alexandrine Marie Tascher de la Pagerie d'Arzoinville, a cousin of the Empress Josephine, and brought her back to almost the position of a royalty in Spain. Believing in the magnificence of a great tradition, he furnished a sumptuous palace, filled his stables with horses, employed an excellent cook and a host of servants. For in spite of his suspicions, he was a large-minded and generous man, with a sincere piety and the most devoted heart,[2] which much unscrupulousness could not chill, and which the ugly look in his face did not altogether hide.

In 1851 a group of his own Conservatives, headed by Bravo Murillo, forced him to flee the kingdom.

[1] Mendigorria ; *Memorias.* iii. 149, 151.
[2] Mendigorria : *Ibid.* Lord Malmesbury : *Memoirs of an ex-Minister.*

But " I am not beaten yet," he wrote in his decisive characters to the Countess of Montijo. " I thank God that He has given me a *head* and a heart and luck," [1] and he promised to make use of them. The Conservatives who took his place attempted a reconciliation with the Church. But politics became a ferment in the next few years.

In May 1852 the Queen wrote from Aranjuez to Bravo Murillo, enclosing a petition from generals and politicians asking her not to follow the advice of her ministers. " They want to complicate the situation," she wrote. " I shall relax it." [2] There had been a question of a *coup d'état* after that of Louis Napoleon ; but Spain did not need one. France, to obtain order, wrote Juan Alvarez to Mendizábal, had been content to resign her liberties. But no one, said Mendizábal, disputed the monarchy of Isabel : there was no turbulent crowd which threatened anarchy. There had been no February 24, and there need be no December 2.[3] " The Spanish people, a model of good sense and prudence, respect the laws and authorities ; the Spanish people live content with the monarchy, which is the sovereign instinct of its soul, and with representative government, which is the supreme logic of its reason." [4] To a happy and obedient nation, he concluded, a *coup d'état* can never be anything but a trumpet-call to war.

This letter is extremely important : it expresses the dominant fact, that under the monarchy of Isabel, Spain was calm, no matter how busy intrigue might be in Madrid. Nevertheless, after ten years of Con-

---

[1] MS. in Palacio de Liria.

[2] Biblioteca Nacional, Madrid : MSS. Legajo 18699.

[3] Feb. 24 was the date of Louis Philippe's fall ; Dec. 2 the *coup d'état* of Louis Napoleon.

[4] Biblioteca Nacional, Madrid : MSS. Legajo 18699.

servative government, the country could restrain itself
no longer.   In 1854 the throne was once again shaken
by a revolution.   The people of Madrid had been
worked up to a sense of outrage, and after some sharp
fighting the Liberals, under old Espartero, and a
younger general, a native of Ireland, O'Donnell,
seized the power.   Isabel knew that she must give
in to them.   On August 26 she published a manifesto,
admitting that owing to bad advisers she had made
mistakes, and that she sympathised with the will of
the nation.   Mendigorria says that " in those terrible
moments she conducted herself in a truly admirable
manner, and was inspired only by the most ardent
desire to tranquillise the country." [1]   From that time
her portrait, with those of O'Donnell and Espartero,
was seen everywhere.   Three days later Espartero
made his triumphant entry into Madrid.[2]

Accusations meanwhile had been concentrated
on Cristina and Riansares.   The extreme Radicals
wanted to impeach her for peculation : it was the
moment for great railway contracts, and they accused
both her and Riansares of unpleasant tricks in connection with them.[3]   They threatened to put her into
jail until she repaid the seventy million reales, out of
which they said she had swindled the Treasury.[4]   A
violent sheet, secretly printed and secretly distributed
even in the palace itself, brought home these charges,
the worst of which was a copy from a contribution to
The Times.

" Of Queen Isabella herself, what shall we say ? "
asked *The Times*.   " She had long fallen as a woman ere
she fell as a Queen.   It is more than questionable if

[1] Fernández de Córdova : *Memorias*, iii. 374.
[2] Angel R. Chaves : *Ilustración Española*, Nov. 30, 1907.
[3] Cristino Martos : *La Revolución de 1854*, pp. 97–9.
[4] F.O. Spain, 72, No. 845, July 19, 1854.

all the trickery of her ministers, all the violent acts of her military agents, would have succeeded in rousing the country against her throne had she been but true to herself. We denounced her in the period of her power as guilty of high treason against the cause of virtue and morality, but in the hour of her humiliation we cannot forget into what hands it was her misfortune to fall. What counsel was she to receive from the lips, what example from the conduct of her mother? What support, what protection, what check from the husband into whose arms she was tricked by an artifice which will remain infamous, even among those of political infamy. Of a truth, the Spanish marriages have borne good fruit to those who planned them, and those who were the objects of their plans." [1]

But since Isabel had given in to the Liberals, the fury of the people was concentrated on Cristina. They howled against her as a cheat and robber,[2] as they had talked of her daughter's vice and egoism. But neither Espartero nor O'Donnell was prepared to hand her over to the mob. With one of the swift changes of attitude characteristic of the Spaniard, to assert now his impatience, now his chivalry, both the new generals were determined to let the Queen Mother escape as she deserved. " I shall leave the country as a Queen, or else I shall not leave it," she said herself.[3] She had offered her house for charity : the mob wanted only to burn it ; they wanted to seize her property and bring her to trial, but she intended to compromise neither herself nor her husband. The new Government did in a moment of weakness allow themselves to present to Isabel these expressions

[1] *The Times*, July 25, 1854.
[2] Record Office, F.O. Spain, 72, No. 845, July 19, 1854.
[3] M. Hume : *Modern Spain.*

QUEEN MARIA CRISTINA IN HER MATURITY

" I shall leave the country as a queen," she said,
" or else I shall not leave it."

of the mob's fury against her mother. Isabel, however, had gone as far as her heart would allow. She
burst into bitter weeping. " You can do what you
like with Doña Maria Cristina," she said, " if the
people insist on your giving them a victim, but you
will not compel a daughter to sign the proscription of
her mother. That disgraceful step would dishonour
me in the eyes of the world and of history, and it is
astonishing that you could think I could agree to anything so outrageous." [1]

The Queen then in a letter of great dignity stated
her position both as queen and daughter : " It is the
deliberate will of my dearest and most beloved mother
solemnly to renounce, as henceforth she does renounce,
all pensions from the State, and all the arrears and
credit due from the Treasury, directing that they shall
be applied to the public needs ; and she directs that
her palace shall become a charitable institution or
serve any pious object that may be judged suitable,
that in this manner there may remain a lasting monument of these days' events, and of the feelings of her
who has been misunderstood by some. To these a
fatal conjuration of events—arranged by stratagem
rather than revealing truth, and alien to her will—
have forced her to appear in affecting scenes when
much of the precious blood of Spain has been spilt.

" In view of these powerful considerations, and duly
conciliating in my royal mind the feelings and veneration of a daughter—which neither could nor should
ever leave my heart—with the sacred obligation which
falls on me as Queen to watch over the peace of the
peoples whose government Providence entrusted to
me and the people have confirmed, I have first
acceded in every particular to the desires of my dearly
beloved mother, authorising immediately her depar-

[1] Bermejo : *Estafeta del Palacio*, iii. 437.

ture from Madrid, and arranging that she shall be accompanied to the frontier, as befits her dignity and station, with the necessary force of my noble army to whose loyalty, as to that of my beloved people, I entrust the guardianship of her who bore me in her womb, and who in times more gracious and serene sat upon the august throne of San Fernando, and laid the first stone in the palace of Spanish freedom." [1]

If the Queen Mother must go, she would go in dignity with her husband, and accompanied by her escort. Of cowardice she knew nothing. Her fortune she had already invested in Paris, her jewels she had with her, and perhaps she would be more powerful as well as safer out of Spain.

On the morning of August 28, Isabel entered her mother's bedroom. Her hair was in disorder ; she was trembling and deadly pale ; it was evident that she had had a sleepless night. But Doña Cristina showed no signs of having wept. The King joined them in uniform, and the Queen, who had brought with her her little daughter, threw her arms around her mother's neck. Riansares, who had made great efforts to keep calm, at last succeeded in disengaging his wife from the Queen's arms, and drawing her out of the room. Espartero with O'Donnell was awaiting her in the throne-room, and led them down the great stair-case to a post-chaise in the courtyard. The Queen and Riansares entered it, the postilions cracked their whips, the escort fell into position, and the cavalcade drove off to Portugal.[2]

She settled at Monte Mor, and from there, during the summer, carried on a vigorous corres-pondence with her daughter in Madrid[3] ; her

[1] Bermejo : *Estafeta del Palacio*, iii. 437.
[2] Conde de Benalúa : *Memorias*, p. 14.
[3] Biblioteca Nacional, Madrid : *Fondo X*, F. 89.

tussles with Espartero were renewed, and she, more than any other, fought hard for her ideals, the ideals of Church and monarchy, to which she adhered while still remembering the rôle she had played against the Carlists, when her blue robe was the oriflamme of liberty.

She then moved over into France. In 1854 Pacheco, who in 1841 had written so ardently in her defence, now wrote to Paris asking the plenipotentiary to send a man to spy on her in Bayonne and Bagnères, a few days later to ask the Emperor to intern her ; but Maria Cristina was as safe with Louis Napoleon and Eugénie as with Louis Philippe. She set herself up at Malmaison, and made friends with Princess Mathilde ; she looked around society, and married her daughter Amparo to Prince Czartorisky. The Revolutionaries accused her, meantime, of financing a rising in Ecuador, of arranging to construct a railway to Aranjuez, and of trying to obtain a monopoly in quicksilver from the Spanish Government—as though she did not know that Spanish Governments were quicksilver themselves.

Meanwhile, they passed their law to confiscate Church property. This Isabel refused to sign. The prelates who protested were exiled, and relations with the Holy See were broken off in 1855. Isabel saw to it that not a month had passed before young Cánovas del Castillo was on his way to Rome as chargé d'affaires.

On March 10 of that year, Don Carlos died in Trieste. And Maria Cristina continued to develop her plans in Paris. Message after message was sent to Olózaga to try to induce the sovereigns of France to treat Maria Cristina as the Cortes were doing. But now through the Countess of Montijo, now through Baciocchi, now through Princess Mathilde, courtesies were sent by Eugénie. The Emperor invited Queen

Cristina to Compiègne, while she united the Orleans family around her with the Duke de Montpensier. Isabel spoke of bringing her back in triumph to Spain, but she herself inserted a notice in *España* : " Queen Cristina does not expect to return in triumph to her old palace in Madrid. Tired of ingratitude, she definitely intends to remain absent from the country where her immense services have been so ill repaid, services for which she was once called the saviour of national freedom."

When Prim still urged her, she answered graciously ; but she had another plan in mind. She went to Rome, announcing that she would visit her brother, the King of Naples. She took with her letters from Isabel, who was determined that by one means or another Spain should once more be on good terms with the Holy See. Cánovas had to communicate to his Government that her welcome in Rome had been enthusiastic.

On December 7 Queen Cristina was received in the Vatican by Cardinal Antonelli and Pius IX. Cardinal Borromeo had received her at the foot of the stairs. The Pope insisted that Riansares should remain while they discoursed in private. That evening, Queen Isabel heard by telegram that relations between Madrid and the Holy See had been re-established.

To make a special manifestation of his pleasure, the Pope offered Maria Cristina a compliment reserved for reigning sovereigns. On December 13 he returned her call in person at the Palazzo Stoppani, remaining with her for an hour and a quarter. But though the Spaniards besought her to return, and promised her every sort of restitution, Maria Cristina kept away from Spain for many years.

3

Her cause meanwhile had triumphed. Democratic government is to the oriental mentality of Spaniards like a drinking bout : they crave it, they imbibe it uproariously in injudicious mixtures ; they are paralysed by it, they vomit it forth, and then they turn away to other things till the craving returns and once again they have their spell of delirium, which is once more followed by impotence. So was it from 1854 to 1856, and then Narváez returned to power. For another ten years he and O'Donnell disputed it between them, O'Donnell being as calculating and suave as Narváez was spectacular and irascible. Liberalism was gaining in force all over Europe. O'Donnell looked shrewdly at it, and arranged his plans accordingly. But Narváez felt only a profound misgiving, and he fell into a taciturn despair. " Neither experience, nor disappointment, nor misfortune, nor in fact anything, will improve the greater part of men," he wrote on October 14, 1860, and again on December 30. " Things are going in Spain now as they always go." The sovereigns of Europe, he said, have themselves joined the revolutionaries, " and then they will complain of ingratitude, and make all the complaints that generally are made by those that make concessions. This will happen everywhere, and we have no choice but to be revolutionaries, too, or groan and howl at the moon." [1] The army worried him ; it was, he said, " rotten to the core."

On March 2, 1863, Miraflores formed a parliament : Narváez came back to Madrid, but did not take a place in the ministry. He was overwhelmed by the sudden death of his daughter at Aranjuez. She was

[1] Mendigorria : *Memorias*, iii. 452.

buried at Loja, and then he returned, writing to Mendigorria on May 15, 1864 :

"I have travelled well, in the sense that I had no mischance on the journey. But I have suffered too much, as I go on suffering since I arrived here. To pass again on the road which one month ago the unfortunate child travelled in my company, and which a very short time ago her remains have travelled ; to come back to Loja, the very sight of which brought back to my imagination an immensity of reminders, as sad as they are dear ; to walk where she is buried ; to enter the house she left for the last time ; in this garden in which I still believe, in my delirium, that I see her play, that she calls me, that she comes to look for me, as she used to do—this is to suffer too much. You will understand. But there is no remedy : in Loja, in Madrid, everywhere, it must be the same. My sad memories are not in the road, or in the house, or in the garden. They go with me always, for they are in my heart. They will go with me always as long as I live. God will give me resignation as He gives to all who beg Him to help them through the misfortunes which He sends. But it cannot be helped. I have much to suffer, much to weep."

4

When O'Donnell and Narváez had both died, Queen Isabel had lost both her champions. Insurrection spread over Spain the more fiercely in reaction to the outburst of reactionary clericalism which had accompanied the uncompromising papal *Syllabus errorum* of 1864. And Isabel, at this moment, threw away her last opportunities by a surrender to a new favourite, Marfori, the son of a pastrycook. Her first fancy, Serrano, had been for a short time the head of the Government; her affair with Puig Moltó in 1856 had again compromised her choice of a Government, and after the birth of her son, he had been exiled—as we saw. Her liaison with Marfori was fatal, because he not only aspired to political power when there were no dictators, but he had also a vulgar and repugnant personality.[1]

Born in 1821 at Cadiz, he had entered the army, and married a cousin of Narváez, in spite of the dictator's opposition. But once he was married, Narváez supported him, and made him Civil Governor of Madrid,[1] and there he had gained the Queen's confidence, and, as many believed, her heart. A man with thick lips, and a heavy jaw which suggested a Moorish origin, he had grown extremely fat. Isabel, too, had now an enormous figure, a heavy face, an eye that looked drugged with sensuality. It is believed that she suffered from a trouble which made normal standards of morality almost impossible for her; and, in any case, had not her marriage placed a woman of her temperament in an intolerable position? That she was good-natured, that she loved her country and its people, and that she always wanted to do the best for them, no one doubted. But as a constitutional monarch she was made the slave of faction, and her position was made weaker still by her indolent and impulsive character. She had no idea how to reign. And yet—how was it; was it in the dignity of her bearing, or in the very monstrosity of her outlines?— she was particularly regal. From that gross form emanated the power to charm and to subdue. And there were many who still ardently admired her. Serious historians as late as 1860 produced accounts of

[1] Marqués de Lema : *De la Revolución á la Restauración.*

her which were not less than panegyric. Angelon, the head of the Liberal Ateneo, wrote a history in which he summed up his impressions of her in the sweeping sentence : " Happy the people of Spain who have for Queen such a mother, happy the children of Doña Isabel who have for mother such a Queen." [1] Another who knew her intimately said : " She was as a woman more a woman and as a lady more a lady than any that I have known." [2] She had always " *très grand air*." [3] Though Queen Victoria did not accede to her petition for the Garter, the Pope allowed her that prize of queenly virtue, the Golden Rose. And long years after her death, her daughter, the popular and able Infanta Isabel, when questioned by an historian, could say nothing but " she was a great queen, she was a great queen." [4]

Though she herself had no political capacities, her reign was not a time of disaster for her country, as her father's reign had been. In spite of all the factions, the face of Spain had changed, and the country had grown wealthy. The application of the advancing science and industry produced an infinite multiplication of abundant veins of fortune and prosperity. Special schools were created, universities, academies, and lycées founded and filled. Sixty-seven thousand kilometres of roads were constructed, 12,000 of railways, 11,000 of telegraphs. The proof of her country's prosperity is in the actual figures of the currency. When her father died, the gold in circulation was some 450,000 pesetas ; in 1845 it was 7,658,140 ; in 1850, 16,224,375 ; in 1855, 21,117,000 ; in 1860, 57,073,425 ; in 1865 it had exceeded 100,000,000.

[1] M. Angelon : *Isabel II*, p. 293.
[2] Conde de Benalúa : *Memorias*.
[3] Agnes Carey : *Empress Eugénie in Exile*.
[4] Private information.

As for the Queen, she had the warmest heart ; in the opinion of the Empress Eugénie, who had had every opportunity to judge, she had also an inborn nobility and many other fine qualities as a woman.[1] Her greatest gift was liberality ; she knew nothing of the value of money, and poured it out with both hands. Between 1844 and 1868, when she was in power, she gave away in alms over 100,000,000 pesetas. They went to relatives, ruined nobility, old servants, monks, friars, nuns, churches, convents, hospitals, and all kinds of benevolent institutions : to poets, novelists, journalists, writers and artists of all kinds, and to politicians of all parties. And many of those who attacked her with the written and the spoken word, and tore her from the throne, were among those who in obscurity and adversity had been able to rise by the direct gifts of her charity.[2] She had the impulse to give, and knew nothing of the value of money till at last they put on her table sacks of coins, and pointed out to her that that was what she was accustomed to give out from day to day.[3]

But neither love of her people, generous impulses, nor popularity could save her from factions when her two great military dictators were gone. The Liberals rose against her, and who was at their head ?—Serrano. Was he jealous of such a successor as Marfori, or did he voice a general feeling of outrage at a position that looked so irregular ? The rumours about the King Consort were never silent : he had very little to do with the Queen, and she showed, in one after another of her subjects, a very warm and undisguised interest. With her spontaneous good nature, wrote the Duke of San Pedro, she had the caprices of a woman spoilt

[1] Agnes Carey : *Empress Eugénie in Exile.*
[2] Pérez de Guzmán, quoted in Opisso : *Historia de España,* xxv. 129. [3] Private information.

by the flattery and lusts which always surround a throne.[1] No one could be surprised if, in such circumstances, there were all sorts of guesses as to the parentage of her children. Nothing could be proved, nothing could be disproved. But the times had gone too far to tolerate such intimacy between scandal and Catholic Majesty.

The Queen had now had five children : the son who died within an hour after his birth ; the Infanta Isabel, born in 1851 ; Alfonso, Prince of Asturias, born in 1857 ; the Infanta Eulalia, and the Infanta Paz.

5

In 1866 an attempt at revolution broke out in Madrid on June 22 ; when it was put down by General Vega Inclan, Prim, who was behind it, escaped to Portugal, but Narváez died in 1867, and with O'Donnell's death in the year following, there was no one left to maintain order in Spain by military force.

On August 9, 1868, the Royal Family, in spite of the King's opposition, left La Granja for the Escorial. They went on from there to San Sebastian and Lequeitio, where, among announcements of mutinies and *pronunciamentos*, they passed the last days of August and the beginning of September. On September 17 the Queen decided to leave Lequeitio for San Sebastian.

Prim, who had been to Vichy, heard that the navy at Cadiz would decide on his arrival what to do. At the same time Montpensier sent another emissary, hoping that Prim would declare in favour of Luisa Fernanda. Prim said, however, that he would leave the question to *Cortes Constituyentes*. He travelled second-class in a boat for India which stopped at Gibraltar, and then took ship for Cadiz. The

[1] Conde de Benalúa : *Memorias*, p. 23.

QUEEN ISABEL II WITH HER SON, DON ALFONSO
After the portrait by Winterhalter in the Royal Palace.

" There were all sorts of guesses at the parentage of her children."

Queen, waiting in trepidation at San Sebastian, heard on September 29 that her partisans had been defeated at Alcolea, and that the people had revolted in Madrid. She decided to leave for Biarritz, where she received a telegram from the Empress Eugénie, offering her the castle of Pau. And so, on September 30, the Queen, with streaming eyes and a broken heart, left the country over which she had reigned as long as she could remember. Her family and the Duke of Sexto were with her. At Hendaye she was received with more than accustomed honour by the French under Castelnau.

" On arriving at the frontier, and noticing the calm and order which reigned in France, his imagination turned back at once in melancholy to that ship of maniacs—bloody, messy, impoverished, and torn in pieces—which was his country." So Pio Baroja was to write on the first page of *La Nave de los Locos*. The words might have been put into the mouth of Doña Isabel. Spain, the prey of factions, had seven evil years before her : it was faction which had turned out a Queen who, though obviously inadequate, loved her people, and was loved.[1] And though the thirty-five years of her reign had been only an alternation of factions with which she had no power to deal, she left her country immeasurably greater and better than she found it. But the people, as Napoleon had said to Fernando VII, " are glad to avenge on us the respect they pay us."

When she arrived at Biarritz and was greeted by the Emperor and Empress, she was more than mistress of herself. The Emperor thought her actually cheerful. But the two little princes, Alfonso and Louis Napoleon, each deadly pale, burst into tears in one another's arms.[2]

---

[1] Donoso Cortés : *Obras Escogidas.*
[2] A. Carey : *With the Empress Eugénie.*

IX

CONFUSION

Unhappy men : they are unable to be just, and they want
to be free.—SIÈYES.

I

THE Spain which accepted the banishment of Doña
Isabel was indeed a raving shipload of lunatics. Serrano, who was the military leader of the Revolution,
had thought of making Luisa Fernanda queen ; that
project was killed by a faction which cried, " Down
with the Bourbons ! " Another party offered the
crown to Espartero, but Espartero refused to take the
crown from her to whom he had in spite of everything
given his loyalty as Queen. There were a few under
Castelar who wanted a republic, and started an insurrection. The great majority, however, decided,
even before the elections, that the choice must be a
monarch. But who ? The Court of Portugal was
canvassed, for still at Lisbon were a Coburg and his
son. They both refused, and were applauded for
refusing. The Carlists came forward again, and
secured the support of the priests and of the Holy See.

And then Bismarck came into the game. Whether
he actually originated the suggestion of Prince
Leopold of Hohenzollern is not quite clear ; but at
least he pushed it, for he knew at that time no desire
so great as to provoke France to war. The Second
Empire, after seventeen years of prosperity and glory,
had fallen into ruin before Spain knew where to seek

a sovereign. Prince Leopold, after having come forward twice, had twice withdrawn.

But before either Espartero or Leopold of Hohenzollern was proposed, Montpensier, who had been plotting against Isabel from the beginning, believed that he could secure the throne. That was more than Don Enrique could endure ; he had had to see his brother sit as a nincompoop on the throne for twenty years ; he had had to abandon his own hopes as a Liberal leader ; he had every reason for a grudge against Montpensier. So he wrote to the papers that Montpensier was fomenting factions against the throne of Spain as against the throne of France, but that " Espartero was the man to whom the nation's veneration turned, and never to a puffed-up French pastrycook." [1]

The dear good Piat wrote, on March 8, 1870, to ask the Duke of Seville if he had written the letter. The Duke answered : Yes ; and received a challenge to a duel, which was fought at Carabanchel at ten in the morning on the 12th. Once the royal Dukes exchanged shots without effect. Again Don Enrique fired and nothing happened ; Montpensier's shot hit his pistol-case. Again Don Enrique's shot went wide, but Montpensier's third ball blew out his adversary's brains. Don Enrique had lost his life, while Montpensier had forfeited the throne.[2] He now declared that the family's claims were centred in Isabel's young son, Alfonso.

It was not without a fierce struggle in her own heart that Isabel resigned her own prerogatives. She was at forty in the full vigour of her age, sovereign by nature, by habit, and by inherited instinct. She had always had her own way in every passing caprice, and

[1] Ortega Rubio : *Historia*, vi. 126.
[2] Ortega Rubio : *Ibid.*, pp. 126, 127.

Marfori, with a certain Padre Claret, whom some called a plotter and some called a saint, was still at hand to urge that she should reserve any sovereign right to herself.[1] The King Consort had melted away. It remained for the Duke of Sexto to convince the Queen of the sacrifice the royalist cause required her to make. Queen Isabel could not go back : as a politician, she was hopelessly ineffective ; as a woman, her name was compromised by her favourites. The Duke of Sexto now took charge of the young Prince's cause. The very man with whom the Empress Eugénie had been for years so passionately (though so innocently) in love, and who had married the beautiful widow of the Duke de Morny, now became the prop of the Spanish throne. The shrewdness of his mind he showed in the argument he put before Queen Isabel, an argument which is of as great interest to-day as when it was written :

> " To lose a single battle has always meant the loss of the throne," he wrote. " So it was in France in 1830 and 1848 and in Spain in 1868. But to conquer revolutions it has needed several battles. And that is very natural. The monarchy is represented by the unity of its government. When that is overcome, then the monarchy collapses, since its party is composed of the settled classes who, by their very nature, are of little help in times of struggle and uncertainty. On the contrary, revolutionary Governments, favoured in Spain, by the spirit of provincial independence, identifying themselves more and more with the masses, in every part of the country, do certainly lack unity, and therefore in one way they are weaker and more disorderly.

[1] Conde de Benalúa ; *Memorias*, pp. 47, 48.

But to conquer them one battle is not sufficient : it needs a whole campaign, above all when the revolutionary organisation is complete, as is now the case.

" But can we therefore argue that I am attempting to prove the revolution invincible ? God preserve me from making such a ridiculous mistake. Quite the contrary, its life will be short and ephemeral. It will not succumb within a fixed time to a movement from without, but on account of its very turbulence, it moves quickly towards the abyss ; and when it stands on the edge, the lightest impulse will hurl it down into the bottomless pit which opens out of its uncertainties. What does matter then is to view it with a serene mind so as to see clearly the final moment at which it will compass its own destruction, that we may save the country the convulsions of its agony.

" For the excesses of revolution destroy its own organism, making it intolerable to the immense majority ; and the classes which by their tradition are essentially peaceful and even timid, are made the victims of vexations caused by others, and by the threat of poverty, so as to awaken all the living forces of society. And with these the revolutionary Government, or part of it, finally unites, because there is no one who in the end is not worn out by the demands of the masses, which, finally, are absolutely impossible to satisfy. This is the eternal history of reactions, and so undoubtedly it will turn out here in one way or another as soon as the horizon clears.

" Up to now, Government and Parliament alike have had only one care, and that is to increase expenditure, with recompenses to the revolution-

aries, drying up at the same time the springs
public wealth. Their only desire has been
satisfy the working classes, in which they cou
their strength and place their trust. With th
object they have puffed it up with the name
the Fourth Estate, to which all the rest should
subordinate. In spite of these cajoleries, the lac
of work is already beginning to be felt, becau
without any plan or agreement, and withou
making provision for public funds, for publi
utilities, or even public ornament, they have, i
the first months of the revolution, sacrificed to th
working classes all the funds of the provinci
governments and municipalities, and lastly, eve
to the percentage due to the State, they hav
renounced the fat revenue from merchandis
from toll-gates and bridges, from salt an
tobacco.

" At the same time, instability and fear para
lyse industry and commerce ; capital is locked u
or goes out of the country, credit is more difficul
wealth decreases. The taxes are the more re
sented, all reduce their expenditure, some
necessity, some for motives of carefulness, and th
Great Fourth Estate, to which they gave suc
pharisaical adulation, is soon left without its pa
because they can get nothing from the im
poverished Treasury, nor from the ruined popula
corporations, and still less from private indivi
uals, whose whole object is to guard and pu
away the diminished remainder of their fortun
which has been cut down enough already by th
fall in the value of all sorts of securities. The
the proletariat, who had been made to believ
that all their fortune was summed up in the re
volution, and which more than any other clas

has to feel the rigours of poverty which is the inseparable companion of disorder, will very soon be bitterly disillusioned."

Such were the arguments with which Sexto accompanied his plea that Isabel should do all to help her son to reign. On June 24, 1870, she made her will, and next day she signed her act of abdication, the Duke being the first to witness it.

2

Don Alfonso, though now claimant to the throne, was too young, of course, to seize it : he was still only thirteen. But he seemed promising. He had a slight spare figure, a graceful carriage, an excellent memory, especially for geography, a quiet pleasantness of disposition even to those who were against him, and not the least of his advantages, the undeviating devotion of the Duke of Sexto.[1] The Duke of Sexto's warmth aroused comment, and some wondered if there was a closer tie than that between a monarch and his liegeman. This talk was louder when the Prince, as he grew up, came to have a greater and greater likeness to the Duke. But there is no evidence whatever that Doña Isabel was intimate with Sexto before Don Alfonso's birth. It was not Sexto but Puig Moltó who was then exiled. Sexto used to write letters of the warmest and most courtly affection to the boy whom he called his *Serenissimo Señor*. Each loved to take the other in his arms for a Spanish hug, but such demonstrations were in Spain not unconventional for a courtier and his prince. The letters of the boy to Don Francisco de Asis were also full of trust and affection.[2]

[1] Conde de Benalúa : *Memorias*.
[2] Biblioteca Nacional, Madrid, MSS. 12978, 61, 62, 67.

The one person for whom the young Alfonso had no affection was the poor, good Piat—Piat who plotted for Isabel's dethronement and then killed his own brother-in-law in the duel. " I don't want to go any where with Montpensier," the Prince would say This did not please Doña Maria Cristina de Bourbon de Muñoz. She had apparently never repented of the mode in which she had brought Montpensier into the family ; and in the tone rather of a schoolmistress than a grandmother, she argued with young Alfonso that he had no reason to find his uncle distasteful.

Queen Maria Cristina's figure was not bowed by years or tumults. She was as different from the lovely girl who, forty years before, had charmed King Fernando and his people, as the Baroness Bernstein was from Beatrix Esmond when she arrived at Castlewood. Her hair, now white, was worn in ringlets which were still combed up in the fashion of an earlier day. " Under the weight of years," wrote an observer, " she sought to hold unbowed her inborn majesty," and the impression she left was neither charm, beauty, nor even respect : it was fear. Such was the last phase of the remarkable woman who first gave Spain a Liberal monarchy, and who, when Don Fernando de Bourbon had left her a widow, for forty years had lived as wife with Don Fernando Muñoz.[1]

3

But Prim could make no terms with the Bourbons. Anxious above all to undermine the Carlists, and yet to have a monarch, he went from the Hohenzollerns to the House of Savoy. No one could expect a son of Victor Emmanuel to be too clerical : Liberalism was in 1870 the keynote of the new Italian monarchy,

[1] Conde de Benalúa : *Memorias*, pp. 28, 29.

and Amadeo, the choice of Prim, was a blameless young man with an agreeable wife. But with the choice of Amadeo, Prim's career came to an end. The very day that Amadeo landed at Cartagena, Prim was murdered at Madrid. The captain of the assassins, Paul y Angulo, was editor of *The Combat*. When he failed to get from Prim the embassy he had expected, his excitable temper, made worse by drink, vented his rancour in an article headed, " Kill him in the streets like a dog." [1] And the deed answered to the word.

Amadeo rode into Madrid in snow, and his first duty was to visit the dead body of the man to whom he owed the throne. A few months later an attempt was made on his own life in the Calle Arenal.

The keynote of his reign was simplicity. The antithesis of the earlier intruder king, he occupied few rooms in the palace, lived simply, received without ceremony, went out sometimes on horseback and sometimes in a small carriage, generally alone, and always without an escort. [2]

But simplicity was not what the Spanish people wanted. Two things they demanded from a monarchy : a Spaniard who, even if he had all the vices of Ferdinand VII, understood them as a people—this for their hearts ; and for their imaginations, the mystic attributes of inherited authority, strong in religious sanction. The excellent Amadeo, like the excellent Joseph Bonaparte, could lay no claim to either. The aristocracy ridiculed him ; the Catholics remembered that he was the son of the dissolute monarch who had made war on the Pope and despoiled the Holy See ; the Army was disgruntled with reforms it had not asked for, and which were particularly irritating to the artillery ; the Carlists had their own allegiance,

---

[1] Conde de Benalúa : *Memorias*. [2] Pi y Margall : *Opúsculos*, i. 10.

as had also the followers of the young Alfonso, and the Republicans did not want a monarchy at all.[1] His position was hopeless from the start. He came as the puppet of the Radicals ; no one really cared for him except one leader, Ruiz Zorrilla. If he broke with the Radicals, or if he were overpowered, there must be an immediate revolution, and he himself admitted to the Cortes that he could neither dominate the clamour of contradictory parties nor find a remedy for the evils affecting Spain. Of course, they said he was weak. But it was his function to be weak. If he did nothing, it was because his own supporters bound him to do nothing ; and his ineffectiveness deserves not blame but pity.[2]

For two years he held out in Spain. Then, to follow his ministers' advice, believing that it was his duty as a constitutionalist, he signed a paper which infuriated the army. In Spain no one can afford to do that, and he realised it almost at once. His wife had just borne another child, and in his solicitude for her, he thought it safer for them all to go. On February 11, 1872, he wrote to the Parliament to abdicate : the two years of his reign, he said, had been a struggle, not against foreign enemies, but against the strife of parties ; all talked of patriotism, and then plunged into fights and tumults for their own advantage, and what the country really wanted he found it impossible to guess. In these circumstances he saw nothing for him to do but abdicate. " My intentions," he said, " are impracticable, my efforts barren." [3]

At six in the morning of February 12 he started for Portugal with his sick queen, in such neglect that a

---

[1] Marqués de Lema : *Cánovas*, pp. 88, 89.
[2] Pi y Margall : *Opúsculos*, i. 81, 82.
[3] Ortega Rubio : *Historia de España*, ii. 462.

KING AMADEO

" It was his function to be weak."

one point he was obliged to get her a cup of tea in a
fonda ; he left the factions behind to try their hand
at a republic under Sagasta and Zorrilla, with Serrano
at the head of the army and Castelar thundering in
the Cortes.

" No one," the orator said, " has destroyed the
monarchy in Spain : no one has killed it.   And I,
who have worked so much towards this moment, I
want to say that I do conscientiously believe that its
fall owes nothing to me : the monarchy is dead
without anyone whatever contributing to its death
except the Providence of God.

" Gentlemen, with Fernando VII died the traditional monarchy ; with the flight of Isabel II the
parliamentary monarchy ; with the abdication of
Don Amadeo of Savoy the democratic monarchy :
no one has brought it to an end.   It died of itself.
No one is installing the Republic : it is due to
circumstances ; to a conspiracy of society, nature,
and history." [1]   Castelar did not recognise, as Sexto
did, that under the providence of God working through
society, nature, and history, the monarchy would be
restored within three years.

4

For the republic soon showed itself unable to up-
hold order against anarchy.   It threw its energies
into making a republican constitution, and when it
had accomplished that, its energy was exhausted.
And it could not guarantee order, so neither could it
hold the country together.   Each province wanted
autonomy, and Andalusia, though it declared that it
wanted only the Canton System of Switzerland, was
already communistic.   In the North, the Church and

[1] Ortega Rubio : *Historia de España,* ii. 154, 155.

bandits made common cause under the Carlist flag
For as yet Catalonia was more Catholic than Radical
Navarre and the Basque Provinces were clerical and
reactionary.　But everywhere alike there was disorder
tumult, bloodshed.　The masses of the people were
out for what they could get by whatever means, and
agitators urged them on to their excesses.　Business
was paralysed.　Carlist war had broken out in the
North, even before Don Amadeo abdicated.　And
though Serrano led an army against it, the frequent
changes of government in Madrid made that army
doubtful of its cause.　Meanwhile the partisans o.
Alfonso were organising.　Doña Isabel herself was
plotting in Paris, while in Madrid Sexto had enlisted
the zeal of Cánovas del Castillo.　As Sexto had
foreseen, the stable and peaceful elements of the
country had strongly reacted against revolution.
They wanted order and peace, to ensure that production, traffic, and trade by which alone men live.
So the tide was with the Monarchists, and the two
leaders made an irresistible combination.

Born in 1825, the Duke was a man of the world
who had taken full advantage of his opportunities as
grand seigneur.　He had three dukedoms and fourteen titles ; he was seven times a *grand d'Espagne*, and
had an enormous fortune.　Though his features were
a little weak, and they were shown up at their worst
by the odious fashion of side whiskers, which had dis-
placed the imperial, he was redoubtable in the inter-
play of sagacity and enterprise.　" I have never
known," said his nephew Benalúa, " a man simpler,
more even tempered or more affable.　He enjoyed
also perfect health, a natural distinction and taste,
good judgment, and a power of reading men and the
human heart.　In addition to all this, he had a
personal magnetism and attraction, especially over

omen." [1]   The man for whom the Empress Eugénie
efused the Duke de Doudeauville, and for whom she
vas ready to sacrifice the crown of France,[2] was not a
nan to be ignored.

Cánovas del Castillo had the more solid qualities
f a man who, by his intrinsic force of character, raised
imself from the middle classes to dominate a parlia-
nentary monarchy.   He had no fortune but his
loquence and good sense.   Spain, however, has
lways been a country for the man of talent to rise,
nd Cánovas at the age of forty, when Doña Isabel
vas exiled, was already a man of mark.   It was his
art to counsel the Queen against bad advisers,
specially those of her own or her husband's family ;
vith Marfori and Meneses always with her, with her
nilitary support depending on a nonentity, the Conde
e Cheste, and intrigues working against her by those
he had most reason to trust,[3] her son's most solid
upport in Spain was certainly with Cánovas.

He went to the North of Europe, and made diligent
nquiries about Don Alfonso : the report on the boy
vas excellent.   After studying at a college in Vienna,
he Prince had entered Sandhurst at the same time
nd on the same terms as the Prince Imperial at
Woolwich.   He lived in one of the instructors'
ottages, with two Spanish servants, and did his drill
nder a Sergeant Mackintosh.   The English had
nade up their minds that Alfonso would return, and
is attractive personality made its own impression.
'wice a week he dined with the cadets.   He visited
he Prince of Wales, and the Empress Eugénie used
o come over to see him from Camden.   He remained
t Sandhurst till Christmas.   Everywhere he had been

---

[1] Conde de Benalúa : *Memorias.*
[2] R. Sencourt : *The Empress Eugénie,* p. 69.
[3] Marqués de Lema : *De la Revolución á la Restauración.*

the same—tactful, quiet, thoughtful, popular, courage
ous. His passion was Spain.[1] In the autumn c
1874 Cánovas came back to Madrid, and knew tha
he had the country with him. He quietly worke
to consolidate the position among the men wh
counted as minds in Spain.

The Duke of Sexto came back, and worked in hi
own way, skating in the gardens of Liria and on
little pond in the Retiro, and planning a ball. Th
Countess of Montijo had fixed one for the same da
as the Sextos, and a heavy battle ensued, in which
however, the aged Countess so far compromised fc
the monarchy as to give hers the evening before. I
December a manifesto addressed to all Spaniard
was signed by Don Alfonso at Sandhurst and brough
to Madrid. It made an excellent impressior
Cánovas had meanwhile been working with the Duk
of Sexto, not in favour of a military intrigue, but tha
Alfonso should be welcomed by the whole country i
freedom, peace, and order.

On December 29 the royalists in Madrid wer
in tense anxiety: all their plans depended on th
attitude of Jovellar, who commanded the army of th
Centre, and of Castillo, who was Captain-General c
Valencia. In Madrid, Radicals and Republicar
placed all their resources at the disposal of the Goverr
ment, counting still on the enthusiasm of the masse
Fernando Primo de Rivera, the Captain-General c
Madrid, came to the Duke of Sexto to say that he wa
doubtful of the garrison of Madrid, but that Jovella
had joined Martínez Campos. Sexto had gone t
the house of Cánovas to warn him that he must hide t
escape arrest. " Pepe," he answered, " if you remai
with them and they imprison me, all the powers wi
be yours, and you will have the full responsibility."

[1] Conde de Benalúa : *Memorias.*

On retiring to lunch at home, they heard that the Civil Governor of Madrid had detained Cánovas. They had not finished their coffee before Romero Robledo arrived, saying to the Duke : " Get out of it while you can : they will be here to hunt you out within an hour." More royalists arrived with the same story. Imperturbable, the Duke thought out his plans. " It is my duty," he said to the Duchess, " not to let them catch me," and with Mesada, Torrecilla, and his nephew Benalúa, he went out into the snow just before dusk. A quarter of an hour later the agents of the Civil Governor arrived to capture him. His brother Nicolas was arrested by mistake as he went out of the house. Then another messenger arrived saying that Sagasta, after holding a council, had decided, in order to avoid bloodshed, to hand over the power to Primo de Rivera. The Duke of Sexto, who meanwhile had come into his house, then quietly took up his hat and walked over to the Ministry of War, where Serrano Bedoya had handed everything over to Primo de Rivera.

Meanwhile, a boy of seventeen who had left Sandhurst for his Christmas holidays had to settle a country which was torn by civil war and waging a war in Cuba ; without knowing how far the movement in the army answered to the deeper feelings of the people, he was hastening to a country which had known nothing of ordered government for seventy years.

On January 9 Don Alfonso arrived in Barcelona from Marseilles. There the " *Viva España !* " he heard had filled him with emotion ; he had no uniform, but young Benalúa was measured for one in Madrid, which was brought over for him.

After a visit to Valencia, where he went first to the Virgen de los Desamparados, he arrived, at ten o'clock in the evening of January 13, at Aranjuez.

Next day he arrived at Madrid a little after noon
and mounting a white horse went straight to the
Atocha, where he was received by the Primate of
Spain.

5

On his arrival in Paris, he had received a letter in
a woman's writing, saying : " *Sire, Votre Majesté a
été proclamé Roi hier soir par l'Armée espagnole. 'Vive
le Roi!'* "

On his arrival in Madrid he found another letter in
the same writing : " *Sire, n'oubliez pas un cœur qui crie
'Vive le Roi!' et qui vous aime.*" From the writer of
those letters he was to hear again.

X

ALFONSO XII AND HIS WIVES

Hunters, where does Hope rest ?
Not in the half-oped breast,
Nor the young rose,
Nor April sunrise—those
With a quick wing she brushes,
The wide world through,
Greets with the throat of thrushes,
Fades from as fast as dew.

But would you spy her sleeping,
Cradled warm,
Look in the heart of weeping,
The tree stript by storm.

EDITH WHARTON : *Artemis.*

I

THE salient fact in Spain's history in the nineteenth century is the rapidity with which the Monarchists of 1875 settled the country's troubles, and established the Constitution which enabled the country to make a continuous advance for well over fifty years. The long torpor into which a people, naturally virile and vivacious, were stunned in the eighteenth century by the batons of the Inquisition, and again by the reaction to it ; the reaction which exiled the tireless fathers of the Society of Jesus ; the austere and spiritual dignity which Goya expressed in one style of his portraits, the verve and passion which he depicted in others— these combined to show that the living spirit of Spain was gathering like the electric forces which gather in the days of heat to drench the earth with fruitful storm. The crisis of bright weather was the administration of Godoy. The storm was the Bonaparte episode. Thenceforward, Spain's soil was no longer arid. Certainly under Fernando VII every shoot and growth of free development was ruthlessly cut back by tyranny, whose pruning knives were cunning, intrigue, and violence. But though there was pruning knife and axe, there was no more drought. Spain became a forest of human growths, where military leaders ruthlessly felled the trees to make arable land and meadows on the borders of the wood. And then the forces of nature had been too strong for them : a forest fire had burnt both habitations and implements, and Spain's most fertile gardens were unweeded. Then followed the slow years when wildness was gradually subdued into fruitful and civilised earth, though as events were to show, the forces of nature could not yet be mastered. The fire and the heat and waters under the earth rolled in thunderings and earthquakes which menaced still another cataclysm even while the work of tillage throve.

For the nineteenth century did not yet attempt to organise society. It still believed in nature and in economic law ; though nations, as if fearing the universal spread of trade, impeded it by tariff barriers, yet they left men free within those limits to make wealth as best they could. Law was for the most part content with the protection of persons and of property. Kings gave unity to national organisations, captained society, focused patriotism. The Constitution of 1876 limited the powers of the King of Spain to the dismissal and the appointment of ministers and to presiding at their meetings. No act of his was valid unless countersigned by a minister, but the disposal of titles and honours was in the King's hands. Below that, a working agreement of a subtle and yet serviceable kind between Liberals and Conservatives, that they should alternate in power under the monarchy, and make common cause against Republicanism.   The ballot box was an amiable formality. The people as a whole took no interest in politics, and the elections were arranged by the returning officers. Let us say brutally that the parliamentary system was a farce : the ministers did much as they liked, by an understanding that neither one party nor the other did it for too long or did too much.

Such was the system which put a small, quiet, bright-eyed boy of seventeen, fresh from Sandhurst, at its head.

His opening task was to stop the Civil War.   He first attempted to make peace, and issued a proclamation : " If you are fighting in the cause of Royalism, I am the representative of the dynasty to which your fathers swore allegiance.   If you are fighting for the Catholic faith, I am a Catholic King, and will right the wrongs done to the Church.   You yourselves love liberty ; you cannot deprive Spaniards of it.   Lay down your arms, and you shall see the prosperity of Cuba revived, and shall forthwith enjoy the advantages that were yours during thirty years under my mother's sceptre.   Before beginning battle, I offer you peace."   But the Carlists did not want peace.   The young King joined his army : he saluted Espartero in Logroño, and received an exposition on the duties of a constitutional monarch, and later he toured the reconquered provinces, and the Holy See acknowledged his accession.

Then came trouble with his mother.   In October 1876 she returned to Spain, engaged in altercation about her pension, and intrigued with the Clerical Party.   But her power and her prestige were gone.

Though the priests did waver in their allegiance when he censured an *alcalde* who had tried to force Catholic baptism on the children of Protestants,[1] the King had all Spain with him, and in 1877 he made a fresh claim on their sympathy by announcing his proposed marriage. For nothing pleases people more than that their royalties should wed. Nothing makes a monarchy more popular than goodness and beauty in a queen. Don Alfonso's choice fell on Doña Maria de las Mercédes, daughter of the Duke de Montpensier. Montpensier's sins and intrigues were passed over both by the King and his people, who were delighted to think that the new Queen was to be a Spaniard. Doña Isabel had lost ground, and the fact that she had accepted a visit from Don Carlos after her last quarrel in Madrid made it impossible for her to be present at the wedding. Don Francisco de Asis returned, however, for the first time since his exile.

The young King was married on January 23, 1878. People crowded into Madrid from every part of Spain : every inn was full. The face of the young Queen was thought to be enchanting in its beauty and in its sweetness of expression. The martial bearing of the King, and his remarkable eloquence, were the praise of all. In spite of a biting wind, the people's hearts glowed ; and they shouted at the top of their voices. And yet in the Calle de Alcalá a bomb was thrown, a woman killed. For weeks after an enraptured King called on the horses of the night to stay their pace.

But before five months had passed the beautiful young Queen was dead. The whole country grieved. The King's own heart was broken. Never again did he greatly care for the task and the prestige that were his : his high spirits changed to cynicism, and his life became irregular, while he watched with

[1] Butler Clark : *Modern Spain*, p. 409.

a listless eye the incessant intrigues of Cánovas against
Sagasta, of Sagasta against Cánovas. He entered
into a liaison with a *cantatrice*, which was continued
till his death. Was it not she who at the moment of
succession had written that she already loved him ?

2

Another marriage was rapidly arranged for him ;
it did not give him back what he had lost, though it
brought to Spain a Queen who broke for ever with
the old traditions which had set the Spanish throne in
such a lurid light. Princess Maria Cristina of Habsburg had been head of a conventual house for noble
ladies in Prague, a house where these ladies lived as
nuns, but with liberty to marry if a husband were
found for them. The Princess had seen Don Alfonso
years before, and welcomed the fate of being both his
wife and his queen. Her marriage took place in 1879.
Her first two children were daughters. Maria
Cristina insisted that the elder of these should be called
Mercédes, after the wife her husband still mourned.
When she was born in 1880 the King was so disappointed to find her a girl that he almost refused to
present her to the Court as etiquette prescribed ; and
when he found his second child a girl, he almost gave
up hope.

In 1883 he travelled to Vienna, to Berlin, to Paris.
Vienna gave him an ovation, and in Berlin the
Emperor William, to annoy the French, made him
honorary colonel of a Strassburg regiment. The consequence was that when he arrived in Paris he was
greeted with hisses. Don Alfonso did not alter his
demeanour in the slightest ; he went coolly through
his programme. The result in turn of this was that
when he returned to Madrid the streets were crowded

with men who, at his approach, welcomed him in a frenzy of enthusiasm.

The next year there was an earthquake in Andalusia. The King insisted on travelling through the provinces of Malaga and Granada, encouraging and helping the wounded. His arrival awoke a deep and general emotion. Without a thought of the disease which was so soon to bear him down, he travelled through the ruins, offering gifts and counsels to the homeless. Later in the year there was an outbreak of cholera at Aranjuez. Although an Englishman wrote to the King that a tablespoonful of salt and a tablespoonful of red pepper in a half-pint of hot water was known to be an infallible cure for cholera,[1] the doctors of Spain, as the world in general, made little headway against the disease. One hot summer morning the King drove with an A.D.C. to the Atocha station, and took two tickets.[2] In his railway carriage he wrote two letters, one to say to the Queen that he was going to visit the sick at Aranjuez, the other to Cánovas, to say he had not told him because he knew the old politician would say no.

He went to the houses where the cholera was raging, gave money, arranged for treatment. The people followed him through the streets with what Francos Rodriguez called the noble excitement of a crowd carried away by gratitude. Meanwhile, the news was running through the streets and cafés of Madrid. There, they said, was a man who was worth anything. "Vale un mundo." Ministers went to greet him on his return. "I did it," said the King, "following an impulse of my heart, but not ignoring my oath to the Constitution."[3] The Queen met him at the station

---

[1] *Royal Palace Archivós* (Madrid), Anónimos, 1884.
[2] J. Francos Rodriguez : *Un Triunfo de Alfonso XII.*
[3] J. Francos Rodriguez : *Ibid.*, pp. 246, 247.

KING ALFONSO XII IN THE ROBES OF THE ORDER OF THE
GOLDEN FLEECE

After the portrait by Padrò in the Royal Palace, Madrid.

" There," they said, " was a man who was worth anything."

on his return, and the two drove back to the palace through a crowd carried away by admiration.

In the autumn of 1885 there was news that Germany had seized the Caroline Islands. Spain was furious. There was a confused uproar of lies and accusations—a general hatred of Germany. But the Government were too shrewd to imagine that was the way out of the difficulty. It was the King who saved them. He arranged with the Emperor William to refer the matter to the Holy See. His prestige in Germany stood Spain in good stead.[1]

But the King's reign was nearly over. His excesses were the outburst of a temperament made hectic by the advances of consumption. Even in the midst of his courtiers, he would lie in white flannel on his couch [2]; he felt his end was near, and that as at the death of his grandfather, the sceptre of Spain would be once more in the hands of a baby girl, while Carlists again made war against her and her mother. One autumn afternoon he was looking out from the red dining-room on to the Plaza de Oriente, watching a young workman who was carrying in his arms a small boy, who kept pulling his father's cap off. The King watched him till they were out of sight, and as he turned back into the room, his eyes were moist. A courtier asked him what was the matter. " Nothing ! " answered the King. " The presentiment that I shall never attain to the joy that workman is having —to kiss my son." [3]

Although Don Alfonso's lungs were almost gone, the ministers could not admit that he was ill, for fear that their enemies might prepare for revolution. In the days of October he retired to El Pardo. The old

---

[1] J. Francos Rodriguez : *Un Triunfo de Alfonso XII*, p. 251.
[2] Vizconde de Guëll : *Perspectives*, p. 10.
[3] *Guia Palaciana*, iii.

Court doctor had resigned, and it was the new one, Sanchez de Ocaña, who advised him to go where he could breathe a calmer air. On November 23 the doctor was forced to admit that he was dying : a council of specialists met, and agreed that the case was desperate. The peseta fell, and all feared a revolution. " What a complication ! " said the King, but he could do no more. Almost as soon as it was announced that he was ill, he was dead. And Serrano died the day afterwards.

3

Cánovas took charge of the situation : the Duke of Sexto was, as he had always been, the head of the palace administration, and they saved Spain from revolution by handing over the government to Sagasta. The Spaniards felt a natural repugnance to taking up arms against a baby—for the Carlists no longer counted. As for the Queen Maria Cristina of Habsburg (the elder Maria Cristina had died a year before the younger one was married), she found herself in a peculiar situation. According to the Constitution, her elder daughter should be proclaimed Queen ; but she had ascertained only a few weeks before that she was to have another child at the end of some five or six months. So Maria Cristina was simply appointed regent. She had been a devoted wife, she was a faultless queen ; she learnt now of her husband's infidelities, but guarded her memory of him intact as a great and good king. It was a judgment in which not all Spaniards acquiesced, though many did so. Francos Rodriguez, who was a Liberal, said that he had " a spirit as great as it was noble, as firm as it was luminous. . . . History, in giving undiluted praise to the unfortunate sovereign, has but obeyed the com-

mands of justice." [1]   He had certainly never quailed
in meeting difficult situations ; he had scrupulously
performed his duties as a constitutional sovereign ; he
had been tactful as well as intrepid, and he smiled in
the face of death, with the fervent hope and warmth
of heart with which nature compensates a young man
dying of consumption.

4

Early in May 1886 there was a devastating hurricane in Madrid.   The Queen, in spite of her state,
insisted on going out to see where the damage was
worst, giving alms, visiting hospitals, and mingling
her sorrows as widow with those of the people.   On
May 16 she was still leading her ordinary life, and
stayed up talking with her brother till eleven in the
evening.   It was at two on the following morning
that a message was sent out that her position was
critical.   The principal officers of State were summoned to the palace.   Madrid woke up to an intense
curiosity—a boy or a girl ?

The morning hours succeeded without settling the
question ;   a crowd gathered around the palace ;
the ministers waited ;   the Ambassadors arrived.
From time to time an official would come from the
palace only to say that at any moment something
might happen, and yet moment succeeded moment
without it happening.   The clock struck twelve amid
a great murmur of impatience.   But before the half-
hour a cannon was heard, a flag was run up on
the staff, and the whole town burst into applause.
Sagasta gave the news.   Rampolla, the Nuncio, was
said to be especially delighted.   But the mother wept.

[1] *Op. cit.*, p. 258.   Cf. Vizconde de Guëll : *Perspectives*, p. 14.

"My poor Alfonso!" she said, "not to be able to see him, he who wanted it so much."[1]

So Alfonso XIII was born a king. Never before in the recorded history of Europe had a monarch come into his cradle to centre the allegiance of his country. So curious an event appealed to the heart and imagination of a naïve people, and Spain, in its enthusiasm for a royal baby, settled the question of its central order. "Where has the new baby come from?" asked the five-year-old Infanta, whose primacy was forfeited. "From your father in heaven," answered the Queen. That adroit answer gave the lead to Spanish feeling.

Five days later the King was baptised with great pomp in the Royal Chapel. The sign of the Cross was made upon his forehead; the sacred salt, the symbol of wisdom, was placed upon his tongue; he was anointed with oil; the water of regeneration was poured upon his head; he was robed in an embroidered chrysom, and a lighted candle was placed in his hand. "Receive this burning light," said the Cardinal who was administering the Sacrament, "and in blamelessness guard thy baptism. Keep the commandments of God, that when the Lord shall come to the wedding-feast, thou mayest meet Him in the company of all the Saints in the heavenly court and live with Him for ever."

The child who was the subject of these holy ceremonies greeted them, as is not unusual, with a continual howl.[2]

5

The Queen Mother, with Sexto at her side, performed her rôle faultlessly. Even the most refractory

[1] J. Francos Rodriguez : *Dias de la Regencia.*
[2] Olmet : *Vida de Alfonso XIII,* i. 81.

spirits felt it would be unbecoming to Spanish chivalry
to take up arms against a baby in his cradle, or against
a widowed mother, to whose detriment no word could
be whispered. Queen Maria Cristina de Habsburg
was indeed a remarkable woman : though correct, she
was never cold ; though dignified, never austere ;
though regal, never imperious ; though a scholar,
always womanly. She looked on her supreme rank
as a hallowed vocation : and though she was only
twenty-eight when she found herself at the head of
the Spanish nation, and directing its government, she
had the tact and wisdom of an experienced ruler.

The situation she had to face was indeed a baffling
one. She had to face it from the depths of sorrow.
The death of the young King, indeed, left a complication. In the words of the Duke of Maura, it " surprised those who feared it, and disconcerted those who
hoped for it." [1] But the statesmanship of Cánovas in
handing the power over to those who alone were
likely to make a revolution saved the dynasty.[2] The
baby King's enemies were only those of his own
family. Don Carlos, of course, made a protest
against his accession. In 1888 Queen Isabel was
asked to leave Spain, for she had become involved in
an intrigue. The Duke of Seville, a son of the man
shot by Montpensier in 1869, was sentenced to eight
years' imprisonment for insulting the Regent, and
even from prison he published another outrageous
letter. And the Duke de Montpensier was also
suspected of fomenting intrigue, though no charge
could be brought against him.[3] There was a spirit
of indiscipline in the Bourbons. But the sagacity of

[1] G. Maura y Gamazo : *Don Alfonso XIII durante su menoridad*,
p. 1.
[2] Ortega Rubio.
[3] Butler Clark : *Modern Spain*, p. 442.

17

Cánovas and Sexto, the premiership of so advanced
a Liberal as Sagasta, and the tact of the Queen
frustrated all their tricks. Her one overwhelming
anxiety was the severe illness of the baby King in
January 1890. When that was cured her great
anxiety was relieved. Her life was responsible and
busy with great affairs, and all sorts of people wrote
her importunate letters.

"Your Majesty (began one of them ; it was
written from Echo, Oregon, U.S.A., May 31,
1901),—

"In your Maj. dear beloved Mother's name,
please answer those few lines I wrote to your dear
beloved Mother Her Maj. the Queen Cristina for
a little pecuniary help that Her Maj. Queen
Victoria told me to do after last New Year, but
I never got an answer. I used to be a Royal
Valet, and is therefore entitled to a little Attension
of *The Royal Houses of Europe ! !* Your Majesty
understand that I am in destitute circumstances
here in Americka and would gladly accept any
small sum that Your Majesty ! or Mother would
have the pleasure of sending me, it would greatly
strengthen the relations between the two countries, simply because I would tell everybody about
it. I was told by *Emperor Francis Joseph of Austria*
a month ago to write Your Maj. a private Letter
for a little help, and please do not forget me, but
remember that I am a European and not a
American, and need it very badly."

6

The boy, who was very like his mother, soon showed
that he had his full share of character, of energy, and
of sympathy. Children soon understand what advan-

tages are theirs : although he loved the Queen to call
him by the German pet name " Bubi," a member of
the Court who used it was answered with the words :
" For Mother I am ' Bubi ' ; for you I am the King." [1]
This, when His Majesty was three. One day he
descended from his carriage screaming with rage at
a whim being crossed ; the officer commanding the
halberdiers came up and said to him :

" *Señor*, what will the halberdiers say of their King
if they see him crying ? "

The child brightened.

" That I ought to give them their commands ? "
he asked.

" But why was the child crying ? " asked the
Queen.

" No, Mama," he broke in. " I was not crying.
I can't cry." [2]

Indeed, when at another time they brought him
arnica to rub on a bump, he sponged the wall so that
it shouldn't feel the bump.[3]

One day, when King Alfonso was nine years old,
he found his drill instructor smoking.

" You don't smoke in front of the King," said the
King.

" *Señor*," answered the instructor, " those are old
antiquated customs of the ceremony of long ago.
The Kings of to-day have to be affable, democratic,
friends to all their subjects, cordial and simple as
Your Majesty's father was. In the old days there used
to be monarchs called absolute, masters of properties
and lives, who lived like gods. But to-day we have a
different idea of royalty. Nowadays the King is
greater than in times gone by, because he has aban-

[1] Olmet and Carraffa : *Alfonso XIII*, i. 103.
[2] *Ibid.*
[3] Pérez de Guzmán : *Illustración Española.*

doned arbitrary, absurd, feudal rights, and has gained
in the love, and in the conscious and true respect of his
liegemen.   To-day the King is an elder brother who
collaborates with his people.   To-day the King is no
longer a supernatural being who lives apart. . . .
Will Your Majesty allow me to finish this cigarette ? ”

“ Smoke,” said the boy with a laugh.   “ And when
I can, I shall offer you my own cigars.” [1]

But brought up as he was with everyone deferring
to him, and the centre of every company he entered,
he needed discipline ; and the Queen saw that he
did not do everything he liked.   Once she had him
locked up in a room at Aranjuez : he protested by
trying to kick the door through.   It was no use.   So
he crossed to the window and threw open the shutters.
The courtyard was amazed to hear echo through it
the loud shout of “ *Viva la república !* ” [2]   For sometimes even kings themselves revolt against the
exigencies of their own supremacy.

With such a boy Doña Maria Cristina’s task was not
a sinecure.   But hers was a character that was not
made for sinecures.

7

Nor had she an easy time with the politicians.
They had passed a law of universal suffrage in 1890,
but even with that there seemed a lack of reality in
the elected representatives.

This system showed itself peculiarly inadequate to
deal with the Colonies.   Cuba had been in a state of
recurring insurrection, like a patient with tertian
malaria.   And the state of Cuba grated on the nerves
of those who, in the home of the brave and the land of

---

[1] Olmet and Carraffa : *op. cit.*, pp. 116, 117.
[2] Béraud : *Emeutes en Espagne*, pp. 189, 191.

QUEEN MARIA CRISTINA DE HABSBURG
From a photograph.

" Hers was a spirit that was not made for sinecures."

the free, measured the duties of America by the doctrines of Monroe and the exuberance of Roosevelt. The American Government sent alarming messages to the Queen, which she referred, with her usual scrupulous correctness, to the leaders of both parties.[1] But neither she nor they could avoid a war—a war which reft from Spain the most important of her colonies after a defeat which came upon the country with humiliating suddenness. From that time forward the thoughts of the leaders of Spain turned to the idea of resurrection. And they waited with impatience for the inspiration which they expected from the accession of the King. For at his sixteenth birthday he was to be invested with full powers. All expected a great change to follow. And certainly it did.

8

Even before the war broke out in Cuba, a leading Liberal, Francisco Silvela, in an address before the Ateneo,[2] an address which has been twice printed, had spoken on what was to make the drama of the young King's rule—his country's contempt for the parliamentary system.

" The fundamental weakness," said Silvela, " was that the Spanish do not believe that the vote counts : they do not believe in what is called the ' exercise of the parliamentary and legislative function.' When they voted it was not for the sake of a political ideal. What interests the voter is what his member will get for his constituency, in the quickness with which he gives an answer, and obtains a favourable issue to the petitions of the local bodies ; but not in any fundamental political ideas."

[1] Maura y Gamazo : *Alfonso XIII, Menoridad*, i. 360.
[2] Feb. 8, 1896.

" Evident, notorious, and every day more sharply outlined," went on Silvela, " is the lack of accord between what we may call the spirit and faculties of the nation, and the conditions of the life of the governments. The principal and fundamental, which in other times were called the necessary, liberties are fully and peacefully exercised. The Press is developing widely, and with a prudence and a respect for the feelings of the country which even the most advanced countries in Europe can envy. The signs of association and reunion are being developed also in the ample measure which gives us a high place among the most advanced people in Europe. And yet all which touches the organisation of the State, of public administration, of the powers which are in direct relation with the State, in all this there are evident trouble, sometimes deficiencies, sometimes absolute disorder which the country is disgusted to observe, and of which from time to time it complains bitterly and even angrily, while at others it is so indifferent that it hardly pays attention to them. This is the disharmony to which I referred."

And yet it was this very system—so stigmatised by a leading parliamentarian—that the young King, from whose youth and enterprise so much was expected, was forced to swear that he would maintain. It was inevitable that Spain, who, with preceding generations, had watched the throne rock and totter under the violence of the human passions of its occupants, should now see it the centre of a new drama : this drama was the struggle of the people whom the monarch represented with the politicians who managed the representation in the Parliament, while revolutionaries—some republicans, some anarchists— did their best to do away with both.

PART III

XI

ALFONSO XIII : ACCESSION AND MARRIAGE

Con Alfons mi señor no querria lidiar.

Cantar de Mio Cid.

I

AT last the time had come for young Alfonso to march out into the field of political manœuvres. He was still the age of a drummer boy, but had the post, if not of a generalissimo, yet a power to suggest and to organise. He was, as it were, the chief of the general staff.

On his sixteenth birthday this boy was to take his place among the monarchs who were at the heart of the Great Powers of Europe. The King of England, the Emperor of Austria, the German Emperor, the Tsar, and with them the King of Italy, the King of the Belgians, the Queen of Holland, the King of Norway and Sweden, the King of Denmark, the King of Greece, the King of Roumania, the Czar of Bulgaria, the King of Portugal. For monarchy was still secure in Europe : apart from the Confederation of Switzerland, France alone was headed by a President. Asia seemed content with absolute monarchy, and only the New World set store by Republicanism, so much of the New World, that is to say, as had separated from the Empires of Spain, England, and Portugal. Those republics were not yet taken very seriously by Europe, and in themselves the standards were more colonial than they realised, much more than they admitted. The prestige of European monarchy was almost unquestioned, its privilege immense, and the King of Spain, though his powers were constitutionally limited, presided in the Napoleonic style over his Council of Ministers. He was not meant to be a figure-head.

The education of a prince can never be the education of a commoner. The perceptions of a child, like the perceptions of most animals, and of some women, are aware of relations for which reason has found no better word than intuition. Children know immediately the essentials of a situation, and of a personal attitude. In the situation and the attitudes which surround a royal family the quality of deference is constant. To an unenterprising character, the demand it makes is exhausting and the result is blankness. But for a powerful character there is no finer food. This boy, in spite of his consumptive father and his tender stomach, had electric blood and thoughts like arrows. From those dim impressionable days, before we can remember, his subtle fibres had thrilled to shouts of enthusiasm and regards of homage. He had known no one, except his mother, who did not bow before him, and even she, when she was most authoritative, meant only to show him that his position was unique. Even she, in other words, was flattering, and his lightest utterances were received as the Sybil's leaves.

His fertile brain was not unequal to the rôle of prodigy, and its sharpness was smoothed by the chisel of a religious conscience. His devout mother, and his Catholic Court, had bred in him a generous and a knightly sense that his years were sacred to the people's good. One of his mottoes in those boyish years was :

" The rights of the weak become the duty of the strong " ; another : " Those who command are great only when they listen to the lowly." The *Testament Politique de Messire Colbert* rested on his table, with a marker at the 129th page to point to this passage : " *Un Prince, à proprement parler, est dans un état ce que le cœur est à l'égard de toutes les parties du corps. Si le cœur est malade tout le corps s'en ressent incontinent : tout du même que s'il y a quelque partie du corps qui le soit, le cœur en souffre à l'heure même. Il faut donc pour établir une santé parfaite que le cœur et toutes les parties soient d'accord ensemble, et qu'ils fassent si bien leurs fonctions qu'ils s'entr'aident mutuellement.*"

This classic ideal of Christian kingship the young Alfonso would develop in apophthegms of his own, apophthegms which sound more like the reflections of Marcus Aurelius in his maturity than those of an adventurous boy of fifteen. " He only can be called a regenerator who succeeds in healing the wounds of time and misfortune." Or, again, he would amaze his tutor with such a sentence as : " One cannot deny the poor the right of improving their condition and rising ; but one cannot rob the rich of their fortunes, and the means of making wealth increase."

An instinct told the precocious boy already of what his reign was to see. " I do not fear," he said, " the fierceness of new revolutions. The resistant powers of the world are shaken ; the new societies have nothing to restrain them ; the spirit of change has penetrated the minds of all, and the innovations of the future will be made by deliberate processes, but without the violent intervention of arms. What is impossible is to be condemned to a perpetual quiet. When the whole world is in movement I cannot remain fixed in our historic immobility. The law of life is the same in the whole nature of the

universe.   One grows or one declines.   To hold back
is to die."

"We have to look beyond our own frontiers," he
said again ; " the world does not begin at the Pyrenees,
or end at the Straits of Gibraltar."   A Daniel, it
appears, had come to judgment in this excellent young
man ; and who could wonder if his tutors made the
delineation of his character into a panegyric : " The
discretion of his judgment and his precocious common
sense had been noticed when he was a child," writes
one of them.   " His mother had trained him to be
circumspect and reserved, and had taught him ease,
distinction, and affability of manner.   He has already
got far in the leading European languages, his knowledge is wide and deep, and all hope that when his
mind has been awakened by contact with affairs the
amenity of his traits will show the happiest combination.   The doubts of his physical constitution seem to be
ill-founded : shooting and riding, he displays a manly
vigour, and he has a great love of the sea.   In the
few public affairs that he has touched, he has already
shown himself strong, resolute, and personal." [1]

Sanchez, the King's tutor, said that " the Queen-
Regent has made every effort not only to cultivate her
son's intelligence, but at the same time with great care
his bodily health.

" Riding, gymnasium, fencing, swimming, shooting
have hardened his skin and developed his muscles,
giving vigour to his vital functions," so wrote another.[2]   " The studies which have formed the base
of his scientific and literary education are such that
at 13 he knows the authors of our golden age, the
best contemporary authors, and French, English, and
German as well as his own language.

[1] *Illustración Española y Americana*, May 22, 1902.
[2] *Guia Palaciana*, iii. 26.

" He has also learnt military drill, and can manœuvre a company of infantry. He has an idea of sailing and naval tactics, and has studied artillery, military geography, and strategy. He gets up at seven every morning.

" The King's character is mild and docile, so that he has never needed either compulsion or coaxing to get him to work. His life has always been ordered and methodical, the plan of it being altered only for extraordinary circumstances. He has great love for his father's memory, and has a real veneration for his mother, not failing in the immense gratitude he owes her. He listens respectfully to his tutors, and is gracious to those beneath him, frank and easy in approaching all, he is able to charm all those who have the good fortune to come in contact with him, and shows not the slightest sign of pride except in being a Spaniard.

" He has an extreme affection for military drill, being devoted to everything that has to do with the organisation or administration of the Army and Navy, and there is nothing to teach him in the elements of commanding and governing our armed forces. He takes pleasure in entering upon his duties as a constitutional King, which he studies under the protection of a prudent instructor, and without anxiety to command as sovereign, he watches with complete trust in the future and serenity the moment of his majority, as indeed he should in view of the difficult periods approaching."

2

On May 19, 1902, on the young King's sixteenth birthday, both Houses gathered together in the Palace of Congress to receive his oath according to the 45th article of the fundamental code of the Monarchy.

The presidential table had been removed. In its place stood two arm-chairs on a carpet of red and gold. On the left of these chairs five others were placed for the Infantas. On the right were two tables bordered with crimson velvet and embroidered with gold, on one of which were placed the crown and sceptre, while before the other stood the Prime Minister attended by the Duke of Bivona, and the Counts of Toreno, Montero Villegas, and Bastida.

Besides the diplomatic representatives accredited to the Court were the Envoys Extraordinary, among them Prince Albert of Prussia, the Archduke Carl Stephan, the Grand-Duke Vladimir, the Duke of Connaught, the Duke of Genova, the Princes of Denmark and Greece, the Duke of Oporto, the Crown Prince of Siam, Prince Eugène of Sweden, the Crown Prince of Monaco, Prince Joachim of Prussia, the Duke of Calabria, and Prince Gennaro of Naples.

As they waited there, rumours reached them that a madman had made an attempt on the King's life; but the President was able to assure them that the procession was continuing amid the acclamations of the people.

At twenty minutes past two the Infantas Isabel and Eulalia arrived, and after them the Prince and Princess of Asturias. Each as they entered made their courtesies, one to the foreign princes, one to the Ambassadors and Ministers, and one to the Chambers. They had hardly taken their places when the King entered in the gala uniform of a Captain-General. He looked so young, and his bearing was so full of life and energy that the whole assembly broke into tumultuous applause, which was renewed again and again. As it was dying down the Queen Mother entered, accompanied by the Infanta Maria Teresa and attended by her ladies-in-waiting.

After renewed acclamations, the King raised his
and, and said in a clear ringing voice : " Be seated."
Then the Secretaries of the Parliament, the Duke
Bivona and the Count of Toreno, opened in front
His Majesty the books of the Gospels, and the
resident of the Congress, the Marquis of Vega de
rmijo, said :

" *Señor*, the Cortes convened by Your august
other are invited to receive from Your Majesty the
ath which in conformity with article 45 of the Con-
itution of the State he comes to take to keep the
onstitution and the Laws."

The King, who had taken his glove off his right
and, placed that hand on the Gospels, and in a strong
ice, which reached every ear, answered :

" *I swear by God, on the Holy Gospels, to keep the Con-
itution and the Laws. If I do so God reward me for it, and
not, may He ask me to give account.*"

At those words there were few who were unmoved,
id the applause and acclamations broke out afresh.

The Sovereigns again took their seats upon the
irone, and when all were seated the President rose
nd said :

" The Cortes have now received the oath which
our Majesty has taken to keep the Constitution and
ie Laws."

Then the Royal Family retired with the acclama-
ons and ceremonies with which they had entered.

The great procession passed to San Francisco el
rande, where they were awaited by the Primate of
pain, Cardinal Sancha, the Nuncio, and thirty-three
relates, and the King, seating himself beneath a
inopy, listened to a solemn Te Deum.

After the Te Deum, the ministers had driven back
ith the King to the palace. Worn out with the
notions of the day, and the heat, which they felt

more in their magnificent uniforms, they naturall
expected to be dismissed when the one remainin
formality had been completed. They moved int
the Council Chamber. A huge fire was burnin
on the hearth, but it could not warm the chill an
melancholy room. The ministers went through th
formality of offering their resignations. The Kin
then formally confirmed them in their powers, an
received their oaths of allegiance and they expecte
to retire, but Alfonso was so anxious to exercis
his privilege that he then said he would immediatel
hold a council. Sagasta was not enthusiastic, but h
was unable to refuse.

The King took his seat at the head of the grea
walnut table, the ministers ranging themselves o
either side. In a low tired voice, Sagasta spoke a fev
words, saying that he had never known the people s
enthusiastic ; then the King, with absolute ease c
manner, as though he had done nothing all his life bu
preside at councils, cross-examined General Weyle
the Minister of War, in a rather imperious tone as t
why he had decreed the close of the Military Acade
mies.[1] And Weyler, who was usually laconic, gav
very full answers. Nevertheless, Don Alfonso was nc
satisfied, and was about to begin again. Respectfull
but strongly Weyler replied, and when the argumer
took a dangerous turn, Sagasta intervened, sidin
with the King, and so overcoming the Minister of Wa

After a short pause, the Monarch, taking the Cor
stitution in his hand, read the eighth clause of articl
54 : " It is the King's right to confer civil appoint
ments and to grant honours and distinctions of a
classes," and then by way of commentary he said
" As you have just heard, the Constitution confers i

[1] Romanones : *Notas de una vida*, ii. 46 ; *Año Politico*, Ma
17, 1902.

n me to grant honours, titles, and grandeeships ;
erefore I inform you that I absolutely reserve for
yself the exercise of this right."

There was a feeling of profound surprise among the
inisters. What was coming next from this boy of
xteen whose tone was so imperious, and who had
een so ready to move central among the leaders of
is country ?   At this point the Duke of Veragua, the
inister of Marine, who was at once a thorough
iberal and a nobleman of the highest lineage—he was,
a fact, a descendant of Columbus—answered the King
ery simply. " I beg your pardon, *Señor*, but may I
ad the second paragraph of article 49 : ' No com-
and of the King takes effect unless countersigned by
minister ' ? "

Sagasta, who took no interest in titles and honours,
nd who appeared to be very tired, had hardly
stened to the words exchanged between the King
nd the Duke. He was too tired to say a word of
arning about the exercise of constitutional power,[1]
nd the Council ended with the signature of decrees.[2]

Next morning the Feast of Whitsuntide was cele-
rated in the Royal palace with great solemnity. In
e afternoon the King went to the Park of Madrid
lay the foundation-stone of a monument to the
emory of his father, finishing with a short speech :
" I shall be able to maintain the glorious tradition
the Spanish monarchy, and my reign will be, in
e shadow of peace, the reign of peace and justice
r all."

In the evening he went to a splendid review at the
ace-course, and was received with the same acclama-
ons. He so performed his first ceremony as head of
e Army and Navy. Two days later he was present

---

[1] Romanones : *Notas*, ii. 48.
[2] Olmet and Carraffa : *Alfonso XIII*.

at a battle of flowers in the Park, and the day following, at a bull-fight. The ceremonies of initiation were completed, leaving on all the same impression that the boy of sixteen was in no way unprepared to take the central position in his country.

3

In the succeeding months, Don Alfonso threw himself with all the energy of his temperament into his fascinating task. He rose regularly at half-past seven, and gave himself with ardour to business, to ceremony, and to sport. He broadened out the life of the palace, and the Marquis de Borja's task of keeping the accounts ceased to be a sinecure. The work of a young prince is always lightened by the claim which youth makes on the instincts of affections ; the old, conscious of their experience, feel something parental even in their deference ; the young are delighted that one so high in privilege shares their youth. And so, amid the same enthusiasm, whether he continued his royal routine in Madrid, or whether he explored the other cities of Spain, the last years of apprenticeship hurried happily on. The King did not at first travel farther than his own realm except to return in Lisbon the State visits of the King and Queen of Portugal. His round of festivities was interrupted in 1904 by the death of his sister, the Infanta Mercédes, just after her first child was born. But after the months of Court mourning, the task of reigning was continued in its brilliant auguries, and broadened out with State visits to Germany and Austria. His Foreign Minister the Marquis de Villa-Urrutia, went with him and coached him in his part. The time had not yet come when Don Alfonso paid the compliment of courtesy to his ministers without paying any attention to what they said.

In greeting foreigners, his initiative added to his
charm, and in Germany, during his official visit in
1905, this winged his tact. It had been agreed that
at the Royal Banquet in Berlin each monarch should
make his speech in French. But when the Emperor
William rose, his impulsiveness got the better of him.
He threw aside his written speech, and spoke in
German in a wholly different strain. Don Alfonso
listened perplexed. When his turn came to answer,
he spoke in Spanish. Although no one outside his
own suite understood a word of what he said, all
felt the fire and enthusiasm with which he spoke,
and gave him great applause.[1]

The Emperor was the first monarch to be visited
by Don Alfonso since his visit to Dom Carlos in
Lisbon ; but the younger monarch did not relish the
Emperor's manner, and neither then nor in later
years, when they met on the Spanish coast, or again
at Windsor, was there any real sympathy between
them.

King Edward understood King Alfonso better.
" No one can deny how charming the youth is," said
King Edward, in spite of noticing that his control of
languages was not perfect, and his table manners
were not yet those of a cosmopolitan Court. Like his
father, the young King would pick out one favourite
dish and stick to that, and he had, like most very
active people, a particularly good appetite. He drank
little wine, but much water, and ate quantities of
bread. His favourite meat was cold chicken, which
he took at every meal, and he even had a plate of it
left by his side at night.

The young man who had charmed King Edward
captivated at once both the people of France and their
President. A bomb was thrown at him as he and

[1] Romanones : *Notas*, ii. 132.

18

Loubet drove away from the opera, but he remained unmoved. He deepened French approval by kissing a Queen of the May, who presented him with a bouquet. At St. Cyr the President had told him [1] that a horse he had particularly admired would be his. " What ! " he exclaimed, " is that superb horse really for me ? " Yet his boyishness everywhere was one with something decidedly regal.

" The courtly flatteries of his childhood have so strongly fixed in the King's mind the idea of his authority that no one could be more jealous of it even in the intimacy of his own hearth," wrote Señor Pérez de Guzmán. " The King feels himself King, and is always King." [2] And yet this authority made him only more tender and affectionate to all the members of his family. He adored the memory of his father. If he needed (and he often needed) to dominate some dangerous desire, to repress some incorrect habit, or to soften the obstinacy of his will, the one expression which conquered him was, " Sire, Don Alfonso XII would not have done it." His one desire was to know, " What would my father have done ? " His intelligence was broader than his father's, but less reflective. In fact, no one could help noticing his ready initiative, his ingenuous enthusiasms, and the integrity with which he submitted to his sense of what is just and equitable. Courtiers were no less struck by the frankness with which he approached every question, and his refusal to have facts veiled.

To this moral energy and openness, Don Alfonso added two qualities even more becoming to a king : sympathy with the poor and suffering, and a daring which kept him at all times prepared to risk his life.

[1] Pérez de Guzmán : *Illustración Española,* July 15, 1906.
[2] *Ibid.,* June 30, 1905.

Driving out at the age of twenty in his car in the snow, he gave a lift to a poor woman and her children. When Moret had first made him an honorary member of the Ateneo, and they were discussing keeping hungry mutineers in order, the young King said, " Hombre, no. What you have to count is how much the cartridges cost to fire the shots, and if with the price of them you can buy bread, and so can dominate the tumult and hunger of the crowd. That is the method I prefer." He showed no fear of the bomb either at the Canaries, or driving with Loubet, or on his wedding-day. Danger, in fact, delighted him.

In the first four years of his reign he had to deal with no less than fourteen ministerial crises, and with eight different Prime Ministers. There was no sign that either in Maura, on the one side, or in Montero Rios, Moret, or López Dominguez (perhaps as yet not even in Canalejas), there was any real power of ideas, or any fixed policy in the politicians except the policy of getting places. Young as he was, the King was more king than his Ministers were ministers. Each change of government meant not only a change of politicians, but of secretaries, sub-secretaries, and civil governors. One thing alone remained fixed : the King in the exercise of his prerogative, the King in relation to the Constitution.

" From the depth of misfortunes in which we have lain so long," wrote a Spanish historian, " the lines of the physiognomy of Alfonso XIII are already so clearly outlined that towards him, and him alone, turn all the eyes of hope in the new situation created by the King since the solemn declaration of his majority, and from his oath, more solemn still, to maintain the constitution of the State." [1]

[1] *Illustración Española*, July 22, 1906.

He was dominated by no one : sovereign con-
sciously and always, he gave to his nation that which
ensures for a nation the solidity of its freedom, the
King's majesty which symbolises the continuance of
its administration and its laws, the dignity of a
people's life in society.   His supremacy was the
expression of the nation's power and wisdom.   He
personified the army ; he was the pledge of intellectual
progress, material prosperity, of the honour and
prestige of the nation.   He focused its hopes, main-
taining its integrity and increasing its greatness,
providing unity behind the variety of its thoughts,
and equilibrium to its effervescing parties.   For such
is the sacred function of a king : his office is to give a
nation what else it cannot have, a life which centres
and consecrates that nation's life ; a heart, as Colbert
said, beating with the blood which flows through every
vein of it, with the rich tide on which its health and
strength depend.   Behind the administration, beyond
the lawgivers, the King, as the head of this society,
gives it a final and continuous unity, because he
authorises its laws and embodies its order.   In a
country like Spain, where changes are so frequent
and politics so arbitrary, the King's function was more
valuable than all the parliaments.   And whether or
not the Civil Servant changes with the change of
government, the country which has a king has a
man trained from youth to assume the attributes
of Majesty, to dispense graciousness, to accumulate
experience by constant acquaintance with both
leaders and affairs, and to nourish the patriot's
imagination by the dignity of his ancient office, and
refresh it with the magnificence of courtly state.

In Spain royalty was exalted to a still higher end.
The King had not only a king's majesty, but Catholic
majesty.   His authority was definitely bound to

exalting life to an end beyond life, where justice, love, and peace should signify a spiritual felicity, and make countless kingdoms beauteous in their accord with the will of heaven, so that civilisation meant not only the temporal wealth of men, but strengthened it and exalted it into unity with the supremacy of Christ and the glory of His Church.

Young King Alfonso knew those things, and was not seldom to refer to them. But in the unworthy intrigues so long associated with the Spanish crown, and which made it so uncertain, he must ensure the principle by proving himself equal to so high an office. Could he overcome the fatal powers which long since had played with, and unbalanced, the pillars above which his throne was set? Or were there in his own attractive character fresh menaces of danger? Men doubted whether so strong a sense of personal supremacy might not be its own undoing. The King's energy was hardly equalled by his patience. Count Romanones questioned whether it would not have been wise to complete his education by sending him abroad to study foreign Parliaments. Señor Sagasta put a subtler point: "The most difficult questions in a palace," he said, "are those that refer to people. In questions of principle there is room for difference of opinion, and you can argue with a sovereign till you convince him. But it costs a great effort to modify his opinions where people are involved." [1]

Apart from this there was in his nature a love of surprise and risk. When his mother had given him a new thoroughbred, he rode it up the palace staircase into her salon, though to get it down again without breaking its legs he had to carpet the staircase. Critical spirits complained that love of sports dis-

[1] Romanones : *Notas*, ii. 49.

tracted him from more serious things. Polo was a
new game for Spanish monarchs, and looked too
perilous for them ; but polo was less disturbing than
the speed with which he drove his car. "Your
Majesty is to be remembered in history," warned a
Conservative Prime Minister, " as a King, and not as
a *chauffeur*." Don Alfonso was not only a *chauffeur*,
but also a *chasseur*. Count Romanones declared that
he was, in fact, the best shot in Spain. Before long
the politicians made a discovery more disconcerting :
their regal impresario was so versatile that actually
in their own business he was the most expert of
them all.

4

His Majesty, they also noticed, had a heart. Perhaps there was something in his Bourbon heredity
that went back to the wife of the Duke of Riansares,
his great-grandmother, though he had the decisive
features of his Habsburg mother. He was devoted to
his youthful friends, the Marquis of Viana, the
Marquis of Tovar, and the Duke of Arévalo. And he
was soon to fall in love. His journeys to foreign
Courts were not mere visits of ceremony : they were
excursions in search of a bride.

Don Alfonso, it was felt, should break with the
family traditions, and strengthen his line with new
blood. What better blood than England's ? England
had sent to the ceremonies of his coming of age him
who was perhaps the finest and most soldierly figure
of all the princes of Europe, the Duke of Connaught.
The Duke of Connaught had a daughter : her mother
was a Prussian Princess. To marry her would unite
the Court of Spain with England, with Russia, and
with Germany. King Alfonso and Princess Patricia

were given many opportunities to meet ; her photograph was made familiar to Spain by reproductions in the newspapers ; and Liberal politicians welcomed the opportunity for a bond with the British traditions.

In June 1905 King Alfonso arrived in England. He was just twenty, he was full of life, and the prestige of royalty in those early years of King Edward's reign, with the Conservatives still in power, stood on a crowning height. Society circled round it, wealthy, powerful, glittering. The social ceremonies of the life which touched the Court were lavish and continual. Its easy but sumptuous ritual absorbed all types of aristocracy, and though the foundations of society were ancient, it was hospitable to all newness that could awaken interest or widen power. Into this King Alfonso was given a swift and splendid initiation. A review at Aldershot, a lunch at Marlborough House, a visit to Windsor, a gala at Covent Garden, a banquet at Buckingham Palace, another at Lansdowne House (for Lord Lansdowne was Foreign Secretary), a ball at Lady Londonderry's, and a Court ball followed close on one another to give Spain's King and England's central society the means of knowing each other. Between these functions, he made visits to the House of Commons, the Tower of London, Westminster Abbey, and St. Paul's ; to the tombs of Wellington and Gordon ; to the present Duke of Wellington at Apsley House, and to that tireless Spaniard who knew and thought so much, the Empress Eugénie at Farnborough.

There was none who scrutinised his fate more closely ; none who realised more clearly that in that moving flash of orders and tiaras, of wine-cups and gold plate, King Alfonso was looking for a bride. It was observed that between him and Princess Patricia things seemed to get no farther. His impressionable heart was developing an attraction for another of King Edward's nieces, and one who appealed to his susceptibilities by being at once more a girl and more a woman. The daughter of Princess Beatrice had a rare combination of high spirits and the grand manner. She bore the names of two of the greatest personalities in Europe, the two sovereigns who had dominated her childhood, Victoria and Eugénie. Who could dispute the regal power in the presence of the ancient Queen, the great lady who was worshipped almost as a divinity by the four hundred million people of the British Empire, and whom Princess Ena knew and loved as her own grandmother? And yet she knew equally well the other beautiful sovereign whom also England loved, although she lived apart, and who was regal too in her sad splendour, the brilliant, continental, Catholic Eugénie. These were the two to whom Princess Ena always said, " Your Majesty." The Empress Eugénie was her godmother, and almost felt like something more. For she and Victoria, it was whispered, had designed that Princess Beatrice should espouse the Prince Imperial when he came back from Zululand.

The Empress, like her mother, was a matchmaker. She no sooner saw an important baby than she began to speculate on its wedding and its progeny. And though she was approaching eighty now, her mind at the King of Spain's arrival went back—how could it but go back?—to sixty years before, when from close at hand she had watched the play of intrigue at Madrid before Queen Isabel was affianced. In her unfading memory Bresson and Mr. Bulwer were clear outlines still. And this time, as she knew, there was not merely, as then, the British choice in question : it was now the choice of a British princess. The King of Spain's marriage naturally absorbed her ; she was hardly less absorbed in the marriage of her god-daughter. The two ideas inevitably coalesced ; and the plan was very soon discussed with Princess Beatrice. When King Alfonso ceased to interest him-self in Princess Patricia, he found Princess Ena was never far away. The plans of Eugénie ran even with the claims of blood : the two young people were soon simply in love.

There was an outcry from the point of view of religion. The Queen of Spain must obviously be Catholic, and how could a British princess forswear her Protestantism ? The influence of Farnborough had long since settled that question. Even in the old days of Queen Victoria, Princess Ena had been allowed, by a special miracle, to have a Catholic godmother. From her earliest years she had felt a peculiar attrac-tion in the Farnborough religion. It was one with the whole life of the little Court and the Spaniards who were never absent from it. Windsor was for every-body, but Farnborough was specially Princess Ena's : she was one with everything to do with it. She had in fact always wanted to be a Catholic. King Edward, who had always been a warm admirer of the Empress, would be the last to disagree if the Spanish crown came into the question. But there were dan-gers in the Spanish crown itself, apart from its religion. He warned his niece in quite uncompromis-ing terms of all she risked : "Don't come back whining here," he even said. But he was pleased that she should wear a crown, and now that his policy of an *entente* with France and Russia was ripening so rapidly, he was grateful for so close a bond with the Spanish Court. King Alfonso was also warned that the Battenbergs were liable to suffer from a curious disease, known commonly as bleeders, and that this disease could possibly be transmitted even when it was

latent. But he was so deeply in love now that he
would listen to no warning of uncertain dangers
lurking in the heredity of a princess so radiantly
healthy. On his return to Spain he did not try to
hide his passion. And even when he sat in council
with his ministers, the photograph of the Princess was
placed before him. The whole Court declared him
madly in love.

5

A visit of Princess Ena to San Sebastian, a tour of
Don Alfonso in the Canaries preceded the marriage
ceremony of 1906. His realms now all knew him, and
they regarded the wedding with a personal keenness.

On May 25 the Princess arrived at the frontier
with her mother, her brothers, and her suite. To
Madrid she made a triumphant journey in the company of her lover. " I know the journey by heart,
but I have never made it so happily," he said. For a
week before the wedding she found a temporary home
at El Pardo, for tradition forbids that a future Queen
of Spain shall enter Madrid before her wedding-day.
Every day Don Alfonso lunched and dined at El
Pardo. From there she drove up to the Campo del
Moro, and so into the Royal Palace, where Napoleon
had exclaimed to Joseph on the staircase : " *Mon
frère, tu es mieux logé que moi.*" A suite in the old
Admiralty House, the Ministerio de Marina, had been
reserved for her to don her wedding dress before the
ceremony at San Jerónimo.

The wedding in the brilliant May weather of
Madrid was a great international ceremony. The
town blazed with the red and yellow banner of Spain,
and with festoons of flowers. Silks, carpets, curtains
hung from every window, while the carriages drove

to make a galaxy of splendour in the Gothic Church
of San Jerónimo.   England had sent the Prince and
Princess of Wales, Austria the Archduke Franz
Ferdinand, Russia the Grand Duke Vladimir, Germany Prince Albert and Prince Henry, Italy the Duke
of Genoa, and there were more than thirty other
special envoys, each with a brilliant suite.

The bride had driven from El Pardo with her
mother in a closed car early in the morning to the
Ministry of Marine to dress.   At half-past ten she
issued from her apartments, followed by the Queen
Mother and Princess Beatrice.   As she went to her
carriage the acclamation was so intense that it was
impossible to keep the horses quiet, the carriage
moved as she put her foot on the step, and in her long
train she was in danger of being tripped.   But this
little contretemps was surmounted, and, within half an
hour, she found herself before the altar with the King.
In due order the ceremonies of espousal, the Nuptial
Mass, and the Te Deum followed.   And then, retiring
to the cloister, they signed the marriage contract.
The ceremonies had taken almost three hours.   A
little after two the great procession started for the
palace in brilliant sunshine, amid the delirious
acclamations of the crowd.

6

The King had received many anonymous letters
threatening assassination, and though he himself had
never turned a hair in danger, he could not restrain a
certain feeling of anxiety.   The Princess too had had
a presentiment, and as she adorned herself as a bride
was restless and preoccupied.   The Government
knew of the danger, and had taken its precautions.
An attempt had been feared at the very door of the

church, and the police had been doubled. As the procession moved off, the Home Minister, Romanones, who was responsible, breathed more freely. He hurried to his office at the Puerta del Sol, and saw the procession pass amid wild enthusiasm. There were only a few hundred yards to the palace. Now surely all was well. He had hardly reached his house when he heard a call to the telephone. He was told that a bomb had been thrown in the Calle Mayor.

Some days before an anarchist named Morral had taken rooms in a *pension* at No. 88 in that street. The evening before, he returned with a large bouquet of flowers. As the royal carriage approached, he threw the bouquet towards the carriage. There was a loud explosion as it touched the pavement, a cry of anguish, a stampede of horses, a cloud of smoke enveloped the royal carriage, and chips of wood, with fragments of harness and of uniforms flew in all directions. The King leant forward and covered the Queen's body with his own, and then drew her up again to sit beside him : they found themselves unhurt, though the bomb had killed one of the hind white horses and wounded some of the others which drew the royal carriage. The surviving horses stampeded, and it was some time before the grooms could bring them to a halt. It was then decided that the King and Queen should change from the gala coach to an empty one which followed it. The King descended, the Queen with him. Her face was deadly pale, her eyes full of tears. Everyone around her was a stranger, except her husband, and even he was talking in a language she hardly understood. Her eyes rested with unspeakable relief on four officers of the English Horse Guards who appeared with the British Ambassador. The King was approached by a Spanish officer, Alvarez de Toledo, whose face was dripping with blood. " Less talk," said Don Alfonso, " and look after *yourself.*" Again the procession moved on. Someone had drawn the curtains across the windows. The King drew them back, and showed himself in full view of his people. That afternoon he drove out again, unguarded, to visit the wounded. Next day he insisted on driving with his bride through the most populous streets of the city.

As the royal carriage went on down the Calle Mayor, it left behind thirty-seven dead and more than a hundred injured among the royal equerries, the soldiers lining the street, spectators on the pavement ; as well as twelve of the inhabitants of the house from which the bomb had been thrown, among them the young and beautiful Marchioness of Tolosa. At the door of the house Romanones, on his arrival, found eight dead bodies covered with cloaks ; pools of blood lay on the street ; he heard groans on every side. As he walked up the staircase he saw that it also was stained with blood. He hurried to the room which Morral had been occupying. The acrid smell of the explosives the murderer had used for his bomb made a sickening mixture with that which he had employed against his syphilis.

Matthew Morral was a Catalan of twenty-seven who had arrived in Madrid a few days before. He was known to the police as an anarchist, but had so far done nothing to warrant an arrest. He took advantage of the confusion caused by the bomb to pass down the stairs and mix with the crowd in the street. He thus passed to the office of a revolutionary newspaper called *Mutiny*, where the editor, Nakens, in a spirit of mistaken generosity, became an accessory after the fact, and helped him to attempt an escape. Two days later a policeman at an outlying village dis-

covered the assassin and arrested him.   But as this
man brought him into the village of Torrejon, Morral
shot the policeman dead from behind, and then shot
himself through the heart.[1]   For several days his body
lay in the morgue.   The face was calm, the features
regular, the hands clean and well cared for.   It was
because he came of a respectable class that he had
eluded the police.   They did not know that when at
Barcelona he had attended an atheist school, founded
by a revolutionary, Francisco Ferrer.   That school
existed to undermine Spain's sanest traditions of
authority in Church and State.   When its doctrine
grew rotten-ripe in a brain further unbalanced by
venereal excess and resultant disease, the outcome, not
altogether surprising, was the crime of the Calle
Mayor ;   aiming at the life of the central authority of
the kingdom, as a step towards general anarchy, it
had succeeded only in the minor consequence of
murder of thirty-seven peaceful citizens, and making
hideous mutilations on nearly three times as many.
Neither King nor Queen could doubt that in the
august task before them royal privilege must be
buttressed by sacrifice.   Every time they appeared in
public, they were facing death like a cavalry subaltern
leading his troops into battle.   Forces of disorder,
inspired by atheism, were determined to hunt them
down.   But they were not unequal to the soldier's
task.   They trusted to the defence of Spanish loyalty.

[1] The policeman had a wife and several small children, for
whom the King provided out of his own bounty.

XII

KING ALFONSO : THE ROYAL DIPLOMATIST

I consider under all circumstances a constitutional monarchy
the best form of government for Spain in its present state of
knowledge and improvement.
WASHINGTON IRVING : *Letters from Sunnyside and Spain.*

I

THE number of persons murdered suggested the
abandonment of festivities for mourning ; but that
would have helped no one, and harmed many ; and
so the great ceremonies arranged continued with all
the splendour with which they were planned. Then
the bride and bridegroom had some quiet days in El
Pardo ; they visited Aranjuez and La Granja, and
they spent the late summer at San Sebastian. "And
don't you remember, Ena," he asked in England,
referring to the chivalrous way he had seized her
when the bomb was thrown, "how for weeks afterwards you had the black marks of my fingers on
your nice white fat arms?"

The young Queen was extremely popular : although
she had still much Spanish to learn, she was learning
quickly, and with a face so charming, a figure so
gracious, and so queenly a bearing, she had done her
part before she spoke. Her days were full from break-
fast-time to tea, with letters, charities, exercise,
affairs, and before long her time-table was dominated
by the fact of her expectant motherhood. The Prince
of Asturias was born some eleven months after the
wedding-day. Another son, two daughters, and

finally two more sons followed in the next seven years.

The King had now developed his personal gifts to great success. He remained much loved ; he was a splendid ambassador for Spain in his tours abroad, and became extremely popular in France and England, to which he paid long visits both in 1907 and 1908.

There was nothing, however, to obscure the fact that the throne of Spain was not the same sort of seat as an arm-chair. Not only did the Governments, and with them the officials, continue to change with disturbing frequency, but in spite of Europe's prosperity, Spanish soil was still volcanic : anarchy might break out at any moment to assassination, as on the hideous eruption of the wedding-day. The political parties, which still depended for their power on the appointments of the mayors and municipal officers, and behind them the political bosses, or "*caciques*," made only so much a pretence of democracy as to weaken their powers of government ; and because there was neither democracy nor government, the forces of anarchy were organising. The police knew that Morral was but one of many assassins who had been suborned to carry out a ghastly scheme.

There had already been terrorism in Barcelona. On February 1, 1908, the King of Portugal and his heir were murdered in Lisbon. The night before he was killed, King Carlos had signed a decree authorising the police to deport anarchists. Could such a decree be signed in Spain ? Yet what was the alternative ? The Lisbon assassinations gave Spain a horrible reminder of the hidden powers at work all over the Peninsula.

Don Alejandro Lerroux, therefore, a leading Republican of Barcelona, who had published in his paper *Rebellión* a subversive article from a Portuguese

QUEEN VICTORIA EUGÉNIE OF SPAIN

After the portrait by M. de Laszlo in the Royal Palace, Madrid.

" With a face so charming, a figure so gracious, and so queenly a bearing,
she had done her part before she spoke."

paper, was sentenced to two years' imprisonment : he
fled to France, and afterwards to America. But his
departure weakened the Government rather than
strengthened it, for Lerroux had combated with the
utmost vigour the Catalan extremists who were
hostile to Spain.

In March, nevertheless, the King went with Maura,
his Conservative Prime Minister, to pay a visit to
Barcelona. He was received with more than the
usual ovation. Yet three bombs burst near him, and
the Mayor, who had asked the King to inaugurate
reform, was himself asked to resign. Even before Don
Alfonso started there had been strong propaganda to
prevent him going : the telephones from Barcelona
to Madrid rang incessantly, but at last the Government lost patience, and the minute that the word
" King," " Maura," or even " visit " was mentioned,
the communication was cut.

Alfonso still followed his mother's constitutional
example. But it was not surprising if the young King
returned from this visit to Catalonia a little more
inclined than usual in the sense of authority which
had been developed from early youth in his personal
imperiousness. On July 12 he gave his cousin, Don
Alfonso, a magnificent Toledo sword as a wedding
present ; but hearing afterwards that when this
cousin married the Queen's cousin, Princess Beatrice
of Saxe-Coburg, he had accepted the Protestant as
well as the Catholic rite, the King applied through
the Court the discipline of the Church. He deprived
his cousin of his Infantazgo, his Grand Cross of Carlos
III, and his Golden Fleece. It was known that the
advice had not come from the ministers ; and this
act awoke criticism.

Meanwhile, on July 14, the King made a speech
of fire to the cadets in the Military Academy at

19

Toledo. Immortality, glory, sacrifice, he said, were
the words that should be engraved in indelible
characters in their hearts as soldiers. Four days later
old memories were revived by the death of his father's
rival, Don Carlos, who claimed to be Carlos VIII, and
almost immediately after that, war broke out with the
Berber tribesmen in the Rif. So did Alfonso approach
the question of that African territory which was to
be so baleful to his power and popularity. It led at
once to a conspiracy which recalled the horrors of his
wedding-day three years before.

2

Whether in the interests of commerce, or of mere
prestige, Spain had begun again to clutch at empire.
The French example in Morocco awoke an effort of
emulation. Politicians had given across the straits a
zone of influence in area equal to Massachusetts, and
backed by the mountain chain of the Rif. Those
mountains were inhabited by hawk-like tribes, who
would from time to time swoop down upon the little
Spanish settlements. Spain's conscripts were called
upon to defend them, though they felt no interest in
risking their comfort or their lives on what they
believed a gratuitous enterprise. When the troops
were ordered to embark, a thrill of protest electrified
the dark tenements where Barcelona's labourers live
in a network of silent defiles. The soldiers could not
mutiny ; but the masses could revolt. Long years of
conspiracy had matured their aptitude to take advantage of such an occasion. On August 2 communications were cut between Barcelona and Madrid, and
the capital of Catalonia became the scene of civil warfare. The police were fought by even the *Somaten*,
that private civil force which was formed long ago in

Catalonia to maintain order, and whose motto was peace. In the name of peace, the *Somaten* fired upon the army, and did as much harm to their capital as if the Berbers had assaulted it. The mob burnt churches and libraries, they desecrated altars and tombs. The disorder spread to Manresa and to Sabadell, where some of the finest churches were destroyed. It was indeed to churches, to altars, and to the tombs of nuns that the mob was especially violent. The crowd, it seemed, was in delirium, and did not know what it was doing. But those who directed it knew what *they* were doing.

The uproar continued for a week. In the first days no one could tell who were behind it. As the enquiries proceeded, however, and as the revolt turned from anti-militarism to anti-clericalism, the evidence pointed to a man who at first seemed remote from the acts of violence. That man was the founder and head of the school in which Morral had been educated. His name was Francisco Ferrer.

Ferrer was then a man of some fifty years of age. The son of a small proprietor in Catalonia, he had become in youth a militant atheist. He had left Spain for Paris. There his wife had shot him, and he had abandoned her for another woman. This second, however, he abandoned also. His influence with yet a third woman enabled him to obtain a considerable sum of money, with which he founded his atheistic school, and for some years he had been running this school while living with yet a fourth woman, a young and good-looking Catalan, with whom not only he, but Morral, had been in love.

Ferrer was, says Count Romanones,[1] up to a certain point an intellectual : " He was endowed with a will of iron and deeply rooted convictions, and was a

[1] Romanones : *Notas*, p. 239.

mortal enemy of those who did not share his views."
He had been in his way an apostle, an apostle of free
love, and of free-thinking, and though by no means
a saint or even a philosopher, he had been self-denying
enough to take no personal advantage of the funds he
had collected for his propaganda.   But his influence
on youth was obviously unhealthy, and in his denun-
ciations of all forms of belief, or of anything associated
with them, he had the insanity of the bigot.   He
might well have been arrested for inculcating doctrines
subversive of morality, but Spanish toleration had
gone so far as to leave him unmolested.

As the enquiries proceeded, it was found that he
had incited the rioters in Barcelona, that he had
acted as an agent of revolution in outlying villages,
and that he had been moving about Barcelona speaking in support of revolution.[1]   He then went into
hiding.

The whole development of the outbreak was in
strict accordance with the anti-clerical fanaticism, of
which he was the known and tolerated leader.   A
number of investigators were convinced that he was
the instigator of the week of outrage.   It is quite
possible to prove that the charge against him of
using violence against the State is supported only by
circumstantial evidence[2] ;   but when a man who is
living a grossly immoral life (adultery is still defined
by the law as gross immorality), who attacks the
most sacred institutions of society, and derides its
highest beliefs, whose partner goes out from their
common school to perpetrate a sensational crime
which kills thirty-seven people and shocks not only
Spain but the world, when such a man is seen encouraging a mutiny marked by pillage and by

[1] William Archer : *Life, Trial, and Death of F. Ferrer.*
[2] *Ibid.*

murder, and then rushes into hiding, he can hardly
expect, in this common-sense world, to be found not
guilty, when he is put on trial, by the rough justice of
either a jury or a court-martial. It was a court-
martial which tried Ferrer, and he was shot next day.
But at that moment the Prime Minister of Spain,
Maura, was a Conservative and a strong Catholic.
This was enough to create the idea that in Spain there
was still a short of Inquisition, and that Ferrer was
a sort of Savonarola. He was exalted as a martyr
among the rationalists of the world. Maura and his
Government, knowing that there was not the slightest
reason for the horror worked up internationally by
indignant Liberal thinkers, paid no attention to them ;
he did not disturb himself for the reasoned protest of
his political adversaries. Don Segismundo Moret,
their leader, had said that considering the war in
Africa and the disorder in Barcelona he would support
the Government in its strong action.[1] But in view of
the excitement which arose in the autumn, he was
tempted to go back on his promise. All combined
against Maura, and his Government fell.

3

A few months later saw the keenest mind in Spain
at the head of the Government. It was now ten
years since Don José Canalejas had first obtained
a post in a ministry, and in whatever ministry he
appeared, he was the leading spirit. His was a mind
at once so scholarly and so eager, his energy was so
full and fresh, that his sincerity as a reformer shone
out among all the men of his time. He was at once a
strong anti-clerical and a devoted Catholic. " One
must," he said, " at the same time curse clericalism

[1] Romanones : *Notas.*

and bless the Church, this Holy Church which clericalism calls mother and exploits as slave." [1] He
feared that bishops, and still more the men and
women of the religious orders, wanted to replace the
movement of the human heart towards spiritual
things by the rules and conventions of their own
calling, that they wanted to command rather than to
share, that in fact they were inclined to restrict the
free development of even what is most promising in
modern life so as to ensure their old position of
supremacy.

Canalejas was at once an ardent Catholic and an
ardent Liberal.   Although he had been converted to
monarchism when he saw the King to be the expression of the national will, he had determined to keep
a respectful distance from Don Alfonso : in a short
time he found that beyond his powers.   There was
about the young sovereign something which no
minister could resist.   He was at once so friendly, so
expansive, and so adroit, that little by little the most
experienced politician found himself charmed into an
exchange of compromise with the King.   And the
youth of the King tempted Canalejas to believe that
Spain was about to evolve an English monarchy.
The King, after all, was still only twenty-five when
he found Canalejas his Prime Minister.   And if
Canalejas had fallen to the King, it was the King
who seemed to be acting at the behest of his
minister.[2]

For on June 16, 1910, Don Alfonso, in a speech from
the throne, actually expressed himself as a Liberal-
Catholic.   He began by talking of his filial respect to
the Holy See, but soon declared that his Government
would strive to give expression to the public aspiration

[1] Romanones: *Notas.*
[2] J. Francos Rodriguez : *Vida de Canalejas.*

KING ALFONSO XIII
After the portrait by Casals

" There was in the young sovereign something no minister could resist."

for the reduction and control of the religious orders, without impairing their independence in spiritual matters. Instructions were sent out to the Civil Governors to enforce the existing rules as to the registration of the orders ; negotiations were opened with Rome for the suppression of convents not needed by their different dioceses. " The Government," said the King, " was inspired by the universal spirit of liberty of conscience."

At this point the clericals of Spain shrivelled with horror ; the ladies of Seville in a formal protest compared Canalejas to Diocletian. The Almighty was implored to have pity on Spain, and, as in times of public calamity, the relics of San Isidro were to be carried in procession through the streets of Madrid. The Chapter of Toledo complained of the King's speech as " threatening the total abolition of the faith of Christ, and an open and shameless persecution of the Catholic Church." So intransigent were Pius X and Cardinal Merry del Val, that on July 30 the Spanish Ambassador was recalled from the Vatican in protest.[1]

But Canalejas and the King were at one. The Republican, Melquiades Alvarez, warned his friends that the great reformer had become the captive of the Crown. And Canalejas was beginning to depend on Conservative support against the Republican Socialists, led by Alvarez and Lerroux. Maura assured him that he could always depend on the Conservative alliance to defend the monarchy. He needed it ; for he was on a tight rope. The Ultramontanes and Carlists, in fact, everyone under the clerical influence, was as hostile to him as the extreme Left were suspicious of him adulterating his Liberal zeal.

[1] *The Times*, Oct. 18, 1910.

It was at this point that the Republicans began to affirm that in such a delicate situation the King would be the deciding factor. Secretly they hoped that the King would drop Canalejas and his Liberal programme ; he would then have all the influences of the Left against him, and place his throne in extreme jeopardy.[1]

But the King was far too astute not to see that for himself. He knew the Republican contention that it was not himself but his office which they were against. They held that nothing good had come out of the monarchy for three hundred years, and that, however Liberal the King's own intentions might be, he could not dominate the clerical and reactionary influences which were entrenched in those who most frequented the Court. Yet it did not need great shrewdness to see that it was not reactionaries who would dethrone the King ; the Left had become too strong for him to be safe without it, and in Canalejas he found that the most prominent brain in the country was perfectly in sympathy. So for a year, in spite of raging conflicts, the Liberal policy—now contained in the monarchical constitution—was gradually crystallising in the sense of an English monarchy, as a boiling conserve of fruits, when placed with the due amount of sugar over a brisk fire, solidifies to keep for an indefinite time.

But the revolutionaries were not going to give in easily.

At the beginning of April 1911 the arguments over the conviction of Ferrer eighteen months before were revived. In spite of the judicial courts having given their final decision, the whole subject was debated afresh in Parliament. Canalejas asked for a vote of confidence. He had to deal with the fact that the

[1] *The Times*, Oct. 18, 1910.

army, on which alone the Government must depend
to maintain order, was having its judicial functions
attacked, not because its courts were unjust, but
because there was a party which was strong against
the army.   When Canalejas offered his resignation,
the King refused to accept it, pointing out that
Canalejas had the majority of the Chambers with him.
The Government insisted that they would use force
to repel violent attacks on law and order.   The
Socialists were still insistent, but their proposition
was rejected by 179 against 23.

As the interest in Ferrer declined, that in Morocco
rose.   Were not the French, it was asked, tyrannising
over the Spanish in the question of Morocco ?   There
was a reassuring speech from a French minister : " As
far as Spain is concerned, we shall continue our cordial
and friendly relations with her, working together in
the most conciliatory spirit, and endeavouring to
improve our economic relations."   But that was all
very well.   The French, behind their camouflage of
courtesy, were increasing their preponderance in
Morocco with a disquieting thoroughness.   And when
the French were alarmed by the arrival of the German
cruiser *Panther* at Agadir on July 1, the Spaniards
were by no means displeased.

4

Just at that time the question of Canalejas's anti-
clerical Catholicism was settled in a way surprising
and significant.   The Church had organised in
Madrid a Eucharistic Congress.   It was one of those
sacred pageants which touch the depths of the Spanish
heart.   In the great procession which passed in such
splendid state through the streets of the capital on

that June afternoon of 1911, there were few indeed
who did not believe that there before them present in
the Host, present in act and power, was He to whose
redemption they owed the pledge and hope of heaven.
Everywhere there was the same deep religious feeling.
From street to street they caught up the echo of the
chant : *Hosanna to the Son of David.* Even Liberal
politicians felt that they had never seen anything
more beautiful or more impressive.[1] The scarlet of
the cardinals' robes, the purple of the bishops and
monsignori, and the glitter of uniforms contrasted
with the black of the priests' cassocks, and of the
frock-coats of the laymen, Don Antonio Maura at
their head. As the procession moved on, the bells
from the parish churches, which were all decorated
as were the streets, rang out their music above the
shrill cry of swifts and swallows, which perched on
the granite façade of the Royal Armoury. A flight
of doves at the palace completed the scene and
heightened the enchantment.

The Cardinal Primate, followed by a splendid
suite, bearing in his hand the gorgeous monstrance
which for so many hours had centred the devout
attention of the people, at last swept up the great
stairway of the Royal Palace, and entered the Throne-
room. There the Royal Family knelt, the King in
uniform, with a candle in his hand. There, too, his
Liberal ministers fell upon their knees, and there
were some who, in the transport of their fervour,
pressed their lips to the floor where the awful Presence
had passed by.

The King himself headed the procession into the
Royal Chapel. Behind him were the Queen Mother,
the Infantes, the nobles of Spain, and the Liberal
ministers. And while he knelt before the rest, his

---

[1] Romanones : *Notas.*

haplain advanced and read the form of national onsecration :

> " Sovereign Lord, alive and present in the most holy Sacrament of the Eucharist, King of Kings and Lord of Lords, Before Thy august throne of grace and mercy, Spain, Thy beloved daughter, bows in adoration.
> " We are Thy people : reign over us, with might to endure from everlasting to everlasting." [1]

Such was the triumph of the Church in the heyday f the Liberal Government : in the face of that riumph anti-clerical legislation was impossible.

5

Yet there was one party which ground its teeth in ury. Liberal newspapers complained that Spain was s backward as Ecuador or Paraguay. On July 9, 911, a banquet was offered to Don Melquiades lvarez. In attacking the King's relations with the rmy and the Church, he voiced the fury of the nilitant agnostics.[2] "The army is the nation in rms," said Señor Alvarez, " and can have no other nterests than those of the national society as a whole, nd no other honour than the honour of all, and no ther extent than the growth and prosperity of the ountry. In the eyes of the army the King cannot be he Head of the Armed Forces : the King must be the irst servant of the nation, and nothing more than the irst servant of the nation. And when the nation, by he legitimate vigour of the people, makes known its overeign voice, the army, which is the depository of

[1] Soldevilla : *Año Político*, 1911, p. 289.
[2] *Op. cit.*

force, must give way before this voice, passing
necessary over existing institutions.

" The Conservative Party, better called the part
of Maura, represent for us class privileges against th
aspirations of the people ; religious fanaticism whic
prevents it from recognising the reality of the clerica
problem ; war which annihilates us for ever :
politic of repression, inhuman, barbarous, an
cowardly. For these reasons we must annihilate i
employing every means and all our energy. Canale
jas represents the policy of deceit, and his conduc
is the conduct of a courtier. One cannot doubt i
Remember what has just happened. He has allowe
the King, of his own will, to close the Eucharisti
Congress, which was not an outpouring of religiou
feeling, but a brutal outburst of the reactionary an
fanatical force of clericalism. He has done an un
heard-of thing—he has allowed the King to read
speech written by none of his advisers ; he has allowe
the King to come to a secret understanding with th
representative of the Church."

During November there was a violent campaig
against Canalejas in the Radical Press ; *España Nuev*
even saying that he was politically dead, after provin,
himself a traitor to his country.

To the Republican writer, Pérez Galdos, wh
was his old friend, Canalejas, on November 3c
made an eloquent reply : "In these days of syste
matic persecution all the newspapers which are hostil
to monarchical government, or out of sympathy wit
the dynasty, enjoy not only the ' sovereign liberty c
thought ' which you advocate, but a tolerance give
in no other country.

" As for the arbitrary persecution of workmen'
societies, none have to submit to limitations, unles
according to the fundamental principles of the Court

f Justice. What the Courts restrain is the illicit
xploitation of the good faith of the Spanish people,
nducing it to paralyse the railway services in agree-
nent with foreign revolutionaries, to deprive the great
:ities of light, water, and heat, to control the work-
nan's liberty by violence, to prevent the concentration
of troops, to take up arms against the forces of the
3tate, including the burning, the attack and the
.ooting of public buildings, and the assassination of
nodest citizens who are placed in authority and die
is martyrs to duty.[1]

" Not a single citizen suffers the penalty of banishment or exile."

All that he said was true ; but, added to the trouble
in the Rif, and the strain with France, the fierce
bitterness of the Left made close observers anxious :
they felt that something terrible might happen. In
the following autumn it did happen.

6

Meanwhile the King had a passage at arms with
his unconventional aunt, the Infanta Eulalia.

On December 2, 1911, *Le Temps* had stated that
the Infanta was publishing a book, *Au fil de la vie*,
written in the simplest style. The book was favourable to divorce. It advocated woman's complete
independence, and the same education for all classes.
There was not in the Royal Palace the slightest
attempt to hide the King's annoyance, or the fact
itself.

The King telegraphed on December 2 :

" Surprised newspaper's announcement that
you are publishing book under pseudonym

[1] Soldevilla : *Año Político,* 1911.

Condesa de Avila, and that, judging other news, it is anticipated it will cause sensation ; desire that you suspend publication until I see it and authorise it."

The Infanta replied next day :

" Amazed that you judge book without seeing it ; on receiving the order I telegraphed to take leave of you."

The King then telegraphed to the Ambassador :

" In view of this, please go and visit her, giving her to understand that I am not disposed to tolerate such an attitude, and that her answer does not correspond to what I said."

The Infanta refused to receive the Ambassador, announcing that she had separated from the Spanish Royal Family and the state of Spain, and that neither then, nor at any other time, would she receive the Ambassador.

The King then announced that he did not censor the publications of his family, and that Doña Paz wrote in books and papers. But in this case, when the publication might cause a scandal, he believed it his duty, as head of the family, to ask her to send him a copy before offering it for sale.

Canalejas then discussed in council the question of depriving her of her rank and of her pension of £10,000 a year. If she had broken with the family and the Government, what else, he asked, could she expect ?

On December 5 *Le Temps* announced :

" As for the title of Infanta, Doña Eulalia declared that she received it at her birth and cannot lose it."

But she telegraphed to Canalejas :

> " I expect to pay the penalty ; but please let
> me know soon what it is, for I am thinking of
> starting on a journey."

Canalejas answered that the Council of Ministers
confined itself to deploring the attitude the royal lady
had taken with the prudent suggestions of the head
of the Spanish Royal Family.
On the 6th she wrote to the King :

> " DEAR ALFONSO,—
> " I do not write to defend myself, but to ask
> forgiveness. I am suffering too much either to
> remain silent or to write a long letter.
> " As an aunt I suffer in my heart, which feels so
> much affection for you, and as a Spaniard who
> loves her country I am suffering too.
> " I need not tell you that, whatever penalty you
> ask me to pay, I shall believe that I have deserved
> it.   And if I have given my submission to you to
> the papers, it is because I want Spain to know my
> feeling towards my King as towards my country.
> " I do not dare to show you signs of affection,
> I should feel it so much if you rejected them.   But
> I hope a day will come in which you will tell me
> face to face of your forgiveness, and I can tell
> you that I am always, your loving aunt,
> " EULALIA."

The book was published, but very few in Spain paid
any attention to it except the Radical papers, which
at first praised it, but threw ridicule on it when they
heard that she had come to an accord with the King.
But Don Alfonso had not heard the last word from

this daughter of Queen Isabel. Not long afterwards she published another, and, as its title suggests,
a franker, book : *J'ai voulu vivre ma vie.*

7

On November 12, 1912, an assassin did for the
Republicans what speeches could not do. The
genius who promised security to Spain and the
monarchy by uniting the King with the party of progress was removed.

The Liberal Premier was so confident of the people's
affection that he was in the habit of going about
Madrid unattended and unprotected. That morning
he was walking to the Home Ministry and only a few
steps away from it where the Calle de Carretas runs
into the Puerta del Sol, he had stopped to look at a
book-case before a shop window. It was almost noon,
and at noon he had a Council of Ministers.

He was still looking at the book-case when a man,
dressed neatly in a blue suit and a dark overcoat,
approached him. That man, Pardinas, a native of
Aragon, as he had known for some time, had been
deputed by anarchists to shoot him.

Pardinas had been expelled from the Argentine.
The police traced him in Marseilles, Bordeaux, and
Biarritz, but there they had lost sight of him. He
had arrived in Madrid two days before.

The moment that Canalejas turned to continue his
walk to the Ministry of the Interior, Pardinas fired a
revolver at him.

Canalejas raised his hands to his face and swayed
but again he drew himself up, and in an attempt to
defend himself moved a step forward. The man fired
another shot. Then several men approached, while
others threw themselves upon the murderer.

The Premier had a severe wound in the temple and another behind the ear. They carried him to the Ministry unconscious, and in a few minutes he died.

The King hurried to the Ministry, and standing beside the body, with his arm resting on the table where it lay, he exclaimed, " How horrible it is ! " His best adviser had been taken from him.

On March 27, 1913, the King had a bad accident playing polo : while he was at full gallop his horse trod in a hole and threw him some distance ; he was stunned, and did not recover consciousness for a quarter of an hour. He was badly bruised all over, and not least in the head and face ; they feared congestion, but after a few days he recovered, and went about as before. There were some, however, who thought that his head had been badly hurt, and that he was never quite the same man again.[1]

His courage was undoubtedly the same. For as murder had taken Canalejas, it came closer, and leered in the face of the monarch. King George of Greece had been assassinated just before the accident. Pamphlets scattered about Madrid all through that spring declared that *Alfonso XIII would die on April* 13 *of the year* 1913. There was a feeling of increasing anxiety, but on the threatened day the King went none the less to a military review. The streets were filled with such an enormous crowd at 1.30 when the review finished, that the troops found some difficulty in keeping the way for the procession open. The enthusiasm was tremendous as the King rode through the main streets on his way home ; he who, as they had heard, in the schools, in the markets, in the meetings of society, was to die that day, rode among them vigorous and triumphant, the symbol of their awaken-

[1] *Año Politico*, 1913, p. 78.

ing country. Then, as he reached the middle of the
Calle Alcalá, just at the top of the rise, a man dashed
out of the crowd with a revolver in his hand, and
fired two shots at close range at the King. As the
officers of his suite closed around him, a third shot
was fired. A bullet had grazed his glove. Another
bullet had wounded his horse, which swerved violently
round as though to kick the assassin. Don Alfonso,
however, was unhurt, his demeanour unchanged.
In a moment the procession had continued, and the
King was received with deafening shouts. Meanwhile, the two Queens drove back to the palace a little
time after the King, by the same route, knowing
nothing of what had happened.

Who was the criminal ? Sancho Alegre, a Catalan
of twenty-five, who had abandoned his wife in Barcelona to carry on an amour in Madrid ; he was un-
shaven and dirty, with long rough hair, lumpy features,
and fiery eyes. His mind, between adultery and ill-
chosen reading, had become unhinged. His object,
he said, was to avenge Ferrer. Later enquiries proved
him to be an epileptic.

The close connection between anti-religious propaganda and organised murder was becoming plain
to all. Nor was it easy to avoid noticing how often
the assassins were living in moral irregularity, and
suffering from venereal disease.

8

The month after Canalejas's death, there had been
another political crisis. But there was a valour in the
King which assassination only strengthened : he did
not waver in his policy. He was determined to side
with the Left, and the crisis therefore was soon resolved by placing Romanones in the place of Canale-

jas. By his sympathy, not less than by his skill, Don Alfonso was disarming his most dangerous enemies : he was approximating more and more to the great model of constitutional monarchy in King Edward, who, being content not to interfere in politics, found in his diplomatic skill a great part to play, and whose personality so genially personified the Majesty of the Head of the State. As for King Alfonso, he declared to an intimate friend that, in making his resolutions, it was public opinion which inspired him. " I am far," he said, " from seeking Oriental crises. I want the crisis to arise in the Parliament, where people can argue out their opinions, and so arrive at an expression of national opinion. So I haven't much taste for giving decisions as to things which cause me anxiety, still less as to any others. I want to live apart from political wrestles, confining myself exclusively to my constitutional obligations." [1]

Had the King abandoned the imperiousness with which on his sixteenth birthday he so jealously guarded his prerogatives ? Or did he think that, in taking the lowest place, he would be asked to go up higher ? Whatever his motives, his policy was a brilliant success. Even the Republican Lerroux declared that the Crown had fulfilled its duties. " And I," he added, " will be the first to recognise it in the Press of the party, and in all my own personal activities for politics." [2]

Up to that time, the Liberals and Conservatives had been able to play for power with one another. The elections were what the polite called a courteous formality, what real democrats knew were a mockery ; but the Home Minister was instructed to arrange a majority for the Government, and did so. Changes of government depended on something subtler than the

[1] *Año Politico*, 1912, p. 565.　　　　[2] *Idem*.

vote of constituencies. They were the results of personal manœuvring with the forces of personal opinion in the capital. This game the leaders of government knew to have its own rules which could not be disputed. So the government of Spain had been carried on for nearly forty years in a seesaw of Conservative and Liberal Governments agreed to maintain the monarchy, to manage the elections, and to check the Republicans ; the convention, in a word, which Cánovas had made with Sagasta, over the death-bed of Alfonso XII, called the Pact of El Pardo, the name of the palace where the King died.

The system began to collapse after the death of Ferrer. When Moret went back on his word and overthrew Maura, the Liberals had sided with the Republicans against the tradition of authority. When Canalejas went farther, and won over the King to support him, the Conservatives began to lose their temper. The Liberals, they thought, had ceased to play the game. Then the Conservatives also abandoned the old compromise. The Liberals therefore were forced to compromise with the Republicans, and as we saw, they dragged the King with them into one of those sporting forays on which he was as keen as on a shooting party in the Cantabrian Mountains. But the Conservatives were getting thoroughly disgruntled, and on January 1, 1913, Maura and fifty of his adherents threatened to resign from public life. On the other hand, the Republicans were enraptured. [1]

Morayta declared at Seville on January 2, the day after Maura's threat : " We have a great King, greater than we deserve." But it was a risky game for a king to play. Suppose the Republicans changed their minds ! Suppose, by the help of *caciques*, the Conservatives should upset the balance of the Cortes in their

[1] *The Times.*

favour, and Maura came back to power.   Romanones
and the King conferred.   They decided on a bold
plan, the sort of plan in which the King's audacious
enterprise delighted.   He decided to summon to the
palace two leading Republicans, Señor Cossío and
Don Gumersindo de Azcárate, and an excellent opportunity was given him on January 12, 1913, by a
speech which Melquiades Alvarez made in Murcia.

"Maura sought in his pride," said Alvarez, " not
to say in his egoism, to make an accomplice of the
Crown.   And listen to me attentively, Republicans.
I would do justice to the King : he has fulfilled his
duty attending to the requirements of opinion and
respecting constitutional principles.   He has been a
sovereign who knows how to inspire the confidence
of his subjects.   I, a Republican enemy of the Government, against which I have struggled day by day (and
I will continue my work unperturbed), beg you to
applaud our enemy ; for one should not omit to do
justice to one's adversaries." [1]

The meeting rose to its feet, and for a long space of
time thundered its applause.

Then the speaker continued :

"The King will be able to make comparisons and
will see how in us the spirit of justice brings us to recognise his shrewdness, and in exchange those who call
themselves his servants vilify him, and when he ceases
to serve their personal interests, they abandon him.

"The King, in the time of his great soliloquies, will
observe the contrast with bitterness, and will recognise
the differences between men united by ideals and those
who feel only the craving of selfishness.

"An honest adversary may say so.

"Those who attempted to govern arbitrarily and
take advantage of the King's support for the sake of

[1] Soldevilla : *Año Politico*, Jan. 12, 1913.

their personal profit, the plutocrats and traffickers, the clerics guilty of simony, all who used to flatter him, to-day, because in the fulfilment of the law he does not pander to their ambitions, to-day they threaten and insult him."

So the King asked the Prime Minister, Count Romanones, to write direct to Azcárate in the most courteous terms, to ask if he would accept an invitation to the palace ; on receiving a favourable reply, the King at once sent an invitation to the palace for six that evening.

The King and the Republican discussed not only social questions, but the army and Morocco, and at last politics in general.

Azcárate had been presented to the King once before, and had already an impression of him which was " extraordinarily agreeable " : the King had shown him every sort of courtesy and attention. This time the King showed himself well abreast of the questions and the projects which the Republican had most at heart ; and the two discussed what should be the action of the Head of the State, whether King or President.

" The same for both," [1] said the King.

They then went on to say that the supreme power should never intervene when there was a conflict of opinion, but occupy himself with the highest interests of the nation as a whole. They touched on the question of religion, and the King advocated the widest tolerance in everything affecting the procedure and measures of government.

As for the Rif, the King said it would have been better first to settle the internal differences of the country, but that they had been obliged to take their present action so as to arrive at an understanding with France.

[1] *Es igual.*

They spoke of making the relations closer between Spain and Spanish America. The King was enthusiastic on the subject. He said he would love to make a tour in America, and was in full agreement with the feelings of the Republicans on the subject.

" My enthusiasm for Spain is great," he said, " and precisely for that reason I want to enter into relations with all Spaniards, and know their opinions, even if it is a question of Republicans, because I am delighted with the result. Therefore it seems to me very good that you should continue in your Republican ideas. Do you think it would be a good plan in cases of crisis to have consultations with those who are hostile to the throne, so as to know their opinions ? "

Azcárate considered it for a moment. Then he answered : " Yes." And he believed that His Majesty had taken his advice.

The King then discussed the programme of education, and seemed to have the most Liberal views. They went on to the question of off-hours and the bakers being saved from work at night.

" We shall all have to put up with stale bread," said Azcárate.

" Then," said the King with a smile, " we must unite to oppose this reform."

And what in general was the Republican's impression of the King ? That he was a most charming and attractive man, with very modern views.

When Señor Cossío went to see him, he talked of museums, and of art, but above all of elementary education. They discussed how Italy, Greece, Sweden, and Bulgaria had all enormously increased the sum they spent on education. The subject was one on which Señor Cossío could not speak except with all his heart and soul. And perhaps such vehemence was hardly suitable he thought on such an occasion.

" Your Majesty," he said, " must pardon me if I express myself——"

" No," interrupted the King, " I am delighted to listen. Your language is that of a Spaniard who loves his country."

Cossío's impression was that "the King was very encouraging ; he shows a lively desire to know what the intellectual level of Spain is, and to raise it. He says that he has learnt much from his tours abroad. He has studied, and he knows the education problem. I pointed out to him that the reforms I had outlined would not bear an immediate result. The fruit will be gathered by others, much later."

" I know," answered the King, and he changed the metaphor ; " but I want to have my mind at rest in knowing I have laid the foundation-stone."

The King's action aroused a great wave of enthusiasm in Spain ; and even abroad aroused many comments in his favour. Never was his prestige higher, nor did the prospects of monarchy seem so promising. Spain was beginning to make great advances, and there were not a few who believed that the King, though he was not yet thirty, had vanquished and overcome his enemies, even if his old supporters spoke of treachery. But never, and least of all in Spain, can power be confident : it needs ever to hold in mind—

> How chances mock,
> And changes fill the cup of alteration
> With divers liquors.

In Don Alfonso's country those divers liquors all were effervescent. Some were poisonous.

XIII

KING ALFONSO : THE BREAKDOWN OF PARLIAMENTARY GOVERNMENT

Government is a contrivance of human wisdom to provide for human wants.

BURKE.

Et sedebit populus meus in pulchritudine pacis, et in tabernaculis fiduciæ et in requie opulenta.

Isaiah xxxii. 18.

I

THROUGH all those years Spain was hastening to take her place in Europe and show herself once again worthy of her golden age. Commerce began to make great advances, electric light appeared in every village, houses and hotels were fresher and cleaner, people began to travel in greater numbers into and out of Spain.

No one could deny that the King and Queen led and personified the advance. Among the masses of their own people, they were both extremely popular, and they were personalities eminent in Europe. Their frequent visits to Paris and London gave them an international place in the days when, as we have seen, the lives of European countries still circled round their Courts, maintaining the tradition of those gorgeous years when King Edward and the Emperor William were the two central men of Europe. Prices were so low, and life so easy, that people used their leisure to elaborate formality, and those rituals of

elegance absorbed the attention of all ranks of social
life. The picture papers were at the height of their
importance because people did not yet care much for
the pictures on the screen, and how often royalties
came into the pictures ! Their movements were all
events which, involving as they did social prestige,
were really accepted as the crowning reality of human
affairs. This system suited Don Alfonso admirably.
He loved its rapid changes, and what gorgeous opportunities it gave to his swift observation, his business
sense, his graceful assurance, and his scintillating
versatility ! It was actually in his person that Spain
began to magnetise the gaze of peoples. In him she
was accepted, and through him she understood.
Modern yet traditional, cosmopolitan yet Spanish ;
volatile, easy, generous, vital, he was everywhere the
King.

The very attacks on his life were one of the great
elements of his success. They came so near and he
met them so coolly. But they were a warning of the
unrest which was boiling under the rich productiveness of Europe, as lava boils below the vineyards
and the blossom on the slopes of Etna. The great
civilised whole of Europe was all volcanic ground ;
nothing was more in danger than those privileged
lives which glittered in royal Courts—the social system
which looked so brilliant depended for its wealth on
monotonous lives spent in noisy factories and sordid
slums. While the conditions of these lives outraged
the very instincts of human nature, unbalanced
human judgment, and made ideals sound like a
mockery, the authority of nations feared them little.
Politics and economics were almost separate spheres.
And nations were organised, not as healthy bodies
living by free exchange, but as armed rivals, jealous
of one another's power, while each of them had

swelling in his vitals the same sorts of ulcer. The strain of competing diplomacies had been made too severe by the growth of the armaments, and the burden which they laid on commerce and industry, which were in themselves unhealthy. The old society in fact was actually elaborating the means of its own undoing. The lives and fortunes of Englishmen were thus at the mercy of political criminals on the borders of Bosnia. So did the productiveness of Europe transform itself into an enginry of death.

Spain's position at the mouth of the Mediterranean, and the fact that her territories marched with modern Africa, meant that she made a heavier weight in the scales of war than the power of her army and resources did in themselves suggest. But there was no reason why she should take sides, and she soon learnt that there were powerful reasons for her remaining neutral. Both sides manœuvred tirelessly for her support, and from the rival embassies in Madrid agents of propaganda stalked and pounced like tigers from their lairs. There was in Spain a certain division of opinion. The Liberals were persuaded that the Allies would make the world safe for democracy : the others therefore took the other side. As early as August 19, 1914, an article appeared in the *Diario Universal* of Count Romanones, saying that neutrality was a murderous risk, while the rival Powers were preparing to remould Europe as they wanted. Lerroux, a week later, in his paper, *El Imparcial*, was much more emphatic : he claimed that not only was Romanones inclined to fight with the Allies, but also the King. And the King, who was often supposed to relieve his feelings with a witty indiscretion, was declared to sum up that he would but could not : " There is no one who wants to fight but the *canaille* and myself." Although his mother was an Austrian, he had few sympathies with Austria ; while France and England were homes away from home, and the Queen's two brothers were both fighting. Indeed, Prince Maurice of Battenberg was killed in October, just at the time that the King's youngest son, Don Gonzalo, was born on the Queen's birthday.

The King found a tactful way to express his sympathy. He organised a great charitable work to better the lot of prisoners of war, and to enquire into the fate of the missing. By December 31, 1915, 150,000 were missing from the French Army alone. Into the case of every one of these every possible enquiry was made through a mediator whose assistance no one could refuse. The organisation which set to work to improve the prison camps was an even greater enterprise. Worship, libraries, schools, theatres, cinemas, work, hospitals, baths, warmth, and food all came into the purview of the King's enquiry, and he exerted a steady influence to see that they were provided. At every step he showed his personal initiative : he wrote many letters with his own hand, especially to those who were anxious and bereaved, and he received the most pathetic and moving letters from those for whom his work was meant :

> " SIRE (said one of them),—
>
>   " *J'ai été touché au cœur en lisant la lettre que Votre Majesté m'a fait le très grand honneur de m'adresser, et profondément confus de ce qu'Elle ait pris Elle même la peine de me donner de l'espoir pour Mlle de Larmier. Les soldats morts, et celui qui survit, frémissent d'orgueil en apprenant quelle insistance est accordée à leur fille, à leur sœur. Pour moi, dans ces lignes pleines de grace j'ai retrouvé tous les traits que la légende française prête avec amour au jeune Chevalier*

qui règne sur les Espagnes. Sire, c'est une chose de la plus haute élégance que cette lettre, pour laquelle, à cause d'un héros, un Roi promet à un poète de protéger une femme." [1]

King Alfonso was hailed in an inscription from two distinguished Belgian poets as the upholder of the innocent, the help of the hungry, the consoler of the captives, and the hope of peoples in distress.

But there were simpler letters :

"God bless father and mother and nurse," said one of them, "and send father back soon from his horrid prison in Germany. And God bless specially the dear King of Spain who found out about father. Amen." [2]

"MAJESTÉ," began another,—
    "*Maman pleure toujours depuis qu'elle a son frère prisonier. Est Majesté, maman vient de recevoir une carte hier qu'il mourait de faim. Majesté, si vous vouliez le mettre en Suisse car voilà deux ans qu'il est prisonier et maman va surement tomber malade, Majesté, je vous remercie d'avance.*
                "SYLVAINE VOTRE SERVANTE.

"*Sylvaine Sartor,* 14 *Avenue d'Autun, Paris. J'ai huit ans.*"

To this the King wrote the whole answer with his own hand :

"CHÈRE MADEMOISELLE,—
    "*Je tacherai de mon mieux de faire que Maman ne pleure pas : mais veuillez bien me donner des renseignements précis sur votre oncle à fin que je puisse faire les*

[1] Espinós y Moltó : *Espejo de Neutrales,* p. 59.   [2] *Ibid.*

demandes nécessaires pour savoir son état de santé et si c'est possible de l'interner en Suisse.

"ALFONSO R. H."[1]

20. iv. 1917.

The feeling of enthusiasm evoked by the King's work brought him many graceful compliments ; but there were few he more appreciated than a letter from an English boy asking for Spanish stamps, and finishing : " You are the King I like the best."

The agile mind of Don Alfonso had realised from the beginning that his charitable work, added to the offices which his Embassies and Legations performed for belligerent countries, would greatly increase both Spanish prestige and his own. In the meanwhile he could not let his attention wander from the effect of the war on Spain's own life. Its chief and embracing result was to pour money into the country. The gold reserve of the Bank of Spain rose from £22,000,000 to £88,000,000. Trade with South America rose to 250 per cent. of its former volume. In fact, the balance in Spain for the five years beginning with 1915 was over £30,000,000. The population of Barcelona doubled.

2

As for the political parties, the old distinctions tended to disappear. The King seemed to be uniting Spain : he kept the sympathy of the Republicans, and he began to make a rapprochement with the Conservatives so as to secure a Coalition Government. This was the more prudent, because with the increase of money in Spain, votes were getting harder to order or buy, and it was becoming impossible to manage elec-

---

[1] Espinós y Moltó : *Espejo de Neutrales*, p. 60. R. H. for *Rex Hispaniarum*.

tions in the old way. It was necessary, too, because the new wealth was concentrated in Barcelona, and Barcelona, under Señor Cambó, the man who had made the greatest fortune out of the change, was demanding self-government for Catalonia ; while at the same time anarchical and Communist movements were stimulated, first from Germany, and after the Russian Revolution from the Soviet ; and lastly, because the army showed a tendency to take power into its own hands. The result of these different movements was political turmoil. Maura came back for a while to power, and was succeeded by other leaders, Dato, Sánchez-Toca, Romanones. But the parliamentary system, which, because of the corrupt coin at the polls, had never really existed, now became a more and more obvious failure, and with fresh troubles arising it soon provoked the impatience of the whole Spanish people.

The King's tone therefore wholly changed. The triumphs of 1913 no longer interested him. He crossed the Sierra, and his eyes rested on an entirely different view. He had been travelling up through a network of overgrown ravines. He now looked down a deep valley, green where it was irrigated from the clear stream which sparkled in sunset light. The stream was authority. The irrigated fields were Church and State, and in them there grew food enough to maintain those austere and virile people who hewed the blue-green pines of the forest, guarded the tinkling flocks, or gathered together in the rocky walls of the village, while a blaze of light shone from the flame-lit cloud above the sanguine horizon. And as the twilight deepened, the moon was a frosted crystal in the walls of heaven to enable Spaniards in glory to look back on the scenes where they had enjoyed a foretaste of eternity. Such a scene at Gredos or among the Picos de Europa had often swelled the heart of Don Alfonso with the inspiration for what he felt a sacred task. Such a scene symbolised the prospect which was created by his exaltation as he thought of Spain as a military and Catholic state, with himself at its head. " All in Spain, from the King downwards," he said, " are moved by religious fervour : to our soldiers nothing is so high an incentive to fulfil their duty as the cross they bear on their swords." [1]

In the year 1921 this idea absorbed the King's whole mind. That year is critical in his history, not only because in it he made a famous speech denouncing Spain's parliamentary system, but also because he allowed his ambition to turn towards military victory in Africa at the very moment when his army encountered its most shocking disaster. The two tendencies were closely related in King Alfonso's mind ; and was it not natural to ask if the disaster itself had any connection with them ?

The whole subject invites close attention ; and the drama begins with the speech which the King made at Cordoba on May 23rd.

" I have devoted a constant study to the problems which affect my country," he said ; " therefore I have been able to realise that in a great part of Spain, and especially in Andalusia, the means of transport are most inadequate and that its deficiencies were at their worst in the war.

" In Spain, communications are slow, and therefore the distribution of products and necessities is not made with the necessary ease and regularity, and this is very important, because all comes back to the stomach. Rich and poor, we are all human beings, and have to eat.

" At this moment, my Government has presented

[1] *Año Politico*, 1921.

to Parliament a project of the most far-reaching kind to deal with this problem. Well now : the King is not absolute, and has no other power than to authorise with his signature the proposals submitted to Parliament. But he can do nothing to make Parliament approve them. I am very happy not to have responsibilities—the responsibilities which have been transferred from the Crown to Parliament. I prefer to dedicate my life to the country without those responsibilities. But it is very hard that what is for the good of all cannot prosper because of the trivialities of politics.

" My Government presents a proposal : they fight it, and it falls. The ministers who succeed those who have fallen can make no progress either, because those who were in power before are now in opposition, and take their revenge. How can you expect them to give their help to those that kill them !

" Some think that, in speaking so, I am exceeding my constitutional duties. But I say that, after having ruled as King for nineteen years, and several times risked my life in them, they are not going to catch me out in not acting constitutionally.

" I believe that the provinces should begin a movement of support to the King and to the proposals, which will do good, and then the Parliament will agree with the mandate of the people, because this is the meaning of your votes. Then the King's signature will be a guarantee that beneficial proposals will be put through." [1]

The speech, which was not correctly reported, made a great stir. The Socialist deputy, Indalecio Prieto, rose and shouted that " Parliament had a higher dignity than the King," but Lerroux agreed with the

[1] *Año Politico*, 1922, p. 167.

King. " What happens here," he said, " is that o
the old story of the good Canons and the bad Chapter
We are all here very clever, very worthy, and very
good. But the Parliament could not be worse."

3

The feeling of Señor Lerroux was very general
though it was natural for the old Parliamentarians to
mutter curses not loud but deep in the face of such
frankness—for, after all, it was almost like a public
rebuke to them. The King's speech increased his
prestige and popularity. And the success of the
speech sent him hurtling down the road he had
obviously chosen. He began to crave and to prophesy
a military triumph, and turned his ambitions toward
Morocco.

Now, in Morocco at that time there were three
dominant personalities. There was first the rebel
chief Abd-el-Krim, an able and enterprising man with
a modern education, living in his African fastness
Ajdir. There was a fine soldier who, like Espartero
had risen from the ranks by dash and daring, who had
received more than sixty wounds, General Silvestre
And there was the skilled soldier who had just been
made High Commissary in Morocco, General Berenguer.

Silvestre and Berenguer in the spring of 1921 had
come to open blows : Silvestre, who had resented the
other's promotion over his head, had come from
Melilla to Ceuta to urge a big offensive against the
Rif. Berenguer, content with pacifying the tribes
around Ceuta and Tetuan, fearful perhaps of the
audacities of Silvestre, had given a definite refusal to
the older general's plans. Silvestre had lost his
temper, and taken his superior officer by the throat,

and in this dramatic struggle, the two generals had been surprised by a junior officer.[1]

But Spain never settles its business by considerations of personal dignity : she accepts such outbursts as part of her people's life ; and Silvestre went in the summer to Spain, and had a long talk with the King. The naïveté of the old General's outburst was hardly less congenial to the King than the romance of his career. Don Alfonso gave his heart to Silvestre ; he delighted in the idea of a big offensive ; in his impulsiveness he gave Silvestre the feeling that it was right to take his own line against, not only the Commissary in Morocco, but also the Minister of War ; the King then allowed him to go back to Melilla, while the royal mind turned back to a still more famous warrior of Spain, no other than the Cid, whose ashes were now to be handed over to the Cathedral of Burgos. In the capital of Old Castile, the Gothic architects had built long since a Metropolitan church whose spires and lanterns bore witness to emotions wild and high. Fierceness had been exalted into a celestial virtue, and so charged stone with images of the wood and the fire that its crocheted finials rose against the sky with a fanciful and signal exquisiteness. " The Cathedral," said the King, " will no longer be simply the work of art whose principal end is to strike such a beautiful note in post card collections of the monuments of Spain. From this moment everyone who has the feelings of a Spaniard will speak of it with words which touch the heart to recall one of the most glorious epochs in the history of our country. . . . My ancestors, Don Sancho and Don Alfonso V, may at that time have had complaints of the hero of Castile. For my part I see in him no more than the patriot and the genial warrior who, in addition to his own work,

[1] Tharaud : *Rendez-vous, Espagnols.*

served with his hosts even as those proud Tercios of Flanders who obtained such triumphs for their country where the sun never set on the dominions of Spain. Do not think that in recalling the empire of my ancestors I am moved by any impulse of ambition. No ; because Spain is great enough still to realise her destiny ; and apart from that, with what Spain is in the Peninsula, and with what belongs to us on the other side of the Strait, we have enough to figure among the first nations of Europe."

4

The other side of the Strait ! On that very day there was in Spanish Morocco a disaster so sweeping as to shake the King upon his throne. He had returned from Burgos to San Sebastian to keep with his mother her annual festival, when he received news that hurried him into the first express for Madrid. The military forces at Melilla had been totally destroyed. General Silvestre had advanced from Melilla to aid the garrison at Igueriben. The Moors had attacked in great force, and with furious energy. Igueriben and Anual had been surrounded and invested. Silvestre had wired to Berenguer, the High Commissary in Morocco, that his position was desperate. Then, in Anual he attempted to evacuate the advanced position : he had been ordered to retire, but had answered that he must get his troops out first. Then with his staff he had been surrounded by the Riffian horde. With the exception of one officer, who broke through to the retreating troops, the General's whole staff was to be annihilated. In the operation, over twelve thousand men were lost, an incalculable amount of munitions and transport was captured, as well as hundreds of cannons and many thousand rifles.

Silvestre alone could have explained the mysteries of his own audacity, and Silvestre chose not to explain. Alone with his staff he was left in Anual. He called for his chauffeur, whose tunic he donned. He gave the man letters for his family. He took his razor and shaved his moustache. After that no more was heard of him. Though the Riffians did not pierce the disguise he had assumed, no one doubted that he had shot himself.

Berenguer hurried from Ceuta. He learnt almost at the same moment of Silvestre's insubordination and of his death. Entering Melilla in advance of his reinforcements, he found himself with only twenty-seven men to withhold the attack of the victorious chieftain. But Abd-el-Krim's daring was satisfied with wiping out the army of Anual.

5

An enquiry was opened. A telegram from the King, " On the 25th I expect good news," and another more colloquial, " *Holá hombres*, I'm waiting," were found among Silvestre's papers. But after all, that said no more than the King himself had said in his official speech at Burgos. What the enquiry did reveal was that, in spite of the large sums of money Spain had so long been spending, the army was disgracefully supplied. It had neither munitions, nor arms, nor cloaks, nor linen, nor tents. " The existences of dictators to the dictated, the submission of the executive, and of the Government to *juntas*, and elements who were irresponsible painted this tragic picture." [1] Such

[1] *Año Político*, 1921.

was the general verdict. But rumours kept multiplying about the initiative and the responsibility being the King's own : Barcelona again remembered 1909, when it had brought the war from Morocco to the streets ; and the extreme element tried once more by bloodshed to force separation.

Indeed, the whole face of Spanish politics was changing. The prosperity due to the European War had passed : that left not only its own malaise. The national finances were disorganised : the war in Morocco, as costly as it was apparently hopeless, dragged on ; anarchical societies spread, and organised a great campaign of murder. It was a time for energetic government in Catalonia ; it was a time, so the King still thought, for the military ideal to develop ; and he was glad to have as the Captain-General of Barcelona a man so clear in his ideas, and so effective in expressing them as General Primo de Rivera, a nephew of the General who, in 1875, had led the garrison of Madrid back to support the monarchy. In the summer of 1922 the King went to Barcelona, and after talking to General Primo, he completed the suggestions of his speech at Cordoba by speaking of the army, and especially the Barcelona garrison, as the model of the nation, and its highest expression.

" If you have taken an oath to your King," he said, " I have taken it before the highest representation of the country, the Cortes, swearing with my hands on the Gospels that I should fulfil the laws. And I say to you that it is an offence to all when we are drifted this way and that, saying that someone has taken such and such a decision : it is an offence, I say, to all and each.

" The army before the attitude of politics and of the country was silent, inclining its head, and waiting until time should do it justice. And so must be the discipline of the army which then listened patiently to all that I said to it, and answered nothing. Time has answered for it ! "

" An electric spark," he went on, " moves a whole body : let the garrison of Barcelona be the spark which moves the whole army so that from to-day it may attain to a new life, submitting to order and military discipline. And I the first, because no one consulted me when I was born to be King. But once I found myself in the position, I had to fulfil my duty, as you should fulfil yours.

" That is all. That is what I wanted to say, and what I have said." [1]

Yes, he had said it ; but what did it all mean ? It was seldom that the King's mind was so obviously confused. No one could quite trace the connection between the different ideas—oaths of loyalty, offences, a patient army, a disciplined army, an obligation for the army as there was for the King. It was difficult to make it cohere ; it was, in the common phrase, hard to see what the King was driving at—even to those who knew that he had made one attempt after another to get the politicians to govern, and had failed in all.

But in a short time the meaning was explained in Rome : as disordered as Spain, Italy was developing Fascism ; she was falling under the spell of Mussolini. Three months later the people of Italy rebelled against parliamentary government. They brought an armed force against it. Was that not what Don Alfonso meant ? He could not dislodge his Parliament because he had sworn to support it. But how if the army dislodged it for him ?

Everyone really was sick and tired of it : even that

[1] *Año Político*, 1922.

Radical reformer, José Ortega Gasset, in Madrid, had written a book to say that parliamentary Spain had lost its backbone,[1] and there was no real patriot in Spain who did not feel it essential for the country to be rescued from the politicians.

[1] See *España Invertebrada*.

XIV

THE DICTATORSHIP OF PRIMO

And, undoubtedly, a concentrated power is necessary in those cataclysmic periods when an exhalation of blood takes possession of the heart of nations, stains the candid robe of freedom, robs the eyes of men of the statue of judgment, and hides the star of intelligence from the sight of peoples. Undoubtedly, a concentrated power is necessary at such a time. . . .

In whom, then, will this concentrated power rest? In the strong man, gentlemen, in the man of strength and intelligence whom constitutional governments do not bring to the top.

Donoso Cortés : Collección Escogida, i. 186.

It is, however, not surprising that great opinions were first formed of the heroism of the Spaniards, and those expectations were greatly augmented by their agreeable qualities. There is not upon the face of the earth a people so attractive in the friendly intercourse of society : their majestic language, fine persons, imposing dress and lively imaginations, the inexpressible beauty of their women, and the air of romance which they throw over every action, and infuse into every feeling, all combine to elude the senses and impose upon the judgment. As companions, they are incomparably the most agreeable of mankind ; but danger and disappointment attend the man who, confiding in their promises and energy, ventures upon a difficult enterprise.

Napier : Peninsular War, iii.

I

In 1923 the Spanish situation worsened as rapidly and unequivocally as that of Italy improved. Abd-el-Krim made himself master of the Rif, and the Spaniards on the coast were at his mercy. At the same time, war strength had to be kept up, and Spanish soldiers were dying without any good coming of it all. A Liberal Government had been in power with a fluent and eloquent speaker, Señor Alcalá Zamora, as its Minister of War. He was so ineffective (for talk, though it may make revolutions, cannot win battles) that his colleagues dismissed him ; but though a general took his place, the tussle still went on, and the national debt was still increasing. The Catalans were making representations at Geneva to be allowed to escape from Spain, and anarchist societies, translating the ideas of Ferrer into the language of the revolver and the bomb, were paralysing business in Barcelona. There were general strikes in the big towns. In a few years five hundred employers had been shot, poisoned, or kidnapped, a hundred and sixty of them in the single city of Barcelona. The murderers once accounted for twenty-one of them in the course of two successive nights. Disgust with Spain's parliamentary government was general and intense. The country was ready for any change.

This was the opportunity for the most dynamic officer in Spain. Born in 1870, Don Miguel Primo de Rivera was the nephew of that Captain-General who secured Madrid for Alfonso XII in 1875. He knew his Spanish history. He knew that the whole reign of Isabel II, with its enormous commercial progress, was a sequence of military dictatorships ; that the parliamentary systems which followed them had been a mockery which was now played out ; and the conclusion was inevitable : the time had come for another dictatorship. If the army were behind him, his course was easy. It was obvious that he need not fear great difficulties from the King. He made his plans for a *coup d'état* on September 14.

The King was still in San Sebastian with Don Santiago Alba, his Foreign Minister. The other

ministers were in Madrid. They knew, and they
must have warned the King, that a *coup* was being
prepared. But they dared not face a crisis, and they
could do nothing against the army. And, besides,
during 1923 Mussolini's prestige had almost mes-
merised a doubting world. Democracy, it was felt,
was no safer for Europe than Europe for democracy.
The Spanish Captain-General therefore did not
need to preach his plans : he did not need to make
flamboyant speeches or march on Madrid. Besides,
he had none of Mussolini's gift for stalking into the
arena and roaring : in the country of the corrida,
men left that to their bulls.

On September 11, the rioting in Barcelona had
been particularly grave. Processions of youths had
gathered in enormous numbers, and begun to
demonstrate. At a banquet in the evening, orators
had shouted, "Down with Spain!" Then the
Captain-General had on his own authority proclaimed
martial law and sent a communication to other
military commanders inviting them to do the same.
Aizpuru, the Minister of War, telephoned to Primo,
and speaking as friend to friend, asked him not to
defy the Government. Primo answered that he was
in a narrow and perilous defile, but that it opened the
way to ampler horizons. The talk went on, but it
arrived at nothing.

"Señor Captain-General of Catalonia," then said
the minister, "it is not Luis Aizpuru, the comrade
who has much affection for you, who is speaking now.
The Minister of War is about to speak." At that
Primo put back the receiver, and said to his officers
that, as he had made up his mind, there was no need
to remain at the telephone. And neither was there.

At San Sebastian, Santiago Alba was talking hour
by hour to his colleagues in Madrid. Next morning

he went to the palace at ten o'clock to offer his resignation. He could not agree with his colleagues in a struggle against the military power. The King meanwhile announced that he was coming straight to Madrid. There had been a ball in the palace the night before. The King had devoted himself to the dance, and though he knew from Santiago Alba what was happening, he did not make further enquiries or take further steps. He went quietly to bed. At four in the morning, however, he was wakened by a message from the Prime Minister, the Marquis de Alhucemas. The Premier was afraid that communications might be cut : he therefore asked the King to come to Madrid at once, and open the Cortes. The King answered that, in view of what had occurred, he would take the express on the following evening.[1]

He arrived by train at Madrid at nine o'clock on the morning of the 14th. The Captain-General received him on the platform. So did the ministers. The King asked his Premier to come straight with him to the palace. There the Premier laid before his sovereign his plans to suspend the rebellious Captain-Generals, while an enquiry was made into the charges. For Primo the day before had published a manifesto.

"But are you sure," asked the King, "that with the suspension of these generals you will stop the movement which has begun ? Can you guarantee that the remaining garrisons will not follow the example of Barcelona and Saragossa ? "

The Prime Minister could guarantee nothing. He argued that the Cortes should open at once. The King listened, but he did not agree.[2] He must, he said, have time to think it over, for civil war had been threatened in so many words, and with him rested the responsibility as to whether it should break out.

[1] *Año Político*, 1923, p. 352.   [2] *Ibid.*

2

To Alhucemas as a politician the issue appeared simply a fundamental question of government ! Where was discipline ? There could, in the mind of the Premier, be only one explanation. It was that the King was privy to Primo's defiance. " I swear to you that I did not know a word of it," said the King.[1] If it were not, in fact, such a novelty, why need he think it over ? The Premier was disgusted. He said that he must at once resign. The King accepted his resignation, and bid his Premier farewell. But his demeanour was so affectionate that, as they parted, the King kissed his minister on the cheek. At twelve the Captain-General of Madrid was summoned to the palace. When he left it, he announced that General Primo de Rivera was to be asked to form a Government.

Such is the story of the change which Don Alfonso was to find so momentous. There were few who believed that it was not his work, or that it had not at least his connivance. But there is no evidence that this was so. Primo conclusively denied it ; so, as we see, did the King. Yet, even allowing the courteous supposition that these two important people were telling the truth, the sympathy of the King was evident. His feeling was obviously that of his people. The dictatorship was accepted by Spain with immense relief, though naturally both parties of politicians were disgruntled. And the *Herald* of Madrid complained that when he laid aside the Constitution to take up the pen which wrote approval of the dictatorship, he had ceased to reign. It was, in fact, a part of the Constitution he had sworn that, after dismissing one Parliament, he should call another within three

[1] *Año Político*, 1923, p. 305.

months. Within three months the two leaders of
Congress, Romanones and Melquiades Alvarez, who
were received in audience, reminded him of his
coronation oath. If at that point he had taken
advantage of the sympathy of the nation, and kept
formally to his word, how much stronger his situation
would have been ! But Primo was so contemptuous
of parliaments, and his power over affairs was so
strong, that the great occasion was let slip. Spaniards
as a whole felt that it was no time to call a Parliament
together.[1]

The Military Directory began by giving Spain the
prize of ordered government. The lawlessness and
violence of years settled almost without a murmur
into order. The police became a power again, and
if a murderer was arrested, he could be sure that
within a day or two, instead of being freed, he would
be shot or garrotted. No one even attempted to do
what had been done almost with impunity under the
old régime. Murder and general strikes ceased.
Banks were no longer held up, and courts, when they
acted, began to give judgment according to the
evidence. Disorders ceased to disturb the traffic in
the streets of Barcelona, Bilbao, or Valencia. Smug-
glers gave up their traffic in tobacco and spirits.
Cocaine, the most lucrative and the most sinister of
contraband, became exceedingly difficult to obtain,
and, not least remarkable, many of the unnecessary
and idle men who secured the pay of Government
faded away from their sinecures. Trials of a few
offenders by martial law, followed by summary
execution, proved salutary to murderers and malcontents. Within a month Spain as a whole was calm.

It was so calm that the King and Queen were able
to go to Rome in the company of their military

[1] *Año Político*, 1923, pp. 407-11.

director. A commercial agreement had been signed between the two countries ; Primo and Mussolini wanted to meet, the Royalties envisaged the possibilities of marriage for princes and princesses, and His Catholic Majesty was enabled to greet the Holy Father. On November 17, the Spanish sovereigns arrived in Rome. " This is my Mussolini," said the King to General Italo Balbo, as he introduced his Primo.

The sovereigns, who were received in the Quirinal, hastened to the Piazza di Spagna, where for centuries had been established the Spanish Embassy to the Holy See. From there they set out for the Vatican. Cardinal Merry del Val met them at the entrance to the Apostolic Palace, and led them into the presence of the Pope. There the King read a long speech which in baroque phrases summed up his conception of his Catholic rôle as King of Spain. It had been, he said, the lot of his people in history to be the soldiers of religion, the unfailing defenders of the Catholic Church. " For the glory of religion, and the greatness of the nation, our universities with their teaching, our artists with their genius, our laws with their Christian depositories, our martyrs with their blood, our missionaries carrying the evangel to the most distant regions of the earth, our theologians who were a monument of learning at the Council of Trent, our mystics who spoke in Spanish the words of angels, our people with their customs and traditions deeply rooted in the ages, proclaim from century to century that all the ideals, all the grandeur, all the glories of Spain have been nourished from sacred earth, with patriotism making a single whole with religion ; for our soldiers, our missionaries, our discoverers, our navigators, and our Kings, more numerous than the sands of the deserts, so glorious that they are a path of shining light in the history of humanity, never planted the flag of Spain without the Cross above it ; and when they discovered the New World so as to create twenty nations on the American continent, in the breasts of those nations they kindled the faith of Christ even before they taught them to speak the vibrant language of Cervantes.

" Holy Father, the faith of our people has not cooled. Not an iota of it has vanished from that which, from my childhood, when my mother taught it me, has burned in my heart.

" Spain and its King," he concluded, " faithful to Your holy commands, will never desert the post of honour marked out for them by glorious tradition, to win triumph and glory for the Cross, which is not only the banner of the Faith, but the banner of Peace, Righteousness, Civilisation, and Advancement." [1]

3

The Dictator had kept announcing that he must deal with an emergency. He had restored order ; insisted on unity in Spain. He now, through one of his able lieutenants, announced a great political reform. In the first place he organised municipal government. Every man of twenty-three, every woman not represented by her husband, was to be given a vote for the Mayor and Municipal Council, and these municipalities were to develop local self-government. Behind this, and formed by the municipalities, was the department, and beyond the department the region which corresponded to the ancient Spanish Kingdom.[2] By this theory the question of Catalonia was settled : its old provincial

[1] *Año Político*, 1923.
[2] *Carta del Régimen Municipal y Provincial.*

parliament was dissolved, but when, in 1924, Primo had come back to Barcelona, his attitude had been conciliatory, though there was a return of severe repression before Catalonia settled down under the Directory.

What meanwhile was the position of the King? He was by no means as free, he had much less opportunity for initiative than under the parliamentary system. It was said that he felt it was worth that sacrifice to be rid of the Parliament, and to have a censorship of the Press. But was he not a little restive? A French journalist, M. Tharaud, secured an audience on April 17, 1925. He believed that even if the King was guarded, some nuance in look or tone would betray his real feeling.

" Frankly," said the King to the Frenchman, " did you notice, as you travelled through Spain, that we are living in a state of siege, under military oppression? I read in the foreign newspapers that our Directory shoots men down, throws them into prison, and that it is a reign of terror. Is that your impression? Here we have changed nothing of the ordinary tenor of our lives, and I would say for my part there is no country where the police are less of a nuisance. You can stop in the middle of the street for a talk with a friend without a policeman insisting that you should move on. You can after midnight drink any liqueur you like, which I defy you to do in New York or London, those homes of liberty.[1] At Madrid you can cry, howl, or sing, if that pleases you, till five in the morning. The only things changed since the Directory are that one can go about with money in one's pocket and yet not risk being knocked out, that there are no more strikes, that our works are running, and the masters do not every morning have to face work-

[1] Jérôme et Jean Tharaud : *Rendez-vous Espagnols*, pp. 22, 23.

22

men who appear each morning with revolvers in their
hands to give orders to their masters or assassinate
them. You must admit that that's something. But,
damn it all, you've got to pay for it. Primo has made
us break the Constitution, and that, obviously, is
serious."

The Frenchman looked in the King's eyes, but did
not notice any expression of great bitterness there.

" What else could we do ? " the King asked. " We
have certainly less Communists than you, but our
climate makes ours more virulent. And while at
Barcelona they assassinated you in broad daylight and
all our economic and social life was breaking up, our
Parliament was busy only with miserable finicky
questions, or in gratifying personal spite. One
couldn't go on like that. So General Primo did what
you know. He said to me then that he thought he
could settle the situation in three months, and come
back to legality within the time allowed by the Constitution. That was not my opinion. I thought that
three months would not be enough. And in fact six
months went by, then another six months, and now it
is nearly two years that we live without Parliament
or Ministers." [1]

" And how long, Sire, do you think that this régime
will last ? "

" All that we ask is to get out of it," said the King ;
" but still we must have the means to do that. The
party leaders, the *caciques*, have not shown us any sign
that they are giving up their old *parti pris*, or their
personal quarrels or their *politique de clocher* to rally to
the idea represented by the Directory ; the protection
of our economic and social life and the defence of our
interests as a whole. I know that among them there
are some of intelligence, whom personally I like

[1] *Op. cit.*, p. 25.

GENERAL PRIMO DE RIVERA, MARQUIS DE ESTELLA
After the portrait by M. de Laszlo.

" One couldn't go on like that," said King Alfonso,
" so General Primo did what you know."

extremely, but they are not separated from any of the detestable elements which make up their *clientèle,* and which they themselves are the first to despise. In these conditions, if one reopened the Parliament, one would see the old parties which led the country to its old undoing begin their disputes again, and recommence their chatter at the point where General Primo interrupted it. All would begin over again. The work of twenty months would be destroyed. The Communist leaders, exasperated by their sojourn in prison, would rouse men up more than ever to crimes and strikes. We should fall back into the anarchy out of which we have been making for two years such vigorous efforts to extricate ourselves."

At this point M. Tharaud put to Don Alfonso the obvious, the crucial question : How could Spain ever change from the Directory ? The King was not embarrassed by it.

"In this country," he said, "we have not yet attained to that idea of public life so familiar to a Frenchman or an Englishman. We have not, properly speaking, a public opinion ; the nation is the happy hunting-ground of the leading politicians. But the Directory applies itself to organise the union of all who are not professional politicians, and who ask only to work for peace and order. The *Union Patriótica* proposes to unite the men of goodwill who are disappointed by our old politics, and the numerous mass of neutrals who never bothered about it. It is open to everyone, Liberals as Conservatives, even to Socialists and Republicans ; and its object is not politics : its only object is to instil a feeling for their vital interests in the people as a whole. It is on that force, which is beginning to be conscious of itself, that the Directory believes it may depend on the day when new elections give back constitutional order to the country. When

will that day come? I know no more than you do.
But don't you think that the country shows no great
impatience to see that moment come? Do you
believe that in the twentieth century a nation like
Spain could endure a government it did not approve
without a movement of revolt—what shall I say?—
without any complaint except from politicians deprived of their ordinary occupation? This peaceful
acceptance, this perfect tranquillity, which you can
observe everywhere, is that not a plebiscite which the
nation gives every day tacitly in favour of the dictatorship? And then, don't you see, the question which
arises for Spain involves something infinitely bigger.
The Russian Revolution has brought Western civilisation face to face with another conception of life, a conception which seeks to dominate by force. To-day
the great problem is to know if parliamentary government has the power to defend the actual order of
things against the Sovietic idea. Italy was the first to
see that it could not. Spain in her turn has come to
her conclusion. Who knows if other nations also will
not be obliged to-morrow to abandon their constitutions? I see the glint of swords appear on all sides.

" But to come back to Spain, here are two eloquent
figures : there are in this country five or six thousand
politicians, believe me, there are no more. For them
the ideal of parliamentary government is inviolable.
But the parliamentarians would let the nation perish
rather than themselves ! On the other hand, twenty
million Spaniards, completely indifferent to political
manœuvres, only ask for one thing, the certainty of
work and respect for their property. To please six
thousand persons, must one sacrifice twenty million?
I leave that to you to settle."

At one point in the interview M. Tharaud had said
that in the view of men who were combating the

Directory, it was the King who was the real master of the house, the true force of Spain. Don Alfonso answered nothing, but the lightning in his eyes said more than any words.[1]

4

The King said another thing : " What we Spaniards lack is a Lyautey ! " Abd-el-Krim was as powerful as ever in Morocco. Primo so far had done nothing. But the summer of 1925 saw a remarkable change. Abd-el-Krim had hardened in his strength : he gloried so excessively in his triumphs over Spain that he gave sentence to open war with France also. But France still had her Lyautey ; that summer he visited Madrid : he had had no small opinion of Berenguer, but thought that the Spaniard failed through lack of understanding the Moorish religion.[2] Lyautey excelled as a combination of organisation and sympathy : the man of action had the soul of a creative artist.[3] He came to an understanding with Primo, and that summer, before the combined attack, the strength of the Moorish chief dissolved. His capital, Ajdir, itself was invested and fell, though he himself was not captured till the succeeding May. The whole chain of the Rif was subdued, and the war, which had roused Barcelona to insurrection in 1909 before the death of Ferrer, ended in a triumph. Don Alfonso's long ambition was satisfied. Never did his prestige stand higher. He had identified himself with the dictatorship, and everywhere it triumphed. The nine thousand Mayors of Spain came to Madrid, and the Mayor of Madrid, speaking for them at a banquet,

[1] Jérôme et Jean Tharaud : *Rendez-vous Espagnols*, pp. 28–31.
[2] *Año Político*, 1925.
[3] André Maurois : *Lyautey*.

spoke of the King having gained universal respect and affection. A plebiscite had been submitted to the people : it gave an almost unanimous declaration in favour of dictatorship. For the Spanish people were indeed believed to be free of the bugbear of democracy. Had not Dean Inge, summing up the new European movement in favour of dictatorship, said that the phylacteries of democracies were fly-blown ? In Spain parliamentary government never had had a solid existence. It was a bubble, a fabric of fluid, soft soap, and wind. Fluid thought, trying to find a level surface ; the soft soap of flattery ; the wind of shibboleth and phrase. These were the fabric of the bubble of democracy. Politicians blew it out into a rainbow globe of racing colours, in which in odd unnatural broadenings and elongations their own appearances took on a not unrecognisable reflection. It escaped from them as their cheeks were bursting, and coursed skywards with the breeze. Naïve admirers were delighted with its soarings, and fancied it arriving in the courts of heaven ; but as it began to move idly on or up, it disappeared and dropped in their faces, its sunrise glories shrunk to a drop of unsavoury dew.

5

The King had his people strong behind him when in the autumn of 1925 the dictatorship was re-established as a civil institution. The one task that remained to it was to reorganise finance. But it was there that the dictatorship came to grief. The peseta rose in value, and so impeded the export trade ; then it fell, and so disturbed confidence. For four years Primo de Rivera gradually lost ground. He began to lose it quickly in 1926, when he engaged in a sharp

conflict with the artillery in attempting to deprive
them of the peculiar privileges they had long enjoyed,
to refuse all promotion except by seniority. He in-
curred strong criticism for his action with regard to
the petroleum monopoly which was said to have
weakened the peseta by arousing the ill feeling of
powerful financial interests in New York and Amster-
dam. Business lost its impetus, and according to an
almost universal rule, the Government was identified
with the economic situation. Nevertheless, he still
found plenty to do. He organised five thousand new
schools, he inaugurated a great new irrigation
scheme in the valley of the Ebro, he pierced the
Pyrenees with a new tunnel so as to bring Barcelona
four hours nearer to Paris, and prepared another line to
halve the distance between Valencia and Madrid, yet
another to bring Madrid nearer to Vigo. Above all—
and this particularly at the instance of the King, whose
keenness on motoring made him alive to the need—he
effected an immense improvement in the Spanish
roads. The main roads which had been impossible
were made excellent, and other new ones were
planned. Inaccessible villages were brought within
reach of civilisation. It was due to the King's own
initiative that the primitive inhabitants of Las Hurdes
were provided with means of decent subsistence :
and the King fathered a much greater scheme in the
University City near Madrid, a centre for all students
in the Spanish-speaking world. To these Señor Calvo
Sotelo added a sweeping scheme for local improvements, so that in the icy blast of the plateau of Leon,
the maternity home at Orense should not remain
without windows, nor the doctor without pay.[1] Such
practical reforms seemed far more interesting to the
King than arguments for increasing the franchise

[1] See *Anuario de Vida Local*, p. 924.

or disestablishing the Church. He had the ideals of a modern business man; and business men were delighted. Throughout the dictatorship Spain made immense material progress, though she paid for it by a heavy increase in taxes and a gigantic tariff. For such are the inseparable accompaniments of a strong nationalistic development; and as Spanish prices rose, the value of the peseta fell.

As the years went on, discipline began to pall on the Spanish people. The six thousand politicians were more and more disgruntled. They had the Press on their side, for under the long censorship it grew more and more restive. When the economic boom passed, in the autumn of 1929, Spain felt the repercussion of slump in the richest countries. And as in every other country, there was a craving for change; the bough which had been pressed so hard by the wind began in the lull of the blasts to swing back.

It was then that the King's position became critical. The old charges, that the King had broken his oath and that he was responsible for the disaster at Anual, began to rumble louder. The King had irritated the intellectuals, both by his speech at the Vatican and his frank talk to M. Tharaud; vague gossip about all sorts of indiscretions spread so far as to include unsavoury rumours about the King's private life. But of these he himself naturally knew nothing: he lived in a Court where criticism was inevitably silent; the tone of all advisers alike was flattering. Although his features had not grown more attractive, still, as his fencer's eyes darted above the thickening nose and heavy jaw, he exerted the same personal charm. His courage was untarnished, his tact almost so. And experience had added to his native adroitness in the conduct of affairs. Although 1926 had seen his fortieth birthday, he still in the succeeding years played the part of the dazzling young subaltern. His car, driven by himself, would drop down into the valley of some distant province at the pace of a bomb. He would be photographed at one moment with a famous bull-fighter and at another in a polo-team. At the race-course, at the casino, on the tennis-court, among the aeroplanes, he appeared perfectly at home as the smart young man, sunburnt and *svelte*, smoking his cigarette and twirling his moustache, and with the same *entrain* he would decorate a veteran from Morocco, carry a candle in a religious procession, or sign the warrant for the exile of a professor.[1]

There was only one thing lacking in the King who could not grow up : he could not pretend that serious people did not bore him. And Spain, when all is said, is a serious country, as its immense landscapes are wild and austere. Even where irrigation fertilises the valley, or the *huerta*, the sterile mountain is in sight, and beyond the mountain there is the roll of arid plateaux. The people who have survived the snow and sun of Spain, and breathe its winds of light, are robust, naïve, and affectionate. But they are both conventional and serious. They are still haunted by the solemnity and romance of death. And when they are not religious, they have an almost tragic sense of the value of gravity. There in the heart of their grandeur, Don Alfonso somehow did not reach them. He was always moving under the immense skies, over the tawny plains, beneath the rocky hills, and through the rough-hewn streets of city or village : proudly loving all, and appreciating the masterpieces of each ; but, though the Court was open to all Spaniards of note, he stopped short somewhere of attaining to communion with his country's intellectual leaders. He had no more patience with the professor than with

[1] Béraud : *Emeutes en Espagne.*

the bishop. His greatest painter, Zuloaga, was never summoned to his Court. His most popular novelist, Ibañez, was provoked to write a vulgar diatribe against him. His most famous scholar and thinker, Don Miguel de Unamuno, was banished. And though through the Directory, one of the greatest of his literary students of life, Ramiro de Maeztu, was won over to his course, neither the King nor the Dictator did anything to apply Maeztu's great doctrine of function to Spanish civic life. Every type of thoughtfulness was alien to Don Alfonso, and even when he visited a school or university, the Duke of Miranda, his major-domo, arranged that he should speak with no one but those in a brilliant social position, or else the successful sportsmen. The scholars did not count. While the leading spirits were awakening to a great creative effort, he hung away from it, and gave his whole confidence to the great agencies of Conservative authority, the Army and the Church. The reaction was inevitable.

6

Nevertheless, the King pressed on with his great project of making Spain the inspiration of the Spanish-speaking world. He inaugurated (as we saw) the University City on the outskirts of Madrid, and, with the Directory, he threw himself with ardour into building up those two superb monuments of the Spanish genius, the exhibitions of Barcelona and Seville. They were opened in May of 1929.

Barcelona concentrated on modern industry. Spain there was shown as taking her part in the world of manufacture. But she was still the traditional Spain, the Catholic Spain of the great artists, where, in the striking architecture of the village, in the fertility of the watered garden, or in chased silver, embroidered silk, or shining armour, she had gorgeously expressed her sense of the beauty of life in the light of its relation to eternal values. And the exhibition was arranged on a hill which had been turned into a beautiful garden, and where, when it was opened in the brightness of May, pigeons were released to the number of sixty thousand, and a hundred fountains raised among the lawns and flowers the ever-changing grace of playing waters. The King, as he opened it, received the greatest ovation of his life.

But Seville was a still more glorious picture of the splendour of royal Spain. Every republic of America and every province of the Mother Country had built and stored a palace. The great Anibal González, in a gorgeous semicircle flanked by towers which recalled Seville's famous Giralda, gives expression, as the Escorial gives expression, to the combination of the Oriental with the Western, which makes Spanish genius unique and fertile. From this palace one might wander through an enchanted garden, a garden of profuse leaves and flowers, either to the monuments of Spanish America, or to the museums of ancient art, where royal armoury, old masters, or the gorgeous sculptures of Beruguete and Montañes, grouped in a magnificent ensemble of jewels, of precious metals finely wrought, and of brocades and tapestries, flashed on the eye in an elaborate significance the wealth of Spanish art. At night the whole great park became fairyland. Golden balls, lit from within, awoke the birds among the dark glistening leaves of the orange trees, coloured lights lit up the fountains and surprised the gold-fish in the streams and lakes ; festoons of silver lamps or rainbow electricity outlined the buildings, and rockets would rise into the air and burst in fronds of flame or coloured stars. But though fancy devised such playful effects in the changes of day to night, the splendour of the great collection was solemn and inspiring. There the Old World met the New World in an idea where traffics, inventions, and discoveries, instead of stifling the soul with a surplus of material production, or deadening it to the beat of machinery, amplified the ranges of the life of men, and served the noble instinct of the spirit to express in the wealth and happiness of earth its sense of an ideal perfection. Never were the possibilities of modern life pictured so promising or beautified more widely by the modern directors of traditions of wisdom. The dream of Columbus seemed to have come true with Spain joining the New World to the Old. It was an inspired creative gesture.

But how often the expression of a triumph marks the advent of disaster! When the King came to open the exhibitions, he was in mourning for his mother. They had been open only a few months when Primo fell. The decline in his prestige had been rapid. It was not alone the reaction of a democracy. The Left had organised its propaganda. The newspapers remained hostile. The trial of Sánchez Guerra, an old Prime Minister, and his internment on a warship; a rising in Ciudad Real; the resignation of Calvo Sotelo after bitter criticism of his financial policy, and above all the economic strain which was felt especially in Barcelona: all these had been gradually weakening the political fabric of Primo. Though business men still applauded him, and the country prospered, he himself grew so doubtful that he sent to each of the Captain-Generals a circular letter, asking if he had his confidence. On Sunday, January 26, the text of this letter was published in all the newspapers.

From the newspapers the King himself first heard of it, and at once summoned the Dictator to the palace. Primo was absent when the Royal Summons was sent. When at last he reached the palace, he found the King, not alone, but with his major-domo and his secretaries. That signified a crisis of the most acute kind. The King was furious. Was he not to be consulted, as the supreme representative of the people, or even of the armed forces ? Was Primo to leave the decision to the generals ? What were the King's prerogatives ?

The answer of Primo calmed Don Alfonso. It was, he said, a measure of precaution in the face of possible recurrence of rebellion ; it was not meant for political guidance.[1]

But not a single general answered favourably. Some refused to answer, some equivocated ; not one spoke warmly. On the following Tuesday the King accepted the resignation of Primo de Rivera. The fallen Dictator went into a voluntary exile. In Paris he wrote a series of articles, confused but not un-dignified, in which he looked facts honestly in the face.[2] But his heart was broken. In two months he was dead. They said he had been poisoned, but it was not a case of poison ; there was no need for it. When an ageing man, after a full and long life, and six years of violent strain, suddenly relaxes in seeming disgrace, nature gives him the *coup de grâce*.

When they brought the dead body of Primo de Rivera back to Spain, the people were greatly moved. Immense silent crowds had greeted its passing as it was brought back to Madrid. A splendid funeral was given to the man who received his due panegyric as the *Saviour of Spain*. But in all those stately obsequies there was one man absent : he who was

---

[1] Gabriel Maura y Gamazo : *Bosquejo Histórico de la Dictadura,* pp. 373, 376.
[2] Primo de Rivera : *Dictadura.*

above all the man whom the Saviour of Spain had tried to save. From that time there were few devotees of the dictatorship who believed that they could rely on Don Alfonso. The politicians had already lost faith in him. And he had ceased to propitiate the Republicans. His position was being undermined by the lack of a continuous policy. " He tires of everything," the Queen herself had said as a bride over twenty years before. " Some day he will tire even of me."

XV

KING ALFONSO : THE FINAL CRISIS

When it is impossible to obtain a clear manifestation of public opinion, and the deficiencies of the voting system oblige the sovereign to intervene in arranging which people and which party will govern, there is an inevitable reaction to this exercise of power, and so, sooner or later, there is unpopularity.

ALCALÁ GALIANO : *Memorias*, ii. 216.

Brevibus momentis summa verti posse.

TACITUS : *Annals*.

I

THERE are many who, wise after the event, say now that if, at the fall of Primo, the King had made an appeal to the country, all would have gone well. The people had swung back to the idea of the Constitution, and safe from the troubles of 1923, and braced by six years of discipline, would have made a successful return to parliamentary monarchy. The Dictator had had his own scheme, a sound one, for organising the country on a new basis, the basis of function, and in this the workmen's organisations under Largo Caballero were supporting him. But since Primo had fallen, even his best ideas were greeted with derision, and the immense work he had done for Spain was ignored. The King felt it imperative, as a representative of the national feeling, to dissociate himself from Primo and all his works. Yet he at once instituted another ministry with another general at its head : Berenguer, the man who had done well as High Commissary in Morocco, and who had tried

351

to save Silvestre from his rashness at Igueriben and Anual. The new ministry was by no means in-effective, but in what was understood to be its special task, the preparation for immediate elections, it accomplished nothing. The fact is, that the new directory believed no more than Primo in parlia-mentary government; in the summer the King, accompanied by the Duke of Alba, now Foreign Minister, paid the usual visit to London. They saw that the country was depressed, and that a crisis was not far off. "The present state of England," they said, "is obviously no advertisement for parlia-mentary government." They returned to Spain, where all seemed well. While England was getting into financial difficulties, Spain's exchequer showed a credit balance of 80,000,000 pesetas. In Barcelona the export of manufactured cotton had nearly doubled. And in December it was announced that the Berenguer Government would go to the country.

That was the signal for tumult. It seemed to restive Spaniards that they were to be under a dictatorship for ever; and knowing how the party in power can manage an election, they were con-vinced that the new election, like the old ones, would be a farce. So far the Berenguer Government had been gently feeling its way. It tried to avoid the brutalities of dictatorship, and indeed all methods of oppression. On the other hand, it had kept a sharp eye on disorder, and in its ten months of function had more than once closed a university, tightened the censorship, and dealt summarily with strikes. But it had no constructive scheme; indeed, as it was supposed to be a makeshift, it could not have one. And its methods were not uncompromising—it allowed the agitators to throw into the drinking vessels of Spain the salts of revolutionary effervescence. It was these which boiled out in Madrid in November and at Jaca in December.

For the Republicans had organised. At their head they had the old Liberal minister, Alcalá Zamora, the well-meaning orator who had been dismissed for incompetence in 1923. With him were Miguel Maura, a younger son of the old Conservative leader, and a number of Republicans and Socialists, headed by the shrewd veteran, Lerroux. These men, believing that they had no certain majority in the country, and that the managers would deprive them even of the support in numbers which they had, organised an armed revolt. They formed a widespread conspiracy to initiate a civil war. For the army was no longer solid with the King : thousands of young officers had been, like the University men, won over to Republicanism.

2

The revolt broke out near a grim little fortified town where the foothills of the Pyrenees meet the barren plain of Northern Aragon. A young officer of thirty-one, who had been brought up in a charity school, whose principles were fiercely Republican, and who had the temperament of an enthusiast with the face of a cut-throat, broke his oath and turned his revolver upon authority and upon the sovereign to whom he had sworn allegiance. The design was that the mutiny should spread to Saragossa and then to Barcelona, which should be the headquarters of a republican army. Galán, in his impulsiveness, began a day too soon. His mutiny was a fiasco. With his companion, Garcia Hernández, he walked back to Jaca and surrendered to the authorities.

Meanwhile, there was a curious demonstration

23

against the sky of Madrid. The King, in his palace, had to watch his own aeroplanes flying the red flag, circling over his head, and dropping pamphlets demanding his downfall. But the capital appeared unmoved. In the palace Don Alfonso presided at a Council of Ministers. They debated for hour after hour what should be done with Galán and García Hernández, and the King came in to luncheon almost an hour late. An English general and an English diplomat, who had once been Ambassador in Madrid, were among the guests. " I am extremely sorry, gentlemen, to be so late," said the King, " but we have had a long discussion over the affairs at Jaca. I have come to the conclusion that if officers in my army mutiny, they must be taught a severe lesson." The lesson was that which martial law is used to teach mutineers—the lesson of death.

General Berenguer now acted with vigour. He still had the artillery firm behind him, and against the artillery no revolt could make way. He prosecuted enquiries into the revolutionary influence at Madrid, and found the elaborate Republican organisation, of which Señor Alcalá Zamora was the head. Alcalá Zamora, Miguel Maura, Fernando de los Rios were arrested, and interned in the model prison where Spanish revolutionaries are placed to cool their ardour, the prison known as the Fan.

But the suppression of the attempted revolution had by no means calmed Spain, and least of all Madrid. Up to now the revolutionaries had been agitating a prosperous country. Now the peseta fell, business was disorganised, and the new movement vaunted two young martyrs. The uncompromising King had provided the revolutionaries with the very appeal to sentiment, the lack of which had been their weakness. The manifesto of the insurgents became public property. " When we clamoured for justice," it said, " our freedom was taken from us ; when we cried for freedom, we were offered as a concession a Cortes manufactured on the pattern of those swept away— formed by adulterated suffrage, convened by a dicta- torship, the instrument of a perjured King, and elected with the help of the old *caciques*."

At the same time, three intellectual leaders, Ortega Gasset, Pérez de Ayala, and Gregorio Marañón, pub- lished a manifesto. They said that the traditional Spanish State was in the last stages of decomposition. "The monarchy," they said, " has become, instead of national, an association of groups living like parasites on the substance of the nation, making use of public power to defend private interests. In consequence the monarchy has become every year more isolated. It is unequal to the task of regenerating the country, which must be undertaken by a republic. It would be childish to expect the monarch gracefully to bow to the new régime, and the people must be prepared to use their full influence."

" Political health can return to Spain," wrote *The Times* on January 25, 1931, " only when King Alfonso submits to a thorough discussion of the posi- tion. With every day that passes the danger to the monarchy becomes greater."

3

Just at that time Princess Beatrice fell on a polished floor in Kensington Palace and broke her arm. Such a shock for a lady of seventy-five was serious, and immediately after she caught a chill. Serious as the position was in Madrid, the Queen felt that the illness of the Princess was more serious still. The unrest of revolution was not grave enough to keep her from the bedside of her mother, and she hastened to Kensington with her deaf-and-dumb son.

On February 11 the censorship was removed in preparation for the elections. The swing was so heavily to the Left that things looked like an immediate revolution. Berenguer, like Princess Beatrice, had had an accident, and could not move from the Ministry of War. Madrid was wild with rumours. Count Romanones, it was believed, was about to ask for *Cortes Constituentes*, and the King to have his constitutional position reconsidered. On the other hand, generals had met at Saragossa with the idea of forcing through a new dictatorship. The King's own position was extremely difficult. The Church advised intransigence, believing that the paramount duty of those in power was to maintain order in an undisciplined country, which harboured an organisation definitely anarchical; the Republicans insisted the King should abdicate ; the Liberals were urgent for a new Constitution. But a return to Liberalism was not really advisable. The King's old counsellors were still astute enough, but they no longer represented the Spain of the day. In turning its back on the dictatorship the country had not yet given back its trust to the politicians of the parliamentary system. Don Alfonso, though he could obviously come to no decision, seemed, however, like the artillery subaltern whose nerves are braced by the rattle of the machine gun, to be still in the highest spirits.

On the morning of February 15, a Sunday, he drove over to the Ministry of War to see Berenguer, whose foot still prevented him from moving. It was obvious that something drastic must be done, something drastic to meet the mood of reaction against dictatorship. Berenguer was ready to resign. At the palace the politicians of the old school—Romanones,

Alhucemas, the Duke de Maura, La Cierva, Bugallal, agreed in advising the King to let the Liberals take charge of the situation.   Melquiades Alvarez insisted on a new Constitution, and to this Santiago Alba wired his agreement from Paris.   In the afternoon the King went for a drive, and again met Romanones.

Next day at noon the released prisoner, Sánchez Guerra, called on the King.   He was now asked to try his hand.   Don Alfonso's tone was courteous, and even cordial, and the old man produced a suggested list of ministers, which the King agreed that he should sound.   When he left the palace, he went first to Berenguer, and from the Ministry of War he went on to the gaol.   To the monarchists the venture seemed fantastic.   Were the governors of Spain, they asked in dismay, to come straight out of prison ?   The place for Sánchez Guerra, said one newspaper, was not a ministry but a lunatic asylum.

But when Sánchez Guerra returned to the palace, he had to admit failure.   The King told him that if he could not guarantee order, he must leave things in the hands of those who could.   Don Alfonso was apparently as confident of his position as ever.

But Señor Alcalá Zamora, in his prison cell, felt more confident still.   The King was so weak that he had consented to ask support from those insisting on his downfall !   The political prisoner found a means to issue a *communiqué*.   He would join no political movement, he said, but would watch for the final triumph of the republic.   He declared that true elections would give the Republicans a majority, and that they would take care that at the last hour no intrigue should tear away victory.

Meanwhile, the Queen left London on her return journey to Madrid.   The King and Queen of England, who, after reading the despatches from the British

Embassy, felt not a little concern, took leave of her at Victoria, and Queen Mary was seen gently patting her on the back. They were advising her to persuade Don Alfonso to act constitutionally. Before she arrived in Madrid on the 18th, the politicians had passed a day of intense excitement. In the words of *The Times* correspondent, confusion had reigned in Madrid from dawn to dusk. While some believed revolution imminent, the Royalists began to demonstrate their strength. At an early hour rumours began to circulate that cavalry regiments and batteries of artillery in several garrison towns had declared their willingness to support the King against whomsoever he should regard as his enemies. In Spain, such declarations, which in other countries might be mere demonstrations of loyalty, were not without political significance. But Madrid knew no more than rumours. Those who enquired at the Ministries were merely informed that the Berenguer Government was in power to maintain order.

The Queen on her return journey had crossed the frontier in the early morning, and spent the day travelling down from Irun to Madrid. She had braced her courage to meet something like a revolution; but at each great station her passing was greeted with unprecedented enthusiasm. At Madrid the station was crowded. She looked out for a moment in amazement, and then a deafening shout broke on her ears : " *Viva la Reina ! Viva la Reina !* " The open space outside the station was a sea of faces, a sea which roared a welcome in long recurring waves. A dense crowd followed her to the palace and made such fervent demonstrations that the King and Queen were forced to appear again and again to acknowledge the ovation. At such a moment, such a demonstration was taken as decisive.

Later in the evening the monarchist leaders met at the Ministry of War. Romanones, La Cierva, Bugallal, Alhucemas, Ventosa, the Duke de Maura, Admiral Rivera, Gascón Marín, and the Marquis de Hoyos agreed to form a coalition. It only remained for the King to appoint a head : he chose a man held in wide esteem, the Admiral of the Fleet, Aznar, who had already had experience as Minister of Marine seven years before. There was a general feeling that all was well for the monarchy. The presence of Ventosa, who was the right-hand man of Cambó in Barcelona, proved that the Catalans were not dissatisfied. The coalition looked a strong one. And remembering the enthusiastic demonstrations which had greeted the Queen, there seemed to be no doubt at all that the majority of Spaniards were in favour of the monarchy. The Republicans, it was believed, were routed, and the third dictatorship prepared to organise elections. The King felt the situation so secure that he went away for a holiday to England, to congratulate, he said, his royal mother-in-law on her recovery and offer her his compliments. There were some, however, who believed that he was preparing for every eventuality.

On March 20 he set out from London on his return journey. That day began also the trial of the revolutionary chiefs. The leading advocates of Madrid were ranged on their side, and Señor Ossorio Gallardo, in an eloquent speech, argued the same plea as had been made for old Sánchez Guerra, that no one could rebel against a Constitution which did not exist. The argument was enough. The conspirators were acquitted.

4

Meanwhile the Republicans and Socialists had swept the country with propaganda, a propaganda both of complaints and promises. Now and again their criticism would squeeze through the censorship of the newspapers, and a thrill of passionate discontent would pass over numbers of the people. But the constant and reiterated force of harangue and pamphlet did the more telling work. The Spaniards wanted a change. They believed the King's immediate advisers to be bad, they had no trust in the old gang of politicians, and they felt the strain of the economic situation. Business, which had done well up to the fall of Primo, had been declining since, and was now almost at a standstill. His nationalistic policy of a high tariff had produced a boom, as a rise in the tariff always does. But from any such boom there is a reaction, and this reaction left the Spaniards with the cost of living, as well as the taxes, enormously higher. This was very bad for their export trade. In spite of Primo's great reforms in communication and education, and his big educational schemes, he had omitted to co-ordinate the producing regions of Valencia with the industrial centres, Barcelona and Bilbao. In addition to this, Spain's invisible exports from investments in the New World had been dwindling away ; the actual exports on which she depended to balance her trade, olive-oil and fruit, shared precariousness with the whole Mediterranean region, and neither the nationalism of Primo nor the uncertainty which succeeded it had encouraged foreign capital to initiate new enterprises.

As for the King, he no longer commanded the enthusiasm of the young who, twenty years before, had shared with him the hopes of youth ; the army's loyalty was shaken ; the old politicians had no enthusiasm for a man who had welcomed a Dictator in their place, and the aristocracy, taking them as a whole, rallied to nothing but amusement. Those few

who, like the Duke of Alba, cut up their estates,
encouraged learning or art, and thought out new
enterprises, were distrusted as masons or anti-clericals.
And yet it was with these rather than with the extreme
Conservatives that the King found his affinity. The
love of polo, and the love of travel which he shared
with them, were taken, like his alertness, as a sort of
remoteness to Spanish tradition. And the health of
his sons was never forgotten. His distrust of Parliament was widely known. He wants, they said, to
reign as an absolute monarch.

The avowed Republicans hardly did the King so
much harm as lukewarm monarchists. While those
around him cut him off from the intellectual life of
the country, their deference, which was not seldom
obsequiousness, gave him no chance to gauge the
change of feeling. Whenever he appeared, he was
greeted with the same ovation as before. And neither
he nor many others guessed how much harm had
been done to his cause by accumulating criticism,
which loaded on his head all the failings of his ancestors. Peoples, as Napoleon wrote to Fernando,
are only too prone to avenge on monarchs the
respect paid to them. " He is more treacherous
than Fernando VII," Don Antonio Maura had
said of Don Alfonso in an explosion of impatience.
Ibañez, voicing the same thought in a vulgar col-
loquialism, had spoken of him as " Fernando VII
and a bit more." [1] Señor Cambó, in an article
in the *Veu de Catalunya*, had once summed up the
gossip against Don Alfonso in a eulogy of Victor
Emmanuel. " The King of Italy," said Cambó,
" never of his own act initiated a military adventure ;
never sent clandestine instructions to the generals

---

[1] This remark is said to have originated with Don Antonio
Maura.

conducting the war ; never intervened in the appointment of diplomatic representatives, or, unknown to
ministers, gave those representatives instructions compromising the interests or prestige of the country ; he
never meddled in the appointment of officers or
officials ; he never conspired against the Governments,
plotting to oust them from power, and he never
brought ridicule upon himself or his country by indiscreet language or improper conduct." The King of
Spain was a man of action, and like all men of action
he sometimes made mistakes. No one can deny that
he had more initiative than prudence. But those who
described him as the worst of the Bourbons were not
aiming at the target. Daring, resourceful, able, he
made himself a man of mark such as few monarchs
are. He did signal service to Spain, and under him
she awakened to a life and energy such as she had not
known since her golden age.

5

From March 20 the days passed quietly. The
Aznar Government had announced that municipal
elections would be held on April 12, while those for
the Cortes would take place in June. The monarchists, divided and apathetic as they were, did nothing
to prepare for the municipal elections. Yet in Spain
it was still the municipal authorities who controlled
the urns and so announced the parliamentary vote,
and Romanones had insisted that the municipal elections must come first. It was the very point which
had led Espartero to exile Queen Cristina, and which
had made her say that she had made him a Duke but
could not make him a gentleman.

All this had been carefully thought out by the
Republicans, whose leaders were once more at

liberty. They were now intensely active : they toured the country ; they founded fresh newspapers, in which lawyers, doctors, writers poured out enthusiasm for the Republican cause. But to all this monarchists paid little attention. They were confident that the masses of the people held themselves aloof from the activities of both the masonic elements. They knew that lawyers, journalists, university men, were a class by themselves ; that they were separate from the Church ; that they lacked also the practical sense of business men. They did not recollect that such men might be the moulders of opinion because they were the voice of opinion, and in the palace they felt so secure that a week before the election the Queen's sister-in-law, Lady Carisbrooke, actually underwent a serious operation.

When the people voted on April 12 (all Spanish elections are held on a Sunday), there was no sign whatever of agitation. There were neither demonstrations in the streets nor uproar at the polls. Count Romanones, who was spending the afternoon shooting in the country, felt his heart sink, and believed he was about to undergo a great misfortune. When he returned to Madrid and found that the *barrio* of Salamanca, a district of the upper and middle classes, had declared for the Republic, he knew at once that the battle was lost. He went to the Ministry of State and called up the Civil Governors. All gave him the same answer. At the Ministry of Government he found the other ministers and the head of the Civil Guard, a colleague of Primo, and a devoted monarchist, General Sanjurjo. " Up to now," said the old Count, " you have answered for the Civil Guard. Can you do so to-morrow when they know the will of the country ? " With the General's answer, the last hope vanished.

Early next morning Romanones went to the palace and saw the King. His Majesty appeared untroubled. The Count spoke in roundabout terms of his own fear. The King interrupted him. " I shall be no obstacle in the road that must be taken ; but I think there are still several roads." When the old politician left the palace, he knew he would not often cross the threshold again.

Not till five in the evening did the ministers meet. Romanones was the first to speak. He spoke with great emotion, saying that the Government must face the crisis, and take a free hand. His contention, he said, was that force could be used against revolution, but not against the result of an election : you cannot attack a ballot-box with a mauser. Other ministers answered that municipal elections could not alter the Constitution. The discussion lasted for three hours. At last the old man wrote down the result of it to take to the King.

Early next morning the Count Guimero called on him with a message from the Count Casa Aguilar, whom Romanones himself insisted on seeing.

" Unless we act quickly," said Romanones to Casa Aguilar, " the life of the King may be in danger. Go to the palace and tell him that there is no other solution than for him to leave Spain immediately. Do not argue with him—warn him of the peril he is running, and which I believe he is running ; for he with his character and courage will make light of it. Tell him simply that the love he has always expressed for Spain demands that he should leave it." And he dictated a message for Casa Aguilar to take.

An hour later Romanones was received by the King, and repeated with all the force of which he was capable the purport of his message. The Minister of Justice came, and reasoned that the King might still

treat with the Constitutionalists : Sánchez Guerra,
Villanueva, Alvarez. Meanwhile the King told
Romanones to discuss matters with Alcalá Zamora,
who, twenty-five years before, had been his private
secretary. They met in the house of Dr. Marañón.

" You have known me very well for twenty-five
years," began Alcalá Zamora, " and you know that
I am a man who cannot keep the truth from the light.
The truth is obvious. You have lost the battle.
There is no way left but for the King to leave Spain,
and to leave immediately. The Republic will be
proclaimed before sunset. The King must resign
his powers to a Council of Ministers. He must not
leave Spain by Irun, for there, as in San Sebastian,
there is a great feeling against him. He would do best
to cross the frontier into Portugal." Romanones
understood that any further discussion would be useless, and went back to the Council.

The revolutionaries were amazed at the extent of
their own triumph. The towns had nearly all a
republican majority, though some, like Cadiz, remained
solidly monarchist. In the country constituencies,
also, the great majority were for the King. But the
people of Madrid were prepared to take things into
their own hands, and the conspirators were only too
gratified that they should.

But if they had hesitated, the news from Barcelona
would have given them decision. Maciá had walked
into the Provincial Parliament and proclaimed
Catalonia a republic. The news made a profound
impression in Madrid, where already, on Monday
evening, a great crowd had surged to the royal palace
and demanded the instant departure of the King.
Troops had remained on guard all night. In the
morning of the Tuesday, crowds filled the streets of
Madrid and rushed at the newspapers. In the after-

noon a lorry with the red-and-blue flag of the Students'
Union drove down the Calle Alcalá, escorted by a
cheering crowd. Almost immediately afterwards,
boys scattered Republican proclamations through the
street. The town burst out into a flame of red, and
the Republican flag appeared on every vehicle. In a
broad flood the crowd moved towards the open space
above the Manzanares, where the royal palace looks
over the valley, the plain, and the sierra to the setting
sun. Inside the glittering grey walls the King was
still debating with his ministers what it was best to do.
The Republican leaders, like the crowd, were insistent
on one thing, that Don Alfonso should leave that
night for Cartagena, and there take ship for France.

If the King did not agree, there must at once be
civil war. A great attack would burst upon the
palace. Not even the army could be trusted to
defend it. Don Alfonso's presence was endangering
the lives of everyone around him.

His own mind was clear. His function was to
represent the people. The people had made that
impossible. The Republican leaders were still guaran-
teeing his escape. He determined to hand over his
prerogatives to his ministers till a more favourable
moment came to take them up. He signed the
manifesto and handed it to his ministers. It was not
an abdication, but a suspension of his prerogatives.

" The elections that took place on Sunday have
told me clearly," it ran, "that I have now lost
the love of my people, but my conscience tells me
that this disaffection will not be lasting, because
I have always acted in such a way as to serve
Spain, my only care being the public interest even
in the smallest matters. A king may make a
mistake, and doubtless I have myself erred some-

times, but I know well that our countrymen have always been generous to faults that are not deliberate. I am the King of all the Spaniards. I am myself a Spaniard.

" I might have used various means to maintain the royal prerogatives and fight my adversaries effectively, but I resolutely want to eschew anything that might throw my countrymen into a civil and fratricidal war.

" I renounce nothing of my rights, because, rather than my own, they are a deposit accumulated by history, and I shall one day have to give a strict account of their keeping.

" I am waiting to learn the real expression of the collective opinions of the people, and until the nation has spoken, I deliberately suspend the exercise of the royal power, and depart from Spain, thus recognising that she alone is mistress of her destiny. Yet to-day I think I am performing the duty dictated to me by love of my country, and I pray to God that other Spaniards may have as deep a comprehension of their duty as I have."

The King held his last council at six o'clock. As he said farewell to his ministers, he embraced them each ; but he showed no sign of his courage failing. "I am leaving with a clear conscience," he said, " having done my best with the legacy left me by my father."

The Prince of Asturias, who had exhausted himself on a shooting expedition, and had spent the whole time of the crisis in his bed, awaited his father's farewell in his own room. Neither to the Prince, nor to any member of the Prince's suite, did he show any sign of emotion. " I must prove to the State," he

said, " that I am more democratic than many who
call themselves so. Since the result of Sunday's
elections, I have seen clearly that there was no alternative but to act as I am doing, or to resort to arms.
And I love Spain too well to shed her blood." The
King alone maintained a calm demeanour. He spoke
to men and women whose hearts were broken, whose
lives were ruined, and whose ideals were shattered.
For in the palace there was no one who swerved in
passionate devotion to the King.

At the last moment he said good-bye to the Queen,
to his daughters, to his sons, Don Jaime and Don
Gonzalo. As he walked from his apartments to the
lift, the guard of halberdiers gave the royal salute.
The officer commanding shouted " *Viva el Rey!* " and
the shout was taken up by all at the top of their voices.
The King tried to answer, but could not. At the door
of the lift he shouted once, " *Viva España!* " And in
silence the lift descended.

On the terrace outside, friends and servitors were
gathered beside the small procession of cars which had
been sent by the Minister of Marine. The last lights
had left the evening sky. It was a little after eight
when the King stepped out into the lamplight on the
terrace. He made his last farewells with the same
calm. The fortitude and serenity which he had
shown at every hour of those trying days did not fail
him at the last. With his cousin Don Alfonso de
Bourbon-Orléans, with Admiral Rivera, the Minister
of Marine, and with the Duke of Miranda, he entered
his car, and, followed by a small procession of vehicles,
drove off into the night.

As soon as he left, the republican flag was flown
over the palace and the guard was withdrawn. The
Queen and her children, amazed at the suddenness
of the events, had been told that they were to leave

by train next morning. The Queen was cut to the heart by the change. " I thought I had done well," she said. They hurriedly packed, while a few friends went round borrowing money for them, for they had made no preparations whatever for the crisis ahead of them. Meanwhile, the mob howled and screamed before the palace, yelling for their blood. It seemed to the Queen in those dreadful hours as though the people whom she had always seen enthusiastic had, like Gadarene swine, suddenly become possessed by the devils of anarchy. " Nothing in nature," her Spanish godmother had said of the last night she had spent in her own palace, " neither storms, nor the elements in fury, can give you the least idea of the horror of a people in uproar against you. Unless you have seen it, no one can imagine what it is to have a whole populace howling for your blood. It is ghastly ! "

The terrible night which, to the Queen's overwrought feelings, threatened the murder of her children before her eyes, revolved its exhausting hours. The preparations had been made. The morning shone out clear in the bracing spring weather. And the sun had already begun to glow when the Queen in her turn went down to the same garden entrance, sheltered from the *canaille*, where just twenty-five years before she had first entered the royal palace. Neither chauffeurs nor footmen wore livery. Another crowd had gathered at the station. Not knowing into what violence it might break out, the Ministers had agreed that the Royal Family should enter the train at the Escorial. As they drove on, they were informed that the demonstrations of the populace had prevented the train from starting. It did not reach the Escorial till noon. The Queen alighted from her car. Sitting on a bank on the roadside, she

24

received the farewell homage of the ladies who had accompanied her. The Prince of Asturias could not move from his car, and finally had to be carried into the train.

To save them from danger, the royal saloon had been sent out to the Escorial the night before, and there was some little delay while they were hitched on to the train. A British officer approached the royal party. " I suppose you have come from your Embassy," said Don Gonzalo. " No, sir, I have not," answered the officer. No one had come from the British Embassy that awful night, that awful morning. The Embassy of His Britannic Majesty was, as those of His Catholic Majesty were soon to be, under the orders of a Socialist. It was simply an unofficial officer from the country of her birth, who reassured her at that moment as one had reassured her on her wedding-day, when the anarchist's bomb had marked her path with Spanish blood.

Aznar and Romanones were the only two officials of the late Government at the Escorial to say good-bye to the Queen. With them were about a hundred others, some serving in the palaces, some habitués of the Court. A great ovation greeted her at Hendaye. " I give you the assurance that the King has not abdicated," she said to a newspaper man, as she had said with equal distinctness at the Escorial. Lady Carisbrooke, in spite of her operation nine days before, also travelled with the Queen. The Prince of Asturias became exhausted with the journey, and when the train reached the frontier could hardly move.

A great company had gathered to meet the Queen at the Quai d'Orsay ; when she arrived she was greeted with wild cheers in the reception room, where a company of the most distinguished society of Spaniards and French had been gathering. It was to these people that the Queen suddenly appeared, moving slowly, with the expression of a woman walking in her sleep. Her mouth was set : her eyes gazed fixedly ahead. Unknowingly she clutched a bunch of red and yellow tulips, the colours of royalist Spain. The women curtsied and kissed her hand. But her only sign of recognition was her tears.

As she moved out into the street the acclamation grew louder and more tumultuous. There was no menace now ; but after all she had borne in Madrid she could react no more to the shouts of " *Vive la reine !* " " *Viva la reina !* " which shook the air. The crowd pressed so close on her that she could hardly reach her car. When she entered, the police could no longer hold back the people, who cheered so wildly and obliviously that, until the police organised for a great effort, no one could move. But the Queen sat immovable and expressionless. She was worn out.

CONCLUSION

The day is lost ?   What then ?
What though the struggling rearguard of the fight
Be whelmed in fear and might
And the flying scouts proclaim
That death has gripped the van ?
Ever the heart of man
Cheers on the hearts of men.
" It hurts not ! " dying cried the Roman wife
And one by one
The leaders in the strife
Fall on the blade of failure, and exclaim
" The day is won."

EDITH WHARTON : *Artemis*.

I

THE King's convoy had driven quickly, and soon after dawn he had arrived at Carthagena, where a cruiser, the *Principe Alfonso*, some distance from the wharf, was already under steam to take him into exile. Careful arrangements had been made to avoid unpleasantness, and the gates of the quay were closed. But the news of the King's presence had leaked out, and as he stepped on board the pinnace, serene as ever, but, as his voice showed, not unmoved, the cry of " *Viva la República !* " could be heard from the crowd pressing against the barricade.

Next morning, at six o'clock, a French watchman above the harbour signalled the arrival of the *Principe Alfonso* at Marseilles.   The sun rose into a cloudless sky, and turned the water azure.   The Château d'If raised its primrose wall from the island in the harbour. The beautiful city showed its roofs and wall against a background of umbrella pines, or hills silvered by the olive ; beyond was the Provençal landscape, over which Carlos and Maria Luisa had driven from Aix over a hundred years before, and high to the right stood out in gold the statue of Notre Dame de la Garde. The King passed the morning at an hotel, and at noon took the train for Paris.

Debonair as ever, he could not pretend that all had been easy. " I left Spain so that there should be no civil war," he said ; " but it is harder to leave like that than leading the charge of a squadron."

Paris had prepared for him a sounding reception : and never since the days of Louis Philippe had such a cry of " *Vive le roi !* " been heard as when, that night, the King arrived at the Gare de Lyon. Enthusiasts followed him to the hotel, and it was plain that if he had lost popularity in Spain, he was sure of the sympathy of France, as he was of that of England.

The King and Queen spent a few quiet days in Paris, and then moved with their family and their suite to Fontainebleau, where they could live quietly while they watched the turn of events in Spain.

2

The country rapidly resumed its normal life. The ministers were perforce changed, but not the functionaries. Indeed, it was a little surprising to find that a couple of days after the revolution, Admiral Aznar, the head of the King's Government, was moving through the corridors of his offices in uniform. Although he had ceased to be Prime Minister, he had resumed his post as Admiral of the Fleet.

For four weeks all went well, though to be sure on May 1 there was a little disorder in Barcelona. But the new Government spoke of adopting Liberal measures. They declared that there would be free-dom of the Press and freedom of speech. It was understood that there was to be no difference in the status of the Church, and private property in general was to be respected. Law and order were enforced, but the prisons were almost emptied by a political amnesty. The people, however, were not allowed to succeed in setting malefactors free. All this seemed so reassuring that a monarchist newspaper of Madrid printed a message from the King that, in view of the known forces of anarchy behind, the wisest thing was to support the republican authority ; and a few young monarchists shouted, " *Viva el Rey !* "

In an hour the situation changed. There were at once a riot in Madrid and unrest in Saragossa ; and, taking advantage of the feeling excited, a small band of anarchists organised a campaign of arson, which burnt to the ground ten churches and religious houses in Madrid.

That movement showed the nature of the new Government. Counsels in its Cabinet were so divided that the police were not allowed even to defend pro-perty against the crime of arson. A minister declared that " all the convents in Spain were not worth the life of one Republican." The thirty-two churches of Malaga were then burnt, and acts of hideous sacrilege performed, while the Civil Governor, appointed by the Republic and responsible for main-taining order, greeted the riot with the cry of " *Viva la República !* " Liberty was everywhere withdrawn from the Press, leading newspapers of Madrid were temporarily suppressed, monarchists were thrown into jail, and it was found that one of the most active incendiaries was the mechanic of the airman, Franco, who was now Minister for Air. The exchange collapsed, confidence with it, and business suffered a set-back from which it has never recovered. While the provincial government of the Republic had soon outdistanced the most repressive acts of the dictatorship, and intellectual leaders were exiled without trial to the tropic island of Fernando Po, leading Liberals and intellectuals complained that their dearest ideals were being flouted. " The dog," they said in the words of a Spanish proverb, which took its origin from Fernando VII, " is the same : he has only changed his collar."

The world of aristocratic fashion had migrated to Biarritz, tourists hurried from the country, and the large number who had lived on the bounty of the King faced famine ; not only this—in the rapid increase of unemployment the poor began to suffer general privation. Although the rapid fall in the exchange should have stimulated exportation, business was stagnant, and prices were prevented from rising by the plethora in the foreign markets, which was reducing the cost of living in the rest of Europe. Decrees to cut down the cumbrous army and reform the civil service, though excellent in themselves, made a new centre of discontent. The King's properties were said to be at the disposal of the public, but no one was allowed to enter them. Arrangements were made for elections ; and when a sweeping majority of extremists were returned, even in those centres which had been devoted to a monarchist, as Orense was to Calvo Sotelo, there was a general feeling that the figures at the polls could no more be trusted than in the days of the old politicians. And it was even cynically observed that at the head of the Ministry of the Interior was Don Miguel Maura, a son of the man who, as Prime Minister, was credited with having brought to a fine point the art of managing elections. And, in any case, as Lord Clarendon observed : " C'est

surtout en Espagne qu'on aime à venir à l'appui du plus fort.''
Following the attacks on Church property, there was
a sudden outgrowth of pornographic literature : the
Minister of Justice, in an interview, declared that one
of the chief reforms he had in mind was a system of
trial by jury in crimes of sexual violence so that due
allowance might be made for those who found self-
control impossible in a hot climate. And it is the
literal truth to say that while business as a whole
languished, there was a boom in the trade of both
newspapers and brothels. There were some who
questioned which of these was in the circumstances
the more sinister.

For the newspapers were filled with panegyrics of
the new régime and abuse of the old. There was
little attempt at sanity of judgment ; and the new
censorship saw to it that no attempt should be made,
no opportunity permitted, to weigh things in the
balance. This in itself was unfortunate, but it was
not the tragedy. The worst was that while all was
effervescence of enthusiasm, no one gave attention to
the real features of the situation, the decline in business, the loss therefore of employment, the breakdown
of the old system of charity, and the general increase
of want and destitution even to the point of famine.
The revolution has meant above all one thing—an
immense increase in the physical sufferings of the poor.

It became clear in the autumn that this economic
effect was to be closely associated with an attack on
religious liberty. Early in May the Primate of Spain
had been warned to leave the country, the Bishop of
Malaga, after the destruction of his palace, had been
forced to flee, and the Bishop of Vitoria had been
exiled. The Primate, when he returned in June, was
arrested, and taken to the frontier. There was, of
course, no proof whatever that any of these had com-

mitted any fault, or that they had even acted in any way against the Republic. But the ministers still insisted, publicly and privately, that they would guarantee civil liberty to the Church, even those ministers—they were the majority—who wanted to disestablish it. In October the drapery of decency was torn off their designs. The two members of the Cabinet, Alcalá Zamora and Maura, who as Catholics had stood against the attack on the Church, were forced to resign ; and it was declared to be a part of the Republican Constitution that the religious orders should surrender their property to the State, that they should not have the right of association, that the chief educators among the clergy, the Jesuits, were to be exiled, and that no religious body had the right to teach. This law would deprive some hundreds of thousands of children of education, and showed that the system of spreading primary instruction, which Don Marcelino Domingo had taken over from the Directory and enlarged, was not so much an increase of schools as an attempt to remove them from moral and religious influence. The attempt made in Navarre and the Basque Provinces to protest con-stitutionally in favour of religious association of any kind was met by the presence of troops, repression by police, and censorship, or more often suspension, of the newspapers. These things, it is declared, were necessary in the interests of the Republic. Primo de Rivera, it is true, also did these things ; but he did not make a revolution with the avowed object of remedying them ; and, in any case, he began with anarchy and established peace. In every case where Primo in his six years' dictatorship had sacrificed liberty to order, the Republic in six months went farther, and left Spain much less happy, much less quiet than at the Revolution. And unless the monarchy had created a feeling of optimism, the revolution would never have been risked.

3

Such reflections bring us to understand the nature and function of kingship in Spain. In a country where practically equality, as Gómez de Arteche called it, was the tradition of the country, where little deference was paid to rank, and pride (especially in the sense of refusal to submit to discipline) was the heritage of all, there was a foreign element in the absolute traditions of the Bourbon monarchy. Nevertheless, that French absolutism had done no harm, and never since before the days of the Emperor Charles V had a monarch been so popular, or made such wide reforms as the benevolent despot who was the father of Carlos IV. That enlightened despotism had been continued in the long ministry of the affable Godoy. From then we have traced the story, a story lurid and fateful. We saw on the one side the sudden irruption of humanist ideas against an almost mediæval system, encased in the armour of the Inquisition ; we saw, on the other hand, that, while the life of the nation was still centred on the King, there was a succession of extremely unfortunate kings : the inadequate Carlos IV, the intruder Joseph, and the unscrupulous traitor Fernando, who lost America and invited a sequence of calamity, undermining the prestige of monarchy in generations unborn.

His daughter never had a chance. Born the victim of bad heredity and inbreeding, her education was ruined by the weakness in the position of her mother, and by the intrigues of faction around her person. When she might have married a man to support her with the character, the principle, and the sagacity she lacked, she was, while yet a school-girl, bullied into accepting as consort a nincompoop, whom everyone alike despised, while her impulsive heart satisfied its cravings as best it could. In such circumstances it was impossible for Catholic majesty to keep its prestige intact.

But what was the alternative? The Duke of Sexto's shrewdness saw that the republican remedy was worse than the disease of the reigning house. The most satisfactory plan was to restore the ancient dynasty, and for nearly fifty years Spain walked forward in the presence of a constitutional sovereign. The responsibility was with the ministers, who arranged things among themselves. This was the system which Don Alfonso XIII inherited from the long and blameless regency of his mother. His powerful personality, his swift and adroit mind, his adaptiveness and enthusiasm, his combination of tradition with enterprise enabled him to give a new significance to his splendid position, a significance which was generally identified with the Renaissance of Spain. "I have not spoken often with the King," wrote Don Miguel de Unamuno, the first among the advanced intellectuals of his country; "but it has been sufficient to show me that one must look elsewhere for the obstacle to certain necessary reforms to establish the supremacy of justice and education. I hope more —much more—from the King than from the Parliament. By his office the King stands—and he knows it well—above classes and struggles : he does not belong more to the nobility than to the people, nor to the army more than to civil use, to the capitalist more than to the earner." "Among all persons," wrote Altamira, "who can to-day have a deep influence on our political and national life, the King is *the only one* in whom many, and perhaps the majority, feel that they can trust." "He is a man in the full meaning of the word," wrote Romanones. "To cry *Viva Alfonso XIII !*" wrote Benavente, "has for good Spaniards to-day the same significance as *Viva España !*"

Such was the general feeling as late as 1923. The people's distrust shrewdly settled on the Parliament : even Count Romanones admitted that, since public opinion had no influence on politics, the politicians had nothing to restrain them in the pursuit of their own profit. And to realise to what suffering this pursuit of political profit brought Spain, we have only to recall the murders, the war, and the financial instability of 1923. The King had done all he could to bring politicians to a sense of responsibility ; but in effort after effort he had failed. His most signal services were yet to be performed ; for it was at this point that he accepted the military dictatorship, as the King of Italy had accepted Mussolini ; and in this, beyond any question, he had interpreted the instinct of the country, and accepted a system which meant also an enormous advance for the country. Yet when that dictatorship became unpopular, it was Don Alfonso once again who interpreted the popular feeling. It was he who, in the following year, gave the instructions to prepare for the new elections which led to his dethronement. By a system of enforced authority, he could no doubt have lengthened a reign which had been of incomparable advantage to his people. But regarding himself as the King of all the Spaniards rather than the leader of a party or a class, he left the judgment to his people as a whole. He would be either their representative or an exile.

4

What reasons were there for the decided anti-monarchical vote of the towns on April 14 ? Why

had the King become unpopular in the towns when
he retained the confidence of the country constituencies ? The reason is not far to seek. The
Socialist organisation was shrewder than anyone had
guessed. The long years of the dictatorship and its
discipline had grated on the instinct for change which is
natural, not alone to the Spaniards, but to all peoples ;
and the Republicans turned this impatience to account
before the Monarchists had guessed what was happening. The great dictator had gone ; but one man
remained, the man whose outstanding position and
striking gifts made him the symbol not only of an
authority grown irksome, but also of privilege and
class. Old memories of scandal surged up from a
hundred years before, and history, according to its
ancient rule, demanded reparation, not from the
guilty, but from their descendants :

> Forgetful is green earth. The gods alone
> Remember everlastingly. They strike
> Remorselessly and ever like for like.
> By their great memories, the gods are known.

King Alfonso fell because the sins of the fathers
are visited upon the children, even unto the third and
fourth generation. It is true that Spanish feeling was
severe on a man, three of whose sons inherited hæmo-
philia ; it is true that his tastes for sport and travel
became unpopular ; it is true that his political
enterprise gave excuse for criticism, and that he lost
the sympathy of thoughtful men. It is true that on
him was revenged the natural grudge of badgered
intellectuals against the high-handedness of a Captain-
General made absolute. But the feeling of the
country was not against him personally so much
as against what it believed was a Court tradition and

a selfish clique. They said that the King was *mal rodeado* ; that he had bad advisers ; and in his own manifesto he confessed that he had made mistakes. Yet few, indeed, had the sagacity to point to them when they were made. And besides, all people make mistakes. Is a mistake a reason for a revolution ? If so, the only remedy is to deprive a king of power.

As we look round, indeed, at the surviving kings of Europe, we see that they are all " Apple-cart " kings[1]— all quiet men, whose influence upon affairs, if they have any, it is impossible to trace. But they are not for that reason inactive, or merely ornamental. The royal system, of which we make such prudent use in England, and which is such a shrewd investment for the taxpayer, never allows the King to take a political step which could be interpreted by anyone as a mistake. And yet his functions are by no means incommensurate with his dignity. He is an official invested with romance and continuity ; he is a unique liaison officer ; and with the elasticity of a single mind and heart, he performs at the centre of the mechanism the nice operation of adjustment.

But the constitutional functions of the King of England are inseparably associated with his prestige as the sovereign of an Empire. Human nature needs the person of His Majesty, as it needs the mystery of his crown, to centre the lives of peoples. A king to whom so many eyes are turned as the symbol of their social unity is no mere figure-head. He is not merely the head of the family over which sentimentalists can have the luxury of slobbering. He is a consecrated

[1] After this book was written, Miss Dorothea Evans pointed out that my own view of the function of monarchy in relation to parliamentary government coincides almost exactly with that of Ireland's clever socialist, Mr. Bernard Shaw, the author of *The Apple Cart.*—R. S.

person, with a sacred office, not for religious mysteries like the priest, but with a religious function such as no ordinary layman can have ; for in a way too august neatly to define and yet too practical to escape, he gives his people the inspiration of united service ; such service, as their instinct knows, is one with the unseen mysteries of life and mind. Loyalty to the King is a nation's call to sacrifice. And the unity of the nation becomes venerable in the King's majesty.

Such has been the deep instinct, not only of the English people, but—even more so—of the Spanish people. It was that loyalty to the Catholic throne which enabled them to play a glorious part in the civilisation of the New World, and which, not satisfied with mere words and figures for a child's essential education, made Spain insist that Spanish life meant Christianity, and Christianity as bond between East and West, so that as earthly wealth increased, it should be brought into the service of ideal wealth, and so that ideal wealth must also mean the physical well-being of the peoples of the world. That was the great function of Spanish kingship. It had an Oriental quality which gave Western Europe, and irradiated into the New World, a conception of nationalism not to be dissociated with spiritual mystery. There is no truth of which the Western world is in greater need.

But the fact that modern invention brought Spain daily nearer to the rest of Western Europe obscured the peculiar nature of her offering to civilisation. At a time when the parliamentary system of universal suffrage is being criticised as government by the brute force of numbers ; when its sudden subservience to personal influence, and its appeal to a short-sighted cupidity are awakening the distrust of thinkers who prefer to assess the national life in terms of the commerce and industry by which men live, Spain, oblivious of her own past, and of the latest development of political instinct, plunged into extreme democracy without even securing herself from corruption at the polls. She robbed herself of the traditions which not only she herself enjoyed, but which she ought to have contributed to the life of her neighbours. That is the tragedy of 1931.

It was no doubt due to very complicated causes that it became finally inevitable ; but it is not hopeless. King Alfonso is therefore the symbol of a great issue. In these days the monarch's function is less spectacular, more grinding ; and he cannot expect to command confidence unless, in season and out of season, his dignity and his devotion are obviously equal to his sacred task as sovereign. He needs to be sympathetic, yet he must walk apart. He must avoid everything that could give occasion to scandal or even gossip. And he must be able to put himself in touch with his people so as to represent their deeper instincts, or else he must make way for those who can. But if he really heads his people, the benefits he performs are immense.

" Those who are placed in the front rank of society," said *The Times* as far back as 1854, " require the greatest amount of requirements—of self-respect and self-command. In no class of men has the progress of the present age been more remarkable, and since Princes have followed the beaten track of knowledge, instead of the royal road, they have become at least the equals of the best-educated men of their age." [1] What was then true of England Don Alfonso XIII made true fifty years later for his own country.

Nowhere is the king's work so necessary, and yet nowhere so arduous as in Spain. The Spaniards are

[1] June 7, 1854.

the most chivalrous, the kindest, the most religious of peoples ; they have in the last fifty years reawakened to make immense advances ; but no one can say they have the qualities which render government easy. That is the fact the Republic has had to face— with what results becomes clearer every day. For a while, few voices were heard for the King ; but no student of Spanish history can think that the Spanish people have yet spoken the last word.

The case for the Monarchy at the present time has not been put before them ; and dark destructive agencies are at work among their masses. In themselves they are sane and virile, but the sense of discipline, like the sense of logic, is lacking. Their changes of mood no one can gauge. "Who," once asked a very sympathetic Englishman, "can ever calculate what this volcanic people will do, who never calculate, but whose impromptu actions are guided by passions which are as fierce as the sun in Africa, and as capricious and instantaneous as the hurricane?"[1]   Spain, in fact, as the Duke of Wellington said, is the only country where two and two do not make four.

It would be vain, therefore, to look too judicially for reasons why the Spaniards acquiesced in the exile of their King and Queen. All one can say is that they already know they are paying dear for it. And, since they are a grateful and good-natured people, chivalrous at heart, their very changefulness may bring them in time to recognise the mistake and to make reparation for it to the blameless Lady and the skilful, devoted, intrepid Sovereign who, in poverty at Fontainebleau, suffer the penalty of having entrusted almost their all to Spain.

[1] R. Ford : *Handbook to Spain*, 1st ed., ii., p. 742.

25

CHRONOLOGY

1807. Escorial Conspiracy.
1808. Carlos IV abdicates.
Fernando VII assumes throne.
Joseph Bonaparte assumes throne.
1811. Battle of Talavera.
1812. Battle of Salamanca.
1813. Joseph abdicates.
1814. Fernando VII restored.
1819. Carlos IV and Maria Luisa die in Rome.
1820. Constitutional attempt.
1823. French army invades Spain.
1829. Fernando marries Maria Cristina of Naples.
1830. Isabel born.
1831. Luisa Fernanda born.
1833. Fernando publishes revocation of Salic Law and dies.
Isabel II succeeds.
1833–1839. Carlist War.
1840. Queen Cristina exiled.
1842. Isabel declared of age.
1844. Queen Cristina returns.
1846. Isabel and Luisa Fernanda marry.
1854. Revolution.
1856. Narváez restored.
1857. Alfonso XII born.
1868. Queen Isabel exiled.   First Republic proclaimed.
1871. Amadeo of Savoy takes the throne.
1873. Amadeo abdicates.   Second Republic proclaimed.
1875. Bourbon dynasty restored with Alfonso XII.
1877. Alfonso XII marries Maria de las Mercédes.   She dies.
1879. Alfonso XII marries Maria Cristina de Habsburg.
1885. Alfonso XII dies.
1886. Alfonso XIII born and proclaimed King.
1898. Cuban War : Spain against U.S.A.
1902. Alfonso XIII assumes power.
1906. Alfonso XIII marries Princess Victoria Eugénie of Battenberg.

386

1909. Mutiny in Barcelona. Ferrer executed. Moroccan War begins.
1912. Canalejas assassinated.
1913. Compact with Republicans.
1914–1918. European War.
1921. Disaster in Anual.
1923. Primo de Rivera becomes dictator.
1925. Moroccan War ends.
1930. Primo de Rivera falls.
1931. Alfonso XIII hands over prerogatives.

SOURCES

PART I

THE STORY OF FERNANDO VII

THE fullest bibliography available, but by no means complete, is Sánchez Alónso : *Fuentes de la Historia de España.* More precisely the authorities followed here are as follows :
Contemporary sources :

Spanish

Alcalá Galiano, A. : *Recuerdos de un Anciano.* 2 vols. A valuable account of the constitutional struggle from an active mason.

Ceballos, Pedro : *Historia de los Hechos y Maquinaciones.* A strong partisan on the side of Fernando VII.

Escoiquiz Juan : *Memorias.*

„   „   : *Idea Sencilla.*
Another strong partisan of Fernando VII, but more eloquent and more reliable.

Fernando Fernández de Córdoba, Marqués de Mendigorria : *Mis Memorias Íntimas.* 3 vols. The most unbiased and intimate record of the whole period.

Godoy : *Cuenta Dada de mi Vida Política.* 5 vols. Far from reliable, but obviously one of the principal sources of the period. There is a valuable appendix to this book in the article on Godoy, *Westminster Review*, April 1836, by W., probably Lord Wellesley.

Llorente : *Historia de la Inquisición.* Contains many vivid touches on the period.

Mesonero Romanos, R. de : *Memorias de un Setentón.* Many vivid details.

Miraflores, Marqués de : *Memorias.* 2 vols. Conventional and dull, but not unreliable.

Pirala : *Historia de la Guerra Civil.* 6 vols.

Toreno : *Historia del levantamiento, guerra y revolución en España.* 7 vols. Excellent, but strongly on Fernando's side.

Vaya, Stanislau-de-Koska : *Historia de la Vida y Reinado de Fernando VII.* 3 vols. The standard history of the period, with many documents of first-rate importance in the appendices, and far more free from bias.

Foreign

Napoleon I : *Correspondence.* 32 vols.

„ „ : *Mémorial de Ste. Hélène.*

„ „ : *Lettres Inédites.* Lecestre.

Bonaparte, Joseph : *Mémoires et Correspondance.* 10 vols.

All obviously fundamental, and not less so is the *Moniteur Officiel*, Feb. 5, 1810, which contains the correspondence of the Spanish Bourbons with Napoleon.

Others are :

Abrantès, Duchesse d' : *Mémoires.* 3 vols.

Beauharnais, Comte de : *Mémoires.*

Beausset, M. de : *Mémoires.*

Coxe : *Memoirs of the Spanish Bourbons.*

Holland, Lady : *Spanish Journal.*

Holland, Lord : *Foreign Reminiscences.*

Laforest, Comte de : *Mémoires.* 10 vols.

Latour du Pin, Marquise de : *Journal.* 2 vols.

Miot de Mélito, Count : *Mémoires.* 3 vols. The best account of Joseph's life in Spain.

Murat, Joachim : *Correspondence.* 10 vols.

de Pradt, Monseigneur : *Mémoires Historiques.* 2 vols. Courtly but not untrue.

Quin, M. J. (M. J. Quintana, a Spanish Liberal of some repute) : *A Visit to Spain.*

Rovigo, Savary, Duc de : *Mémoires.* 10 vols. Full but unreliable.

Stendhal : *Promenades dans Rome.* A few details.

Ticknor, George : *Life and Letters.* A discerning American man of letters.

Walton : *Revolution in Spain.* 2 vols. Contemporary but unreliable.

The Spanish archives of the period have already been well worked over, and leave little more to be discovered : in Spain, as well as in London, the principal worker is the Marqués de Villa-Urrutia, who has embodied his researches in several excellent books :

Relaciones entre España y Inglaterra. 4 vols.

Fernando VII ; *Rey Constitucional.*
María Luisa.
Mujeres de Fernando VII.
El Rey José Bonaparte.

See also :
Gómez de Arteche : *Historia General de España.* A classic.
  Only second to these is :
Geoffroy de Grandmaison : *L'Espagne et Napoléon.* 3 vols.,
  which embody twenty-five years of work among the memoirs
  and archives of the period, especially the Parisian archives.
  Another who has worked with equal care over the period is :
Fugier, E. : *Napoléon et l'Espagne.*
Ducéré, E. : *Napoléon à Bayonne*, is another admirable work,
  though not based on researches into MSS.
  See also :
Custine, Marquis de : *L'Espagne sous Ferdinand VII.*

  In English there are four good accounts of the period :
Oman, C. : *Peninsular War*, 8 vols., of which the first is occupied
  with the Spanish monarchy. It has a valuable reference
  to papers at All Souls' College, Oxford.
Butler Clarke : *Modern Spain.* A business-like work, corrected
  by Fitzmaurice Kelly.
Hume, Martin : *Modern Spain.* A vivid story of high authority
  from a scholar on the spot.
d'Auvergne, E. B. : *Godoy : the Queen's Favourite.* Another vivid
  and reliable story.
  But none of these gives a satisfactory account of the documents
on which they are based, and each ignores certain essential
sources of information : none is up to date.

Part II

From the Accession of Isabel II to the End of the Regency of Maria Cristina de Habsburg, 1833–1902

Contemporary sources :

Spanish

Angelon, M. : *Isabel II.* Though written by a prominent
  historian of the time, it is only a panegyric of the Queen.

Benalúa, Conde de, Duque de San Piedro : *Memorias.* Only
1 vol. published. Fundamental and intimate with regard
to Isabel II and Alfonso XII.

Bermejo, A. : *La Estafeta de Palacio.* 3 vols. This extraordinary
work, written in the form of letters to Alfonso XII, is the
best source on the period, though it contains some inventions, frankly acknowledged. But it is the only frank record
of a difficult period.

Burgos, F. J. de : *Anales del reinado de Isabel II.* 6 vols. Good.

Casa Valencia, Conde de : *Memorias.* Reliable.

Donoso Cortés, Marqués de Valdegamas : *Obras Escogidas.*
2 vols. One of the best writers of the period. Eloquent,
and not widely known ; a defender of Cristina.

Espóz y Mina, Condesa de : *Memorias.* A vivid and accurate
story from a royal governess, with an important introduction.

Eulalia, Infanta : *J'ai voulu vivre ma vie.* A princess's intimate
memoirs, privately published.

Fernández de los Rios : *Luchas Politicas en España.* 2 vols.

Flores, S. S. : *Vida de Espartero.* 4 vols. Dull but not inexact.

Rodriguez, J. Francos : *En Tiempo de Alfonso XII.*
        „   „   : *Cuando el Rey era Niño.* Very vivid.

Fernández de Córdova, Marqués de Mendigorria : *Mis Memorias
Íntimas.* 3 vols.

Excellent on this period also :

Gómez de Arteche : *Historia General de España.* A classic.

Washington Irving : *Letters from Sunnyside and Spain.*

Lema, Marqués de : *Estudios Históricos.*
     „   „   „   : *De la Revolución á la Restauración.*
        Studies by a competent Spanish historian.

Miraflores, Marqués de : *Memorias.* Discerning view of this
                                period.
     „   „   „   : *La cuestión de la sucesión.* A collection
                                of documents.

Peréz de Guzmán : *Un Matrimonio de Estado.*

Pi y Margall : *Historia de España en el Siglo XIX.*
   „   „   „   : *Opúsculos.*
        Books of high authority by a great Spanish historian of
        the period.

Romanones, Conde de : *Notas de mi Vida.* 2 vols. published
so far. Fundamental.

Rubio, Carlos : *Historia Filósofica de la Revolución Española de* 1868.

Foreign authorities dealing with this period are almost confined to the episode of Queen Isabel's marriage. They are :

Bulwer, Sir H. (Lord Dalling) : *Life of Lord Palmerston.* 3 vols.
Greville, C. C. F. : *Journal of the Reign of William IV.*
    ,,   ,,   : *Journal of the Reign of Queen Victoria.*
    Extremely precise in knowledge obtained through talk.
Guizot : *Mémoires pour servir à l'histoire de mon temps.* 8 vols.
    Brilliant apologia.
Hall, Sir John R. : *England and the Orleans Monarchy.* A record
    of documents on France and Spain in the Record Office and
    the Quai d'Orsay. He was wrong in thinking the dossier of
    the Spanish marriages missing. Bresson corresponded
    direct with Louis Philippe. Of these letters no trace has
    been found. Philippe's correspondence with Guizot about
    the marriages is in a book called *Revue Rétrospective. Archives
    Secrètes du Dernier Gouvernement,* 1848.
Martin, Sir T. : *Life of the Prince Consort.* 5 vols. A full record
    from documents handed over by Queen Victoria.
Maxwell, Sir H. : *Life of Lord Clarendon.* 2 vols. Contains
    highly important letters.
Russell, Lord J. : *Correspondence,* edited by Dr. G. P. Gooch.
    2 vols.
Stockmar : *Memoirs II.*
Queen Victoria's Letters.
    See also :
Cecil, Algernon, *Six Foreign Secretaries.*
Guedalla, Philip : *Palmerston.*
Woodward, E. Ll. : *Studies in European Conservatism.*

    The Queen was gradually led over to take Palmerston's view, though she had Bulwer's letters before her.

    The Foreign Office also published a blue book on this episode, but it is not complete.

    See also *The Times* on this period ; though its correspondents were often partisans.

    The Spanish archives of the period are not yet available, and those in Paris and London are only very partially explored ; those in Vienna not at all. There is, however, some authoritative writing on the period, notably :

d'Auvergne, E. B. : *A Queen at Bay.* A good life of Cristina de
    Bourbon.
Benoît, Charles : *Vie de Cánovas del Castillo.*
Butler Clarke : *Modern Spain.*
Chaves, M. : *Bocetos de una Epoca.*

Hume, Martin : *Modern Spain.* Excellent on this period, which he knew personally.
Lema, Marqués de : *Cánovas del Castillo.*
Marvaud, Angel : *L'Espagne au XX⁰ Siècle.*
Mortera, Conde de la, now Duque de Maura : *Reinado de Alfonso XIII durante su minoridad.*
Peréz de Guzmán : Articles in *Ilustración Española y Americana.*
Thureau-Dangin : *La Monarchie de Juillet.*
Villa-Urrutia, Marqués de : *La Reina Gobernadora.* Finally authoritative on the Regency of Queen Cristina de Bourbon.
Eugenia de Montijo, Emperatríz de los Franceses.
Serrano.

PART III
RULE OF ALFONSO XIII

The best account of the period is in the newspapers gathered together in the Hemeroteca at Madrid.

Excellent for the whole period is *The Times*, the *Ilustración Española y Americana*, 1902–1912, and also *Soldevilla : Año Político,* of which there is one volume for each of the twenty-nine years. Count Romanones' *Notas de mi Vida* is also of paramount importance ; another valuable book is J. Francos Rodriguez' *Vida de Canalejas.*

Don S. de Madariaga gives an extremely partisan account of the period in his *Spain,* as does also the Duque de Maura, in his *Bosquejo Histórico de la Dictadura.* The best on the other side is Primo de Rivera's own pamphlet ; see also José Calvo Sotelo : *Anuario de Vida Local* and *Carta de Régimen Municipal* ; and Salvador Canals : *España, la Constitución y la Monarquía,* is impartial.

Extremely clear-seeing books are :
Béraud : *Emeutes en Espagne.*
Angel Marvaud : *L'Espagne au XX⁰ Siècle.*
Jérome et Jean Tharaud : *Rendez-vous Espagnols.*
The two best lives of King Alfonso are in English :
Major D. Chapman-Huston and Princess Pilar : *Alfonso XIII.*
Mrs. Erskine Stewart : *Twenty-nine Years.*
Both of these appeared in Nov. 1931.
See also A. F. Calvert : *The Spanish Royal Marriage.*

A good Spanish account of the King up to 1914 is : Olmet y Carrafa : *Alfonso XIII.*

There is a good account of the King's part in the war :
Espinós Moltó : *Espejo de Neutrales.*

On the whole century, there are standard histories of Spain by :
Ballester.

Ortega Rubio.

Don Pedro Aguado Bleye. With an excellent bibliography at
   the end of each chapter.

Miss Catherine Moran and Mr. H. D. Sedgwick have each
written reliable short histories of Spain.

INDEX

A

Abd-el-Krim, 322, 325, 329
Aberdeen, Lord, 190, 193, 196, 198
Abrantès, Duchess d', 9, 31, 32
Aizpuru, Don Luis, 331
Alagón, Duke of, 106, 150, 161
Alba, Duke of, 352, 361
Albert, Prince of Prussia, 268, 283
Alcalá Galiano, 122
Alcalá Zamora, Señor, 330, 353, 357, 365, 377
Alexander, Czar, 30
Alfonso XII, King, 215, 230, 231, 237, 242, 243, 245–6, 249–54
Alfonso XIII, King, born posthumous, 255 ; baptised, 256 ; a precocious child, 259–60 ; assumes power, 263 ; a prodigy, 264 ; a Christian king, 265 ; a Daniel come to judgment, 266 ; fond of drill, 267 ; mild and docile, 267 ; swears the Constitution, 270 ; asserts himself, 271 ; visits Lisbon, 272 ; visits Germany, 273 ; pleases King Edward, 273 ; authoritative and impulsive, 274 ; courageous and sympathetic, 275 ; his function as king, 276 ; his pitfalls, 277 ; his rashness, 278 ; visits England, 279 ; affianced, 280 ; married, 283 ; in danger of assassination, 275, 284–6, 288, 305 ; highly popular, 288 ; rebukes his cousin, 289 ; addresses Military College, 289 ; wins over Canalejas, 294–6 ; adores the Holy Eucharist, 298 ; rebukes Infanta Eulalia, 301–4 ; has an accident at polo, 305 ; disarms his political foes, 307–12 ; everywhere the King, 314 ; helps the victims of Great War, 316–18 ; changes his policy, 319–20 ; denounces parliament, 321 ; his relation to Anual, 324–6 ; makes an enigmatic speech, 327 ; has news of *coup d'état*, 330–2 ; accepts dictatorship, 333 ; imperils Constitution, 334, 338 ; visits Rome, 335–6 ; receives Tharaud, 337–41 ; finds his position in danger, 344 ; versatile and smart, not serious, 345–6 ; helps Las Hurdes, 343 ; inaugurates University City, 343, 346 ; annoyed with dictator, 348–9 ; lacks perseverance, 350 ; institutes Berenguer dictatorship, 351 ; uncompromising against rebellion, 354 ; in danger as king, 355 ; faces crisis, 357 ; believes crisis surmounted, 359 ; becomes unpopular, 360–1 ; unpopularity undeserved, 362 ; his life in danger from mob, 364 ; suspends prerogatives, 366–7 ; leaves Madrid, 368 ; arrives Marseilles and Paris, 372–3 ; his acknowledged success, 379–80 ; his adaptability to the people's moods, 380 ; the injustice of his fate, 381 ; he has bad advisers, 382 ; his historic achievement, 384 ; he suffers for trust in Spain, 385
Alfonso, Don de Bourbon, 289, 368
Alhucemas, Marquis de, 332–3, 357
Altamira, 379
Alvarez, Don Melquiades, 295, 299–300, 309, 334, 357, 365
Alvarez de Toledo, 285
Amadeo, King, 238–9, 240
America, United States of North, 261
Angoulême, Duke d', 121, 122
Antonelli, Cardinal, 224
Antonio, Don de Bourbon, 47
Anual, 324–5, 344
Aranda, Count, 7
Arévalo, Duke of, 278
Argüelles, 123, 186
Arteaga Palafox, 155, 156
Asturias, Prince of, 367
Augusta, Princess of Saxony, 9, 21, 47, 48
Augustín Iturbide, 125
Aumale, Duke d', 191
Azcárate, Don Gumersindo de, 309–11
Aznar, Admiral, 359, 362, 370

B

Baroja, Pio, 231
Barrios, 61
Bastida, Count, 268
Beatrice, Princess, 280, 282, 283
Beatrice, Princess of Saxe-Coburg, 289
Beauharnais, Count de, 21, 47, 48
Beausset, 57
Beira, Princess de la, 83, 84
Belgida, Marchioness de, 172, 183
Benavente, 380
Benavides, 213, 214
Berenguer, Count de Tetuan, 322–5, 351, 354, 356
Berthier, 14
Bismarck, 232
Bivona, Count, 268
Bolivar, 105
Bonaparte, Princess Charlotte (Lolotte), 86
Bonaparte, King Joseph, 66–8, 71, 73–5, 79–81, 88–90, 239
Bonaparte, Empress Josephine, 54, 56, 79–80, 217
Bonaparte, Queen Julie, 86, 115
Bonaparte, Lucien, 86
Bonaparte, Empress Marie-Louise, 79
Bonaparte, Princess Mathilde, 223
Bonaparte, Emperor Napoleon, 1, 13, 24, 25, 30, 32, 33, 34, 40, 47–9, 50, 51, 53–4, 65, 74, 75, 76, 77, 79–80, 231, 361
Bonaparte, Princess Zenaïda, 86, 87, 88
Bourbon, Cardinal de, 96, 97
Brancimonte, 101
Bravo Murillo, 217, 218
Bresson, Count, 191, 196–7, 198, 199–202, 203, 280
Brougham, Lord, 199
Bulwer, Sir Henry, Lord Dalling, 196–7, 199–200, 202, 203, 206–7, 210, 280

C

Caballero, 24, 25
Cadiz, Cortes de, 77, 121–3
Calabria, Duke of, 268
Calomarde, 124, 126, 136
Calvo Sotelo, Señor, 343
Cambacérès, 14
Cambó, Señor, 311
Campo Alange, 102, 103
Canalejas, 293–6, 300–1, 303, 304–5

Canning, 82
Cánovas del Castillo, 223, 224, 242, 244, 258, 308
Carbonell, 155
Carisbrooke, Marchioness of, 363, 370
Carl Stephan, Archduke, 268
Carlos III, 7, 378
Carlos IV, 1–2, 4, 5, 6, 7, 11, 18–20, 21–4, 26, 28, 54–6, 99–103, 108–12, 129, 134, 373
Carlos, Dom of Portugal, 272, 273, 288
Carlos, Don, 126, 129, 139, 140, 145–9, 153, 187, 223, 290
Carlota, Queen of Portugal, 9
Carlota, Princess of Naples, 129, 130, 131, 135, 136, 186, 190–1
Casa Aguilar, 364
Castanedo, Señora, 158, 160
Castelar, 240
Cazes, Duke de, 202
Ceballos, 41, 51, 52, 54
Cerralbo, Marquis de, 115
Chamartín, 74–6
Champagni, 51
Chateaubriand, 121
Clarendon, 4th Earl of, 194, 199
Claret, Padre, 234
Clémentine, Princess of Belgium, 130
Colbert, 265, 295
Collignon, Louis, 84–5
Connaught, Duke of, 268, 278
Constancia. *See* Campo Alange.
Cortina, 168, 169
Cossío, Señor, 309, 311–12
Cowley, 1st Earl, 200
Cristina. *See* Maria Cristina.
Cuba, 260
Czartorisky, Prince, 223

D

Dato, 319
Diego de León, 172–80, 183
Domingo, Marcelino, 377
Dulce, Domingo, 173

E

Edward VII, 273
Ena, Princess. *See* Queen Victoria Eugénie.
Enrique, Don, 197, 200–1, 204, 233
Escalera, 166
Escoiquiz, 8, 22, 29, 41, 45, 48, 52–4
Escorial, 15–17, 150
Espartero, Duke of the Victory, 153, 164–9, 184, 197, 219, 233, 249, 362

Espoz y Mina, Count, 172
Espoz y Mina, Countess, 173–80
Estella, Marquis de. *See* Primo de
    Rivera.
Etruria, Queen of, 65, 101
Eugénie, Empress, 21, 206, 207, 222,
    223, 229, 243, 279, 280
Eulalia, Infanta, 230, 268, 300–4
Evans, Miss Dorothea, 382 n.

F

Feliú-Bardaxi, 123
Fernández de Córdova, Fernando,
    204–6
Fernández de Córdova, Luis, Mar-
    quis de Mendigorria, 132, 143,
    146, 152, 159, 163
Fernando VII, 7–10, 11, 18–20, 21–4,
    25–9, 39, 42–4, 47–50, 55–7, 65,
    84–6, 91–9, 113, 115, 116, 120–2,
    124, 127, 133, 134, 136–40, 145–50,
    231, 239, 248
Ferrer, 291–3, 296, 297, 306, 341
Floridablanca, 7
Francisca, Infanta de Braganza, 106,
    127, 130
Francisco de Asis, King, 197, 199–
    201, 209, 213–14, 237
Francisco de Paula, Infante, 2, 129,
    131, 188, 210
Francos Rodriguez, 254
Franklin, Benjamin, 47
Franz Ferdinand, Archduke, 283
Frere, Ambassador, 29, 34

G

Galán, 353
Garcia Hernández, 353
Gennaro, Prince, 268
Genoa, Duke of, 268, 283
George III of England, 83
George V, King of England, 283,
    357
Godoy, Prince of the Peace, 4–5, 8, 9,
    13, 14, 15, 20, 21–3, 24, 25–7, 28,
    31–2, 34, 38, 39, 40, 101–3, 108–12,
    113, 134, 248
Gómez, Sergeant, 162
Gómez, politician, 184
González, Anibal, 347
González Bravo, 186, 211
Gonzalo, Infante Don, 316, 370
Guimero, 364
Guizot, 189, 190, 191, 199, 203, 204

H

Henry, Prince of Prussia, 283
Holland, Lady, 9, 29, 31, 129
Holland, Lord, 31, 34
Hoyos, Marquis de, 359

I

Ibañez, 346
Igueriben, 324
Imperial, Prince, 231
Indalecio Prieto, 321
Infantado, Duke of the, 21, 28, 36,
    41, 74
Inge, Dean, quoted, 342
Inquisition, 67, 75, 80, 83, 97, 98
Irving, Washington, 208, 287
Isabel of Braganza, Queen, 106–7
Isabel II, Queen, 134, 147–8, 149,
    152, 172–81, 182–7, 190, 196, 202–
    4, 206–7, 208–9, 214–15, 218, 220–
    2, 227, 228–30, 231, 233–4, 241,
    242, 250
Isabel, Infanta, 214, 230, 268
Isturiz, 194
Italo Balbo, 335
Izquierdo, 12, 13, 31

J

Jarnac, Count, 199
Jaruco, Countess, 78
Joachim, Prince, 268
Jourdan, 88
Jovellar, 244
Junot, 31 n.

K

Kolli. *See* Collignon.

L

Lacépède, 12
Lacy, 106
La Forest, 91
Largo Caballero, Señor, 351
Leopold I, King of the Belgians, 204
Leopold of Coburg, Prince, 191, 199
Leopold of Hohenzollern, 232
Lerroux, Señor, 288, 289, 295, 307,
    315, 321, 322, 353
Lieven, Prince, 121
López Alia, 106
López Dominguez, 275
Londonderry, Lord, 121
Loubet, 273, 274, 275
Louis Philippe, King, 131, 152,
    187–8, 191–2, 195–6, 199–292,
    203, 215

Luisa Fernanda, Infanta, 134, 135, 172–80, 181–2, 196, 201–2, 203, 230, 232
Lyautey, Marshal, 341

M

Maciá, 365
Maeztu, Ramiro de, 346
Marañón, Don Gregorio, 355, 365
Marcus Aurelius, 265
Marfori, 227, 234, 243
Maria Amalia, Queen, 115, 116, 117, 128
Maria Antonia, Infanta, 9–10
Maria Cristina de Bourbon, Queen, 130–4, 135, 137–8, 149, 153–8, 159–63, 164, 165, 166–72, 181, 186–7, 188–91, 193–5, 197, 199–200, 202, 212–13, 219–24, 238, 254, 362
Maria Cristina de Habsburg, Queen, 251–2, 254, 255–6, 257, 260, 283, 298
Maria da Gloria, Queen of Portugal, 142, 180
Maria Luisa, Queen, 2–3, 4–7, 9, 10–12, 15, 20, 23–4, 28, 32, 44, 54, 99–103, 108–12, 129, 154, 374
Maria de las Mercédes, Queen, 250
Marie-Amelie, Queen, 131, 203, 206
Marmont, 82
Marracq, 50, 55–7
Martínez de la Rosa, 122
Masséna, 82
Masserano, Prince, 12, 32
Maura, Don Antonio, 275, 278, 289, 298, 309
Maura, Don Miguel, 353, 377
Maura, Duke of, 257, 357
Maurice of Battenburg, Prince, 316
Mendigorria, Marquis de. *See* Fernández de Córdova.
Mendizábal, 160, 161, 218
Meneses, 243
Mérimée, 207
Merry del Val, Cardinal, 295, 335
Mesonero Romanos, 128
Metternich, Prince, 105, 121, 193, 205, 215
Miguel, Dom, of Portugal, 142, 145
Miot de Mélito, 90
Miraflores, Marquis de, 117, 124, 128, 147, 150, 225
Miranda, Duke of, 346, 369

Montehermoso, Señora de, 78
Montero Villegas, Count, 268
Montijo, Countess of, 218, 223, 244
Montijo, Eugenio, Count de, 21, 36, 37, 183
Montpensier, Duke de, 196, 201, 202, 230, 233, 238, 250, 257
Moore, Sir John, 77, 82
Moret, 275
Morral, Matthew, 284–6, 288, 291
Mortefontaine, 190
Muñoz, Don Fernando, 155, 156–8, 160–3, 170, 196, 210, 215, 219, 222, 224, 238, 278
Muñoz, Doña Amparo, 223
Murat, 13, 29, 34, 44–6, 47, 48, 62, 66, 67, 75, 101
Mussolini, 327

N

Nakens, 285
Nancy Derrieux, Mme, 78
Napier, Sir Charles, 142
Naples, Queen of, 10, 13, 14, 18, 30, 31, 44
Narváez, 164–5, 186, 193, 211–12, 216–17, 225, 226–8, 230
Nelson, 31, 44
Nesselrode, 121
Norwood Young, 79 n.

O

O'Donnell, 219, 222, 225, 226, 230
Olózaga, 184–5, 188, 189, 223
Oporto, Duke of, 268
Ortega Gasset, Don José, 328, 355
Osma, Duchess of, 39
Ossorio Gallardo, 359

P

Palmerston, Viscount, 152, 198–204
Pardínas, 304
Patricia, Princess, 278, 279, 281
Patrocinio, Sor, 153, 216
Paul y Angulo, 239
Paz, Infanta, 230
Pedro, Emperor of Brazil, 142
Pepa la Malaguena, 106
Pérez de Ayala, Señor, 355
Pérez Galdos, 300
Pérez de Guzmán, 275
Philip II, 17
Pius VII, Pope, 98
Pius IX, Pope, 215, 224, 226, 232

Pius X, Pope, 295
Pius XI, Pope, 335
Pozzo di Borgo, 121
Prim, 230, 238, 239
Primo de Rivera, Fernando, 244, 245, 326
Primo de Rivera, Miguel, 326, 330-1, 333-4, 335-50, 360, 377
Puig Moltó, 215, 227, 237

Q
Quintana, 172, 183
Quiroga, 118, 119

R
Rampolla, 255
Riansares, Duke of. *See* Muñoz.
Riego, Rafael del, 118, 119, 123, 133
Rif, 290
Rivera, Admiral, 368
Romanones, Count, 277, 278, 284, 285, 310, 315, 319, 334, 356, 362, 364-5, 380
Ros de Olano, 211
Rovigo, Savary, Duc de, 47, 48, 49, 74
Ruiz Zorrilla, 240, 241
Russell, Lord John, 210

S
Sagasta, 241, 255, 270-1, 277, 308
San Carlos, Duke of, 21, 28, 36, 41
Sáncha, Cardinal, 269
Sánchez-Guerra, 348, 359, 365
Sánchez de Ocaña, 254
Sánchez-Toca, 319
Sanjurjo, General, 363
Santa Cruz, Marchioness de, 183
San Teodoro, Duke of, 13
Santiago, Alba, 330, 331, 332
Sartor, Sylvaine, 317-18
Serrano Bedoya, 245
Serrano, General, 209, 210, 214, 227
Seville, Duke of. *See* Don Enrique.
Seville, Duke of (his son), 257
Shelley, 110
Silvela, 261-2
Silvestre, 322-5
Sotomayor, Duke of, 209
Southern, George, 194

T
Talleyrand, 14, 21, 55, 65
Tascher de la Pagerie, Rose Françoise, 21, 86
Tharaud, 337-9, 344
Ticknor, George, 88
Toreno, Count de, 5, 159, 160
Toreno, Count de (contemporary), 268
Torrijos, 268
Tovar, Marquis de, 278
Trápani, Count, 193

U
Unamuno, Don Miguel de, 346, 379

V
Valençay, 65, 84-6, 91
Vargas Laguna, 103
Vasco da Gama, 30
Vega de Armijo, Marquis, 269
Vega Inclan, 230
Velazquez, 3
Veragua, Duke of, 271
Viana, Marquis de, 278
Victoria, Queen of England, 190, 191, 193, 196, 202, 203-5, 228, 280, 281, 283-5, 286
Victoria Eugénie, Queen of Spain, 280, 281, 282, 283, 313, 350, 357-8, 368-71, 385
Victor Emmanuel, King, 131
Vidal, 106
Vienna, Congress of, 99, 103
Villanueva, 365
Villa-Urrutia, Marquis, 272
Vladimir, Grand Duke, 268, 283

W
Wellesley, Marquis, 34, 84
Wellington, Duke of, 81, 88-9, 113, 121, 279
Weyler, General, 270

Y
Yandiola, 106

Z
Zea Bermúdez, 151, 159
Zuloaga, 346
Zumalacarregui, 153
Zurbano, 181

Printed and Made in Great Britain by
Hazell, Watson & Viney Ltd. London and Aylesbury

A